FATHERING A NATION

BARBADOS AND THE LEGACY OF ERROL WALTON BARROW

Foreword by the Prime Minister of Barbados
Introduction by The Rt Excellent Sir Garfield Sobers

Edited by Guy A.K. Hewitt

First published in Great Britain by Hansib Publications in 2016

Hansib Publications Limited
P.O. Box 226, Hertford, SG14 3WY

info@hansibpublications.com
www.hansibpublications.com

ISBN 978-1-910553-63-3

A CIP catalogue record for this book
is available from the British Library

Production by Hansib Publications Ltd

Printed in Great Britain

The twentieth century has been rightly called the Century of the Common Man. The elemental desire for *freedom, prosperity* and *security* has, in our time, been turned into the creative energies which we see at work in emergent countries. This upsurge has to be properly directed into productive channels, so that ordinary folk may build up their own communities with the greatest speed, and with the least distraction. They can best do this under the leadership of political parties which, both by origin and outlook, are firmly rooted in the people.

The story of the Democratic Labour Party is a saga of struggle and service. But, in a wider sense, it is part of the History of the People of Barbados at the point at which they shook themselves awake and alert. Something has been achieved. Much more remains to be done, but [we] have shown that the human spirit can create its own best future, so long as diligence, loyalty and perseverance are its watchwords.

Errol Walton Barrow
1965

The soul of this community has to be laid bare, and there is no better time to do that than when we are preparing for Independence, so that we know what we are, who we are, and where we are going.

Errol Walton Barrow
4 January 1966

For creative men like Errol, there can be no final arrival. They represent great continuums and are not to be mourned. When we speak of them in the past, it is because the grammar of language dictates it, not the grammar of life.

Sir Kenneth Stuart

Dedicated to: the youth of Barbados, and youth of the Caribbean, for we in our area [the Caribbean] have long had young men [and women] who dreamt dreams and saw visions. They have all grown older as [Errol] did, but there has always been another generation. I know therefore that Errol rests in peace, for that generation has received education, experience, pride in a nation, which is now theirs to carry forward.

Dame Nita Barrow

CONTENTS

CONTRIBUTORS

Sir Frank W. Alleyne, KA, was Professor of Economics at the University of the West Indies. His long and distinguished academic career includes being a co-founder of the Faculty of Social Sciences at the Cave Hill Campus, Head of the Department of Economics, and Dean. He is currently the Chairman of the Financial Services Commission (FSC). This article draws on the DLP 10th Anniversary publication.

Mr Ian DeVere Archer, GCM, is an Attorney-at-Law with specialist training in Air and Space Law. His career was primarily in the Civil Service where he retired in 1989 as Permanent Secretary in the Ministry of International Transport. He was a Director, Managing Director and Chairman of LIAT (1974) Ltd, the Caribbean airline.

The Rt Honourable Owen S. Arthur, MP, was the fifth Prime Minister of Barbados from 1994-2008 and Leader of the Opposition from 2010-2013. He was a principal architect of the Caribbean Community Single Market and Economy (CSME).

Dame Maizie Barker-Welch, DBE, BCH, CHB, was a teacher, politician, and advocate of women's rights. A Parliamentary Secretary in the Ministry of Labour and Community Development, she was also President of the Barbados National Organisation of Women and the Business and Professional Women's Club of Barbados.

The late Dame R. Nita Barrow, GCMG, FRCN, was the only female Governor-General of Barbados, serving from June 1990 until her death in December 1995. A sister of Errol Barrow, she was President of the World YWCA and the World Council of Churches, Ambassador to the United Nations and a member of the Commonwealth Group of Eminent Persons on South Africa.

Professor Mary Chamberlain is Emeritus Professor of Caribbean History at Oxford Brookes University. A Fellow of the Royal Historical Society, she has been a consultant to the Barbados National Oral History Project, a member of the UK Government's Caribbean Advisory Group and has held visiting professorships at the University of the West Indies and at New York University. A former resident of Barbados, her article is an extract from her book, *Empire and Nation-building in the Caribbean: Barbados 1937-1966*.

Mr David A. Comissiong, is an Attorney-at-Law, author and founder of the Clement Payne Movement. He was a Senator and served as head of the Commission for Pan-African Affairs in Barbados.

Sir Stephen E. Emtage. KA, GCM, was Director of Finance and Planning in the Ministry of Finance and Economic Affairs, and Senior Vice-President and Deputy CEO of Life of Barbados. He served as a Director of the Central Bank of Barbados and Director/ Alternate of the IMF, World Bank and IDB.

Sir Henry de B. Forde, KA, QC, served as a Member of Parliament from 1971-2004 including Leader of the Opposition from 1986-1993 and a Cabinet Minister with the portfolios of Attorney General and Minister of Foreign Affairs. He is the sole surviving Adviser to the 1966 Constitutional Conference.

Dr Ayana Gibbs, MBChB, PhD, is a medical doctor with specialist training in psychiatry from the Maudsley Hospital in London. A recipient of a Research Training Fellowship Award from the Wellcome Trust to pursue doctoral research in neuroscience, in 2010 she joined the medical faculty at the University of Sussex in the UK as Clinical Senior Lecturer in Forensic Psychiatry.

The Honourable Ralph E. Gonsalves, MP, is the Prime Minister of St Vincent and the Grenadines, and leader of the Unity Labour Party (ULP). A Member of Parliament since 1994, he became Prime Minister in 2001.

Mr E. Evelyn Greaves, GCM, was Deputy General Secretary of the Barbados Workers Union (BWU) and Head of the BWU Labour College. A Member of Parliament from 1971-1994 and Cabinet Minister from 1986-1994, he most recently served a High Commissioner for Barbados to Canada from 2008-2014.

Sir Philip Marlowe Greaves, KA, QC, was Deputy Prime Minister of Barbados and is the sole surviving Delegate of the 1966 Constitutional Conference. His parliamentary career spanned 39 years and includes numerous Cabinet posts and the unique distinction of holding the position of Leader of Government Business in both chambers of Parliament. He has acted as Governor-General on a number of occasions.

Mr Harold Hoyte, GCM, is Editor Emeritus of The Nation Newspaper. He has spent his entire life in journalism in Barbados and Canada and was one of the founders of The Nation, retiring as its President and Editor-in-Chief. An author of four books including two on politics in Barbados, he was conferred with an honorary doctorate by the University of the West Indies.

The Honourable Donville O. Inniss, MP, is a Cabinet Minister of Barbados; appointed Minister of Industry, International Business, Commerce and Small Business Development in March 2013. Prior to this appointment, he served as Minister of Health, and Minister of State in the Ministry of Foreign Affairs and International Business. Prior to entering Parliament he worked in the public and private sectors.

The late Carl E. Jackman, CBE, had a distinguished administrative career at the University of the West Indies retiring as University Registrar in 1985.

The late Oliver Jackman, was an outstanding diplomat and jurist. During his twenty years in the diplomatic service, he was Permanent Secretary of the Ministry of Foreign Affairs and also Ambassador to the European Community, Belgium, and United States, High Commissioner to Canada, and Permanent Representative to the United Nations and also to the Organisation of American States. He was a judge of the Inter-American Court of Human Rights and Personal Representative of the UN Secretary-General on the Border Controversy between Guyana and Venezuela.

The Honourable George Lamming, CHB, OCC, is a Barbadian novelist, essayist, poet and a leading Caribbean literary figure. A former distinguished visiting professor at Duke University and Brown University, he has lectured extensively and held academic posts around the world. He is the author of six novels including the much acclaimed, *In the Castle of My Skin* the coming-of-age story of a boy and a region. In June 1986, he wrote the tribute to Barrow included in this publication.

Dr Peter Laurie, GCM, was Permanent Secretary in the Ministry of Foreign Affairs from 1989-1999. He was also the Ambassador to the United States, China and Cuba and a member of the Inter-American Commission on Human Rights from 1999-2003. An author of multiple books and plays, he was a columnist with the Barbados Advocate and the Sunday Sun, and now writes occasionally for Barbados Today.

The late Most Honourable Michael N. Manley ON, OCC, was the fourth Prime Minister of Jamaica from 1972-1980 and from 1989-1992. The son of Norman Manley and close friend of Errol Barrow, he served in the Royal Canadian Air Force during World War II and attended the London School of Economics.

The Rt Honourable Sir James Fitz-Allen Mitchell, KCMG, was the second Prime Minister of St Vincent and the Grenadines and the founder of the New Democratic Party (NDP). He became Prime Minister in 1984 and was re-elected for a fourth successive term in 1998. One of the longest serving prime ministers in Caribbean history, he retired in 2000 and stayed on as Senior Minister until 2001. He also served as Premier of the then colony from 1972-1974.

His Excellency The Honourable Robert L. Morris, CHB, GCM, is the Ambassador for Barbados to CARICOM and the ACS. He was Deputy General Secretary of the Barbados Workers' Union, a personal assistant to the Rt Excellent Sir Frank Walcott, and Vice-President of the Caribbean Congress of Labour. He served as a Member of Parliament from 1986-1994.

Ms Alicia Nicholls is a Caribbean trade and development consultant.

The late C. Asquith Phillips, QC, shared legal chambers with Errol Barrow. He was the second General Secretary of the DLP and also served as Deputy President of the Senate.

Mr George A. Pilgrim is the General Secretary of the DLP and the Principal Political Advisor to the Prime Minister of Barbados.

Sir Shridath Ramphal GCMG, AC, ONZ, OE, OCC, QC, served as Commonwealth Secretary-General from 1975-1990. He previously was the Foreign Minister of Guyana from 1972-1975 and Assistant Attorney General of the West Indies Federation from 1958-1962.

Sir David A. C. Simmons, KA, BCH, QC, is a distinguished Caribbean jurist and politician. A Parliamentarian from 1976-2001 and a Cabinet Minister including three terms as Attorney General, he was also Chief Justice of Barbados and set a record in becoming a Queen's Counsel after only 14 years of professional practice. He is currently a Member of the Regional Judicial and Legal Services Commission of the Caribbean Court of Justice.

Mr Alan Smith is a banker and a Fellow of the Royal Society for the Encouragement of Arts, Manufactures and Commerce. In 2015, he and the late Sir Frederick co-authored the book *"Dreaming a Nation"* on the Barbados journey to Independence.

The late Sir Frederick Smith, KA, MBE, QC, was a founding member of the Democratic Labour Party. He was its first Chairman and served on the first Provisional General Council. He held numerous Cabinet posts including Attorney-General at Independence and Leader of the Opposition from 1976 – 1978. He also served as Chief Justice of the Turks and Caicos Islands, and President of the Court of Appeal of Grenada.

The Rt Excellent Sir Garfield Sobers AO, OCC, heralded as the greatest cricketer ever, is a National Hero of Barbados.

The late Honourable David J. H. Thompson, QC, was the sixth Prime Minister of Barbados from January 2008 until his death on 23 October 2010. He entered formal politics in 1987 in the St John by-election following the death of Errol Barrow. During Erskine Sandiford's (now Sir Lloyd) Administration, he served as Minister of Community Development and Culture and as Minister of Finance. He became leader of the DLP in 1994.

Professor Pedro L. V. Welch was Dean, Professor of Social and Medical History, and Deputy Principal of the University of the West Indies, Cave Hill Campus. A Commonwealth Scholar and Johns Hopkins Fellow, he has written or co-authored several books and articles on the history of Barbados.

SOURCES OF IMAGES

Portraits of Errol Barrow: Barbados Government Information Service (BGIS)
With his sisters Nita, Sybil and Ena: Frank DaSilva
Barrow and Sobers: Willie Alleyne
A Diverse Man: The Nation Publishing Co. and Frank DaSilva
Barrow with Bomber Crew: The Nation Publishing Co.
Barrow with Second Barbados Contingent: Barbados Postal Service
DLP Founders: The Democratic Labour Party
Of the People: The Nation Publishing Co.
The Parliamentarian: BGIS and The Nation Publishing Co.
Constitutional Conference: Royal Commonwealth Society Cambridge University
    Archives
Independence: BGIS
United Nations: BGIS
White House: BGIS and US Naval Photographic Unit
The Caribbean Man: BGIS, Jamaica Gleaner and CaribbeanElections.com
Queen and Commonwealth: BGIS, Commonwealth Secretariat, Getty Images and Frank
    DaSilva
CARICOM: CARICOM Secretariat and CDB
Titans: James Mitchell
Farewell: The Nation Publishing Co.

KEY TERMS

Barbados Labour Party (BLP) – The BLP is the current official opposition party which was founded in 1938 and until 1944 was called the Barbados Progressive League.

Democratic Labour Party (DLP) – The DLP is the current governing party which was founded in 1955 in a breakaway from the Barbados Labour Party and which led the island into Independence. It was mostly led by Errol Barrow from the late 1950s until his death.

CARICOM – Established in 1973, the Caribbean Community (CARICOM) is a fifteen-member territory organisation whose main purposes are to promote economic integration and cooperation among its members.

CARIFTA – The Caribbean Free Trade Association, the precursor to CARICOM, was formed in 1965 and dissolved in 1973.

CSME – The CARICOM Single Market and Economy is an integrated development strategy adopted in 1990 towards: i) deepening economic integration by advancing beyond a common market towards a single market and economy, ii) widening membership towards expanding the market, and iii) strengthening trading links with non-traditional partners.

Commonwealth of Nations – The Commonwealth of Nations is a voluntary association of 53 independent and sovereign states, mostly former British colonies, working under common values, goals and development objectives. Her Majesty Queen Elizabeth II serves as the Head of the Commonwealth and convenes a biennial meeting of Heads of Government. The principal agency is the Commonwealth Secretariat led by the Commonwealth Secretary General.

House of Assembly – The Lower House (Chamber) of the Parliament of Barbados

Little Eight Federation – Following the independence of Jamaica and Trinidad and Tobago in 1962 another attempt was made to join the remaining so-called Little Eight islands (Antigua and Barbuda, Barbados, Dominica, Grenada, Montserrat, St Kitts/Nevis/Anguilla, Saint Lucia, and St Vincent and the Grenadines) into the Federation of the Eastern Caribbean, with Barbados playing the leading role in the organisation's Regional Council.

Parliament of Barbados – This is the national legislature of Barbados. The Parliament is bicameral in composition and is made up of an appointed Senate (Upper House), and an elected House of Assembly (Lower House). It is second only to the Palace of Westminster as the oldest national parliament in the Commonwealth of Nations.

Senate – The Upper House (Chamber) of the Parliament of Barbados

Tenantry – A tenantry, normally a plantation tenantry, is an area of land, vested in the Crown, in a statutory board or a private person, which is subdivided into more than 5 lots for letting as sites for low-income wooden dwelling (chattel) houses.

UWI – The University of the West Indies was formally established in 1948 as the University College of the West Indies. It now comprises four campuses: Cave Hill, Barbados, Mona, Jamaica, St Augustine, Trinidad, and an Open Campus coordinated from Barbados.

The West Indies Federation – This was a short-lived political union from 3 January 1958 to 31 May 1962 of the then British Caribbean colonies (Barbados, Jamaica, Trinidad and Tobago and the Leeward and Windward Islands), with its capital in Port of Spain, Trinidad and Tobago. The expressed intention of the Federation was to create a political unit that would become independent from Britain as a single state. Belize (then British Honduras) and Guyana (then British Guiana) held observer status within the Federation.

ACKNOWLEDGEMENTS

Assembling this manuscript was a profound experience. The text demanded a certain reverence given the standing of the contributors but also because it holds an energy for it is more that the testimony and tribute to a legend; it is also the story of a people who over the span of time sought an expression of who and what they were, which was ultimately manifested in and through The Right Excellent Errol Walton Barrow.

Bringing this manuscript together was a unique honour and privilege and I need to express my sincere thanks all those who made it possible.

The Barrow family for supporting this publication and encouraging those close to our 'Father of Independence' to contribute to it. Allow me to use this opportunity to again thank the Barrow family, on behalf all Barbadians whom Errol Barrow adopted as his own, for sharing him with us which I appreciate at times may have been demanding. I am thankful also for access of the tribute delivered by the late Dame R. Nita Barrow, GCMG, FRCN.

The Rt Honourable Freundel Stuart, QC, MP, Prime Minister of Barbados, for his insightful contribution and also his commitment to the legacy of Errol Walton Barrow and to Barbados as a whole.

The Rt Excellent Sir Garfield Sobers, AO, OCC, National Hero of Barbados, for being part of this work and allowing himself to be swayed by an insistence that the narrative of Errol Walton Barrow and 1966 would be incomplete without reference to him and his role as the captain of the West Indies team. Cricket embodied our aspiration to affirm our greatness and particularly to outplay the English at their own game. His humility in genius is as inspirational today as it was then.

The current and former Prime Ministers and leaders of the region for their distinguished contributions: The Rt Honourable Owen S. Arthur, MP; The Honourable Ralph E. Gonsalves, MP; The late Most Honourable Michael N. Manley ON, OCC; The Rt Honourable Sir James Fitz-Allen Mitchell, KCMG; Sir Shridath "Sonny" Ramphal, GCMG, AC, ONZ, OE, OCC, QC; and The late Honourable David J. H. Thompson, QC.

To the current and former members of Cabinet and the Parliament of Barbados, for their rich and diverse reflections and tributes which gave immense depth and breadth to this work: Dame Maizie Barker-Welch, DBE, BCH, CHB; Mr David A.

Comissiong; Sir Henry de B. Forde, KA, QC; Mr E. Evelyn Greaves, GCM; Sir Philip Marlowe Greaves, KA, QC; The Honourable Donville O. Inniss, MP; His Excellency The Honourable Robert L. Morris, CHB, GCM; the late C. Asquith Phillips, QC; Sir David A. C. Simmons, KA, BCH, QC; and the late Sir Frederick Smith, KA, MBE, QC.

To the writers, public servants, academics, and researchers, in particular The Honourable George Lamming, CHB, OCC, for sharing his wisdom, knowledge and critical insights: Sir Frank W. Alleyne; KA; Mr Ian DeVere Archer, GCM; Professor Mary Chamberlain; Sir Stephen E. Emtage; KA, GCM; Dr Ayana Gibbs, MBChB, PhD; Mr Harold Hoyte GCM; the late Carl E. Jackman, CBE; the late Oliver Jackman; Dr Peter Laurie, GCM; Ms Alicia Nicholls; Mr Alan Smith; and Professor Pedro L. V. Welch.

To all those who supplied photos including Barbados Government Information Service, Barbados Postal Service, CaribbeanElections.com, CARICOM Secretariat, Caribbean Development Bank (CDB), Cambridge University, Commonwealth Secretariat, The Democratic Labour Party, Getty Images, The Nation Publishing Co., Jamaica Gleaner, US Naval Photographic Unit, Frank DaSilva and Willie Alleyne, and also related materials: His Honour Michael A. Carrington, MP, the Speaker of the House of Assembly and Mr Pedro Eastmond, the Clerk of Parliament for granting access to the 1987 Parliamentary Tributes; Professor Emeritus Barry B. Levine of Florida International University for the use of the article from *Caribbean Review*; and the *Old Harrisonian Society* particularly Ralph Jemmott, Andrew Hart and Michael Tull who provided access to invaluable manuscripts. Dr Ayana Gibbs, for her contribution then and now, and most significantly to another fellow Harrisonian and friend, Dr Kurt A. Lambert and the Forlam Foundation for making it all happen.

To the Democratic Labour Party particularly Mr George Pilgrim the General Secretary.

To Hansib Publications, Arif Ali, Kash Ali, Ansel Wong and the late Yussuff Haniff for loving the Caribbean as I do and sharing my passion for this book. Twenty-one of the speeches by Errol Barrow, and the tribute by Michael Manley, reproduced in this volume, were first published in *Speeches by Errol Barrow* (Hansib Publications, 1987) and edited by Yussuff Haniff.

Thanks also to the High Commission staff: Ms Simone Lewis for trying to keep up with me and Mr Peter Sealy for keeping me going.

On a personal note, I have to mention a few individuals who have been beacons in my life: Philip Greaves who exemplifies humility, David Simmons who exemplifies integrity, Griselda Barrow and Carol Haynes who exemplify compassion, Tyrone

Mapp who exemplifies resolve, and John Mayers and the late E. Eugene Ward who exemplify family. To my mother who pushed me and to my wife, Michelle, son, Dominic and daughter, Maya whose distance is an incredible struggle, I owe you all so very much. Thanks also to my sistren and brethren all.

Finally, to the Creator – for the life of Errol Walton Barrow and for being our people's Guide – we praise and glorify your name.

In Deo Fides

FOREWORD BY THE PRIME MINISTER OF BARBADOS

Mine is the especial privilege of writing the foreword to this very important publication, *Fathering a Nation: Barbados and the Legacy of Errol Walton Barrow.*

The appearance of this book coincides with the celebration by Barbados of fifty years of nationhood. The focus of the book is on Errol Barrow who led Barbados into Independence and saw the nation through its first ten years. To that extent, he is the Father of the Nation and was in the year 2000, not surprisingly, voted the Man of the Century in Barbados.

It was the German Philosopher, Hegel who, in his book, *Elements of the Philosophy of Right*, defined the great man of the age as follows: "the one who can put into words the will of his age, tell his age what its will is and accomplish it. What he does is the heart and essence of his age, he actualises his age." By that measure Errol Walton Barrow was a great man. He told Barbados what its will was and he accomplished it. He actualised his age and Barbadians recognised and acknowledged it.

Presiding over the destiny of a small island, post-slavery and post-colonial society is not easy. There is usually so much to undo at the institutional level, and so much to exorcise at the mental and psychological levels! Destiny, therefore, is very careful in its identification of those whom it will select for that exacting task.

From the time he returned to Barbados after military duties in World War II, and studies at the London School of Economics and the Honourable Society of Lincoln's Inn, it was clear to all that, like Hannibal, Errol Barrow was "clothed in that indefinable splendour which marked him out as a man destined for great enterprises". Whether in the Courts of Law or in legislative councils, Errol Barrow always manifested that spirit of combativeness that sent a clear signal to the masses of the people that he intended to be their champion. He took the side, in both law and politics, of the poor, the voiceless and the disadvantaged.

Recognising that the most powerful and effective route to empowerment was through education, immediately he acceded to office he broadened access to secondary education, created the means by which Barbadians could access tertiary education locally, and made primary education a more congenial experience for our youngest school children.

Since he had come to office in 1961 on a Manifesto that proclaimed "The road to destiny is the road to Independence. Towards this goal the country must press on", the pursuit of that goal was his continuing concern. He achieved Independence for Barbados on 30 November 1966.

Fifty years later, none but the churlish or undiscerning will deny that Independence has worked for Barbados. It has worked because while Errol was introducing projects and pursuing programmes, he was at the same time being the teacher of his people. He appealed not only to their pockets and to their material tastes, but also to their heads and to their hearts.

Errol Barrow is as much remembered, therefore, for what he said as for what he did. He understood that the needs of his countrymen were not merely material but were especially "spiritual" in the broadest sense of that term.

Small wonder then that, just shy of thirty years after his death, he is still the most quoted politician in Barbados. What is contained in the pages of this book, made up of things he has said, and of what others have thought about him, will provide evidence, at once eloquent and moving, of the greatness of the Father of our Nation.

Even stronger evidence exists around us of the social, political and economic impact he made on Barbados and the Caribbean in his time. To detail this evidence is not the purpose of a Foreword and should not detain us here.

His legacy is a challenge to any lethargy, indifference or casualness which may exist among the politicians of today in Barbados and the Caribbean. It is a reminder also that what will distinguish the great politician and leader from the very ordinary one, is what lessons, what principles future generations can say that politician or leader taught. To put it differently, the extent to which he was able *"to raise people's gaze to new and hitherto unimagined horizons"*.

A great man, our National Hero, the Right Excellent Errol Walton Barrow, fits that bill perfectly.

The Rt Honourable Freundel J. Stuart QC, MP,
Prime Minister of Barbados

PREFACE

Errol Walton Barrow's name is synonymous with the growth and development of Barbados and the modern Caribbean. This courageous, sophisticated, soft-spoken yet sharp tongued, intellectual giant was the extraordinary leader of a quiet revolution in Barbados and the English-speaking Caribbean.

He provided the vision and framed the mirror-image of Barbadians and how they should regard their Caribbean brothers and sisters. He proclaimed a gospel of self-esteem, self-reliance, and ultimately Independence. *"We were far on the road to achieving a level of understanding in this country where every man, woman and child felt that he or she counted for something; where he or she felt that here in this country existed possibilities for self-realisation and fulfilment".* This was his ideology.

Influenced by his family, particularly his uncle The Rt Excellent Dr Charles Duncan O'Neal, himself a national liberator and National Hero, and exposed to Garveyism and the 1937 riots, that would be a watershed in the political and socio-economic development of Barbados, as a teenager he would abandon the comforts of further education and instead enlist in the Royal Air Force. He flew 45 operational bombing missions over the European Theatre during World War II rising to the rank of Flying Officer.

After the War, he read economics, then a relatively new academic discipline, at the London School of Economics and Political Science at a time when it was traditional for Barbadian scholars to opt for an Oxbridge education in law or medicine. While there, he would be exposed to democratic socialism and build lasting friendship with his contemporaries including Forbes Burnham, Michael Manley, Pierre Trudeau, and Lee Kwan Yew. He also read for the Bar at Lincoln's Inn.

In 1950 he returned to Barbados and in 1951 was elected to the House of Assembly. Following a rift with his then Party leader over the

25

gradualist approach to change, in 1955 he became a founding member of the Democratic Labour Party and its Leader in 1961 when the party won the General Election. He served as Premier of Barbados from 1961-1966 when after leading the country to Independence, with his now famous statement that Barbados would *"not be found loitering on colonial premises after closing time"*, he became the first Prime Minister serving continuously for the next ten years as well as Minister of Finance and, initially, also as Minister of Foreign Affairs.

A dedicated regionalist, he was the principal architect of the Caribbean Free Trade Association (CARIFTA) in 1965 and thereafter the Caribbean Community (CARICOM) in 1973 which he described as a *"giant step for us all"*. Following the oil-crisis and the ensuing economic downturn which affected the countries in the region and also the highly controversial constitutional amendments on the appointment of senior civil servants and judges, his Party was defeated in the 1976 General Election.

An influential voice even as Leader of the Opposition, his ongoing advocacy for sovereignty and regional unity manifested itself in his opposition to the 1983 United States invasion of Grenada that he concluded would *"damage Caribbean sovereignty and self-respect."*

And through it all he never lost his common touch. George Lamming notes, *"...in person, he is the least offensive of men; easy, accessible, almost ordinary in his style of discourse. Be it fish market or supermarket, back alley or modern highway, the humble chattel home or posh ministerial office, he moves through these different orbits with a total lack of pomp or ceremony."*

Oliver Jackman captures the embodiment of Errol Barrow as a man 'of the people, by the people, for the people' stating, *"Everybody has his or her own very personal, totally authentic, Errol Barrow story, and future historians are going to go out of their minds as they try to grapple with the volume of contrast and paradox that awaits them. That is the way it is with heroes..."*

In May 1986, after ten years in opposition, he was re-elected as Prime Minister in a landslide victory; his "Mirror Image" speech was a seminal moment in the political campaign. His re-election would witness a continuation of his previous call for regional unity and self-reliance.

Regrettably, on 1 June 1987, a year after his re-election, he returned to his ancestors.

In his honour, Barbadians observe his birthday as a National Holiday and have a constant reminder of his life and service in his likeness on the Barbados fifty dollar bill. In 1998, by an act of Parliament, he was named as one of ten National Heroes of Barbados.

In this our 50th Anniversary of Independence, the Rt Honourable Freundel Stuart, QC, MP, Prime Minister of Barbados, called on Barbadians as a people to look backward, look inward, and look forward. He urged us to *"look backward to see those features of Barbadian life which we have lost and need to reclaim...look inward to see those features of Barbadian life that we need urgently to discard...and look forward to see those features of Barbadian life which we have not lost and need, at all costs, to retain."*

This introspection would be best achieved with a firm grasp of the phenomenal life and legacy of The Right Excellent Errol Walton Barrow. This publication provides a small glimpse which I hope, in time, will form part of an *Errol Barrow Archive* in which the many addresses, writings, photographs, and audio and video clips of the Father of Independence, and the reflections of those who couldn't make this publication, could be catalogued and made available for generations to come – those for whom Errol Barrow dreamt dreams and saw visions.

Guy A.K. Hewitt

With Sir Garry Sobers

With his sisters Nita, Sybil and Ena

Portrait of a Hero
The Rt Excellent Sir Garfield Sobers

Some are born great, some achieve greatness, and some have greatness thrust upon them.

WILLIAM SHAKESPEARE

I have walked with giants and have been called a legend in my own lifetime by people whose opinions I respect. While my list of giants especially those in cricket is endless, there are three in public life, in a class apart, that I want to mention.

Her Majesty The Queen is a treasure to Barbados. Beyond being our Head of State, Barbadians of all walks of life are drawn to her for her selfless sense of incredible service, her dignified leadership and the extraordinary grace with which she carries out her duties. Whenever I have had the opportunity to interact with her, we talk about our common joys and interests: Barbados, the West Indies, and horses in particular. Occasionally cricket will come up but her husband, the Duke, is by far a keener fan of the game.

Although I only met Nelson Mandela for a brief period, I felt that I knew the man. He was a gracious, serene man and I could feel the sincerity that came from deep within him. On meeting me, he related how he had followed my exploits from the confines of his prison cell. Possibly our triumphs on the pitch, symbolic of the pupil surpassing his master, reassured him that his time too would come. I looked at him and wondered how he could achieve all he had done. To be so upright, to stand for justice and to not want revenge on the people who had imprisoned him, I always thought was remarkable. That's why he is so revered by so many around the world.

Last but by no means least, is the motivation for this particular publication, the Right Excellent Errol Walton Barrow. I am sure he was the unanimous choice once Barbados embraced the concept of National Heroes and he will forever sit in the top of our pantheon of honour. As the only living National Hero, I hope that my reflection of him helps people to understand the enormity of the man but more so, to inspire others to pursue their own 'greatness'.

It was as if the same hand of destiny was guiding West Indies politicians and cricketers in the 1950s and 1960s. Indeed, you can see how our exploits on and off the pitch have been aligned, those periods of greatness along with those of uncertainty. Looking back on the 1960s, whether on or off the pitch, we were working to the same outcome – to show that the West Indies had come of age.

I am not interested in politics but it is important to understand the link between West Indies cricket and its politics, specifically the aspirations of West Indians as a people. CLR James' *Beyond a Boundary* speaks to the interconnections in our lives as he poses the question "What do they know of cricket who only cricket know?"

CLR approaches West Indies cricket as an art form but also examines its many impacts. Everything, including family, race, class, culture, politics, and the process of decolonisation are examined through the prism of West Indies cricket. He held that cricket is fundamentally unthinkable outside of the context of British colonial rule much in the same way that West Indian colonialism and decolonisation are unthinkable without cricket. For him, cricket was both an instrument of colonial power as well as our means of resisting it.

In those years, the intense social and political passions expressed themselves fiercely in cricket and stimulated the West Indies team. Race and class battles could be fought on the cricket field without violence or lost, except for pride and honour. The opposition of batsman and bowler was charged with social and political significance and served as a symbol for the broader struggle between the coloniser and colonised.

Errol and I were born worlds apart both geographically and socially. He hailed from the north of the island, St Lucy, born and raised around a plantation great house. He was the son of a priest and nephew of a doctor and national leader. I, on the other hand, was of humbler means born in a small wooden house on the old Bay Land plantation tenantry near our capital Bridgetown, the fifth child of Mr and Mrs Shamont Sobers.

My father, a merchant seaman, decided I would be called Garfield St Auburn Sobers. Most Barbadians have unusual names and I was no exception. We had no money for luxuries, only for necessities, but we were happy, well fed and adequately clothed. When I was five, my father's ship *The Lady Hawkins* was torpedoed by a German submarine and was sunk with all hands. The War would bring Errol's and my world together and they would intersect time and time again as destiny would choose to write my name on history's page, near his.

As teenagers, we both had to prepare for battle. Errol in the true sense, who at nineteen joined the RAF during in World War II while I, at seventeen, began my campaign with bat and ball, making my international test debut against England at Sabina Park. I ended up making a good impression as a pace bowler in Jamaica while Errol's Squadron Leader Alfred Barnes would remember him as *"A bloody good Navigator – first class. Get you there, get you back. Never saw Barrow get in a flap ... a good man to have along."*

Errol's intellectual and oratorical gifts are legendary but I will leave others to speak to those talents. But what is clear is that he, like me, lived according to the precept "to whom much is given much is expected" for he gave much, expecting little in return.

Some critics use to say I was an instinctive player. I do not know where my natural ability came from or who gave it to me. Perhaps only God knows, but I do believe that it is what you do with it that counts.

There was a class system operating in cricket in Barbados at that time. Empire and Spartan were the top teams and all the Combermere School boys (like Wes Hall) would go to Empire while the Harrison College boys (Errol's alma mater) went to Spartan. The boys, like me, from Bay Street elementary school had nowhere specific to go but from an early age I thought constantly about my game and what I should do to improve myself.

Errol was a brilliant man, a genius I would argue not because he was bright but because he knew how to use what God gave him. People often don't realise that top level cricket, much like golf, is 99 per cent above the shoulders. It doesn't matter how much ability you have; if you don't channel it in the right direction you will never be successful, reasonably good maybe, but never able to reach the highest heights. To do that you have to have the mental and emotional capacity to match the skill and the ability. If a player can work the two together, there is a chance of being a world-beater.

I would watch how batsmen moved. I never watched the sixes or the fours fly to the boundaries; I watched how they moved their feet, how they picked up their bat, how they got behind the ball and generally what they did. I would rather see what bowlers were bowling than cheer the boundaries. There were few coaches in those days and you learned by watching. That was my education. It wasn't something I was told to do; it just seemed natural. I watched how batsmen got into the position to hit the ball and then I would go into the nets and practice what I had seen.

When I reflect on my and Errol's accomplishments, I realise it is more than just ability, or in his case genius, for you can have all the ability but if your temperament is suspect you will never make it, whether as an international cricketer or statesman. Confidence is vital, and that comes from being in form and believing in what you are doing.

I never suffered from nerves but there was always that little bit of tension because you want to do well for yourself and your team. It is that tension that keeps you safe from doing something stupid. With that and the right confidence, you will hardly ever make a mistake, even if you are playing at the very highest level.

I also had an additional motivation. For most of my international Test career I was playing for two – myself and my great friend Collie Smith, who would have been a great cricketer, but who died in England one night in a car that I was driving. Following that tragedy, I was deeply depressed but then I realised that the West Indies had already lost Collie and I would be letting both him and my country down if I disappeared into the mists of despair. It suddenly struck me forcibly that I no longer had just to play for Garry Sobers but that I had to do two men's jobs – Collie's and mine.

That perspective helped me put my life back together and I willingly shouldered the responsibility. I started to bat and bowl for Collie and myself, and that reality probably improved my cricket to the level I reached during my career!

I suspect that Errol had a similar motivation. He laboured not for himself but for all the people of Barbados, but I also think that he, like me, had a personal motivator in the form of the Barbados Second Contingent in the RAF. They were a team of twelve, including Errol, and six were killed in action. Like Collie, Errol may have battled in the name of Cuke, Cumberbatch, Dunlop, King, Miller and Walrond who made up the 55,573 air crewmen of RAF Bomber Command who gave their lives for us during World War II.

I have heard much said of the influence of Errol's father, uncle, Harold Laski and the RE Sir Grantley Adams on him. What they did for him, Sir Frank Worrell most certainly did to me. The emergence of the West Indies as the world's best team began in Australia in 1960/61 under Frank, the greatest captain I played under.

Before Frank took over in 1960, the practice was to give the captaincy to amateurs of independent financial means like John Goddard, Gerry Alexander and Denis Atkinson. The great cricketing nations of the West Indies, with primarily Afro- and Indo-Caribbean people, had always been captained by a person of Euro-Caribbean extraction. Learie, later Lord Constantine, the West Indies cricketer, lawyer and politician who became the UK's first black peer, said after Frank led the West Indies to victory in 1963 that *"he changed the whole philosophy and structure of West Indies cricket."* A piece of the colonial past had gone.

West Indies cricket was very important to me, I played for the West Indies and not for myself. Anyone could have captained the team and I couldn't have cared less. I was ready to do the job and pull my weight for my country because I had been asked, not because I wanted the job.

I never intended nor wanted to be captain but without realising it, I started my tuition with Frank from the moment I went to England to play league cricket for Radcliffe. I learned a great deal from him while I was there and when we went on tour we spent a lot of time together. At the end of a day's play Frank would call me to have a drink and talk about the match because, he said, I knew more about the game than anybody else in the side.

Like a trusted lieutenant, Frank would discuss most things with me, asking what I thought and what I would do if I were in his place. More often than not we had exactly the same ideas. From the time Frank took the captaincy until he retired in England at the end of the 1963 series, we continued to collaborate.

When the West Indies played Australia in 1965, I was captain and Frank, knighted in 1964, was manager. I had never thought of being captain and I had no prior experience of the job, not even at the club level. But I had served the best apprenticeship of all under Frank and was confident I could do the job, especially with him at my side.

When the Board wrote and offered me the captaincy it took me six or seven weeks to reply to their letter. It was not an easy thing for me to accept because, in order to set an example, I would have to change my lifestyle, something I was not sure that I wanted to do. I have always been a free spirit and maybe not always the conventional professional cricketer. If I went to bed too early, I couldn't sleep and if I had energy to burn, I would burn it.

The players in the team knew what type of person I was and how I behaved under previous captains, ploughing my individual furrow and I wouldn't be a hypocrite. When I took the job I never imposed curfews or anything like that. I believed that if you want to play cricket for your country, and play for a long time, you must know your own limitations. If you know you cannot perform the day after a night out and you still go, you are not made for a career in cricket.

I knew it would be an additional challenge because when you captain an ageing team, half of whom think they should be in charge instead of you, there was bound to be problems. But I always looked for the positive and tried to squeeze everything out of them. Cricket is a team game and I knew that I couldn't bowl or bat at both ends neither could I keep wicket to my own bowling.

Batting at five and six, I rarely ran out partners because I gave them confidence. I believe that if you have faith in your partner and do not try to farm the bowling, he will come to the conclusion that the captain trusts him, and so will trust himself. If you keep refusing singles or pinching the bowling, he will know you have no faith in him and he will either fail or there will be a run out.

My commitment to the West Indies was always total whether I was captain or not. A bad stomach interrupted an innings once but I believed that my job was to be out there and it would take something special to take me away. I felt that my presence was always needed but I would not say I was fit when I wasn't because I would put the West Indies team in jeopardy.

That was always it for me – West Indies first and Garry second. How many others, particularly those on the Board, can say that and really mean it.

When Clive Lloyd's West Indies side beat England 5-0 in England in 1984, it was said that his team was the best ever to come out of the Caribbean. In truth, Clive's team had a phenomenal record – I would not dispute that but the outstanding West Indies team in my opinion was the one I captained between 1965 and 1967. It had a better-balanced attack than Clive's side, better batsmen and a better wicket-keeper. Also the opposition we played in those days was superior. 1966 was my favourite tour in England.

On reflection, 1966 was not just about cricket but about showing Barbados' "pride and industry" particularly against an English opposition. While I had forced England to change their captain three times in that series, over at Lancaster House at the Constitutional Conference, vintage Errol had indicated that his *"Government will not be found loitering on colonial premises after closing time."*

Without sounding insular, what was also significant as we battled on and off the field was that apart from me as captain and Conrad Hunte as vice-captain, nine Barbadians made up the team and it could have been more as some argued that Tony White and Robin Bynoe deserved places. By the end of the fourth Test at Leeds we had retained the Wisden Trophy. England were thoroughly outplayed.

Apart from the joy of our teams victory, and my contribution of three centuries (161 at Old Trafford, 163 not out at Lord's and 174 at Headingley) as well as taking the most wickets, there was the memorable sixth wicket partnership of 274 with my cousin David Holford and the fifth wicket partnership of 265 with Seymour Nurse.

I share all this to show how in 1966, Errol and I did battle on different sides of the boundary, however, I never expected him to play the crucial role that he would end up playing in my cricketing career.

It was not often but occasionally I misread a ball which I did in 1970 with my decision to accept an invitation to play in a double-wicket competition in Rhodesia, as Zimbabwe was then known. This turned out to be the worst period of my cricketing life. I was there for only 36 hours but it caused massive repercussions that threatened my reputation and my international cricket career.

I was living in England at the time and was unaware of the attitudes in the Caribbean to Rhodesia. My decision to play, taken for financial reasons, was applauded by the British press while the then Secretary of the West Indies Cricket Board of Control issued a statement saying it was my decision and had nothing to do with the Board. Further, they had given others the assurance that Rhodesia did not have the apartheid problem of South Africa. I thought I had no worries. It was the first and only time I found myself embroiled in politics.

Following press reports of my visit that highlighted my interaction with the then Rhodesian Premier, Ian Smith, who I described as a great man to talk to, all hell broke loose. It was a personal opinion and had nothing to do with me playing cricket in Rhodesia, nor was it an opinion of his politics.

Political leaders across the region rose up against me, saying I should be disqualified from captaining the West Indies and that I would no longer be welcome in their country unless I recanted and apologised. Even Indira Gandhi threatened the cancellation of the Indian tour of the West Indies. Cameron Tudor (later Sir James), the then deputy prime minister, described the attack on me as an affront to the people of Barbados.

Wes Hall (now Sir Wesley), who has and always will be a giant of a friend, was then living in Trinidad and was sent by the Trinidian Prime Minister to try to resolve the situation. Wes was frank, *"Have you hit Forbes Burnham? If you have, you would have to apologise, but you hit nobody and you do not have to apologise to anybody. We all knew you were going there and if we didn't want you to go, we should have called you and told you not to go."* However, he rightly indicated that in the interest of cricket something had to be done.

Errol, who was in the USA at the time, cut short his trip and returned home when he heard about the growing furore. When we met he agreed that I didn't have to apologise but agreed as a compromise to prepare a letter which I agreed to sign. The matter was resolved but to this day, I will always remember the unswerving loyalty of those including Errol and Wes who stood by me.

Since my retirement, I have been given a number of great honours of which I am proud especially those given not only for my success at cricket but also for fulfilling my obligations as a person and an ambassador. These include my knighthood, the Order of the Caribbean Community and the Order of National Hero of Barbados and let me put alongside these acknowledgments, of equal importance to me, is that those I have played with and against have described me as one of the most honest and gentlemanly persons in cricket.

People say that I have been a role model, an icon even, but I can honestly say that I never expected to be named a National Hero of Barbados, especially in my lifetime. I suppose it was Barbados' way of showing to youngsters that you don't have to go to war or be a revolutionary or a politician to be a 'Hero'. It takes all sorts of people to build a Nation and if you have been a successful sportsman and achieved things in your life, it is just as important for you to carry your country's flag and fly it to the highest standard.

I have never found these accolades including The Might Sparrow's *"greatest cricketer on Earth or Mars"* a burden to carry. I believe these honours were bestowed on me because of the way I am and the person I am not because I have put on any airs or graces or deliberately went out of my way to achieve fame. What people see in Garfield St Auburn Sobers is what they get. I can walk down the road or go to stores in sandals because people have always seen me that way. Those honours were given to me for what I was then, so why would I change now?

I like to think that I have lived my life in an orderly and well-intended way. This was me, not someone I tried to be, but me. I was born that way. Like Errol, no one will be allowed to take away my common touch; I achieved everything as a common man and the friends I had when I was growing up are still the friends I have today. I happily mix with those at all levels including the top but I never forget those elsewhere.

I have always been grateful to God for giving me the ability, the strength, the knowledge and the will to achieve what I have. Without Him, I know I could not have done it. Don't get me wrong, I am not overly religious but belief in God has been one of the most important cornerstones of my life.

As we approach of our 50th anniversary of Independence, I personally remember Errol, as one who was immersed in the struggle to take Barbados from a village to the state of a Nation while at the same time fighting for Caribbean togetherness. I certainly owe him an unrepayable debt of gratitude for his tremendous interest in my own life and career and for ensuring that the twin dangers of 'politics and penury' could not forever define the future of ordinary Caribbean people, including sportspersons like myself.

There is no better time than now for a publication in honour of The RE Errol Walton Barrow, National Hero and the Father of our Independence. I therefore sincerely congratulate the editor, publisher and all of the contributors and I heartily commend this book to every household in Barbados, the wider Caribbean and our diaspora.

Having Dreams and Visions

Dame Nita Barrow

Tribute delivered at the State Funeral

The tributes paid to Errol from every walk of life in Barbados, the Caribbean and all over the world during the past week have been overwhelming.

On behalf of our immediate family and to our extended family many who have come from other parts of the Caribbean and the United States, I thank you and all of those who have given tributes, for their generous words and acts in appreciation of Errol's life and work.

They have expressed it so eloquently and so sincerely, the esteem in which he was held, that there is little I feel I can do or say, except now some words of thanks for Errol as a brother, as a family man, as a friend, and as a human being who was wonderful to know and care for.

I say wonderful, for Errol who at times seemed almost simple in his manner, was also a complex person, a man of many parts full of surprises. So being close to him meant being a part of his rich adventure of living. It was an adventure in which people mattered most. All of you here this evening are a tribute to that.

I always felt that it was his voice which first struck you as the key to the sort of man he was. A soft, low-keyed voice, the voice of a gentle person. This was confirmed only two weeks ago in New York when a friend of mine, a Barbadian living there for many years heard his voice for the first time on the telephone.

She exclaimed in surprise when I got on the line, 'I couldn't believe that he was speaking. He has such a quiet voice. I thought I'd hear a great big one.' But there are many who know that that sort of speaking voice could also cut like a razor. He would listen quietly, then come out with some sort of biting comment.

I well remember on one such occasion he seemed very quiet when our grandmother was reprimanding him. She had rather an acid tongue like him, and he came out with a comment. And quick as a flash she said, 'your tongue is like the pen of a "ready write" (a term for ball-point pens)'. But that same voice could call you very early in the morning with a kind request.

Such a one came to me over one year ago, the voice simply said, *"how many extra beds have you got? There are some families burnt out."* It was a soft spoken voice, but it contained a royal command. He came himself to collect those beds.

He was a man of kindness and of compassion to a fault almost. That was the nature of the man, a people's man who genuinely enjoyed the simplest pleasures of all Barbadians – the sea and the land. But he had qualities of a patrician as well who loved beautiful things while never allowing those tastes to distort his priorities and undermine his public responsibilities as a leader of a small nation.

I think if you check the only house in his name to which he holds title in Barbados, is what I call an oversized, traditional, wooden chattel house by the seaside which he was always happy to open to family and friends.

His scholastic achievements have been widely extolled, but one of the family's strongest memories is of that day when we expected him to take up the Island Scholarship which he had won to Codrington College. He calmly announced, as I the big sister who was packing his clothes, *"those clothes which you have marked for college are going to England instead. I have joined the Royal Air Force".*

And so he went off on his voyage to do what he saw as his duty. No discussion with anyone else beforehand, he had made up his mind.

But the word and the mind and the intellect remained for him always a priority. And he found the time for academic assignments.

I visited him when he was in Florida at the International University there. He was conducting seminars. His colleagues and some of his students clustered around me and said to me, 'How can a Prime Minister take time off to teach and do it so well?'

On another occasion, later at Yale University someone made the remark to me again in a social gathering around him, 'he seems to know so much about so many subjects, but his presentations are always wide and never above the heads of his audience'.

As his friends know well, he revelled in the cut and thrust of debate, but also had a remarkable gift for drawing people out. And again I feel it was that gentle voice that fooled them, it gave them confidence. He probably was storing up the answers.

Although he was not always demonstrative, he had a strong sense of family and an enormous respect for its older members; our oldest surviving aunt in the family can attest to that.

But all of us throughout our lives lived with his great sense of humour, particularly his sisters. He used to say when the days of 'women's liberation' came, that he never had to do anything else because he had three sisters. When he had to say something about us he, who was ever against nepotism, would always say that none of us then worked in Barbados. This is my first assignment for my Government. He visited us in our various venues.

On his first visit to Geneva when I had left the Caribbean, a person who didn't know him well asked him whom he was. He said, *"In Jamaica I am Nina Barrow's brother. In St Vincent I am Ena Comma's brother, in St Croix I am Sybil Barrow's brother, only in Barbados am I the Prime Minister."* It was in words like these that he showed his pride in what we had done.

I cannot forget my telephone conversation with him on the morning of his death. Of course we discussed matters of State, relaying messages that were being passed on, but his concerns were of a personal nature. In fact I had been bidden by a Consul General to call him because I was coming back from Mongolia and the week before when he was with me he said, *"what are you doing going to Mongolia. Two and a half days for a three day meeting?"* And I said 'yes'. He said *"you know you are making a liar out of me. I once made a speech and said no one ever went to Outer Mongolia."* And so I think that he was relieved that I had returned.

But during that conversation there was an activity which involved cooking. We spoke about that for the last time following up on something we talked about the week before. I think that is an activity many members of our family share, our passion for cooking.

For we are a kitchen clan and he was the head chef, forever inventing recipes as some of you know, tossing things together in fresh ways, producing very delicious dishes, very often of the fish which his faithful adherents caught for him in the waters around Oistins and which he never tired of preparing.

Our island, its men and women, the challenge to make its slender resources nourish its people well, was the driving force behind his incredible capacity for hard work. He was his own greatest taskmaster, he never spared himself because he knew that the youth of Barbados above all, deserved nothing but the best. I am reminded of his little granddaughter Nadia who told me today she is going to write a poem to her granddad.

In Barbados we recognise that we are few in numbers and in acreage. We have no great oil wells or gold mines, but we do have great resources of mind and body and spirit. Our richest assets which Errol knew well had to be nurtured and developed with imagination, hard work and absolute integrity.

Throughout his life he was inspired by this visons of a bright and proud future for his beloved country. And all that Errol envisioned for Barbados, he wished and worked for as a Caribbean man who lived and died with his dream of a truly free and integrated nation.

A close friend of Errol's and the family, Sir Kenneth Stuart, sent a telex because he regretted that he could not be here today. He asked to include these words of tribute. They so well capture what we feel that I quote them: *"For creative men like Errol, there can be no final arrival. They represent great continuums and are not to be mourned. When we speak of them in the past, it is because the grammar of language dictates it, not the grammar of life."*

For those of us who knew Errol so well and loved him so deeply: as friends, as father, as husband, as brother, there is no past tense. His life has been a blessing and will always be a present joy.

I commend him to the youth of Barbados, and youth of the Caribbean, for we in our area have long had young men [and women] who dreamt dreams and saw visions. They have all grown older as he did, but there has always been another generation. I know therefore that he rests in peace, for that generation has received education, experience, pride in a nation, which is now theirs to carry forward.

Portrait of a Prime Minister
The Honourable George Lamming

Parents have no idea what damage their love may inflict on children. Similarly, we do not know where an influence begins nor can we trace with any certainty that subtle process whereby it works an effect on the choices we make. My own political curiosity didn't start with the man's interest in philosophy which dominated my reading after the 1950s.

But it may have had something to do with the boy who loitered among the crowds in Queen's Park learning the acid embattled language of men who aspired to be our leaders. And I had watched the riots at close quarters. Or even at an earlier date, when I had feared and distrusted those white priests who led us in prayer at the apartheid church of St Cyrpian's. Belleville is still a difficult memory for me.

A reflection on the source of influence is appropriate to any serious observations of Errol Barrow, the Prime Minister of Barbados.

He had been here before, from 1961 to 1976. Even in Opposition he sometimes gave the impression that he had lent the office to his successor. A man of slow voice and very gentle manners he surprised and often shocked Barbados by the things he said.

Once he apologised to an immense crowd in Independence Square for an unfortunate appointment he had made to the public service. On a similar occasion he has lamented the fact that he helped to draft the Constitution which gave special liberties of speech to Members of Parliament, explaining that he didn't anticipate the Chamber would so quickly accommodate such a great variety of vagabonds.

I have heard him warn the poor to avoid taking their disputes into the law courts. He appeared to have doubts about the honour of his own profession, and he has said so.

And yet, in person, he is the least offensive of men; easy, accessible, almost ordinary in his style of discourse. Be it fish market or supermarket, back alley or modern highway, the humble chattel home or posh ministerial office, he moved through these different orbits with a total lack of pomp or ceremony.

It is difficult to think of a public figure in Barbados who commands such a wide and genuine affection from his people. But there was a complex personality behind his veneration, and one example is provided by his relations with the Press. *"If the media do not make you, they cannot break you. Consequently, even well-meaning and honest journalists find it difficult to secure interviews or responses from me as they will all confirm; chiefly because in public life, I am a private person. If my name never appears in the Press, even if I won a prize of great value, I would remain completely unconcerned."*

This is a very revealing admission, and it says more than Barrow may have intended. In the first place, I do not think it is true that the Press selects its targets with such care. The Press can reason. But the passage is drawing our attention to an important aspect of Barrow as 'a private person'.

A public figure who can remain completely unconcerned about neglect or critical dismissal is making a declaration of astonishing self-assurance; a quality which might otherwise be perceived as arrogance.

And Barrow did have a degree of social confidence which is rare in most Barbadians, who always need to check out each other's origins before a relationship can be approved.

It is as though he had escaped the pervasive inferiority complex which cripples the mind and imagination of most of the black middle class.

Barrow had a powerful sense of his social and ancestral connection, and at the heart of his security is the O'Neal clan, and especially the heroic figure of his uncle Dr Charles Duncan O'Neal.

O'Neal, who was born in 1879, graduated from Edinburgh University as a medical doctor and returned to Barbados in 1924. For the next 12 years his life became the example of sacrifice and dedication which has never been surpassed in the political history of Barbados.

He declared himself a socialist, identified with the cause of longshoremen and field labourers and every sector of wretched black life in the island. He launched the Democratic League, created the Working Men's Association, and fought to teach a voteless black populace the importance of organisation.

Almost alone, O'Neal confronted the merciless citadels of white power, demanding the abolition of child labour; free medical and dental care of old people and children, a universal pension scheme, and the disestablishment of the Church on the grounds that no man should be asked to pay for another man's religion.

Barrow was the nephew, in a sense the son, of a man who came to be known as the father of democracy and who had earned that honour. He absorbed this influence as a boy and must have come to see O'Neal as the rock on which he would one day build his own spiritual house.

Barrow has this innate conviction that he has come from great stock. It is not at all surprising that many years later, in a public appeal to CARICOM Heads of Government, he would say: *"I place special emphasis on defending the dignity and self-respect of our people, since it must never be thought that poverty is a good enough excuse for abandoning these virtues."*

His preparation for public life has another and quite different source of influence. The journey to Britain is critical in understanding the mental climate of his generation. Barrow didn't arrive as a student. Like any other loyal colonial of his time, he went to serve in a war. Crisis is a good opportunity for learning the anatomy of a society. The rigidity of the British class system would have been temporarily dislocated, narrowing the social distance between men and women, and people of different origins. But the English are branded on the tongue, and accent immediately betrays every citizen's social formation.

Barrow would have met English people of all classes, now forced into various forms of social intercourse which would have been impossible in more normal times.

A product of Empire, he caught a glimpse of those who had made the rules by which his own childhood had been indoctrinated. The next stage was inevitable. He would become the colonial revolt. If he did not wish to be revolutionary, it is also true he did not degenerate into that status we call conservative. For the colonial has nothing to conserve unless he consciously settles for a life of voluntary enslavement.

45

By the end of the war, Barrow would be a student with a difference. He was ripe for the influence of the London School of Economics, dominated at the time by the socialist theoretician, Professor Harold Laski. It was an influence which bore strange fruit across more than one continent.

It was here, too, that the triumvirate of friendship, later known as the Barrow – Burnham – Manley axis, found its earliest soil. Years later, they would have settled many a discord by recalling the political intimacy of the London days.

It was a period of great change. The British people had repudiated their war hero, Winston Churchill, in as decisive a manner as the people of Barbados in 1986 dealt with the party of 'Tom' Adams.

The anti-colonial struggle was irreversible. London was the city and the intellectual training camp of many men who would become the dominant influence on the liberation struggles of their countries until independence was conceded: Jomo Kenyatta, Kwane Nkrumah, and his political advisor, the great pan-Africanist, George Padmore. This was the political environment which Barrow knew personally and whose influence he had never been quite able to escape.

The radical tone of many of his statements has a root and a line of continuity from Duncan O'Neal to Nkrumah and Padmore, and the honourable and courageous visit he made with his old friend, Michael Manley, to the Debt Conference in Havana. This could only have provoked controversy from commentators whose general backwardness included a specific ignorance of Barrow's political ancestry.

It is important to remind a younger generation in all territories that his political career is an inseparable part of history of the regional integration movement; from his first meeting with Sir Alexander Bustamante, Dr Eric Williams and Cheddi Jagan in 1963, to the formal launching of CARICOM at Chaguaramas in Trinidad in 1973.

Until 1975, he had played a central role in helping to convene no less than 13 Heads of Government meetings which bore fruit in a variety of Caribbean institutions: the Caribbean Free Trade Association (CARIFTA), the Caribbean Development Bank, the Caribbean Meteorological Institute, the University of the West Indies (UWI), Cave Hill Campus, the UWI Faculty of Law, and the Common Market and the Caribbean Community (CARICOM).

46

DIVERSITY

Jamming with friends and son, David

The Equestrian

The Aviator

Leading by example

The Summation
Professor Pedro L. V. Welch

There can be little doubt that the task of nation-building in post-colonial societies requires the creation or reconstruction of icons of the past. The creation of such icons reflects the need to restore pride in an historical contribution which was all but obliterated under a regime imposed by colonial overlords. In elevating the contribution of Errol Walton Barrow to the status of National Hero, the Government of Barbados sought to address this need.

COLONIALIST ORIGINS: THE CONSTRUCTION OF A HERO

Errol Barrow was born on 21 January 1920 in the Parish of St Lucy, into a prominent middle class family whose roots go back to Samuel Jackman Prescod, the black social reformer of the mid-19th century. He was born to Reginald Grant Barrow and the Ruth Alberta Barrow nee O'Neal in the maternal family house located on a farm in Checker Hall, called The Garden.

His birth occurred within the context of an island society which was still steeped in the norms and values of an earlier colonial age. This was a Barbados with an economy based on plantation agriculture which offered at best seasonal work at relatively low wages. This was a Barbados which the franchise, due to a property qualification, was out of the reach of most persons of African descent and some Caucasians. This was a Barbados where women were completely excluded from the vote. Certainly, F.A. Hoyos, that pioneer of modern Barbadian historiography could say of some democratic reforms initiated by a white parliamentarian, C.P. Clarke, in the early 1920s, that: *"Clarke lived and worked in an age when the plantocracy sat in the seats of the mighty*

49

and controlled the Legislature, when the powers of privilege were entrenched and sought to hold at bay all the forces of liberalism and democracy..."

For most Barbadians the only outlet from the misery they confronted was emigration to Panama, Cuba or further north, to the United States of America. Despite the bleak picture, this was also a dynamic era in which the masses were using their native creativity to fashion room-to-manoeuvre options for themselves. This was a period in which independent organisations such as the Friendly Societies and the Barbados Landship were expanding their membership. This was a period in which an unsung hero, Clennell Wickham was championing the cause of the working class as editor of the Herald newspaper. Moreover, the Universal Negro Improvement Association (UNIA) organised by Marcus Garvey was busy planting its roots throughout the Caribbean. By the early 1930s, seven branches of this organisation had been established in Barbados. Indeed, as research by David Browne's has shown, the UNIA was able to assemble a membership of over 500 persons at a meeting held at the Olympic Theatre in Bridgetown in 1921.

When we add to this picture the agitation for improved conditions for Barbadian workers, led by Barrow's uncle, the RE Dr Charles Duncan O'Neal and the Democratic League, we get a clearer picture of the contending forces which would have had an impact on the life of a young Errol Barrow. Charles Duncan O'Neal's influence on the young Barrow is attested to in the words of his brother, Reginald Graham Barrow, who recalled that *"Errol got many of his ideas from O'Neal. In those days O'Neal was associated with C. A. (Chrissie) Brathwaite, J. A. Martineau...people like that who were interested in the Barbados Democratic League and the Barbados Workingmen's Association..."*

Another aspect of Barrow's early upbringing was the strong influence of his father, Rev Reginald Barrow. He entered Codrington College in 1909 to prepare for ordained ministry, an achievement in itself because by this time, 70-odd years after emancipation, priests of African descent were uncommon. His graduation and subsequent appointment as Curate at St Lucy's Parish Church and later, as Head of the Alleyne School, speaks to the capacity of the man who was also acutely aware of the socio-economic and political inequalities of Barbadian society. While his training and social background placed him within the upper echelons of coloured society his race still constrained him but it seems like Rev Barrow was not averse to using the pulpit to challenge the prevailing order of society.

In early 1920, Reginald Barrow was posted to the island of St Croix in response to a request from the Bishop of that diocese. There he continued to wield a theological cudgel against racism which ultimately led to his dismissal as priest, after which he became a member of the African Methodist Episcopal (AME) Church. He founded a branch of that church in St Croix and continued his assault on the social inequities of the day while also becoming Editor of the Herald which, like its Barbadian counterpart, held a radical pro-worker position. His activities led to him being deported from St Croix in 1922 and the family returned to Barbados. Although Rev Barrow would go on to pursue his ministry in the USA there can be little doubt that the radicalism of his father contributed to the unrepentant militancy which Errol would demonstrate in later life.

PREPARING THE POLITICAL BASE

There were several inputs in the training of the young Errol Barrow for entry onto the political stage. Notwithstanding the impediments which every Afro-Barbadian faced in a society structured along racial lines, the Barrow family had several assets. A well-known medical doctor as an uncle and a father whose antecedents, no less than his own formidable achievements, placed him ahead of most of his peers. He was able to acquire a sound primary education at the Wesley Hall Boys' School and a secondary education at Harrison College, the education mecca for the children of elite families and the black working and middle class who were bright and fortunate enough to win a scholarship.

It is evident that the academic preparation which he received at Harrison College, heavily influenced by a reading of the Classics, provided a solid foundation for his entry into tertiary education in England. As proved by Grantley Adams (later the RE Sir Grantley) the sole Prime Minister of the West Indies Federation, and Dr Eric Williams, Prime Minister of Trinidad and Tobago, the academic base provided in elite colonial schools was more than adequate for the intellectual challenges of the Mother Country. It is noteworthy that when Cameron Tudor (later Sir James), was elected the first black President of the Oxford Union in 1942, later becoming Barrow's deputy prime minister, the news bulletin ranked Harrison College with the best English public schools.

In 1939, the year that World War II broke out, Barrow won an Island Scholarship in Classics but instead of going on to Codrington College like his father before him, he opted to enlist in the Royal Air Force. The experience formed part of a matrix which was to play an important role in transforming him into a leader. While in the RAF he was promoted, in turn, Observer Navigator, Leading Aircraftsman, Sergeant, Pilot Officer and Flying Officer. His was a distinguished service which culminated in his assignment as personal navigator to the Air Chief Marshall, Sir Sholto Douglas, during the Allied occupation of Germany.

This was a noteworthy achievement and a rarity at that time for someone of African descent to be given a position of such responsibility. Perhaps his easy mixing with persons of various racial backgrounds was due, in part, to his experiences in the RAF. When Barrow was demobilised after the war, Peter Morgan (a Minister in Barrow's Cabinet) advised that he was seconded to the Colonial Office where he acted in a supervisory position in a training programme for ex-servicemen. Such experiences were preparing him for the assumption of much heavier responsibilities.

The leadership training which Barrow received in the RAF and in the Colonial Office along with his formidable intellectual skills nurtured at home were honed in London. He graduated from the London School of Economics and Political Science with a Bachelor's degree in Economics and Industrial Law in 1949 while concurrently reading Law at the Inns of Court and being called to the Bar in 1950. Law was an important signpost in the career development of the young man as, like medicine, it was considered to be a prerequisite for entry into the political arena as it provided the financial independence as a bulwark against the ostracism which followed those who dared to challenge the existing social and political order.

Of seminal importance during his English sojourn was the impact of one of his mentors, Professor Harold Laski of the LSE, on his intellectual and ideological development. Laski, a chairman of the British Labour Party, was Britain's most influential intellectual spokesman for socialism in the interwar years and his teaching greatly influenced men who later become leaders of new nations in Africa, Asia and the Caribbean including Jawaharlal Nehru, Barrow and Michael Manley (also a former WWII pilot), among others.

London was also the global hub for the intellectual elite. As a student Barrow served as Chairman of the Council of Colonial Students where his contemporaries included Forbes Burnham, Michael Manley, Pierre Trudeau, and Lee Kwan Yew, all destined to become political leaders in their home countries and lifelong friends. He would also come to know Abubakar Tafawa Balewa of Nigeria, Seretse Khama of Botswana and Kwame Nkrumah of Ghana, all future leaders of their respective countries.

FROM LAWYER TO PARLIAMENTARY REPRESENTATIVE: THE YEARS OF FULFILMENT

Barrow's return to Barbados in 1950, with his wife Carolyn and daughter Lesley, introduced Barbados to the young radical who would slowly evolve into the personality known affectionately as "Dipper". It would seem that Grantley Adams, then the acknowledged leader of political reform in Barbados, took Barrow under his wing, perhaps recognising his future political leadership potential despite the subsequent criticisms of each other's leadership. They also shared some of the tenets of Fabian Socialism and could probably identify with each other's philosophical underpinnings.

It is important to appreciate that the political culture of Barbados in the early 1950s was evolving, that is, the elements of the political party system were still heavily influenced by an earlier colonial political tradition. The three political parties which had contested the 1948 elections, namely, the Electors Association, the Barbados Labour Party (BLP) and the Congress Party, were subscribers to what might be termed a "liberal constitutionalist" philosophy that places emphasis on the individual rights and freedoms by law.

Although the winds of change were on the political horizon, the planter-merchant elite still held the balance of power and represented a formidable opposition to radical reform. Adams appreciated their ability to be a major hindrance and adopted a political stance which might be best described as pragmatic, if not cautious. It was into this political culture that Barrow inserted himself, firstly by launching a career as a lawyer and then by joining the BLP.

In the elections of 1951, the BLP won sixteen of the twenty four seats in the House of Assembly including Barrow's seat as the Senior Member of the constituency of St George. Barbados then had a double-member constituency system in which two persons were elected to represent each constituency; the candidate with the highest number of votes became the Senior Member.

Barrow's first speech in the House of Assembly does not reveal the radicalism which was later to drive a wedge between himself and Adams but it does reveal something of his wide ranging interests. In this maiden speech, the debate was on a Bill to establish third-party insurance. His presentation revealed his intimate knowledge of the workings of the legal system but what is more significant is that the speech also revealed a restlessness of spirit which could not be confined to the matter under discussion but would also seek to address other wider constitutional issues. He asserted: *"There is another point which is not germane to the present issue; but at some very early date, we shall have definitely to revise and amend the Separation and Maintenance Act, 1950 and make its provisions more widely known to the community. However, I do not intend to dwell on that issue, but having had a cursory glance at the present Act, I say that there are certain things which need to be amended..."*

The young Barrow, trained as he was under Laski, and having developed his own socialist agenda, could not long be held in check by the leadership of the BLP. Within a few years he, along with other young intellectuals of the Party, were at loggerheads with Adams over the pace of reform and the direction of Party policy The disagreement between the 'left wing' faction of the party, led by Barrow is also associated with a growing conflict between Adams and the then General Secretary of the Barbados Workers Union (BWU), Frank Walcott (later the RE Sir Frank).

In his *The History of the Barbados Workers' Union*, Francis Mark chronicles the factors which led to Adams's resignation from the Presidency of the BWU after his assumption of the Premiership of Barbados and his break with Walcott. Apparently, with the commencement of the ministerial system of government in Barbados, it was expected that Walcott would have been appointed as a minister. This did not happen and, moreover, as F.A. Hoyos records, *"no member of the Party's far left was selected as a minister."* Hoyos continues: *The Siamese twin relationship between the BLP and the BWU was terminated and this marked the beginning of a period of bitter hostility between Adams and Walcott. Nor did the relations between Adams and Barrow show any improvement. Indeed, the rift in the party grew wider and deeper, with Barrow eventually announcing in March 1954 that he was renouncing all ties with the BLP..."*

The formation of the Democratic Labour Party in 1955 marked the formal separation of party politics in Barbados into two relatively distinct political camps. As both were labour parties it could be presumed that they would pursue essentially similar policies. However, it is clear that in the opinion of leaders and masses of that era, the BLP with its base in the agricultural sector and the DLP with a stated social democratic outlook had clear philosophical and ideological differences.

A crucial factor in the political debate that pitted Barrow and the DLP against Adams and the BLP was the perception that the BLP had capitulated to planter interests, leaving the black masses at the mercy of their economic masters. However, the perception that the BLP was a tool of the planter-merchant elite was unfortunate as there can be no question that tremendous socio-economic strides for the people of Barbados had been made under the leadership of Adams.

However, the political rhetoric which was hurled from one side to another had its effect. Sir Hilary Beckles would later say of Barrow's disaffection with the BLP and the emergence of the DLP: *"Barrow's entry into the mainstream of middle class anti-colonial and black nationalist radicalism...was directly associated with an attempt to rescue the political wing of the labour movement from the rapidly encroaching white conservatism..."* Yet, Beckles goes on to say that Barrow was not a socialist "in the Marxist use of the term; neither was he advocating the restructuring of the Barbadian socio-economic landscape." It is against that observation that we may focus our attention on the years from 1961-1966.

POST-1961: THE HEROIC YEARS

Barrow was defeated in the 1956 General Election as the DLP faced the might of the BLP election machine, which was allegedly supported by the planter-merchant class. The fledgling DLP was badly wounded, ending up with only two seats in St Lucy held by J. Cameron Tudor and J.E. Theodore Brancker. Barrow re-entered Parliament in 1958 after winning a by-election in St John. Thereafter, with the support of the leadership of the BWU, the star of the DLP would continue to rise until in 1961 with Adams in Trinidad as Prime Minister of the West Indies Federation and the BLP led by Dr H.G. Cummins under fire from the labour movement, the DLP won the General Election. The margin of victory was fourteen seats to the combined opposition total of nine. Frank Walcott had campaigned and won his seat as an Independent which effectively boosted the DLP total to fifteen.

While the DLP under Barrow continued to build on the policies of Adams and the BLP, it can safely be asserted that the years between 1961 and 1975 belonged to Barrow. More than any other personality of this period, his influence loomed large on the political landscape. Under his inspired leadership, social initiatives launched by the DLP captured public imagination and linked a growing middle class and an aspiring working class to the fortunes of the Party. The first of these initiatives to bear fruit was the lowering of the voting age from 21 to 18 years and the decree of free access to education at all of the government-supported secondary schools.

The abolition of tuition fees at government schools opened up opportunities for thousands of Barbadians to enter the local grammar schools and had such a profound effect on the Barbadian voting public that it cemented their allegiance to "Dipper." In a tribute to Barrow, Oliver Jackman an eminent Barbadian jurist and diplomat observed: *"My late mother who had no truck with politics and little time for politicians... considered that there were really only four events in her long life (from 1902 to 1985): two world wars, the riots of 1937, and the introduction of free secondary education in Barbados in 1961. 'Barrow free the people' she would say; and that was the beginning and end of her politics."*

In the debate over the reduction of the voting age from 21 to 18 years, Barrow revealed some of the philosophies which girded his policy-making. The issue as far as he was concerned was not simply a matter of lowering the voting age. It had to do with the question of furthering the democratic process. Referring to the Act which governed local government elections, he observed that its provisions favoured the owners of plantations. Moreover, a significant proportion of the voter cohort was excluded, namely those in the 18-21 age group. What was striking, according to Barrow, was the fact that many such persons were gainfully employed and were tax payers: It was only fair that this group should be enfranchised, especially if the principle of "no taxation without representation" was followed to its logical conclusion.

There is no questioning that Barrow's perspective of democracy which included the extension of the franchise to young adults was progressive but his response to attempts by the United Kingdom to reassert colonial dominance over Grenada demonstrated that his vision was one of sovereignty for the people of Barbados and the Caribbean. On 19 June 1962, he introduced a resolution condemning the British Government's suspension of the Grenada Constitution. This suspension took place against the background of charges that Eric Gairy, the Premier of Grenada, had mismanaged public funds.

Barrow asserted that he was *"not in favour of any form of imperialism, whether it [was] British imperialism, American imperialism, or Russian economic imperialism"* and that he was *"opposed to imperialism in any form, shape or disguise, no matter from whatever quarter that imperialism happens to emanate."* The issues in Grenada, he argued were not *"the business of the United Kingdom, the people of Barbados, the people of America, nor the people of the Soviet Union."*

These remarks, coming as they were from the black Premier of a small island, and directed as they were to the seat of British colonial power in the Colonial Office, were nothing short of heroic. In fact, they pre-figured the eventual debates on Barbados' Independence in which

Barrow would assert that the policies adopted by the Barbados administration would be fully informed by Barbadian interests.

There are other statements made by Barrow on the issue of colonialism which expose the inner workings of his mind.

In the speech made in Parliament on 4 January 1966, calling for the convening of a conference to discuss Barbados' Independence, he drew a sharp distinction between his views on constitutional independence and those of Adams. Indeed, he accused Adams of supporting a reversion to Crown Colony status for Barbados in 1939. This accusation needs to take into consideration the context of Adams' then position which was a political system still dominated by the local planter-merchant elite. There is no doubt however, that Barrow was convinced that a sharp ideological divide separated him from his political opponents over the question of Independence.

In the January 1966 speech, Barrow goes further in articulating a view which was strongly anti-imperialist. He delivered a scathing indictment on the colonialist agenda of the United Kingdom. In particular, he pointed out that British efforts to federate Barbados with seven other island-territories, following the collapse of the West Indies Federation, were based on the *"worst kind of political immorality."* The charge of "political immorality" was based on his view that the new federation plans sought to saddle Barbados with financial and other burdens which were primarily the responsibility of the Mother Country. Barrow argued that: *"...these [were] countries which [had] been exploited until the last drop of blood [had] been squeezed out of them, and under these circumstances you [could not] be surprised if the British Government [wanted] to palm off these islands and [wanted] others to take them on..."*

The compelling reason for Barrow's push towards Independence was not an anti-federalist sentiment but rather, the rational consideration of the problems that would face Barbados as the administrative centre of a grouping of small island states. At best, in his view, such a federation would have replaced one imperialist structure with another which would be manifestly tied to the Mother Country through a state of dependency. The answer with which Barrow proposed to counter the British colonial disregard of the interests of Barbados was to assure the Independence of Barbados. *"Colonialism [was] the reason for the...impasse in West Indian affairs, and [Barbados] could not afford to wait."*

Barrow's rationale is contained in his contribution to the 4 January 1966 House of Assembly debate on "Securing Nationhood within the Commonwealth", where he argued: *"And whereas the Government [of Barbados] has from January 1962 to April 1965 engaged in discussions with the Governments of the Windward and Leeward Islands on the establishment of a new Federation... And whereas these discussions have proved fruitless for several reasons among which are: (a) the failure of the Government of the United Kingdom to indicate the quantum of development finance which would have been available to the new Federation..."*

In making this contribution to the debate, the Premier quoted from a letter written by Sir John Stow, Governor of Barbados, to the Secretary of State for the Colonies in the United Kingdom that stated: *"...there is no prospect or little prospect of the discussions coming to a satisfactory conclusion unless Her Majesty's Government made a clear and unequivocal statement on the quantum and duration of financial assistance which would be provided for the Federation..."*

Given the realities revealed above, it was clearly best that Barbados *"not [be] found loitering on colonial premises after closing time."* It may also be noted that notwithstanding Barrow and the DLP's general commitment to a regional Federation, the DLP's Manifesto of 1961 clearly espoused a vision of eventual Independence, possibly within a federation, but given the realities of the time, outside of it. The Manifesto stated, unequivocally, *"The road to destiny is the road to Independence. Towards this goal the country must press on."*

Barrow's views on Independence found further expression in his speech to the United Nations on the occasion of Barbados' admission to that august body where he asserted that Barbados *"will be friend of all, satellites of none."* It is within such a context that Barbados' celebration of this unrepentant nationalist who carries the title "Father of Independence", in addition to the official designation of a National Hero, is fully deserved.

FOR KING AND COUNTRY

With Bomber Crew during World War II

The commemorative stamp of the Second Barbados
Contingent in the RAF including Errol Barrow

A Colossus

HE The Honourable Robert Morris

June 1987 Parliamentary Tribute (abridged)

No longer mourn for me when I am dead
Than you shall hear the surly sullen bell
Give warning to the world that I am fled
From this vile world with vilest worms to dwell.
Nay, if you read this line, remember not
The hand that writ it, for I love you so
That I in your sweet thoughts would be forgot
If thinking on me then should make you woe.

WILLIAM SHAKESPEARE, Sonnet 71

Errol Walton Barrow had myriad qualities that made him a role model for persons of my and any generation, but the one attribute that set him apart, in my estimation, was that he dared to choose a political philosophy that was controversial in his time. He espoused that philosophy in whatever forum he found himself, and in his practice as a politician he tried, with a great deal of success, to embody that philosophy in practical action.

Errol Barrow was a democratic socialist. He was aware of the negative stigma attached to the word 'socialism' and the constant attempt to portray socialists as rabble rousers and, generally, destructive persons, but he was not afraid to assert that there are variants of socialism, including the one which he personally espoused and made the philosophy of this Democratic Labour Party, which puts the masses at the centre of a development strategy while at the same time emphasising an integrative and holistic approach to our society.

Like his uncle before him, he was an instinctive socialist, but his feelings were strengthened by his life experiences and the education which he received in Britain at the London School of Economics. The greatest tribute that can be paid to him is to say that he remained unswervingly faithful to the philosophy he espoused in the practice of his politics and, indeed, his life.

As a point of interest, I read Errol Barrow's maiden speech delivered in the House of Assembly on February 7, 1952. He spoke on the Bill entitled an Act to make provision for the protection of third parties against risks arising out of the use of motor vehicles and for purposes incidental thereto. He made a lengthy and useful intervention, full of practical advice based on a clear grasp of the law, but the two following extracts from that speech are in the vintage Errol Barrow tradition, placing full concern on the interests of the masses.

He stated firstly: *"The interest of the community must be considered, and will always be considered, by members on this side of the House."* Then he went further: *"I hope that since the recovery of damages under this Bill depends upon the success of litigants in the courts of this island, the cost of litigation in the higher courts of this island will soon be made less burdensome to the average citizen than it is at present."*

That is the kind of concern that was expressed in Errol Barrow's maiden speech. Whenever he spoke, and wherever he spoke, there was much to learn from what he had to say. His wide intellectual grasp, his facility with language, his turn of phrase, were a virtual laboratory of learning for those who had an equal concern for form and substance.

There is much to be said of this colossus, whom I revered from the time I was a third former at the Boys' Foundation' (Secondary) School. There could not have been close personal contacts between us, because of age difference and other considerations, but such as there were, I have always treasured them. Certainly, my first contact will always be a memory for me. To be called at home by a Prime Minister returning a phone call on a Sunday afternoon to a research student whom he did not know, and then being given a wide interview at his home, did not seem a normal occurrence to me, and it gave me an early indication of the mettle of the man.

I recall two recent conversations with him on the occasion of May Day 1987, when he seemed determined to share some of these thoughts. He spoke then of two occasions when he deliberately stayed away from school. One was to hear Marcus Garvey, when he spoke in Queen's Park in October 1937. He recalled Garvey wearing a full-length coat, a fur coat, with a felt hat, in spite of the heat, and commented on the fact that Garvey understood the attraction of novelty and the unusual. I think, perhaps, that is why he rode his horse and went into the aeroplane. He understood that.

However, he stressed a statement which Garvey had made which had impacted on his own life. He recalled that Marcus Garvey said that the difference between black people, like ourselves, and white people was that blacks went to sleep early and woke up late while the whites did the opposite and continued to maintain their lead in vital areas of our endeavour. This was not said in a pejorative way about the race which he loved, but it was said in the same vein that Garvey spoke in, that they both wanted the best for our people, and he realised that the best could only come from discipline and self-reliance. We heard him on those themes several times.

He then said that the second time he deliberately stayed away from school was to hear evidence being given before the Moyne Commission in Queen's Park. The experience of the unbarring of the social, economic, and political realities of the lives of the masses of the country was to leave an indelible impression on his mind.

Errol Barrow was very conscious that he stood in a great tradition, in the line of Marcus Garvey and Charles Duncan O'Neal. He took up the standard and carried the banner further than his illustrious forbearers. He piloted the education revolution, which is still in process. It is not completed. He created social legislation second to none in this area. He gave us infrastructural development and he diversified our economy and, of course, he did a great deal of work in terms of continuing the task set by others in regional integration.

More important than all these, however, was a vision of teleological change towards a better living in the future for the masses of this country, to be achieved through peaceful yet revolutionary means. He saw housing as the next stage of the revolution, houses for the masses of the people in this country, and then, somewhere in the distant future, more equitable distribution of economic power in this country, which must be our final goal. His mantle is now to be borne by all of us in the Democratic

Labour Party, who will unite behind our leader and the visions of that great man.

He was not a man of the region or of Barbados, he was a world figure. In ending I must again say, in the words of Shakespeare, of another mortal genius: *"Farewell! thou art too dear for my possessing, And like enough thou know'st thy estimate..."*

Insurance for the pedestrian

*First address in Parliament, on 7 February, 1952, as
the senior member for St. George. (Barrow was then a
member of the Barbados Labour Party (BLP).)*

Sir, I do not think that many members of the general public who have
listened to this debate in this chamber today, and I doubt whether
many members of this House, really appreciate all the ramifications of
this bill. Some honourable member – I cannot remember who it was –
made some reference to the Third Party Insurance Act being on all-
fours with the with the Workmens' Compensation Act. Mr Speaker,
nothing could be further from the truth. Whereas the spirit of that
legislation, and its objects and motives might have been similar to this
legislation, this Bill seeks to place the less fortunate members of the
community, in so far as accidents being suffered, particularly by
bread winners, may not cause suffering to their dependants; while
the motives of the Workmens' Compensation Act may be similar, I
disagree that the objects are in any way the same as this Bill.

I will first explain this point. This Bill indemnifies the user or driver
or owner of any motor vehicle against any liability, and I use the word
advisedly because it is a word which appears time and again in this
Bill. Already many users and owners of motor vehicles in this island
indemnify themselves by taking out insurance policies, but there is
no enactment in the laws of this island which makes it compulsory for
the driver of a motor vehicle to insure against Third Party risks, the
third party being some person other than the insurance company on
the first part and the driver or owner of the motor vehicle on the
second part.

If I may give a simple illustration: If your Honour were proceeding
along one of the more busy highways of this city and someone
dashed across the road suddenly and Your Honour was not insured
against Third Party risks, that unfortunate person would be entitled
to go to the Courts of Law and sue Your Honour – I do not mean to be
personal in any way – for negligence, for a breach of that care which
has to be exercised by every user of the highways. If that person, his
executor, administrator or dependents, recovered damages, he

would then have to go against Your Honour's estate, if such exists, in order to indemnify himself, in order to execute the judgement of the Court. Your Honour can appreciate that if a man of straw such as myself, were driving a car along one of the more busy highways of this city, and were unfortunate enough to be involved in a collision with some even less fortunate person than myself being the third party, the injured person who recovered damages in the Court against me would not be any better off, because I have nothing to go against. The whole object of Third Party insurance is to make sure that there will be some fund for the injured party to go against.

I wonder if the dim light of revelation has dawned on the members of this Assembly yet. Before the unfortunate person who is injured can recover damages, he has to prove that the accident was due to negligence on the part of the person who was in charge of the car. That is why we must distinguish this Bill from the Workmens' Compensation Act; under that Act, if a workman is injured in the course of his employment as the result of an accident he is entitled to compensation whether the accident is due to his negligence or not. The employer has to indemnify the workman as long as the accident took place during the course of the workman's employment. There are over 7,000 reported cases of Workmens' Compensation in which the actual problems arising before the Courts were the problems of this nature: Was the injured person a workman under the Act? Did the accident occur during his employment? And did the accident occur out of his employment? But once these three essentials are proved, except in borderline cases as to the relation between master and servant and between the injured party and the employer, the workman was always entitled to compensation.

On the other hand, we are faced with the anomaly that in Barbados, if a man walks across the street in front of a motor car and he is injured and the other party sets up as his defence that the man's own negligence contributed to the accident, we have the rather inequitable doctrine which will deny that man the right to recover anything at all. You have to prove absolute negligence on the part of the person who knocked you down, but if he sets up that your negligence in any infinitesimal measure contributed to the accident, then you would not be entitled to recover anything at all. If the negligence of the car driver is 99 per cent, and the negligence of the pedestrian is only one per cent, the pedestrian recovers nothing at all.

We see, therefore, the anomaly to which I referred earlier in my speech; although we are passing an Act to make sure that an unfortunate person who is injured may have some fund to go against, he has to be successful in the Court of Law.

I do not think that insurance companies are run on the line of provident associations; my experience is that they always fight cases bitterly even when they have been advised by their own legal staff that they are in the wrong. As a matter of principle, they always resort to some legal subtlety in order to escape paying money out of their coffers. An insurance company does not like to settle claims outside the Court, and in nearly 100 per cent of the cases, the accidents will end by litigation: it is only when judgement is pronounced in the court that liability is brought home to the insurance company. I just want to say that it has been my experience in this island that we, with the best intentions have adopted certain social measures which have been enacted in the United Kingdom for the benefit of the different sections of the community and for the community as a whole, but very often we have adopted those measures without looking at the supporting and ancillary enactments which already exist in the United Kingdom so as to make these measures which we now propose a reality. I am suggesting, Mr Speaker, that instead of repeating the mistakes which we have made so many times in the past, we should, as soon as possible, enact a Law Reform Contributory Negligence Act which states, in my own words, that where any accident occurs which is partly due to the fault or default of the other party, instead of throwing the plaintiff or the injured party out of court because he has in some manner contributed to the cause of his injury, the Court would be entitled to allocate damages, as it were, in proportion to the extent to which each party has contributed to the injury. If one were riding a bicycle and by his negligence he contributed only 10 per cent towards the cause of the accident, and a motorist by his negligence contributed 90 per cent to the cause, instead of the cyclist being denied the right to recover any damages at all, he would recover nine-tenths of the damages which the court would normally have given him if he had not been contributory to his own injury.

That is the first point which I would like to make. There is another point which is not germane to the present issue; but, at some very early date, we shall have definitely to revise and amend the Separation and Maintenance Act, 1950 and make its provisions more widely known to the community. However, I do not intend to dwell on that issue, but having had a cursory glance at the present Act, I say that there are certain things which need to be amended.

To come back to the Bill before us, the various points will be gone into by a Select Committee. Far from Honourable Members on this side of the House being opposed to referring this Bill to a Select Committee, I would like to assure the Honourable Senior Member for the City that it was the intention of the members of the government to propose that the Bill may be referred to a Select Committee. The interest of the community must be considered and will always be considered by the members on this side of the House; if the members on the other side have made the proposals that this Bill will be referred to a Select Committee before we did so, we do not grudge them that bit of praise.

I was surprised that the honourable Member for the City even thought of referring this Bill to a Select Committee because we on this side have fully discussed this matter a long time ago. We have no intention to stampede or steam roller through this House legislation which is so far-reaching in its social consequences.

Although I am not going into the details of the Bill, in respect of Clause 4 (I) (b) (ii) some persons might be tempted to believe that it means that people who are riding on a bus and are injured would not be able to recover damages; but that is not so. That particular sub-clause refers to people who are merely joy-riding or who are friends or invitees of the driver of the vehicle. In Sub-Clause (n) (v) of the same Clause 4 – I would make this last point – the liability of the insurance company is limited to £1,000 sterling which is rather surprising; because if a person who is injured went to the Court and recovered £5,000 sterling damages, he would only be able to go against the insurance company to the extent of £1,000 sterling and would have to take proceedings against the injured himself for the other £4,000 sterling. There may be cases in which people may not be in a position to pay this amount, so that this particular sub-clause may seem to defeat the whole object of the Bill; but I understand that if the full liability of the insurance company were not limited, the premiums would be so high as to make it impossible for a normal member of the community like myself, who earns a moderate income, to subscribe to such a scheme.

But there is a penalty for not being insured; if the members of the community who own and drive cars are called upon to insure, then you have to make it possible for us to do so. I hope that since the recovery of damages under the Bill depends upon the success of litigants in the Courts of this island, the cost of litigation in the higher Courts of this island will soon be made less burdensome to the average citizen than it is at present.

DLP: THE FOUNDERS

J. C. TUDOR

W. A. CRAWFORD
(Deputy Premier)

F. G. SMITH

A. E. S. LEWIS

C. A. PHILLIPS

Genesis: The Origins of the DLP
Sir Frank Alleyne

On the night of 27 April 1955, twenty-six persons met at "Glenhurst" in Lands End, St Michael representing varied backgrounds and outlooks. Some had already had considerable experience in politics; four were then Members of the House of Assembly and two were previous Members. By the time the meeting ended, the twenty-five agreed to start something that would change the course of history for Barbados.

Thus, the Democratic Labour Party (DLP) was born. Yet, before this historic meeting was convened there had been previous discussions and tentative agreements. Before this there was, albeit fragmented, dissatisfaction with the policies and leadership of the Barbados Labour Party. Soon after the General Election of 1951, Grantley Adams (later Sir Grantley), the then Premier, had bluntly told his parliamentary colleagues that if he had to choose between their advice and that of the Governor, he would opt for the Governor's. By 1952, some members of the BLP had lost confidence in the leadership.

Furthermore, outside of the narrow parliamentary circle, for some time there had been a growing radical movement of young men. Over time, the movement had had different names but it was essentially the one group of radical young men who shared a common voice of protest. For a time it was known as "The Citizens' Association" with Brain Alleyne as its President, at other time it was the "Christian Socialists" under the leadership of C.A. Gill and C.L. Brathwaite, and then there was a regrouping with a less radical body known as the "People's Common Law Parliament" under the nominal leadership of Hugh Blackman and Chappie Clarke.

At different times, O.T. Allder, then a member of the House of Assembly was affiliated with these various organisations as was L.B.

Brathwaite and Ulric Grant, the latter known as one of the 'martyrs' of 1937. However, the desire to organise a political party was only seriously entertained by O.T. Allder, C.A. Gill, L.B. Brathwaite, Dr R.B. Caddle and C.L. Brathwaite. For Grant, Alleyne and Blackman, the perceived need for political struggle was almost at an end.

The weakness of these groups lay not in any lack of energy or sincerity or support but in their psyche. They were a protest organisation. They did not appreciate that if a political party is to be taken seriously it must include active and well-known political figures, preferably with a national profile. Among this radical group only Allder was prominent and it was probably for this reason that he and L.B. Brathwaite and C.A. Gill supported C.L. Brathwaite's assertion that they should combine their efforts with people of wider and different traditions. It is noteworthy, however, that O.T. Allder, L.B. Brathwaite and C.A. Gill would leave the Democratic Labour Party within a year of its founding.

Meanwhile another tributary began to flow in the same direction. Cameron Tudor (later Sir James) had severed his association with the Barbados Labour Party in October 1952 and would later challenge and defeat the BLP candidate in what is now the famous St Lucy by-election of 1954. However, before this Adams had invited A.E.S. (T.T.) Lewis to take part in a public meeting in Queen's Park at which Adams devoted his entire speech to a public excoriation of Lewis, then sitting next to him, and which unsurprisingly led to a parting of the ways.

Early in 1952, Barrow began to entertain serious doubts about the policies and purposes of the BLP leadership. With his renowned candour, he had on several occasions challenged these policies in caucus, and occasionally dissociated himself from them in Parliament. A sense of loyalty to his constituents in St George restrained him for some time but the inevitable break engendered since 1952 came early in 1954 when Adams left Frank Walcott out of the first Cabinet.

In 1955, Barrow made one of his more important statements in the House of Assembly, stating, *"I am going to make a serious statement now and because I regard this situation (unemployment) as the most pressing problem facing this island at present, and in view of the fact that I am completely dissatisfied not only with the Honourable Minister of Labour, but with the whole attitude of Ministers of the Government and their complete disregard of the suffering of the people and of the Party. Because of that, I no longer want to be associated with them politically or otherwise...."*

After the St Lucy by-election, in which Allder, then an independent Member of the House played a full part, it was now thought propitious to launch a new political party. Barrow, Lewis, Tudor and Smith already shared a common perspective. However, there was another group, of which Allder was the leading figure also organising themselves. The question arose of whether there should be one party or two; a matter of importance as two new political parties would compete for the same allegiance, whereas a single party, provided that there was common ground among the founders, could galvanise a wider base of support.

Accordingly, Barrow, Lewis, Tudor, and Smith initiated conversations with Allder's group which, by February 1955, had accepted C.L. Brathwaite's suggestion of seeking wider affiliation. Following two months of discussions and negotiations it was agreed that a single political party, democratic and socialist by nature, would be organised. With aims and objects agreed on these, a name chosen, a constitution drafted and several persons expressing interest in joining, on 27 April 1955 the "Glenhurst" meeting was held and the Constitution of the Democratic Labour Party, which came into force on 1 May 1955, adopted. The founding members who formed the first Provisional General Council of the DLP were:

O.T. ALLDER *(with reservations)*
E.W. BARROW
J. BEST
O. BLACKMAN
J.M. BONNETT
L.B. BRATHWAITE
C.L. BRATHWAITE
L.D. BURROWES
H. COULSTON
D. FARRELL
C.A. GILL
D. HOLDER

A.E.S. (T.T) LEWIS
A.H. LEWIS
F.G. SMITH
H. SPRINGER
J.B. SPRINGER, Snr.
J.B. SPRINGER, Jnr.
D. STRAKER
Miss E. TUDOR
J.C. TUDOR
L. WOOD

On 27 April the Provisional General Council also elected from among their number, the following Provisional Executive Committee:

F.G. SMITH	Chairman
L.B. Brathwaite	Vice-Chairman
J.C. Tudor	General Secretary
C.A. Gill	Assistant Secretary
J.B. SPRINGER, Snr	Treasurer
E.W. BARROW	Committee Member
C.L. BRATHWAITE	Committee Member
A.E.S. LEWIS	Committee Member
O.T. Allder	
J.B. SPRINGER, Jnr	

The Provisional Executive met the following day and made the first management decisions of the Democratic Labour Party. These included arranging a press conference, the arrangements for acquiring a headquarters building, and a public meeting to launch the new Party. This inaugural meeting was held in the Steel Shed in Queen's Park on Friday, 6 May 1955 and was presided over by Allder who, because of his reservations, did not feel able to participate in the meeting more fully. Barrow, Tudor, A.E.S. Lewis and Smith spoke and the Democratic Labour Party set off on its journey into history.

Allder's reservations were based on his opinion that D.P. Lynch should not be admitted to membership of the Party as he felt that Lynch's race coupled with his social background and position would impact on the Party. Despite the provisions of the Party Constitution, Allder and L.B. Brathwaite sought to make an issue of this. The Executive Committee thought otherwise and Douglas Lynch (later Sir Douglas) became the first person formally admitted to membership of the Democratic Labour Party. He would go on to contest the Christ Church seat in the 1956 General Election.

The period between the founding of the DLP in 1955 and the formation of its first Administration in 1961 was a stern test of the resolve of the founding fathers to transforming Barbados towards creating opportunities for the majority of its people. Those years required unimaginable sacrifice. Errol Walton Barrow recalled that during the early years the young leadership shared their time between earning a living to support their families and developing the Party.

Barrow recounted that one day after returning from the law courts he discovered the Party's headquarters, then on Roebuck Street, had padlocks placed on the entrance by the landlord as they had fallen behind on the rent. An SOS message was broadcast over the sole wireless broadcasting outlet at the time, the Barbados Rediffusion, to Cameron Tudor, requesting him to come to the Party's headquarters immediately with the ownership documents for his motor car. Tudor responded promptly and thereafter headed to Barclays Bank on Broad Street where they raised a loan against his car to clear the rental arrears and regain access the headquarters.

The 1956 General Election were contested on the dual membership system (two members for each Parish and two for the City of Bridgetown). The DLP candidates were follows:

Christ Church	D.P. Lynch
Bridgetown	A.E.S Lewis
St Andrew	F.G. Smith
St George	E.W. Barrow
St James	A.G. Johnson
St John	C.A. Speede
	A.H. Lewis
St Joseph	J. Kellman

St Michael	C.F. Broome
	J.A. Tudor
St Lucy	J.E.T. Brancker
	J.C. Tudor
St Peter	T.S. Chandler
St Philip	W.A. Crawford
	C. Fields
St Thomas	G. Pilgrim

However, only four would be successful: Brancker, Crawford, Smith and Tudor. By far most disappointing losses for the Party were the defeat of A.E.S (T.T.) Lewis in the City and Barrow in St George.

Lewis, a founder of the trade union movement and leader of the Clerical Workers Union, was elected to Parliament in 1942 for Barbados Electors' Association, in 1944 for the Congress Party and in 1948-55 for the BLP (he lost his job for joining this predominantly Afro-Barbadian Party). His a firm grasp of public affairs, legislative procedure, and the world of commerce, had, when combined with his profound empathy for the masses, moulded a man of considerable stature. Regrettably, plagued by ill-health, he died suddenly in Saint Lucia in 1959.

The Barbados Labour Party, recognising that Barrow represented the single greatest threat to them, combined with the Conservative Party to successfully launch a unified assault against him in the St George election. But their efforts would be short-lived as in the 1958 by-election, held to fill vacancies created by the departure of Members to the ill-fated Federal Parliament, Barrow handsomely won the St John constituency which he would represent until his death.

During this period, C.F. Broome was Party Chairman and J.E.T. Brancker (later Sir Theodore) the Leader of the Opposition. Following the death of Charles F. Broome in 1959, Barrow was elected Chairman and from this position led the DLP into the momentous 1961 General Election. The following were the 1961 candidates:

Christ Church	C.E. Talma
Bridgetown	L. Carmichael
St Andrew	J.W. Corbin

	DaC. Edwards
St George	W.R. Lowe
St James	E.L. Carmichael
St John	E.W. Barrow
	J. Yearwood
St Joseph	D. Payne
St Lucy	J.E.T. Brancker
	J.C. Tudor
St Michael	G.G. Fergusson
St Philip	W.A. Crawford
	R. Weekes
St Peter	G.V. Batson
St Thomas	G. Pilgrim
	N. Boxhill

Three days after its victory on 5 December 1961, Errol Barrow announced his first Cabinet:

The Hon. E.W. Barrow	Premier and Minister of Finance
The Hon. J.C. Tudor	Minister of Education
The Hon W.A. Crawford	Deputy / Minister of Trade, Industry, Labour & Development
The Hon. G.G. Fergusson	Minister of Communications, Works & Housing
The Hon. A.DaC. Edwards	Minister of Social Services
The Hon. H.A. Vaughan	Attorney General

"Operation Takeover" the DLP campaign slogan, was now in effect.

DLP EARLY YEARS

The DLP Headquarters at Roebuck Street

The DLP Cabinet at Government Headquarters, Bay Street, 8 December 1961

How Men Dream a Nation

Sir Frederick Smith and Alan Smith

In 2016, in Barbados' 50th year as an independent nation, there are, give or take, around 200 independent, sovereign countries. The ambiguity in the number is a reminder that sovereignty, independence and democracy are not the natural or permanent order of things. As Professor Norman Davies, in his book *"Vanished Kingdoms – The Rise and Fall of States and Nations"* reminds us "Successful statehood, in fact, is a rare blessing. It requires health and vigour, good fortune, benevolent neighbours and a sense of purpose to aid growth to reach maturity". So, when Barbados started on its remarkable project to democracy and independence in the 1930s, leading to where we are today, it was an improbable journey. The odds were not good.

A few statistics, published in the doctoral thesis of the distinguished, now-retired Barbadian diplomat, Dr Peter Laurie, remind us of this:

- *Wages: In the 1930s the average daily wage for male agricultural workers was only 5 cents more than in the 1830s. Wage rates for plantation workers: men – 1-2 shillings a day; women – 10 pence – 1 shilling and 3 pence a day. Yet the minimum cost of living was officially estimated to be 10 shillings a week.*
- *Working Conditions: Hours worked were long. Bakers normally worked between 65-85 hours a week.*
- *Health and Housing: The West India Royal Commission of 1938-39 (the Moyne Report) appointed to inquire into the riots that had run throughout the Caribbean in the late 1930s noted the high infant mortality rate, extreme malnutrition, and deplorable health and housing conditions for the working class.*

- **Social Security**: *There was no unemployment insurance, nor old age pensions, and poor relief distributed by the parochial vestries was limited to the very old and infirm.*
- **The Franchise**: *1937 franchise was based on property, education and income not derived from 'employment of a menial nature'. It included just 10 per cent of the adult male population.*

Roll forward to today and the story is very different. The United Nations 2013 Human Development Report in presenting the Global Human Development Index, ranked Barbados at number 38 out of 187 countries and territories, classifying it as having "very high human development", the highest category. Its Gross National Income per capita in 2012 was US $17,308. By way of comparison, China ranked number 101 with a GNI per capita of US $7,945. India ranked number 136, with GNI per capita of US $3,285.

Transparency International in its 2013 Corruption Perceptions Index ranked Barbados at 15 out of 177 countries, with a score of 75 out of 100 (where a score of 100 means that the country is perceived as very clean). This placed Barbados just below the United Kingdom, which ranked number 14, with a score of 76, and above the United States, which ranked 19, with a score of 73.

A few years ago, Niall Ferguson, in a Financial Times article discussing democracy and freedom in the modern world commented, *"The countries with the maximum Freedom House scores (an independent think tank which awards scores to the countries of the world according to their degrees of political freedom) are, with the exception of Barbados, the rich countries of north-western Europe."*

The Barbados story of how it built a modern day democracy is one of history's remarkable journeys. It should be studied in the same way as how democratic Athens at the beginning of the Peloponnesian War (431 BC) – which contained perhaps 50,000 adult male citizens, 200,000 free native inhabitants, and perhaps 300,000 inhabitants in all, including slaves and foreigners' – is studied when thinking about how democracy grows.

The story of the amazing project is the story of many men and women, of whom the most remarkable is Errol Barrow, Independent Barbados'

Founding Father; the island's George Washington. Many of us alive today are older than our country and because we have lived, walked and talked with the likes of Errol, we often forget and be sanguine about what a remarkable man he was and what he created and helped us to achieve.

To dream a nation, move it from vision to reality and then establish laws, values and practices so that such a nation sustains itself and grows takes special men. Errol was such a man.

In building a newly independent country and a democracy there was no play book, in particular for a country where the majority of the country was of African descent. Laws had to be written, a central bank created, a free education system set up among other crucial national priorities. A site for a university had to be selected, and then built. Errol did all this and more.

He had his own style, in particular in Cabinet and Government. Strong leaders have their own style. He was a man who, while he thought deeply, preferred action, knowing that in building a country there is an urgency and need to get the foundations right.

Errol was also willing to take risks. All projects of democracy involve risk. Above all the pursuit and support of freedom, in particular for those who were excluded from it previously, is worth the risks taken. This was embodied in one of Errol's finest moments as a leader, his leadership and direction of Barbados' provision of logistical support to the Cuban government in 1975 in its defence of Angola against the incursions of the then racist government of South Africa.

This action was fully consistent with the principles on which Errol and Barbadians were seeking for themselves. It was him at his most sophisticated and clear sighted. It was the ultimate example of Barbadian and its people living out of his statement at Independence that Barbados is *"friends of all and satellites of none"*. It was the value of a man who left the comfort of Barbados to join the Royal Air Force and fight in World War II, knowing that freedom is not free. US President Lyndon Johnson, in welcoming Errol to the White House in September 1968, described Errol as *"a very remarkable leader of a remarkable people"*.

As Barbados approaches its 50th Anniversary of Independence, we must recall and celebrate Johnson's words and above all we must celebrate Errol. We should give the last word though, in reflecting on Barbados and Errol to the great African writer Chinua Achebe: *"There is that great proverb – that until the lions have their own historians, the history of the hunt will always glorify the hunter. That did not come to me until much later. Once I realised that, I had to be a writer. I had to be that historian. It's not one man's job. It's not one person's job. But it is something we have to do, so that the story of the hunt will also reflect the agony, the travail – the bravery, even, of the lions"*.

Errol Barrow is Barbados' lion. His and our story must continue to be told. Through his leadership, his vision, his actions we have our own story. We triumphed over our hunters.

"No taxation without representation"

Address in Parliament January 30, 1962, on the
measure to lower the voting age from 21 to 18 years

It has been declared as part and parcel of the policy of members of this Party, and we had a mandate from the people, for the reduction of the voting age.

The honourable senior member for St Peter dealt exhaustively and courageously with this Bill not only on this occasion, but in 1961 when the Government rejected the one which he introduced and it is not necessary for me to go over the ground which he so adequately covered both in that debate and in this one.

When Her Majesty's Secretary of State for the Colonies was in Barbados not so long ago – within the last three weeks – we pointed out to him that we had got the mandate of the people for the reduction of the voting age and we were committed to supporting a Bill on the floor of the House by an honourable member for that purpose. The Secretary of State for the Colonies intimated to us that it was entirely a domestic matter, and in view of the fact that it would not be necessary to change anything in the Letters Patent or in the Instruments within which the Constitution of Barbados is written – such as the Executive Committee Act – it would be a matter for us to go ahead if we so cared.

When the matter was put before the Government, the then Solicitor General appeared to be of the opinion that the amendment would involve the preparation of three separate registers – a register for the Federal Government Elections, a register for Local Government Elections and a register for the General Assembly Elections. The law relating to the register for the Federal Government Elections – and I cannot see that it would be necessary in these present circumstances – is that the register for the Federal Government Elections, should be the Local Government Register as existing in January, 1958. Therefore, if the Federal Government Elections were to be held any time within the next six months, or I would say within the next twelve months, which in my opinion appears now to be extremely unlikely, the position would be that even although we made the amendment to the Representation of the Peoples Act in respect of this, it would not entitle those of the age of 18 years to 21 years to vote in the Federal Government Elections. However, I do not think that that election is one which should cause any concern because, as I have said before, it is extremely unlikely that such an election will take place. This, of course, is just a personal assessment of the situation according to the way things are shaping at the present moment.

When we come to the question of the Local Government Elections, we have just passed through the Local Government elections and we are not due to hold another election for Local Government Councils until the year 1964. That gives us adequate time to prepare a separate register or alternatively to amend the Local Government Act and perhaps any consequential amendments to other Acts. There again, I do not think that can be a valid objection to the passage of the Bill at this particular time.

However, it is obvious to anyone who has made a study of the Local Government Act that there are several provisions in that Act which are repugnant to our ideas of democratic government in Barbados – ideas of this Government and ideas which I am sure the honourable senior member for St Peter will be quite willing to support. There are several provisions in that Act which tend to make it appear that Local Government Elections are more important than the elections to the General Assembly of this Island. There is such a thing as the qualifications which they have laid down for one to be a member and there are other things such as the method of taxation, the relief which is granted to owners of plantations and matters of that kind. It is, therefore, obvious that several major amendments, in the light of the policy of the present Government would have to be made to the 1958 Local Government Act under which we are now suffering.

The procedure when a Private Bill is introduced is that that Bill should be sent to a Select Committee; this Bill, therefore, has to go to a Select Committee. When the Honourable Leader of the House made the motion, it was an act of supererogation on his part and, as one of my friends on my right would say, it was done out of an abundance of caution. It was, in the light of the provision of our standards, not entirely necessary, but it was only emphasising to honourable members that we do not intend to stampede Private Members' Business until both the public and the members of this House have had full opportunity to debate, discuss, analyse, criticise and make recommendations on measures of this kind. I have already given instructions that all the consequential amendments attendant upon the passage of the Bill, without in any way anticipating the will of the House, should be prepared, so that when the Select Committee reports, we will be able to introduce within a very short time, the legislative amendments which would make this provision for the reduction of the voting age to 18 years a practical proposition.

Mr Speaker, I entirely agree with the honourable senior member for St Peter that if there is any political illiteracy in this island, if there is any political agnosticism or atheism, it is to be found in the age-group 50 to 80 rather than in the 18 to 21 age-group. If there is any age group which has had the advantage of some kind of formal education to the extent of 100 per cent, that age-group must certainly be the one from 18 years to 21 years. I agree that in our archaic system of the Mosaic Law, a man can suffer capital punishment at the age of 18 years, he can marry at the age of 18 years, he is also subject to the payment of income tax, and if we follow the principle of no taxation without representation to its logical conclusion, it is clear that we cannot disenfranchise the people who are taxpayers of this colony. The average age of young people who are leaving school in Barbados is 14 years and in Secondary schools it is about 17-and-a-half to 18 years. We anticipate an economic condition in this country that young people will be absorbed in the avenue of gainful employment immediately on leaving the Secondary Schools and the Primary Schools of this island; if they are going to be absorbed in the avenues of employment, then they will become taxpayers and it is only logical that these young people should have some say in the running of the country in which they live. I, therefore, have great pleasure in supporting the second reading of the Bill which has been moved by the honourable senior member for St Peter, and it is only an indication that this Government does not intend to fall into the thinking of the previous government that whenever a private member introduces a Bill they would automatically oppose its passage. The past government has gone to the extent that they, rather than support legislative matters on the Order Paper, have prorogued the House so that they could kill every possible item of Private Members' Business on the Order Paper. We do not intend to follow that practice. We now see that members of the erstwhile Government are going into the reverse now; they no longer have the power to advise the officer administering the government of the country as to the dissolution of the Legislative Session; so they climb on the vanguard of the 'holier than thou-ers' or the new frontier men and they even second the motions moved by private members.

It is true that they are lagging rather far behind but we welcome them to our ranks in the same way that we would welcome the 18 to 20 years old into the ranks of the progressive way of the exercise of the franchise at the present time.

Errol Walton Barrow – Patriot, Friend of working people and outstanding politician

A tribute by Michael Manley

In a world increasingly dominated by the superpowers there is a tendency for it to be assumed by the unthinking that the personalities of political significance are to be found only amongst the ranks of the mighty. At the same time the interaction between the democratic political process, the power of the mass media and the influence of the opinion poll is producing a kind of politician whose mediocrity reflects the perpetual search for compromise and the need to be all things to all people.

The Caribbean continues to confound both these assumptions. Earlier in this century Jamaica's Marcus Garvey fired the imagination of the black world, laying the foundations for the independence movements in the African homeland and the struggle for rights and recognition throughout the diaspora.

Trinidad's George Padmore played a vital role, building upon psychological foundations which Garvey had laid, in the development of the various political institutions which waged and eventually won the struggle for independence in Africa.

In the Caribbean itself Alexander Bustamente, Uriah Butler, and many others threw down the gauntlet on behalf of the working classes, the most direct victims of colonial exploitation. Norman Manley, T. A. Marryshaw, Grantley Adams and others issued the demand for political independence and commenced to fashion the political organisations which would first win and later manage freedom.

Caribbean nationalism was, accordingly, born of the need to create societies founded in freedom. Similarly, Caribbean politics proceeded on the assumption that freedom must open the doors to social justice. Finally, there emerged early a consensus concerning democracy as the means by which the people would pursue both justice and self-realisation.

Nationhood would not be achieved without struggle, thus the 1940s were a time of ferment and trouble in Barbados and the wider Caribbean.

At the same time, there were a few people of vision who, while committed to the ideals of nationhood for their own territories, also saw that the aspirations of the workers for a better life and the people as a whole for a world with larger horizons could be better served by a region united than by one divided into a number of parts. Standing tall in this company was Errol Walton Barrow.

Errol Barrow yielded pride of place to no person in his support for workers' causes. The long friendship and close association between himself and Sir Frank Walcott of the Barbados Workers' Union and, in the eyes of many, the dean of Caribbean trades unionists, is ample evidence of the late Prime Minister's commitment. That Errol Barrow was a deep, passionate and unwavering Barbadian statesman is impatient of debate. He was as unapologetically Barbadian as any person one could ever hope to meet. However, the region has produced countless men and women who reflected this peculiarly Caribbean sense of social justice and national independence as two sides of a single coin. What set Errol Barrow apart was his understanding that social justice must rest upon economic foundations if it is to be more real than rhetorical. This led him, in turn, to a commitment to economic integration as the only viable framework within which economic development could be pursued. Following the same inexorable logic, Barrow grasped the relationship between a regional economic framework and a political environment in which the sovereignty so newly won by the Caribbean could be defended.

It can be seen, therefore, that the commitment to social justice led his pragmatic mind to the conclusion that economic development pursued in a regional context would best accommodate the demands which social justice makes upon the body politic. At the same time his patriotism led him to examine the nature of sovereignty and in particular how this could best serve regional economic development and, no less important, how that sovereignty might best be defended.

To those who knew him, therefore, it came as no surprise that whether in opposition or upon his resumption of power, Errol Barrow opposed the invasion of a piece of English-speaking Caribbean soil by forces of the United States of America. Of equal logic and force was his unrelenting insistence that the Caribbean should be a zone of peace and not an area for ever-increasing penetration by foreign forces, from whatever source and however cunningly disguised. I believe that history will vindicate him abundantly on both scores.

By the same token his avowed intention upon his return to power of working to rebuild CARICOM trade and the integration process were simple extensions of his philosophy and his view of the Caribbean and its possibilities.

It is in his unrepentant view of the invasion of Grenada, along with his unswerving commitment to regional co-operation and to peace, that we find the final evidence of the qualities which made Errol Barrow so special. For he was, in truth, more than a politician in the ordinary sense of one circumscribed by the narrowest interpretation of what is immediately possible. Like all great politicians, who we choose inaccurately to rename as statesmen, Barrow made all his calculations of short-term political advantage subject to his deeper principles and the causes which they led him to uphold.

He will be remembered as the man who led Barbados into independence. He will be extolled as the author of free education and many other elements of the welfare state re-enacted in this tiny island in the Caribbean. But his claim upon history will extend far beyond the boundaries of Barbados. He will take his place amongst the significant heroes of Caribbean history. When we are brought finally by circumstance, by common heritage and by the logic of history to the point where we are the region which was foreseen by the deeper thinkers of the '30s and '40s he will take his place as a major architect of the process.

So much for the politics of the man. To the countless people who regarded themselves as privileged to share Errol Barrow's friendship, he was a very special person. Typically Barbadian, he had a dry wit and seemingly inexhaustible reserve of good humour. A hearty raconteur, the exterior of humour and story telling were often a facade for a nature generous to a fault. Once you were his friend, it were as though loyalty were underwritten in perpetuity.

Then, again, there was his intellect. A man of wide reading and real scholarship, he could confound his opponents with a flash of repartee. He was equally quick to deflate the windbags of humbug, who litter any political scene, with a single thrust, no less cutting because of the laugh with which he could round off some sally of wit. When he died, we mourned a significant patriot and grieved for a true friend.

'You cannot draw up an indictment against a whole nation'

Statement to Parliament on June 19, 1962, introducing a resolution condemning the British government's suspension of the constitution of Grenada

An emergency meeting of the Cabinet of this island was held this morning because during the past twenty-four hours, there was released from London an Order-in-Council which indicated that the United Kingdom government had decided as from today's date, to suspend the constitution of the neighbouring territory of Grenada and to dissolve the Legislative and Executive Councils of that island.

I am sure that honourable members would forgive me and other members of the Cabinet if, as Westindians and if as persons who are looking forward to the eventual emancipation of the area from imperial rule under which we have suffered so long – and I make no apologies for stating unequivocally that I am anti-imperialist; as a matter of fact, even the leaders of the Conservative Party in the United Kingdom are anti-imperialists in their declaration when we see the rapidity with which they are dissolving the British Empire.

I, therefore, make no apology whatsoever to the members of the Opposition in this House, to the members of the public or to the United Kingdom government, if I reiterate what the general public already knows – that is, my stand in matters of this kind. I am not in favour of any form of imperialism, whether it is British imperialism, American economic imperialism, or Russian economic imperialism. I am opposed to imperialism in any form, shape or disguise, no matter from whatever quarter that imperialism happens to emanate. The terms of the resolution which the Cabinet has agreed upon, read as follows: –

> *'Resolved that this House strongly protests against the action taken under the authority of the Westindies Act, 1962, by the Government of*

*the United Kingdom in suspending the Constitution of Grenada and in
dissloving the Legislative and Executive Councils of that island.'*

Mr Deputy Speaker, that is the Resolution which we will be calling
upon members of this House to support. I think, Sir, that you will
forgive a little background history of the dissolution of the executive
and legislative councils of Grenada and the drastic action which the
United Kingdom has elected to pursue. Sometime in 1961, subsequent to the London Conference of that year, the United Kingdom, in
its wisdom – and I use that word in its very loosest sense – decided to
permit the re-enfranchisement of a gentleman, who, at one time,
enjoyed the confidence of the majority of the electorate of the island
of Grenada and who had been disenfranchised by the electoral law of
that colony and was still suffering under the disability of that
disenfranchisement.

Mr (Eric) Gairy, the Chief Minister of Grenada, attended the
London Conference in 1961 as an adviser to the Government of
Grenada, and it would appear to me that, with the connivance of the
Colonial Office in London, the law under which Mr Gairy was
suffering this disability was abrogated and a new enabling Act passed
in the Grenada Legislature so that Mr Gairy – with whom the Colonial
Office could have been in no agreement on any constitutional matter
in view of the fact that it was the Colonial Office which had elected to
banish Mr Gairy to the neighbouring island of Carriacou some seven
or eight years previously – it was with this collaboration and
connivance that the electoral law was flouted and the legislature was
allowed to pass a Bill which enabled Mr Gairy to take over the reins of
government in Grenada. That was taken by people in the outside
world as an indication that the Colonial Office was, at that time,
satisfied that Mr Gairy had manifested his intention to behave like a
responsible politician and statesman and that the Colonial Office had
now become enamoured of Mr Gairy's claim for leadership.

So said, so done, Mr Deputy Speaker; and after the victory of Mr
Gairy's Party in the election campaign Mr Gairy was duly chosen as
the Leader of his Party and as the elected leader of the people of
Grenada. In that capacity, he attended all our conferences on
federation and made some kind of contribution towards the conclusions at which we arrived at the London Conference held in May this
year. Subsequent to the election of Mr Gairy as the leader of the
Grenada Movement, the people of Jamaica manifested an intention to
turn their backs on the rest – I should say, on the Eastern Caribbean –
and to pull out, as it were, of the Federation which was then in

existence by a Referendum held in the last quarter of last year, sometime around the 11th and the 13th of September. We all know from recent history that the United Kingdom government, after receiving a clear expression, not from the government of Trinidad or from the people of Trinidad – and I offer this as no criticism at all, although criticism may be justified; I am merely making a statement of fact as to what took place – after receiving, as I say, an expression from the General Council of the Peoples' National Movement which is the party of the government of Trinidad, a clear indication that, not one, but two members of the Federation of the Westindies were anxious to dissociate themselves from that most unfortunate grouping, it was at that stage that the United Kingdom government decided that the only thing which could be done in the circumstances was to break up the existing Federation in a manner which would leave no doubt as to its existence or non-existence.

Mr Deputy Speaker, I do not think that it would be entirely keeping faith either with history or with the members of the public in Barbados, if I did not disclose that there was no Westindian man or woman of goodwill who would be entirely in agreement with Mr Gairy; but it is clear that there is no Westindian politician in the Windward or Leeward Islands or Barbados with whom I happen to be associated at the time, who was in disagreement that steps should be taken to dissolve the existing Federation, provided that they were legitimate steps.

It was, moreover, the opinion of most people who had some kind of acquaintance with the constitutional aspects of the matter that as long as one member of the partnership withdrew from the partnership, the Association automatically ceased to exist. There was no provision in the Federal Constitution for a referendum, neither was there any provision for secession of any territory, neither was there any provision for a declaration to continue with the association of the territories at any stage; and in view of the fact that we have now considered that at this stage of the 20th century we could not, as some ill-advised persons and sections of the Press wanted people to do, that is, enforce the territory of Trinidad and the territory of Jamaica to remain in an association reluctantly, in view of all these considerations, Mr Deputy Speaker, I said – and I repeat – that not only were men and women of goodwill, but also responsible politicians with whom I happened to be associated, were in agreement with the dissolution of the existing Federation, and that is still our point of view.

The Federation as it then existed, moreover, had become associated and tainted with the suspicion that it was not working in the best interest of the Westindian people, particularly those people from the Windward and Leeward Islands and Barbados. So, Mr Deputy Speaker, amidst some kind of protest, but with firm resolve, the United Kingdom government pressed through first in the House of Lords and later in the House of Commons, a Bill which provided for the dissolution of the Federation, *inter alia*, a Bill which provided for the suspension of Unit constitutions, if necessary, and a Bill which was known at that time as the Westindies Bill, 1962, and later became the Westindies Act, 1962. Under Section five of this Act, an Order-in-Council was made in May, 1962 which dissolved the existing Federation.

We in Barbados as members of the government scrutinised the provisions of this Bill. Members of this Honourable House expressed fears that this Bill was capable of being employed as the thin edge of the wedge, which, driven right home, would divest Unit Legislatures of their constitutions and authoritative functions of presiding over their own destinies which they at that time happened to enjoy. It was because of these fears and because of our own suspicions that I decided on my own initiative, and after consultation with the members of my Cabinet, to address a telegram to the Secretary of State on the 21st of March, 1962, the contents of which I have already disclosed to the members of the House, but which perhaps, it would not be inopportune to read at this stage.

This telegram, Mr Deputy Speaker, reads as follows:

> 'While it may be necessary to make provision for certain limited aspects of government in individual islands consequent on dissolution of existing Federation, I strongly urge that to allay fears and dissipate suspicions you should give firm assurance – as result of my representations to you – that nothing will be done by Order-in-Council to render inferior or retrogressive the constitutional gains already achieved in Barbados, the Windward Islands or the Leeward Islands. As I am receiving almost daily protests from Chief Ministers of Leeward and Windward Islands, it would be greatly appreciated if assurance could be given immediately.'

No member of the House, therefore, could be in any doubt during the course of this debate as to what attitude I would adopt if an occasion such as the instant one arose. On the 26th March, some five days later, I received a Priority Telegram, also confidential, addressed to me which read as follows: –

'No. 60 PRIORITY Telegram No. 43
'WESTINDIES BILL
'PLEASE PASS FOLLOWING TO PREMIER.
'I can give you the assurance you are asking for in respect of Barbados.
Indeed, the Minister of State speaking on Clause five in Lords on March
7th said: –
It is not the intention of H.M. Government to use any of the powers
under this clause to derogate in any way from constitutional status those
territories which are already enjoying full internal self-government.
'I cannot, however, give any such assurance in the case of the
Windward and Leeward Islands. One of the effects of the Bill is to
transfer responsibility for administration of grants-in-aid back to the
United Kingdom. In the circumstance, I must have the power ultimately
to ensure that moneys voted by Parliament are properly spent especially
in view of growing evidence in recent months of mismanagement in some
quarters. I shall be seeking for an opportunity in Parliament this week to
make the point plain.'

You will notice, Mr Deputy Speaker, that that was a confidential telegram addressed to me personally; but as I have said on frequent occasions, except where the security of the realm is threatened, I do not believe in government by conspiracy; I believe in government by consent. I do not believe that the affairs of the people should be conducted in a conspiratorial atmosphere, and I consider that by addressing a confidential, private telegram to me, the Secretary of State was not aware of my attitude on matters of this kind, and if he was aware, he was placing me in a rather invidious pattern vis-à-vis, my other colleagues from the Windward and Leeward Islands. Because of this, I could not make a disclosure to the House as I had already some weeks ago indicated, and I sent another telegram to the Secretary of State which reads as follows: –

'FROM GOVERNOR ADDRESSED TO SECRETARY OF STATE
Sent 12th April, 1962 (1600)
No. 56 PRIORITY
'Your telegrams No. 60 Westindies Bill and No. 67 Conference of
Eight.
'Following from Premier begins.
'Prior to receipt of your telegram I had promised the House of
Assembly to make public your reply to my request for assurances
regarding change of constitutional status of these islands by Order-in-
Council. This promise received newspaper publicity and I must now say

what is your reply.

'Two. I am meeting Chief Ministers of Leewards and Windwards in Antigua April 16th to discuss arrangements for providing Migrant Services in U.K. on dissolution of Migrant Services division of the Westindies Commission in London and also to discuss the general situation in regard to Federation of the Eight. Chief Ministers are becoming increasingly restive at the present uncertainties.

'Three. Grateful if you would send me by telegram repeated to Administrator Antigua, a reply to be made public in Barbados as well as at the meeting of the Eight on April 16th.'

I received the next day from the Secretary of State for the Colonies the immediate telegram worded as follows: –

'Secretary of State
    'Sent 13th April, 1962 (1640) Addressed to GOVERNOR.
    'Received 13th April, 1962 (1500)
    'No. 75 IMMEDIATE
    '2. On the question of the exercise of powers under the Westindies Act, 1962, I have no objection to your releasing reply given in my telegram 60. You can also draw attention to my comments on this matter in Hansard on March 26th column 855 to 856 and April 2nd Columns 146 and 147.'

Mr Deputy Speaker, as soon as I received this reply from the Secretary of State for the Colonies, I came into this House and I disclosed the full background and all the relevant information. I also managed to secure in a remarkably short time, copies of Hansard for the relevant dates and I stated what the Secretary of State said in the House of Commons which was substantially in accordance with what he disclosed to me in his telegram, No. 60.

If I may be permitted just to sum up the attitude of the United Kingdom Government, it was that Clause Five of the Westindian Act of 1962, which was then a Bill – it had not yet become law – and which had been initiated by debate in the House of Lords and then filtered down to the lower regions of the House of Commons, gave the United Kingdom government power by Order-in-Council to dissolve the constitution of any Unit Legislature in the Westindies and to set up in substitution therefore some alternative form of government which would be entirely at the discretion of the United Kingdom government for as long a period as the United Kingdom in its discretion thought fit. It was also stated that these provisions were not meant to apply to the people of the island of Barbados, but they could give no assurance that they did not intend to use them against the Windward and Leeward Islands.

The effect of the disclosure which I was permitted to make was to make the people of the Windward and Leeward Islands view Barbados with a certain amount of suspicion, and the Barbados delegates at subsequent meetings of the Chief Ministers and their delegates, whether in the Westindies or in London, had the greatest difficulty in impressing upon the people of the Windward and the Leewards and their representatives that the Barbadians were not, if I may be colloquial, sucking up to the Colonial Office, that the age of Uncle Tom in Barbados was over and that we were no imperialistic stooges who were prepared to sell the other islands so that we could get some advantage for ourselves.

I think honourable members will bear me out that in reply to the Secretary of State for the Colonies at the London Conference, I had to remind him that it was not a question of not giving Barbados some special privilege, but that we were anxious to see that the constitutions of the other islands were brought up to the same constitutional advancement which we are now enjoying. We were accused by the same Mr Gairy of sitting down and not saying anything because we had been promised something, and I asked Mr Gairy what it was that the Secretary of State had to promise us which we did not have already. I asked that because in this colony we have only been inhibited for the past sixty years, not even for six months or fifteen years, by our own philosophy of accepting that certain things are not for us.

Even now, we have people in Barbados who do not understand the politics of nationhood and who are pusillanimous of the advantages of independence. Perhaps the only Barbadian politician who in the last sixty years can claim that he has done something for the constitutional advancement of this colony is the late Deputy Speaker, Mr A.E.S. Lewis, a former junior member for Bridgetown. He insisted at all times that Barbados had got to the stage where we should be given universal suffrage as the major and perhaps the only real constitutional advancement in Barbados in the twentieth century. The introduction of ministerial status, the paying of salaries to Ministers and to members of the house and such things, I do not regard as any substantial constitutional advancement because you should not have to ask anybody for those things. The Executive Committee Act of 1891, which I think is Chapter 22, is the real mainspring of the constitutional advancement of this island, although

I would like to disclose that I have not been an admirer of Sir Conrad Reeves who has been the author of that Act. However, we must recognise that this is the real instrument which puts control of the economy of this island firmly into the hands of the elected representatives of the people of this island.

Mr Deputy Speaker, I very much appreciate that you have permitted me to digress somewhat from the original theme, but I was merely pointing out that the telegram of the Secretary of State sent to me as Premier of Barbados, was one which I did not view with any joy at all, and I regarded it as another attempt, even although it may not have been done deliberately, to create the impression that there were two grades of citizens in the Eastern Caribbean: one, the citizens of Barbados, and the other, the citizens of the Windward and Leeward Islands. As I have said, with the assistance of the independent members of this Honourable House, like the honourable senior member for St Peter, the honourable junior member for St George, who attended one of our conferences, and the honourable leader of the Opposition, I think we were able in some measure to dispel some of the fears which existed in the minds of the leaders of the Windward and Leeward Islands.

During the currency of our discussions, both here and in London, a Commission of Enquiry had been set up to enquire into certain allegations of mismanagement by the government of Grenada in general, and by the Chief Minister in particular, at the instance of the Federal Government and a Barbadian judge was appointed to preside over that enquiry. That enquiry made one or two false starts, but if eventually got off the ground; and while we were in the middle of the conference in London, Mr Gairy, the Chief Minister of Grenada, was greatly agitated throughout the proceedings, and he could hardly sit in his place because the Sword of Damocles was hanging over his head: and if at times he appeared to be slightly on edge, we were very appreciative of the position in which he found himself and to which he could have somewhat contributed himself.

I am not making any pronouncement or passsing any judgement. When the report was released, it more or less castigated the Ministers and the Chief Minister of Grenada for mismanagement of public funds and for attempting to intimidate members of the public service of that island. The Commission made no recommendations what-soever, neither was the evidence of the Commission published. Anyone who has any knowledge of the procedure of these Commissions of Enquiry or who has had a nodding acquaintance with the procedure in a Court of Law, anyone who has been aware of the publication of the reports of the Commissions of Enquiry in the island of Barbados would realise right away that that slender document, which was elevated to the plane of a Stationery Office Publication, issued by authority of the United Kingdom government – any such person would realise that that publication must have been a very much abridged version of the Report which must have been originally submitted to the United Kingdom government by the Commission of Enquiry.

It was a remarkable document in that none of the evidence was published, and it made no real recommendation except that there should be a tightening up of the financial provisions relating to the government of Grenada. When I was approached by members of the delegations, by members of the United Kingdom delegation as well as by other people in the United Kingdom as to what was going to happen when the Grenada Report was published, my answer was always the same. A Commission of Enquiry has no right (of) indicting anyone; the purpose of such a Commission is to bring in a forcible manner to public opinion any irregularities which may have been existing in the body politic. The next step was that, having elected not to proceed by way of indictment in a Court of Law, you set up a Commission of Enquiry because you do not consider that the behaviour complained of merits such a drastic step as the prosecution of an individual or of two or three or four persons, but it is a matter which is sufficiently grave that the electors of the area should be acquainted with and get their information on an authoritative level. That is my personal view of the invoking of the machinery of a Commission of Enquiry. I think it would be very high-handed for any government to short-circuit a legitimate prosecution of a person before the Courts of Law of the territory and save that person from incarceration or a fine or some kind of punishment which the law would demand, by setting up a Commission of Enquiry.

A Commission of Enquiry cannot act as a preliminary magistrate's investigation; you cannot set up a Commission of Enquiry and ask an Attorney General of an island to take proceedings on the findings, when the Commission has already fully ventilated a case in the public arena of the territory itself and right through the stratosphere; the matter is disseminated by the press and the radio, not only in the territory, but outside the territory as well.

Therefore, it would be placing a prosecutor in a highly invidious position if after a Commission of Enquiry has gone into the matter, he is asked to prosecute the case; the minds of the jury would have been prejudiced already. I do not know of any instance – there may be some – where a Commission of Enquiry in the island of Barbados has been followed by an indictment in the Courts of Law; that is why I say that one would only take the step of setting up a Commission of Enquiry if the matters complained of were of so nebulous a character or one did not consider them serious enough to make a public prosecution. One may allow public sentiment at election time to take control and decide who is wrong or who is right, or on the other hand, whether the people elect a particular person to manage their affairs, whether he mismanages them or not. The sovereignty of the electorate is such that the electorate sits down in Barbados and chooses people, even although it is manifest that those people are not acting in the interest of the masses who have put them there. We in Barbados have to suffer because of this built-in foundation in the democratic system of government – the freedom of the people, whose representatives may pass a law to expropriate property or send people to a cross. Each and everyone of us has paid that price by having governments who were not interested in carrying out the wishes of the people.

The purpose of my illustrations and argument is to demonstrate that having elected to set up a Commission of Enquiry as to what was going on in Grenada, it is clear that the Commission of Enquiry has not got the power to indict anyone. It would be highly undesirable for a prosecution to take place when the intention is to bring matters to public notice. My idea is that the gentlemen who were appointed to sit on the Commission of Enquiry were members of integrity, who had sifted the evidence, and they were making it available so that public sentiment and public opinion would be brought to bear on any future occasion that these mismanagers may offer themselves to the people. I have spent sometime explaining the background because I want my premises to be clear.

Unless members of this House understand the premises from which I am arguing they would not be able to understand the Resolution which is now before the House, and at this stage perhaps it would be advisable for me to state that this Resolution is in no way intended to condone or connive any mismanagement which may have taken place in the island of Grenada. But all of us feel as government ministers, having met in Cabinet and considered this matter from the constitutional and every other point of view from which it should be considered, that this is a matter for the people of Grenada themselves. It is not a matter for the Colonial Office or the people of Barbados whether they approve or disapprove. The ballot box is the place where this should be decided, and nothing should be done by anyone to try to influence the exercise by the voters of that territory of their democratic right to elect whatever form of government, whether it be a communist government, a fascist government, a democratic government or any other form of government that they want.

Mr Deputy Speaker, it is neither the business of the United Kingdom, the people of Barbados, the people of America, nor the people of the Soviet Union. It is a matter for the exercise by the people of Grenada of their democratic rights and privileges, and I want to get that clear, because if one does not understand that, this resoultion does not in any way cast aspersion on the integrity of the members of the Commission. I am prepared to accept that everything that the Commission said has been proven by the standard which is demanded in a Court of Law for all criminal offences. It has been proven without any reasonable doubt, because I do not imagine any of those gentlemen, knowing some of them in the way I know them, would accept any kind of third or fourth hand evidence that certain irregularities occurred in the matter of the finances in the colony of Grenada.

I am not a personal friend of the Chief Minister of Grenada, neither is he or anyone else my enemy. I am not prepared to defend the suppressing of the constitution, whether or not I agree with what he has done. I see only constitutional issues which are involved; and if any member of this Chamber wants to wash his hands of this matter and say that he could never agree with Gairy, and that he could never agree with what was done in Grenada, I am urging upon him that that is not what we are being called upon to consider now. What we are being called upon to consider is this: when you hear the bell ringing, ask not for whom the bell tolls: it only tolls for thee.

Mr Deputy Speaker, it is not my intention to continue any longer on this matter, because I am sure that other members both on this side and on the other side of this Honourable Chamber will want to express an opinion for or against this Resolution, and it is our intention to allow them to do so. I am sure that your honour will not in any way curtail debate on this matter, except in so far as your honour considers that a speaker is being irrelevant, or alternatively, that he is in breach of the Standing Orders of this House.

In order to highlight the action which we are asking the House to take, I want to invite honourable members to cast their minds back to certain similar actions on the part of the United Kingdom government. Now as you will know, the historian of my party is the Honourable Minister of Education (J. Cameron Tudor, now Foreign

Minister, Sir James Tudor). I am entirely innocent of any knowledge of historical dates, because from the time I was at school, I found it impossible to consider dates of any importance except roughly to indicate different phases in the world's history which may have taken place. But if I remember rightly, sometime between 1953 and 1954 the constitution of British Guiana was taken away by a Conservative government in the United Kingdom. I am reminded by the Honourable Minister of Education who is a walking encyclopaedia on these matters, that it was in October, 1953. If that date is wrong, he must take the responsibility for it; but according to him, in October 1953, the British government decided to take away the constitution of British Guiana after the British Guiana government had been in office for a mere six months.

Mr Deputy Speaker, the difference between that occasion and this one – or the differences, because there are several differences – are that on that occasion they were not alleging that there was any financial irregularity. I understand that a senior Government official who was an Englishman was invited to bring a glass of water for the now President of the Senate, and that they felt that was lowering the prestige of the public servants from the metropolitan country; not that that was the only reason, if that is a reason at all. But there were a lot of silly little bagatelles – somebody painting the statue of Queen Victoria in one of the streets of Georgetown, or somebody writing something on a wall. Well, Barbadians and people from England as well, are in the habit of writing all kinds of things inside the doors of public lavatories all the time, and no constitution is taken away for that. There were a lot of silly, annoying incidents which one would normally expect from a country like British Guiana – I am not being derogatory in any way – which did not have the long history of constitutional development which we have enjoyed in the island of Barbados. Here was a trading post of a company like the Hudson Bay Trading Company where the contractors carried their furs; British Guiana was the tropical trading post of the Hudson Bay Trading Company which suddenly found itself with a large measure of internal self-government after a fairly bitter struggle by the political parties and the different sections of the community. Therefore, if they did not have a long period of tutoring, it was only natural that there would be certain expressions of enthusiasm, if we may put it that way – and I challenge any honourable member here to tell me that I am wrong – and it was seen that there was no allegation of fraud or of financial irregularity.

Mr Deputy Speaker, there was neither riot, nor civil commotion.

But certain entrenched, vested interests – and I am not now referring to Bookers-McConnell Limited, because it now appears that they are the most enlightened apostles of the constitution in British Guiana and are carrying the banner way in front of the Premier of British Guiana himself in the advancement towards socialism of some kind or another, whether Eastern or Western, I am not sure yet. They are carrying the banner for reasons which I have not had sufficient time to analyse, but it is a very happy augury for British Guiana that we find the entrenched interests now being prepared to carry the banner of socialism in advance of the political party itself. In October 1953 no indictment was made against the leaders of the government of British Guiana on the grounds that there had been any financial irregularity or anything like that. There was no riot or civil commotion.

The constitution of British Guiana was taken away. The other difference is that we were assured by the then Secretary of State for the Colonies that he did this after consultation with the leader of the government of Barbados, Sir Grantley Adams; the leader of the government of Jamaica, Sir Alexander Bustamente; the leader of the government of Trinidad, Mr Albert Gomes; and he also added the rider that he had even called up the leader of the opposition of Jamaica, Mr Norman Manley. The impression given by the Secretary of State was that all of these leaders had not only approved, but some of them had heralded him and even urged the British government to take away the constitution from the people of British Guiana. Are we, therefore, suprised now that these architects to the destruction of the constitutional rights of the people of British Guiana, that these people who found themselves as leaders of the Westindian embryonic nation, that these people as soon as birth was given to the Westindian nation, decided to strangle it in its birth? How can we be surprised when they strangled the constitution of the people of British Guiana after it was only given to those people six months previously?

Members of this Honourable House must be abundantly clear about the principles involved in the passing of a resolution of this kind. Mr Deputy Speaker, when the constitution of British Guiana was taken away, I along with some other members of the then government, backbenchers as we were at the time in this Chamber, gave expression to our disgust over the action taken by the British government. I remember saying on more than one occasion – and some honourable members who are not fitted with short memories will remember that I said, echoing the words of Mr Edmund Burke in the House of Commons – you will forgive me if I consult my historical encyclopaedia – that in 1780 when Mr Burke was protesting against the action of the British government in the United States, the then American colonies, what he said was that you cannot draw up an indictment against the whole nation. If I had chosen a theme here today as the theme of this Resolution, I would borrow the words of Mr Burke and say: you cannot draw up an indictment against a whole nation.

Sir, what I said on the floor of the House of Assembly in 1954 and 1955 and subsequently was that if an individual minister of the United Kingdom officially expressed adoration for those little things which he knew and things such as hegemony which he knows little about, if he expressed admiration for forms of government over which he had no opportunity to exercise any authority, if this was seditious or illegal, the good Lord in Heaven knows that the laws under the British constitution are so watertight that sometimes if you did not stand up quickly when they played God Save the Queen, you may be hauled into the court and charged with sedition. No one can deny that.

But my attitude was that the laws of the constitution should not be revoked if there were any seditious practices or something which is called seditious libel in the laws of British Guiana, Barbados, Trinidad and other Westindian colonies. Not only seditions, but actions are noticeable; even painting Queen Victoria's statue with red paint, as I understand, was done in British Guiana was noticeable – and even the statue of Lord Willoughby. All of that can be construed to be seditious and you would not have much trouble in getting an indictment under the colonial statues under which we are suffering. But my contention is that if you are guilty of an action which was susceptible of public prosecution before a Court of Law, it is not only right but it is the duty of the members of the Attorney General's Department, and it is the duty of the officer administering the government of the island or the territory, as the case may be, to invite such public prosecution in order to bring the person to boot. The purpose of my saying that is that I think it is grossly unfair that if some little school teacher in Berbice, who one day hopes to be a lawyer and is burning the midnight oil reading constitutional law, exercises his right to choose whom he wants to represent him, somebody should sit down in England and on the advice of a certain administrator take away from him his right to choose the person he wants to preside over his rights.

That is why I echo the words of Mr Edmund Burke. No one has devised a way of drawing up an indictment against a whole nation. Adolf Hitler was the only person who did it, but the way in which he did it was to sign the death warrant of six million people without an indictment at all. The next step to taking away a constitution is to exercise that kind of authoritative function which Adolf Hitler and other dictators exercised.

Sir, you will understand why I say, if the people of British Guiana had done something, then you would have been justified. If the people had taken arms against the sea of troubles which we call the Colonial Office – those are troubles at sea – if the people of British Guiana had made dykes and prevented a landing of British troops or businessmen or had expropriated property of the Crown or done anything of that kind, perhaps you then would have investigated the drawing up of an indictment against the whole people or you would be justified on the banner of public opinion in the taking away of the constitution from the colony.

We would have mismanagement in these islands of ours. In the United Kingdom, a sum of STG£2,000 million was voted between 1935 and 1940 for armaments to protect Great Britain, and when the British Army was confronted by the forces of the enemy at Dunkirk, apart from about three squadrons of the Air Force, and the small pond boats which pushed out from the east coast, they hardly had parasols to hold over their heads because that money was misspent. Up to now that money has not been accounted for. I want to make that clear. I invite you to read your history. Such things do not percolate down to the colonial press, but they send out pictures of the Queen shaking some old lady's hand.

Mr Deputy Speaker, between 1947 and 1958, when the Federation came into being, we witnessed in this Federation, with the active benevolence of the United Kingdom government, a seduction of British Honduras and the rape of the constitution of British Guiana.

In that period both of these (states), through their elected representatives and heads of government had expressed a willing-ness to join the Westindies Federation. The Rance Report was published in January 1948 – I am speaking purely from memory. In 1953, in the Legislative Council of British Guiana, Dr (Cheddi) Jagan was the only member to vote in favour of the federation. Those leaders I have mentioned did nothing to encourage Mr Richardson or Dr Jagan who became Chief Minister of British Guiana; they did nothing to assist them to make their countries available to the people of the Westindies, but they connived not only at the taking away of the constitution of British Guiana, but they actually assisted to make sure that the Westindian nation was starting off as a puny infant without these territories in which to settle their people or to assist the people of these territories to develop. I say that the doom of the Westindies was sealed when those leaders decided to take away the constitution; but, of course, Dr Jagan is now in complete control of British Guiana. To take away the constitution from British Guiana is to take away the constitution from the electors; you take away the constitution from the people who have the right to vote because you do not give them the right to say how they want their country to be managed when you take away the constitution. I was privileged to witness within a couple of years the same British government under the same political party give back the constitution to the same country of British Guiana.

I was further privileged to witness that, in this year of grace, 1962, a lot of people not necessarily including myself, but not necessarily excluding myself either, you have fought and you have had bloodshed, civil commotion, and a clear expression of the tendency of the government in power to go against the wishes of the people; there was greater justification then for suspending the constitution, even if temporarily, of British Guiana. But the same Conservative government in Britain sent in British troops by plane at the expense of the British taxpayers to shut down the constitution. Just imagine that when the leaders do something, you do not punish the leader, but you take away the constitution of the people. Can you blame any member of the government of Barbados if we do not repose any kind of confidence whatsoever in the discretion of the United Kingdom government which appears to be so preoccupied with the defence of liberalism that they did not have any attention to pay to what they were doing in these areas? As a matter of fact, they have reached the stage of being so demoralised that they want to let go of these colonies like some kind of hot potato, but they want to squeeze out all the pulp before they let them go. That is how it appears to me.

Mr Deputy Speaker, the constitution has been taken away from the people of Grenada by an arbitrary act of the United Kingdom government. What is more deplorable to us in Barbados as a government of the people of this island, is that within twelve months, the United Kingdom government, the same government which we now have re-enfranchising the leader of the Grenada government, in the same manner they have overruled the judgement of a Judge of the Supreme Court in St Lucia. You must ask if we must have any respect for their pronouncements on democratic procedures.

In the neighbouring colony of St Lucia, a Judge of the Supreme Court ruled that there was a breach of the election law and that certain ministers would have to forfeit their seats because of that breach. There is no law which is passed in any of the Windward or Leeward Islands which does not have to be approved by the United Kingdom government. Their election law is actually sent down, like the Decalogue from Mount Sinai, from Church Street. It is not as it is in Barbados where any private member can pass a Bill, and if we do not scrutinise it carefully, we have to abide by the consequences which follow; there are only certain Bills which are reserved for the Royal Assent or Signification; there are very few of them. A law like the awarding of the Princess Alice Scholarship, as the honourable senior member for the City would know, has got to be reserved for Royal Signification; but all the Bills which deal with the constitution of the island, we can decide to pass and make a lot of mistakes; but it is not so in the Leeward and Windward Islands. These Ordinances are sent down from the United Kingdom. Under that law in St Lucia certain Ministers had to forfeit their seats; but because they had somebody in Trinidad, in the Federal Government whom they could not do anything to offend, because the Deputy Prime Minister of the Federation was a St Lucian who rejoices under the name of Dr LaCorbineire, they turned the whole law upside down. Despite what Justice Chenery found – Barbados always seems to be on the wrong end of the stick; we seem always to have Barbadians involved in these things. Mr Justice Chenery ruled that the Ministers should lose their seats; and the Colonial Office said that, despite anything which Mr Justice Chenery did, despite anything which he may have ruled in a Court of Law – and it could not be challenged – the Ministers can still be Ministers. In those circumstances, can we repose any faith in those people? They are playing the game of politics strictly by ear all the time; they have not settled their policy on anything. Those of us who have been following what is taking place in St Lucia, in British Guiana, or in Grenada – well, I cannot say that it came as a surprise to me.

I cannot pretend it is anything that has surprised me, because last week the Secretary of State said he did not like this kind of thing that was going on, and that was five or six days before they actually exercised the Order-in-Council in this matter.

What we regard as being particularly depressing in this matter, Sir, is that we are now trying to build a nation, and by taking arbitrary action of this kind, they are focusing some strictures which are already levelled at the Caribbean area as a whole. We had Mr Castro in Cuba, Sir Grantley Adams in Trinidad, and Mr Jagan in British Guiana, and now they say we have Mr Gairy in Grenada, giving the impression that the Caribbean area, because of the failures and lack of appreciation for the finer points of democracy by some of the people, if not all of them, that I have mentioned, is an area which is always seething, dissatisfied, bordering on Spanish South American Republicanism, and an area in which no one should repose any kind of confidence, because of the gymnastics of a few irresponsible people, and people who, every time they open their mouths, are prone to put both of their feet in them. They now want to project an image as they always do unconsciously, due to their ignorance of the real aspirations of the people of the Westindies, and the real solid basis of Westindian advancement, something which is based on the struggles of the masses of the Westindies, and not on the political leadership of the Westindies. I want to make it clear, and that goes also for this or any other government in Barbados, that any advancement which we have attained has been due to the demonstration of the submerged tenths of the populations and not anything that a leader has condescended to give to the people of the Westindies.

Mr Deputy Speaker, you will always find a leader; and a lot of these governments have been crisis governments. Their political parties have been crisis organisations; they have never had any sound basis either from a business point of view or from a political point of view. There have always been crisis organisations in the Westindies. The idea is: We are having a federal election; so let us get together, although we are not birds of a feather; that is to say, we belong to certain political parties. That is the kind of theory that gave rise to the Bolshevik group in the Soviet Union. We are not really birds of a feather; we are of different plumage; we are, as one member of the opposition has said, blackbirds, among the pigeons all over the place.

I have no hesitation in moving any vote of censure against a Conservative government in England, because I am not a socialist in Barbados, and like some ex-honourable friends of mine who, by the time they get to Canada or the United Kingdom, say that the people in Barbados accuse them of being conservatives, and they are really more conservative than the leaders of the Conservative governments in these countries. When I go to England, I ask them if they know to whom they are talking and tell them they are talking to people who, in the days when police used to be armed with bayonets and bullets, stood up for the masses of these countries.

When Mr Gairy went to Grenada there was a political vacuum. The middle-class people in Grenada had abdicated their right to leadership by ignoring the sufferings of the people of St George's. It is in that kind of atmosphere, where people do not recognise their political responsibilities and their responsibility to the community, that you get dictators and people who are perhaps not fully ripe for leadership issues.

If it is the same people who inspired the British government to think that they can treat the representatives of Grenada with disdain and contempt and to go one step further and take away the constitution not only from the representatives, but from the people of Grenada, then I say that it is time when we must raise a protest; and even although the same people who abdicated their right to leadership by ignoring the masses are the people from whom the constitution has been taken away, I say it serves some of them right, because they are too anxious to play a single game.

A lot of people, Mr Deputy Speaker, accuse me of talking the same way now that I am in government, as if I am still in opposition. They say that I do not remember that I am in government. I did not know that you had to change your tone when you got into government, or that the same tonic *sol-fa* which you had been singing, you had to change to sing some other kind of *oratorio*. I do not understand that at all. I thought that the people had put us on this side because they liked the way we were talking, because of the things which we wanted to do, and the harshest criticism which we can get is that we are still in the opposition. We will be in the opposition until we get the things which we want done, and stop those things which we say that we do not want to be done against the people of the Westindies and the people of Barabdos.

Mr Edwin Burke said: 'I do not know of any method of drawing up an indictment against a whole people.' I say that I do not know of any method of drawing up an indictment against the people of Grenada, and nowhere in the report which was released on the 6th June, 1962, do I find that the commissioners had any indictment to make against the people of Grenada. It is in that sense and spirit and those phrases underlined in this Resolution that I move that this Resolution do now pass.

Federation and the democratic way of life

Statement to Parliament on 20 June, 1962 introducing a resolution to approve the report of the Eastern Caribbean Federation Conference

Mr Deputy Speaker, it is now my privilege to move the passing of this Resolution to approve the Report of the East Caribbean Federation Conference, 1962. It is not necessary for me to go into the history of the development which led up to the dissolution of the Westindian Federation on the 31st of May, 1962. The document which we have before us does not attempt to set out a detailed history of the developments leading up to the establishment and the dissolution of the Westindian Federation. There are certain significant dates which every school child in the Westindies should learn and should know about, and I think that these significant dates would be briefly repeated during the course of a debate of this nature.

In 1947, at the invitation of the then Secretary of State for the Colonies, Mr Creech Jones, delegates from this House and from other Legislatures throughout the British Caribbean area from British Honduras in the north to British Guiana in the south, met in conference; some of the delegates from this Honourable House are still members of this House, and others, although still alive, have gone to other countries, and retired from politics. This Conference took place in 1947 and it was agreed to set up a Standing Closer Association Committee under the Chairmanship of Sir Hubert Rance who was Governor of Trinidad and its dependent territory, Tobago. Perhaps, Mr Deputy Speaker, you will allow me to do something which honourable members of the Legislatures of these islands have appeared to be reluctant to do.

Perhaps you will permit me to acknowledge a debt which they were unprepared to admit, and that is the debt to those Westindians in the United States of America who contributed a substantial amount of money in order to make it possible for the Standing Closer Association Conference to be held in Montego Bay (Jamaica) in 1947.

The Colonial Office – or the British government – is often accused of forcing the Westindies to federate. Personally, it is a view which I do not entirely share, because on an examination of the history and the development of the Federation, you will find that the Colonial Office and the British government were as uncertain about the establishment of a Federation as they have exhibited those uncertainties today in the granting of independence to the East Caribbean, and the shape of a Federation for the East Caribbean. The Secretary of State for the Colonies in 1947, Mr Creech Jones himself, was a Federationist. It is very doubtful whether any of the Caribbean leaders of that day had given the serious examination attendant upon the establishment of a Federation; and the fruit of that has been the result of a total unpreparedness for leadership, a total lack of knowledge of the intricacies of statesmanship demanded of a federal Government. But there is one group of Westindians, quite apart from the students who were studying in the United States of America, Canada and the United Kingdom. This group of persons existed in the areas of New York, Boston, and Chicago; those persons had been brought together by the events in the Westindies of 1937[*] and have stuck together right through the dim period of the Second World War, taking a very active interest in every political development in the British Caribbean area and, indeed, in a wider context, in the Caribbean as a whole.

It was a result of the efforts which they made, and by the contributions which they made to the cause of Westindian nationhood, that that conference was the success it was in 1947, and indeed it was due to their efforts that the conference was held at all. Westindian governments at that time had not got it into their heads that it was the duty of these governments to take the initiative in matters of constitutional advancement. They were always waiting for leadership from the United Kingdom. Every effort made by political parties in the Westindies up to 1937 had been condemned as being seditious, racial or rebellious and it was up to our American cousins to teach us to clear the mat.

Mr Deputy Speaker, when the history of the Westindies is written, despite our long association with the British Commonwealth of Nations, it will be realised that there was a long, dark period of Westindian history between the end of the First World War and the beginning of the Second World War when there was absolutely no economic assistance of any kind flowing from the United Kingdom in this direction, and when the Westindies' economies were sustained to a very large extent – almost entirely, I should say – by the

---

[*]This refers to a series of popular rebellions in several Westindian countries, including Barbados.

remittances which relatives of Westindians resident in the area received from those abroad. First, the Westindians went to build the Panama Canal. From Panama, just about the beginning of the First World War, they moved on to Cuba, and from Cuba they moved to the United States.

Mr Deputy Speaker, that wave of migration did not come to a halt on the introduction of the restrictive Immigration Ordinances by the government of the United States. It continued almost unabated until the time of the depression between the year 1929 and the year 1934 when the flow began to ebb and began to move almost in the opposite direction, because of the vast number of unemployed people there were in the United States and in other countries.

From 1934 until 1937, therefore, we had a period of political and economic stagnation in this island. There were attempts by a few brave souls to enlighten the masses, but the majority of the people who should have been giving leadership to the masses of the Westindies, were content to sit back and do their duty in that state of life to which it had pleased the Almighty to call them, pay no attention to what was going on around them, and accept the status quo as being a pre-ordained and natural state of affairs.

I have always held the theory, Mr Deputy Speaker, that any progress which has come in this Caribbean area, has always been the result of the spontaneous expression of disgust with a situation by the masses, popularly called the 'submerged tenth' of the population of this island. Unfortunately for those who consider government as a natural preserve for one stratum of society, the submerged tenth is now emerging as nine-tenths of the population and not one-tenth at all. No Alexander Hamilton has risen. There has never been the need perhaps for a George Washington as the General of a Westindian army. It has always been the movement of people within and without the territory which brought into focus the very dire economic conditions under which the majority of the people in these islands suffered.

The Panama Canal was built substantially by the toil and sweat of Westindian labour. But it was the income which the workers on the Panama Project managed to earn between the seven years immediately preceding the First World War which prevented the people of these islands from demonstrating, in rebellious manner, their disgust against the conditions under which they were supposed to exist.

Then during the First World War, large numbers of Westindians rallied to the Flag. I think that the British government ought to be reminded of this sometimes, because when we see the craven way in which the British government is today crawling at the feet of their oppressors, the people who tried to destroy the British Commonwealth of Nations on at least two occasions in a quarter of a century, and when we look at the disdain and the contempt with which they are prone to treat peoples whom Rudyard Kipling described as the lesser members without the law, and in the words of the hymnist, the people who inhabit the countries where the heathen in his blindness is supposed to bow down to wood and stone, when we regard all of these things on one side and look at the almost childish loyalty of the Westindian masses on the other, the way in which they rallied to defend what Mr Churchill said is the bastion of freedom on more than one occasion in twenty-five years, I do not see how anyone who has the honour of participating in the administration of these areas can be so much out of his mind as to deprive the people of their constitutional rights.

Westindians were not reluctant in answering the call, whether in the armed services or in factories or on the beaches. The Westindians, the Barbadians, St Lucians, Antiguans could be found whether in the steaming jungle of Malaya or in the cold regions of the North Atlantic on convoy patrols, on the upper deck welding steel ships which the Americans so graciously made available to the British Merchant Shipping Service; wherever the conflict was being waged the Westindians were there. Not a single Westindian has ever been impeached for selling secrets to the enemy, for any disloyalty to the Flag or doing any of those things which would be inimical to the successful prosecution of a war.

I am not going back 150 years or 200 years to talk about the blood and the sweat, to talk as Dr (Eric) Williams has done in his famous treatise about 'Capitalism and Slavery', to show how the industrial wealth of Great Britain was financed by the unfree labour of the workers of the Westindies; those are matters which are accepted by the most rabid, reactionary Conservative in Great Britain, and there is absolutely no point in our re-emphasising the industrial debt which the industrialists owe to the ancestors of the people of the Westindies. It does not get us anywhere. That is as true of John 3:16. That was never a matter for argument; and if the Premier of that territory of Trinidad and Tobago has made any contribution to the economic history of mankind, it is in underlining and documenting the foundation on which that industrial development has been built up.

During the dark days of the depression, during the inter-war period, the period of stagnation, there were no development and welfare organisations, there was no economic policy, no Colombo

Plan. Many of these things we in the Westindies are still without and bereft of. We were just regarded as geographical areas to which school masters in the United Kingdom could say that the sun never sets on the British Empire. The Westindies, apart from the cricket field, first came into prominence because the ordinary men and women in the street, and not any political leader, decided to revolt and rebel against those conditions, although they were not revolting against any individuals or any countries. In 1937, they called them disturbances. In another country, they would call them insurgents, revolutionaries or rebels because the jargon of nationalism is very often qualified by the impression which the person who is being protested against wants to give to the rest of the world.

Out of that rebellion, out of all that social protest, came the appointment of the Royal Commission of very highly qualified persons of integrity in the public life of the United Kingdom who published a very forthright report on the conditions which they found in the Westindies and who recommended that the economic salvation of the Westindies lay along the road to Federation; and the Montego Bay Conference, coming as it did nearly two years after the end of the Second World War, was the first direct recognition that the recommendations of the Royal Commission should be implemented.

The Standing Closer Association Committee met frequently in the territory of Trinidad under the chairmanship of Sir Hubert Rance and published a report in 1948 which lay on the shelf of the Westindian Legislatures for a very long time. It was not until some time in the 50s, around 1952 and 1953, that the Legislatures, including the Barbados House of Assembly, got around to the job of even discussing the Standing Closer Association Committee's report which, had been published some years before; and it is symbolic of the attitude of the Westindian leaders of that era that they had to wait for a directive from the Secretary of State for the Colonies before they had the courage to present the idea of a Federation of the peoples of these territories.

I had the privilege along with at least 40 per cent of the honourable members whom I can see around this horseshoe table in this Assembly of making some kind of contribution to the debate which took place on the Standing Closer Association Committee's Report.

There was not a single dissenting voice at that time and I hope that, by the time we conclude the discussion on the report which I now hold in my hand, there will be some measure of unanimity for the necessity – rather, the plausibility – for Barbados to join the Association with our brethren across the seas; we will be setting the clock back if, at this stage of our development, we are going to stop and hesitate and wonder what are the advantages to be derived from an association of this kind.

If the Westindian leaders who jumped into the Federation when it was clear that there was a certain amount of status for them, and that certain Imperial honours would be attendant upon being recognised as a larger area – if they had done their job to educate the people of the Westindies in the exercise of a Federal Constitution, there would not be any need for my discourse this afternoon.

The government does not intend to steamroller or stampede through with this discussion. We are going to give everybody, even the slow-witted, sufficient time to read, mark, learn and inwardly digest the contents of this document, because once we put our hands to the plough there cannot be any turning back this time. We have to plough a very straight furrow which will have no bends or crookedness.

Mr Deputy Speaker, there are a lot of mealy-mouthed politicians and people in the newspaper world who only believe in indulging in cheap sensationalism, and who believe there is a thing called the freedom of the Press. I do not know whether you went to some legal institution where they were able to tell you what this mysterious freedom of the Press is supposed to be; but as far as I know, there is no such thing as the freedom of the Press. The Press does not enjoy any more freedom than any other citizen in this country. The Press has the same right to criticise anyone, the same right to use their own property in a way which does not interfere with the proprietary rights of their neighbours, the same right to say things provided they fall short of the laws of libel and defamation; but the Press does not enjoy any special status or any special freedom. The Press, however, has a responsibility, a responsibility which they do not always appear to be conscious of; and when they indulge in exercises of this kind, and allow even correspondents in the Readers Columns to write disparaging articles about the Westindian people, and to write poems about 'Ten Little Countries', they are only concealing their contempt like Agatha Christie when she wrote a book about 'Ten Little Nigger Boys'.

A Press which allows advertisements to appear stating that only people of a certain racial origin need apply for certain jobs is not exercising freedom; that Press is abdicating its responsibility and duty to the people of the country where that Press is making a profit for its Directors. In this Year of Grace, 1962, we want someone to write a National Anthem; we do not want clever correspondents doing like

Agatha Christie and writing about 'Ten Little Nigger Boys'. I want to tell them that there are eight countries and not any 'Little Eight', and these eight territories, despite anything that may happen, are not falling off any wall, because if there was anything we decided in London as presented in this Report on the Federation Conference of 1962, we have decided to build a monument more lasting than bronze and certainly more lasting than that erected by the late architects of the destruction of the Westindian nation.

Anyone who does not understand the economic, political and geographical background of the Westindies will not readily appreciate why these islands should want to come together in a federal system of government. If there were one area which a federal system of government eminently suits, it is the Eastern Caribbean.

There has been little communication culturally between one island and another but when you look at the broad masses of people in the Westindies, they do have a common affinity, although in individual islands they have their own way of looking at things. We are, therefore, bound together by some ties of consanguinity, it is true, but we are bound together by similar conditions and similar economic background more than anything else. We are bound together because we believe that most of us were displaced from some part of Africa, some may have come from Dahomey, some from Uganda, some from Gambia, some from the Ebou nation, some from Mozambique, some from Dakar, and from all parts of the continent our ancestors may have been brought against their wishes. But when you look at a country like Barbados and you realise that the average Barbadian is completely detribalised and has more cultural standing and is allied more closely to those people in western industrial nations, one cannot really go on with that nebulous affinity in order to prove we have a common destiny. It may have been established that we have a common past, but we have been bound together by historical and physical accidents, because we have looked to one metropolitan country for control and leadership, and because the pattern of jurisprudence, the pattern of constitutional institutions and parliamentary institutions which we have followed all along has been the pattern which has been given to us by the government of the United Kingdom. Therefore, having one system now of parliamentary democracy (we) are bound together by a common respect of law, and being still in a relatively low state of economic advancement, we now aspire under these common bonds, however slender they are, to weld ourselves together in a nation in which each man would have his self-respect and so that we can assist each other in uplifting the standard of living for the people of the area.

The Finance and Economic Man

Sir Stephen E. Emtage

My first recollection of The Right Excellent Errol Walton Barrow was in 1957 when having won a Barbados Scholarship and thinking of studying Economics, I was advised to speak to him as possibly the only person in Barbados who had such a degree.

On my return to Barbados in 1962 from the London School of Economics (LSE) and Oxford University, I joined the Ministry of Finance. This was a fairly predictable choice as my father and several other relatives were public servants and the only real career options, at that time, was either a profession or the Civil Service.

On becoming Premier in 1961, Mr Barrow also held the portfolio of Minister of Finance and as such was my Minister from 1962-76 and 1986-87. He was a man of eclectic interests, who had considerable experience of the wider world from both his military service and as a university student. This period also brought him into close contact with many future leaders of the Commonwealth: Pierre Trudeau (Canada), Lew Kwan Yew (Singapore), Michael Manley (Jamaica) and Forbes Burnham (Guyana), among others.

I was fortunate as a young, junior official to have had direct access to Mr Barrow as a member of the original Economic Planning Unit (EPU) when it was established in 1962. The EPU was required, *inter alia*, to make recommendations on relevant financial and economic issues going before Cabinet, prepare and publish annual Economic Reports and prepare the National Development Plans. Mr Barrow was very supportive of the work of the EPU and encouraged its personnel to further our professional development.

FINANCE AND DEVELOPMENT

I consider Mr Barrow to have been fiscally conservative. It is true that there were institutional and legal constraints in the choice of fiscal policy measures as up until 1966 Barbados was still a colony and until 1972, when the Central Bank was established, monetary policy was restricted by the fact that we were members of the Eastern Caribbean Currency Board and as such did not have the facility to borrow from the monetary authority. Temporary financing for Government was then mostly provided by the commercial banks. Furthermore, the only tool available for changing interest rates was the Usury Act which set maximum lending rates and which was eventually repealed. The Central Bank did not begin to fix interest rates until 1976.

In furtherance of this view, between 1961 and 1976, in only three years did current expenditure exceed current revenue and the surpluses recorded on current account financed a considerable part of our capital expenditure. As a result, the National Debt which was some BDS $50 million in 1965 only reached BDS $258 million by 1976. Similarly, debt to GDP ratio was about 30 per cent at the end of the period and interest payments on the debt did not exceed 10 per cent of current expenditure.

In summary, fiscal policy during the period under review, was characterised by:

1) the pursuit of the goal of achieving current surpluses to finance a significant percentage of capital expenditure, especially in the period prior to 1972/73
2) the fiscal deficit financed largely from domestic sources and foreign financing, provided mainly through project, not market, loans and grants, and
3) the form of the Budget presentation was modified to show the objectives as (a) the provision of an accounting framework for ensuring accountability, (b) to serve as a tool of management and (c) to serve as a major statement of the Government's objectives and policies.

After 1972, the institutional arrangements for formulating economic policies were strengthened by the establishment of an integrated Ministry of Finance & Planning and the creation of the Central Bank of Barbados. The Bank, led by Dr Courtenay Blackman, was staffed by competent economists who worked closely with the Ministry in providing projections of economic variables and advising the Minister. Mr Barrow actively promoted and supported the Bank as an institution, although he did not support the subsequent headquarters building.

STRUCTURE OF THE ECONOMY

Between 1946 and 1980, the Barbados economy underwent some significant structural changes. GDP at factor cost which was estimated at BDS $40 million in 1946 had by 1980 increased to BDS $1.5 billion. The population had grown from 192,800 to 248,893 persons over the same period and the fertility rate had declined significantly from 5 live births per female to 2.6 live births per female. With regard to the occupational distribution of the labour force, there were significant changes with Agriculture, mainly sugar, declining from 28 per cent to 8 per cent and Services (Government and Domestic), Manufacturing and Tourism significantly increasing.

With regard to the macro economy, Barbados experienced average real growth of between 3 per cent and 5 per cent in the two decades up to 1980. Against a largely favourable international background, the economy became more diversified and although the unemployment rate did not change significantly, there were marked increases in labour productivity as labour shifted from lower- to higher-earning sectors. The main factors underlying this impressive performance were:

1) the economy continued to be competitive
2) capital formation mainly in the productive sectors averaged 20-30 per cent of GDP and foreign capital inflows remained largely positive
3) public finances remained strong with foreign borrowing mainly project-related in the form of long term loans, and

4) despite the fact that the balance of payments came under pressure in the early 1970s as a result of the first oil crisis, early adjustment was undertaken without excessive borrowing.

The basic aims of Government policy were articulated in successive Development Plans which were restricted to public sector investment, but outlined a broad strategy for national development. This strategy was aimed basically at reducing over-dependence on sugar by diversifying the economic structure and had three broad objectives:

1) expansion of the tourism sector
2) promotion of industrial growth, and
3) diversification of the agricultural sector through the search for new export crops and the increased output of food crops for domestic consumption.

The over-arching objective however, was to improve the social condition of the population by using re-distributive taxation to finance mainly education, housing and health projects. The modus operandi for implementing these policies was for the State to provide the physical and social infrastructure and tax and other incentives to support private investment.

Mr Barrow did not, in my opinion, favour a policy of public sector direct investment and ownership as a means of achieving growth in the productive sectors of the economy. On the lighter side, I recall as Secretary to the Central Planning Committee, the discussion concerning a financial problem at the Government-owned Haggatts sugar factory arose and Mr Barrow remarked *"if Government owned the only funeral home in the island, it would still make a loss!"* However, if an investment was critical and key to attracting increased private sector interest, as in the case of the Hilton Hotel, he supported the State taking the lead.

With regard to industrial policy, this to a large extent was inspired by the experience of Puerto Rico which was also adopted as a model by other Caribbean countries. The main elements of these policies were:

1) promotional efforts to attract investment at home and abroad, tax relief and exemptions, impositions sometimes of protective Customs tariffs or quantitative restrictions and the provision of soft loans, and
2) additional provisions for "enclave" industries which operated outside of the domestic economy, for example INTEL and Playtex.

When he was responsible for the portfolio of industrial development in the 1960s, Mr Barrow would meet with investors. In the case of large foreign firms, such as those mentioned above, which eventually employed over 1000 people, he would make himself available to assist with negotiations with their principals. Changes in technologies and loss of competitiveness in labour-intensive manufacturing led to its decline and to the virtual disappearance of the "enclave" sector. However the base was laid for a continuing growth in the sectors that where competitive.

TOURISM

As far back as 1932, administrations recognised the potential value to the economy of expenditure by non-residents and a Publicity Committee was created to promote the island. Before World War II the annual number of long-stay visitors was around 10,000 but by 1950 the figure had reached about 18,000.

The steady rise in incomes, the increasing popularity of foreign travel, the decrease in fares due to the introduction of jet aircraft and the strategic location of the Caribbean allowed the region to become a popular holiday destination. The quality of Barbados' physical and social infrastructure gave the island a competitive advantage which realised an increase in visitor arrivals from 37,000 in 1960 to 224,000 in 1976.

Institutional support for the sector included the establishment of promotional institutions at home and abroad and the Barbados Development Bank was established to provide loans to this and other productive sectors. Of particular note was the major upgrading of the

Airport, which enabled Barbados to become the hub for intra-regional air traffic. Mr Barrow played a major role in mobilising finance from the Canadian Government, whose Cabinet members he knew personally and who vacationed regularly in Barbados.

AGRICULTURE

From working with Mr Barrow for so many years, I concluded that he had a somewhat ambivalent attitude to the sugar industry. His May Day speech at King George V Park where he told the crowd that he hoped to see the day when he could look from St Philip all the way to St Lucy and *"not see a single blade of cane"* illustrated the historical antipathy which many Barbadians held because of the well-known historical antecedents of the industry. Yet, as Minister of Finance he was very aware of the importance of sugar to the economy.

In 1960, for example, sugar and non-sugar agriculture contributed 20 per cent to GDP, employed 21 per cent of the labour force in crop season and earned 53 per cent of the country's foreign exchange. The principal support of the sugar industry was the Commonwealth Sugar Agreement, which grew out of the wartime need of Britain to secure a reliable source of sugar. This agreement secured for Barbados an overall agreement quota (OAQ) and a negotiated price (NPQ) which guaranteed prices "which shall be reasonably remunerative to efficient producers." However, in relation to our average annual production of sugar (155,000 tons in 1961-64) our OAQ was more than 100 per cent and NPQ 80 per cent. Under Mr Barrow's Administration, the Government participated with and supported the Caribbean Sugar Producers in negotiations with the British Government to fix the NPQ price.

The proceeds of sale of sugar, apart from its indirect contribution to the general economy also made a direct contribution as a result of the imposition of special levies, on the annual earnings of the industry, which were:

1) Capital Rehabilitation Fund – a fund intended to finance capital improvement within the industry

2) Price Stabilisation Fund – intended to support falling sugar prices (in fact used only once in 1976 for this purpose, but instead used for other sugar-related purposes e.g. Bulk Sugar facility).
3) The Labour Welfare Fund – to improve the welfare of sugar workers, and
4) Sugar Workers' Provident Fund, which provided pensions

Between 1947 and 1980, the total contribution of these levies to these Funds amounted to BDS $121.6 million.

In 1974/75 when the economy was facing difficulties, as a consequence of the stagnation in the main markets for exports from Barbados and the effects of the OPEC-fuelled oil crisis, the island was facing significant budgetary difficulties. This coincided with a big increase in the world market price of sugar (from BDS $477 per ton to BDS $1,464 per ton). Mr Barrow imposed a Special Export Levy on all sugar sales exceeding BDS $720.00 per ton which yielded BDS $30 million, half of which was transferred to the Consolidated Fund to help finance the budget and the balance mostly earmarked for housing.

This served Barbados well at a time of fiscal stringency, but most sugar producers, who depended on this income from the few years when tonnage produced or world market prices were exceptional, to fund capital renewal and general plant and field rehabilitation, felt that they did not get a fair share of the "windfall" with long-running consequences for the efficiency of the industry.

TRADE AND INTEGRATION

On 4 July 1965, Mr Barrow invited me to a meeting at Government Headquarters which involved Mr Forbes Burnham, Premier of Guyana, together with a few other officials from Barbados and Guyana. This was the first step on the road to forge a West Indian Economic Union, which evolved in 1968 into the Caribbean Free Trade Association (CARIFTA) and culminated in the establishment of the Caribbean Common Market and Community (CARICOM) in 1973.

It was apparent that Mr Barrow was a dedicated regionalist, whom Sir Arthur Lewis described as "a West Indian Patriot". With Jamaica opting out of the Federation after their 1961 Referendum and Trinidad and Tobago effectively doing the same in early 1962, Sir Arthur Lewis, acting in the capacity of an Advisor, submitted proposals for a Federation of the remaining "Little Eight" countries, "in the belief that they are, in the main, acceptable to the Government of Barbados and the Windward and Leeward Islands." Indeed, Sir Arthur reported *inter alia*, that all these territories had confirmed a desire, should Trinidad and Tobago withdraw, to continue in Federation under the leadership of Barbados.

As a consequence of the dynamics that undermined the "Little Eight" Federation, Mr Barrow turned his attention towards economic integration and functional co-operation. He was still keen to pursue the idea of economic co-operation as a means of enhancing wider market access, which led to the 1965 Agreement of Dickinson Bay which established CARIFTA and of which I am one of a few remaining witnesses.

Another important institution which was established to promote economic development and integration which Mr Barrow also played a key role in creating, was the Caribbean Development Bank. The original proposal arose out of the Commonwealth Caribbean/Canada conference held in Ottawa in 1966. The Bank was established in Barbados in 1970 after Mr Barrow successfully lobbied for the headquarters to be located in Barbados rather that Jamaica.

CONCLUSION

Mr Barrow was, in my opinion, a pragmatist and realist. Although trained at the LSE at a time when the fiery Marxist, Harold Laski, held sway, he understood the limits of radical policy in a small, developing country, emerging from centuries of colonialism. He avoided current policies being advocated by some to "seize the commanding heights of the economy" by some of his colleagues and contemporaries in the region, who did so, with dire long-term consequences to their economies.

Mr Barrow was decisive and held strong views but was not obdurate or unwilling to consider advice tendered by his officials once rational, sensible and well researched. However, when dealing with financial advisors from multilateral institutions he would brook no condescension.

One such occasion comes to mind. During the inaugural visit of the World Bank technical team and in the wrap-up meeting with him, the leader of the team, in a haughty manner, likened economic policy to the four wheels of a chariot: financial policy, monetary policy, incomes policy and exchange rate policy. He then suggested that the wheels of the Barbados chariot were not going in the same direction. Mr Barrow refrained from comment.

At the IMF/World Bank Annual Meeting of Governors held in Washington DC later in the year, it was Mr Barrow's turn to speak on behalf of the Caribbean Community. The officials present from Jamaica, Guyana, Trinidad and Tobago and Barbados duly produced a draft statement. With minor amendments, the Ministers approved this draft, but Mr Barrow had added a section in which he forcefully chastised the World Bank delegation which had visited Barbados, for their arrogant attitude, dogmatic presentation and their presumption when speaking to small countries.

The other Caribbean Ministers declined to be associated with these remarks and when Mr Barrow delivered the speech he made it clear that he was speaking on behalf of Barbados only! Mr Robert McNamara, then President of the World Bank, was in the Chair and invited Mr Barrow to breakfast the following day. Rumour had it that there were senior staff adjustments later in the year.

However, when Mr Barrow returned to office in 1986, I recognised his health seemed to be deteriorating. The last time I spoke to him was on the day he died. For a number of reasons I had been considering an offer from the private sector and having served as Director of Finance & Planning for over 15 years had the option of taking early retirement.

As I entered his office he seemed preoccupied and he asked me *"Are you ready to go down to the Central Bank now?"* – the post having recently been vacated by Dr Courtenay Blackman. I was taken aback as we had never previously discussed the matter and I told him I was considering another offer. He asked me not to decide anything then, but to come back to see him the following morning. Later that afternoon we were shocked to learn of his passing.

I retired from the Civil Service in June 1987 and joined Life of Barbados Insurance Company as Vice President. I had served for 25 years and during that time had the privilege of working with Mr Barrow (15 years), Mr Adams (9 years), Mr St John (2 years) and Dr Haynes (1 year). Although, inevitably, there were times when the Minister of the day and I disagreed, I was always able to give advice freely, whether it was accepted or not and maintain good working relationships.

The years I worked with Mr Barrow as a young economist were particularly exciting, since I entered the Service at an historic period when the constitutional future of the region was being determined. These were, the collapse of the Federation, the failure of the "Little Eight" and Barbados' decision to 'go it alone'.

Although we were well prepared for the responsibilities of Independence, there were many who doubted our capacity to manage our own affairs. However, the quality of the Civil Service, at that time, and the leadership skills of Mr Barrow ensured that we met the challenges of Independence with confidence.

The Pragmatist

The Rt Honourable Owen S. Arthur, MP,

June 1987 Parliamentary Tribute (extract)

As an economic thinker, Errol Barrow was a difficult man to classify. At the end of his days, he declared his unrepentant commitment to the principles of Keynesian economics, a school of thought that grew out of the depression of the 1930s and made possible some of the recovery in the North Atlantic economies after the war. However, it is also a school of thought which has not found universal support among Caribbean thinkers, and which has come under critical comment from the University of the West Indies, in which tradition I proudly stand.

Despite his unrepentant commitment to Keynesian economics, Errol Barrow had perhaps a very curious contempt for economic theory. He was a pragmatist. He had a capacity, if any, to reduce difficult economic issues to bread and butter matters, and to draw from economic theory not so much the sterile aspects of theory as theory, but the working precepts that could inform economic strategy and also inform the country's development path.

I consider him therefore not as an unrepentant disciple of John Maynard Keynes, but as an economic pragmatist who, like so many other Barbadians, had the genius of being able to reduce difficult economic issues to their most simple dimensions, to sift out the bread and butter issues of a particular matter, and to be able to work to the country's advantage by maintaining the clearest possible grasp of the bread and butter issues.

He was not an ideologue. I had the opportunity in Jamaica to work with a leader who was also a product of the Laski School, which also informed Barrow's initial intellectual socialisation, and one was struck really by the tremendous difference between the statements by persons in Jamaica influenced by Laski and the statements by Errol Barrow.

For some persons democratic socialism is an ideology which has more to do with the broad transformation of societies, massive changes in the social relations of production, movements of modes of production from one mode to another, and the understanding of democratic socialism as a theoretical concept which can only explain the movements of society in very broad terms. I call those persons ideologues.

Barrow was not an ideologue. Hardly ever in the House of Assembly did we hear him speak of democratic socialism as an ideology. I really believe that there was not a very deep ideological commitment on the part of Errol Barrow to democratic socialism as a political theology, that if there was anything, there was a pragmatic commitment on the part of Errol Barrow to socialism as a working way by which to approach the problems of poor people.

The First Barbados Budget (Abridged)

First financial statement and budget proposals, delivered in Parliament on 26 June, 1962*

I promised honourable members of this honourable House that before the end of June 1962, I would be introducing the real budget proposals and the Development Plan of this government. It is in keeping with that promise that I rise today to make this Financial Statement. One honourable member has referred to the fact that there has never been this procedure before; that is not very difficult to understand because there has never been a budget. What happened in the past is that the Leader of the House or the Premier brought in a conglomeration of statistics which glorified in the name of Colonial Estimates, and in the course of disgorging a mass of statistics he would, in passing, mention that certain fiscal measures would be carried out. I was never in charge of the finance and indeed there was no Minister of Finance.

Mr Deputy Speaker, this island of Barbados is to a large degree dependent on external trade, on the amount of money which tourists are able to spend in the island, and on the remittances which we obtain from relatives, friends and well-wishers abroad. This is not a manufacturing economy wherein the people consume the product of industry, and where we get a turnaround of the money in the country entirely independent of external trade.

The proposals which I intend to make, therefore, must be read in

---

* (Errol W Barrow was the first Finance Minister of Barbados, serving in this capacity for 15 unbroken years from 1961, until his Democratic Labour Party – DLP – was voted out of office in 1976.

He turned over the Finance portfolio to Dr Richard C Haynes when the DLP was returned to office in May 1986, but kept a close oversight on the country's finances as Minister of Economic Affairs.

Dr Haynes resigned three months after Mr Barrow died, complaining of a breakdown of communications between himself and the new Prime Minister, Mr L. Erskine Sandford.

Mr Barrow intoduced the annual Financial Statement and Budget Proposals with the above presentation in 1962. Today, 25 years later, the format for this exercise remains largely unchanged).

the context of the peculiar nature of our economy. I propose to deal with the economic developments in this island and outside which have bearing on our position today. When we look at the world economic position in the light of our own circumstances, we find that the major problem is a shortage of capital, a shortage of money which emerging countries and highly developed countries all need in order to increase their national incomes by way of investment. This shortage of capital has made itself felt in no uncertain way on the economies of the Caribbean area, because we look primarily to the United Kingdom as a source of our investment capital. At the present moment the trend is for short term investment, thereby accentuating the shortage which already exists. Not only do we find that private institutions, private companies and public companies and private manufacturers are indulging in this exercise of short term investment and short term borrowing, but it is a marked feature of the United Kingdom economy today. Everything today is very much in a state of flux, and it is only natural that the people who have the propensity to save, the people who accumulate surplus will much sooner invest in a short term security than in a long term one. This new feature is most attractive to would-be investors, because the average person who has this amount of capital, or a certain amount of capital to invest, would much sooner know he is going to get back all his capital in two years' time with the opportunity to reinvest if conditions are changing as rapidly as we have seen them change, than to invest in Government securities.

Mr Deputy Speaker, not only do we find in the public sector that this trend is now becoming the order of the day, but private industrialists, private entrepreneurs and private businessmen themselves are offering short term borrowing at very attractive rates of interest which makes it all the more difficult for people in our position. The next factor which I think has made its influence felt on the economic position of these islands in particular, is the proposal of the United Kingdom to venture into the European Common Market. The British government, as you know, Sir, has been negotiating for a long period – I think perhaps over twelve months – with the Inner Six in Europe over the conditions under which Great Britain will be permitted to enter the European Economic Community. The effect on us is that these negotiations have generated an atmosphere of uncertainty over the future of the colonies. British investors, therefore, are looking more towards the East in the direction of the Common Market countries than to the overseas territories, as places where investment should take place.

The third factor, Sir, is the uncertainty of the movements, political and economic, in the area in which we live. It is most unfortunate that quite a large number of people in the United Kingdom, in Canada, and in the United States of America are completely ignorant about the geographical and political facts of life in the Caribbean area. This lack of knowledge on their part is due mainly to the distance which separates us from them and because our economic plight and our political situation do not enter in their day-to-day thinking, or make any impact on their standard of living from time to time. The Westindian area is a very small microcosm in the language of international trade. More recently and closer to us, there have been unfavourable movements in the United States money markets.

The average price of investments has fallen to new lows at least twice during the past six weeks. The uncertainty of the investment atmosphere in the United States and in England must, therefore, reflect on the possibilities of these territories being able to urge the necessity for immediate investment capital in the region as a whole.

The fourth factor, Mr Deputy Speaker, has been the chronic over-production of sugar in the world. Sugar being our main export from Barbados, when we get over-production, although we have a guaranteed price under the Commonwealth Sugar Agreement for a substantial amount of the sugar which we produce, yet we have had to sell a considerable amount of that sugar at the World Market Price, and this year it would probably be in the vicinity of ten or twelve thousand tons at World Market Price under the Commonwealth Sugar Agreement. Indeed, this year, the World Market Price is less than half of the negotiated price and, therefore, the small producer, the peasant in Barbados, is very often adversely affected by World Market Price, although he was not aware of it.

Our production this year has fallen well below the estimates of the experts and the planters of Barbados, although there were some planters who were very pessimistic when everyone was calculating on a very good crop indeed. However, the revised figures for sugar production this year are 159,000 tons. This fall in production is largely attributed to the poor quality of the juice, to the pests and parasites who alone in the Westindies are learning to dwell together in unity.

We now come to tourism. This year 1961 was a record year when 37,060 tourists came to the island. In the first quarter of 1962, 12,323 tourists arrived as compared with 10,750 in the first quarter of last year.

When we come to our trade outlook and our trade figures for the past year, our imports were in value $80,281,000. We exported

$43,177,000 in value leaving a trade gap of $37,104,000.

The value of our imports of food alone was more than $23 million. The value of our manufactured goods was $20 million; the value of machinery and transport equipment was $12 million. I do estimate that the amount of the adverse trade balance in 1961 was covered by our net invisible credits; such matters as our income from tourism, our dividends and interest payments from abroad and remittances from our dependents – or should I say our supporters because we are the dependents – our friends, and relatives in the United Kingdom and the United States.

If I may now turn to the population figures. At the end of last year, the population was estimated to have been 241,655, rather less than the previous year's figure of 242,274. The natural increase of 4,344 was covered by our net migration of 4,493. In the first quarter of 1962, 173 more people have come to the island than have left. This may be due to the fact of the United Kingdom Emigration Act which comes into force in about a week's time. At the end of 1961 there were 131,922 females in this island and 109,733 males; in other words, 22,187 more females than males in Barbados. I do not know whether we should advertise this to attract more people from the other islands, but I wish it will rejoice the hearts of some of the honourable members in this Chamber.

The index of retail prices rose by 1.7 points, one per cent between March 1961 and March 1962. That would seem to compare itself with some of the wage increases of the magnitude of 35 per cent and 38 per cent which were recently given to some of our workers in this country, and, therefore, one will see quite readily that there will be quite a lot to cushion the shock of some of the proposals which I intend to make. The wage increases have imposed a great strain' on the resources of the island. In other words, they have reduced the amount of employment which could be provided. I think that that will be obvious to everyone.

At the 31st March, 1962, loans and advances by commercial banks totalled $44,475,000 while deposits were $44,246,000. Of these deposits, $20,551,000 represent savings deposits; As to current expenditure, the actual amount was $27,219,000; the revenue was $26,515,000. The deficit on current account, therefore is $1,004,000. We have estimated this year, of course, for a deficit of over $2.3 million.

As far as capital expenditure last year is concerned, the total amount of capital expenditure in the island by government was $6,732,000.

Mr Deputy Speaker, the issue of Treasury Bills, the primary object of which is to assist in the promotion of a local securities market, is proceeding slowly but satisfactorily.

I will now go on to give the Treasury prospects for the year 1962-63. Although the crop has been smaller than expected, I do not wish at this stage to revise the approved Estimates of Revenue and Current Expenditure for the year 1962-63. The Customs Revenue will to a great extent be dependent on the expectations for next year's crop and the next tourist season and the income tax yield will reflect the profits of last year. In the Approved Estimates for 1962-63 the Revenue is estimated at $25,543,778; the estimated expenditure was $26,895,967, leaving an excess over revenue, or what we call in normal language, a budget deficit of $2,352,189. This is the background, Sir, against which my fiscal proposals will relate.

I now turn to the economic prospects for the year 1962-63. I have already mentioned the world position and our inter-dependence for the advice of international trade. I should also mention that the United States of America is becoming of great importance to the economy of this island. You will remember, Sir, that the Secretary of State issued a statement about three months ago over our proposals for federation of the Windward and Leeward Islands and Barbados and said in that statement quite bluntly that these islands, no doubt because of Great Britain's proposed entry into the European Economic Community, would have to look more and more to the United States and other countries for economic assistance and technical assistance.

Another aspect of the economies of these islands – and when I mention the area as a whole, it is because we cannot exist in a vacuum here in Barbados – is the aspect of confidence which people must have in the area. This is the most important question in all financial matters. It is true that a large degree of the lack of confidence exhibited sometimes is due to the lack of knowledge, or, if I may put it in blunt English, the ignorance of the people in the metropolitan countries about the facts of life in these areas. But we also have to admit that a lack of confidence sometimes is induced by the behaviour of our people inside the area and by people who should know better. It is induced by irresponsible writings and statements and by irresponsible actions on the part of our politicians.

I think that we in the Westindies should not be afraid to speak our minds. I think that we in the Westindies should not be looking around for somebody else to lead and work out our own political and economic philosophy and I do not think that it pays any Westindian politician either to look too rapidly in the direction of European or Asiatic countries for our basic philosophies of life. We have to work out the way of life which is congenial to the people who live in these islands, and we have to act in a responsible manner without, of course, losing our self-respect and grumbling to people who should be on the same terms as ourselves.

The basic situation, however, financially speaking, is not unfavourable. As far as Barbados is concerned, in our economic prospects for 1962-63, the weather has given us a good start for our sugar crop; the tourist trade is expanding; but we must always bear in mind our inter-dependence on international conditions, and recession even in the Dominion of Canada or in the United States of America would adversely affect our tourist prospects for the current year.

The trade with the Windward and Leeward Islands is small in comparison with our total trade – our visible trade – but nevertheless it is a valuable trade for us.

We need in the context of limited migration, in the context of necessity for capital investment and to pay the interest charges which will necessarily be attendant upon the borrowing of money from abroad or locally – the greatest need, therefore, is to find productive employmnet for our increasing population. If I could sum up the government's attitude towards the general economic position in three words – Your Honour will forgive me if I am a little political – I say that our programme must be for discipline, loans and production: it must be the D.L.P.** on other words.

I now come to the discipline. As I told members of my Cabinet an hour before the House began its sitting, you can now fasten your seat belts and prepare for take off. I have considered various methods of raising the large amount of revenue required to meet the increased salaries and wages of government employees and to pay debt charges on the loans which have to be raised to defray the capital expenditure.

I forgot to mention Sir, 'no smoking', but you must still keep your seat belts fastened. My promise not to increase the rates of income tax will be kept, but something must be done about the arrears. At 31st March, 1962, they reached the enormous figure of $1,285,722; that was the amount of taxation owing to the Commissioner of Inland Revenue.

It should be clear that this government is faced today with an exceedingly tough problem, and investigation of the island's finances

---

** A play on the abbreviation for Barrow's Democratic Labour Party.

has shown that if prompt measures are not taken to right the situation, Barbados will either have to go cap in hand to some other country for annual budgetary support or, alternatively, to introduce a drastic reduction in salaries and wages, either one of which will tend to pervert our political and financial outlook. If anyone had doubts as to the determination of this government to put our finances on a very sound basis, he will now realise that he was mistaken. Those who have been studying what has been happening in this island should not be shocked at what I am now about to propose in my first budget. I do not propose to take half measures. It is not just a few additional dollars that are needed from taxation, but between two million dollars and three million dollars per annum, for this year alone.

As much as any other member of the community, being a taxpayer myself – I know that there is a popular myth that politicians do not pay any taxes, but we have to pay our taxes before anybody else – I regret the necessity for these measures.

Of the People

The Honourable Donville O. Inniss, MP

As a boy growing up in the 1970s in rural Barbados, specifically Bayfield, St Philip, the name Errol Walton Barrow resonated in our home, school, church and community, with the greatest of respect and admiration. By the age of ten, I was yet to meet the man but from listening to the adults around me he was a colossus; a man who was obviously revered as a person and leader who had been making major strides in transforming our country.

In September 1977, when the results of the Barbados Secondary Schools Entrance (11+, Common Entrance) Examination came back and it was announced that I was to enter Harrison College (Barrow's alma mater), amidst all of the congratulations was my father's simple summation that, *"had it not been for Barrow, the Lord knows where you would have been going to school because I would not have had the money to pay for you".*

My father's statement encapsulated the depth of gratitude that many working class Barbadians of the 60s and 70s had for Mr Barrow and his Democratic Labour Party for the provision of free school meals at primary school and free secondary education. Had it not been for his vision and leadership, truly only the Lord knows where my parents' six sons and two daughters would be today.

As a teenager, I became attracted even more to Mr Barrow and his policies and found myself after school heading off to the Public Gallery at Parliament on Tuesdays to listen to the debates. It was fascinating and intellectually stimulating to both watch and listen to political heavy weights like Mr Barrow, J.M.G.M. 'Tom' Adams, 'Bree' St John (later Sir Harold) *et al* debate matters of great national import. Mr Barrow clearly was a man who had a plan and was determined to see it through on behalf of his people.

In the late 1970s, he was then in Opposition but that never stopped him from not just keeping the BLP as the Government of the day in check but also continuously exposing the differences between his DLP and Adams' BLP. His grasp of current affairs and his ability to provide a historical perspective on any issue, was an invaluable experience for me; one that every citizen and aspiring politician ought to benefit from. Back then I had no known desires to be a politician, but perhaps was quietly being edged into politics by the vision and statesmanship of Mr Barrow.

It was during the early 1980s, in my days as a supporter of Warwick Franklin, the then representative for the constituency of St Philip North, that I finally encountered Mr Barrow whom I eventually came to be a passionate and vocal supporter of. Once a year the St John and the St Philip North constituency branches of the DLP would meet at Bath, St John for a good old fashion Bajan "lime" – a beach picnic where there was an abundance of food and drinks.

It was at one such event that I met Mr Barrow as he manned the BBQ grill, bedecked in an apron and serving up the dishes he was renowned for. One would have expected our nation's first Prime Minister to be seated in a plush chair being waited on as he spoke with the great and the good. Not Mr Barrow. He was bedecked in short pants, sandals and engaged everyone in sight. For a man who revolutionised our education system, introduced a national insurance scheme, enacted modern labour laws, championed the equal rights of women, and pioneered CARICOM, amongst other feats, he was ever so humble.

It was then I truly appreciated how he derived his power which came from a people who appreciated his humanity, his respect for their views and his championing of their causes.

When I told him my name and where I was from, he has a sense of who my parents and relatives were and knew every major shopkeeper, priest and artisan within a four mile radius. His ability to remember names, faces and events was phenomenal.

It was during my tenure as a member of the Young Democrats (the DLP youth arm) and a member of the Party's General Council that I really got to see and understand him as a leader; how he rallied his troops and created policies and programmes. As Party President, in a very calm and steadfast manner, he would elicit views from ordinary members, entertained divergent views and summarised the outcomes. He made time to listen to the rank and file making them feel valued and also guided them, where necessary. When he made a decision, few challenged him.

Many of the Party's policies on issues such as agricultural reform, the construction of lower income housing, the expansion of healthcare, increasing technical and vocational training, and stronger foreign policies, were all conceptualised and developed on the floor of the DLP Auditorium under the leadership Mr Barrow.

As we journey towards our 50th Anniversary of Independence, Barbados will forever be indebted to the vision, fearlessness and decisive leadership of Errol Walton Barrow. He remains truly the Father of Independent Barbados.

OF THE PEOPLE

By the people

For the people

Land Rights, Conservatism and the Church

Address to Parliament 23 June, 1964 on the acquisition of land for the establishment of the Cave Hill Campus of the University of the Westindies (UWI) (Slightly abridged)

I have been very distressed over the remarks which I have heard during the short time that I have been listening to the debate. I am distressed, Sir, very much because of the unkind remarks which were made against the government to the effect that the government wanted to expropriate people's property. We are not concerned with the political parties in Barbados, but with the social philosophy which should exist in this island. This is a speech which I could have made if honourable members on the other side of the House were not interested in personalities, but in principles, at the time when the Land Acquisition Act was amended by this government.

The Land Acquisition Act, 1949, was amended by this government for the simple reason that it was our experience that the provisions of the Act were such that the whole community could be held up to ransom by recalcitrant land-owners. I may say I am not putting the gentleman concerned in this particular transaction in that category; I am not being personal at all. This government has embarked on a development programme.

The only acquisition not involving compensation which has ever take place in Barbados, is the 92 acres reclaimed at the Deep Water Harbour.

We have inherited a social and economic system whereby the large plantations, or 80 per cent of the plantations, or of the arable land in Barbados, belongs to 360 people. I am not including the gentleman with whom the official opposition is so much concerned, he being a member of their party, I believe.

Let us look at this matter in its right perspective. We have an island of 166 square miles, and with a population of 240,000. We have an average of 14,000 people to the square mile and the average Barbadian has no chance of ever holding a sizeable proportion of this island on which he could rear two cows and three pigs. If you win money you can buy land from somebody who wants to dispose of it or you can make use of the Court of Chancery in order to increase your holdings. There are many people who have gone to the United States of America and have helped their grandsons and their aunts and they have come back here and found that their relatives have passed their land through the court and acquired title. Barbadians are land hungry.

We have large numbers of people who cannot afford to buy land at the existing prices; we have people in the lower brackets, who, if this government did not have a policy of providing for housing areas, would not have owned any of this land. The word 'conservatism' just means holding on to what you have at all costs or at a special price to the detriment of everybody else in the community.

In 1794 the conservatives resisted the introduction of income tax as they did later to Mr Gladstone's Reform Bills and the Education Act. Because I speak to conservatives, it does not mean that I accept the philosophy of conservatism. You have a majority who never had any chance of owning anything. That is the kind of situation which is endemic in a community such as this and that leads to much more serious things than acquisition. It leads to what is taking place in British Guiana, that is to say, 53 deaths within a few weeks. You have people owning thousands of acres of land on the one hand, and on the other hand, you have the man who is never in possession of sufficient money, some of which he can save so as to buy shoes for his children; and you cannot persuade him that even those responsible agitators, such as they are in British Guiana, who come along and say: 'look at what this man has, and what the other man has', are not Messiahs.

In all this you make room for the Jagans, the Brindley Benns and the Castros. The philosophy of conservatism is such that it creates that kind of situation, but what we are trying to do in Barbados, is to give the people in this country an opportunity for education, a chance of getting a square meal, a chance of living in a decent house, and a chance of getting a job for which they are qualified, without any discrimination whatever. Those are the things we have been trying to do and we have not created any revolution in this country.

I would not even try to pretend that a social revolution has taken place in this country. All that has taken place in Barbados in the last two years, is that we have managed to satisfy the people in this country that all is not lost and that something can be done to ease their lot, although we cannot guarantee them pie in the sky or mansions in Spain.

Now let us be honest and straightforward about this whole thing. The reason why I am speaking in this debate – and I intend to speak at some length – is because this debate has highlighted the fundamental differences in the social and economic philosophies existing between the major parties in this House, in other words, between the government on the one side, and the official opposition on the other. Therefore, this is a good opportunity to have a restatement of why we think as we think, why we know that we are right, and why we know that if we were not here, the people who have vested interests would be completely oblivious to the low living standards of the rest of the community, completely unconcerned that their indifference has created the gun powder that might actually make them insecure and blow them through the roof.

They themselves create the conditions, and unless you have a group of people in this country who are prepared to redress the imbalances, to see things in the broad, social context, to see the economic importance of legislation, the economic importance of development, the psychological importance of removing distinctions between one class of the community and the other, then you are asking for trouble.

All that those people on the other side are doing this afternoon is inviting trouble, because they do not seem to know how the masses of people think. We have been the safety valve and we are prepared to act as the safety valve, but we must be satisfied that there is some reconditioning going on on the other side, and there is some kind of rethinking and a restatement of their own position being satisfactorily made in their own minds and the people they are supposed to represent.

For this particular small parcel of land which was producing nothing, which has no services, no roads, no light, and no water, in my humble opinion, the price which was offered by the government was generous and far from being absurd as some honourable members would suggest.

Now I want to clear the air on certain fundamental matters. I regard this as a personal debate for this reason – the members of the conservative party are not going to like what I say; as the honourable senior member for St Peter has often said, and I join with him in this.

I am not looking for any friends now that I am in government because I did not have any before and those whom I had, I have clasped them to my bosom with bonds of steel. But I do not waste my time with each new-found, untried comrade. If I get up here, therefore, and have to offend some people in stating what the philosophy of this Party is, it does not worry me, because all the time that these individuals were growing wealthy, they were not with you. When we were fighting the battle of the masses, they were not with us, because after they reach a certain stage, their social ideas and economic philosophies crystallised and not only crystallised, but they coalesced into groups and the more acquisitive they are, the more unconscious they are of the basic needs of a community.

They are all of them extremely acquisitive but we expect this. We are not saying that it is a crime, but in every democratic society, you will find people like this who do not take the trouble to look around the world and see what is happening, and you will always find them adopting this holier than thou attitude, that you are coming to take away what thay have, that you must go and work for it.

Mexico is one of the richest states today, but they were not talking about that in 1923 when the oil fields were taken over. One of the greatest oil-producing countries in the world is Venezuela, but you have about 70 per cent of the population illiterate, and some of the people have to walk miles to the centre of town to get a bucket of water.

Are we going to let people who have been able to amass money come in from outside and when the public programme demands that something should be done, hold up the progress of this community on the basis that somebody can take an aeroplane trip to America and persuade somebody to pay more money than the government is able to pay for a parcel of land? It is as simple as that.

I will tell you something right now, Mr Speaker, even if His Lordship the Bishop may get offended. When I see some of the people who go to the Anglican Church in this island, my infrequency of attendance rises, because I notice that they, like the Republicans in the United States, and the Southern Protestants, are always the most acquisitive people, and if you want to find people who have a little more social philosophy, you have to look for the Baptists or Methodists, because the established church in Barbados has been for generations a church of vested interests. It is a property owner, and, therefore, all the property owners tend to congregate there, and they think it is not respectable to go somewhere else.

I was born, baptised, and confirmed in the Anglican Church, therefore, I speak without any impunity. The infrequency of my attendance at church is because I have noticed that good Protestants are the most acquistive people. So, you will see that we have a religious organisation, buttressing up these people and you will never see in the Anglican Church, anybody being critical of the landed gentry of this country. I have never heard of one Anglican Priest saying that you should have canteens for workers at factories and plantations, but I have heard of ministers, like the late Francis Godson, from other denominations talking of old age pensions for the people.

We are getting more trouble from the people in the Anglican Church over this same question of land, than from anybody else. We are saying this about these pious Anglican politicians going into church so that you should know that there are going there to have a sense of security. You have rectors who want to charge the government more for land than the biggest capitalists in the United States would want to charge their government. Therefore, I have to say these unkindly things but I am speaking facts. I want to be like the late Prime Minister of India – I want my ashes scattered all over the sea thus relieving the City Council of the pressure with which they are now faced of finding more land for a burial place.

The reason I have mentioned the Anglican Church is just because I want to show that its philosophy was so deeply engrained in the sanctity of private property ownership; that it has become glorified in its religion and it has actually been sponsored and promoted by the Anglican Church. As a matter of fact, they want us to pay three million dollars for their property now, when they have kept it for all these years in the state of condition which it is now. Who are their advisers, but the same people that come in here and who write letters to the newspapers talking of the iniquities of socialism?

We realised what the programme of development of this government would be over the next four years, and we introduced a bill to amend the Land Acquisition Act of 1949 because we had been experiencing difficulties, and so as to give a more realistic method of compensating owners without in any way depriving them of the benefit of a reasonable return for their investments. The whole philosophy of conservative capitalism is based on getting a reasonable return for your investment. What is a reasonable return? There is no capitalist who will quarrel with you if you say that you should get a percentage of your money.

In this particular case the land is in the middle of nowhere. The owner ceased to use it even for agricultural purposes three years ago; the land is not even fit for grazing two heads of sheep, and I see people grazing 20 or 30 sheep on a quarter acre of land or even less than that.

However, as far as these 19 acres of land are concerned, you could not find two sheep grazing there between 1950 and 1961. I have never seen any landowners in Barbados give up anything out of which they are making money. Far from that, you cannot show me any land owners, people who were firmly entrenched and have their roots deep, and their tentacles high in the economy of this country, giving up anything by gift or otherwise that they can make money out of.

The average Barbadian has a reputation for being hard working because he has no other alternative. He cannot go out into the forests and carve out an existence for himself like the homesteaders did in the United States of America.

If you were to examine the social and economic structure in this island, you will find that the pattern has not been so radically changed over the past 100 years. Some people have inherited land, some people have won land, some people have been able to speculate and accumulate a little money and buy land and others have used the courts to expropriate the legitimate owners of land, which is a disgrace to any civilised society.

Now we are offering a man £300 an acre for land on which we probably have to spend $50,000 in order to get this land developed, but he is asking $10,000 an acre for land which did not bring any income over the past three years, and which he acquired at a price which is less than one-tenth of what the government is offering him. Where is the justice in this matter?

This government is putting terrific pressure on land owners because we want living space for the people of this island. There are more people who are working now than have ever worked before in the history of this island, and we are not going to allow 360 people who own 80 per cent of the land to exploit the other 230,000.

You only hear about exploitation when somebody's corns are getting crushed. You do not hear about exploitation in other circumstances.There are people who feel that if a man is born in a house 16' x 9' no government is to give him the opportunity of having a little more expansion because he is a man living in a house 16' x 9', while they are the 300-acre men.

Politics is a question of what is the basic philosophy; but some people have not got any philosophy at all. Some of us have basic philosophy and there are people who have a lot of money but no philosophy at all; those are the ones who do not want to hear of anything which challenges the sacred institution of private property. It does not matter how courteous you are; you can drive a man to commit suicide by putting him in a bad financial position and that is regarded as good business ethics; but whenever you have to interfere with the sacred institutions, you hear this talk about robbing a poor man.

THE PARLIAMENTARIAN

In the Precincts of Parliament

Addressing the House of Assembly

A meeting of Heads

With thanks

Entering Parliament with F.G. Smith

The Last Steps to Freedom

HE The Honourable Robert Morris

The National Heroes of Barbados form part of a continuum in the struggle for the freedom of Barbados and Barbadians. The Rt Excellent Errol Walton Barrow was charged with the negotiation of freedom from constitutional colonisation. He and his supporters in this struggle were well aware of their task following the breakdown of Federal negotiations among the territories of the Leeward and Windward Islands, Barbados and the British Government after three and a half years. It was he who pointed out that: *"The relationship between the people of this country (Barbados) and the Government of the United Kingdom has been a relationship of Contract and not one of Status."*

It was the then Philip Greaves (now Sir Philip), Minister without Portfolio, who in the Senate debate on the resolution calling for Britain to grant Independence to Barbados, asked the question: *"What are we fighting for?"* stating that Barbados *"had already achieved full internal self-government but had no control of defence and external affairs."* He concluded, *"We are merely asking to be accorded our Freedom."*

As one who has spent many years engaged in negotiations, I wish to examine the negotiation of freedom for Barbados by a principled, qualified, passionate, and outstanding son of Barbados who has been deservedly accorded the title of 'Father of Independence', a title to which no other can lay claim. I also want to assert that while personal freedom had been achieved at emancipation, without constitutional decolonisation, personal freedom still remained compromised.

A good negotiator must have personal qualities, including expert and academic knowledge, leadership characteristics, the capacity to build a winning team, persuasiveness and the grasp of strategies and tactics to persist towards the desired objective, in this case the achievement of constitutional decolonisation.

Errol Barrow's knowledge of the constitutional history of Barbados was clearly seen in his all-day speech in the House of Assembly in January 1966. He even referred to the fact that as far as he was aware, Barbados had been granted Independence since 1652, which had not since been revoked. His leadership capacity was mainly responsible for a fourteen to eight favourable vote in the House, and a seventeen to three favourable vote in the Senate, on the question of whether Barbados should proceed to Independence. Any reading of the debates demonstrates his intellectual grasp of the issue and his expert marshalling of his argument.

We must not underestimate the difficulty he faced in building a united Barbadian team in approaching the British for Independence. Even within his DLP, then a relatively young Party, Errol Barrow had to deal with the Cabinet resignation of Wynter Crawford, his then Deputy Premier, and also Erskine Ward, a highly respected politician, who with Crawford resigned from the Party. This could hardly have been a surprise to him as he would have weighed the possible impact on his decision on the Party and Government, and would have decided that the loss would not have been sufficient to impede the journey to Independence.

The votes in the House and Senate clearly indicated that the Government could not count on the full support of the two opposition parties, the Progressive Conservative Party, then led by Ernest Deighton Mottley, and the Barbados Labour Party, led by Freddie Miller. The strategies and tactics used by the opposition politicians included personal attacks on Errol Barrow, suggesting that in case Independence was granted he would become elected "President for Life" and run the country as a dictator. There was also the arguments that it would be more economically beneficial for Barbados to enter Independence as a member of a Federation of the Eastern Caribbean States but with no attempt to show how and when this Federation could become a reality.

However, Barrow could point to evidence that he had tried his best to achieve that same result, without success. It was interesting that a number of parliamentary representatives, descendants of the planter and mercantile interests, such as Douglas G. Leacock, Kenneth R. Hunte, E.

Lisle Ward, and E. Stanley Robinson, admitted the possibility of Barbados going to Independence alone. It is ironic and noteworthy, that the Independent Senators, of similar privileged background and heritage, voted for the Resolution. The argument can be made that Barrow got more support from representatives of the old planter-merchant oligarchy than from the popularly elected working class politicians in the Opposition.

As for the labour movement, the former staunch trade unionist, Kenmore Husbands spoke out against Independence alone, while Frank Walcott (later the Rt Excellent Sir Frank Walcott), was caustic against the naysayers, and gave full support to Barrow, both in Parliament and in the hustings. One effective tactic used by Barrow was to accuse Grantley Adams (later the Rt Excellent Sir Grantley Adams) of many years before supporting a retrograde position for Barbados to become a Crown Colony when as Leader of the Progressive League he addressed the Moyne Commission.

An important component in the accomplishment of the change in constitutional status was the preparation of the case. Before the presentation of the new constitution for negotiation, Barrow had established his intention in the 1961 Party Manifesto, and interpreted his victory at the polls as support for his intention. He also encouraged civil society, and the young intelligentsia like the "Under Forties", comprising young university graduates like Keith Hunte (now Sir Keith), Nigel Barrow, Colin Williams and Colin Reid, and the "Under Privileged", a more grassroots mix, to have a strong voice through their community education exercises.

He topped this off with his gaining Parliamentary approval for the intention to move towards Independence for Barbados alone. He did not support the obstructionist call for a referendum, but one of his closely guarded strategies was the timing of the General Election due after 1961.

The next step in the negotiating process was the preparation of the draft constitution for Barbados. Barrow created a drafting team which included Cameron Tudor (later Sir James), Philip Greaves (later Sir Philip), Hilton Vaughan, Leroy Brathwaite, and Frank Walcott. The team was supported by public servants Denys Williams, Fred Cozier, and Edmund S. Burrowes and external advisers Roy Marshall (later Sir Roy),

Keith Patchett, and Sir Lionel Luckoo (who became the first joint Guyanese/Barbadian High Commissioner to the UK). Harold Brewster and Jean Holder were also co-opted. This was a quality team in terms of related qualifications and experience, as well as persuasive capacity.

The Opposition team comprised Ernest Deighton Mottley, and Freddie Miller, with advisers Henry Forde, and Jack Dear. It is noteworthy that neither of the Opposition parties took part in the Parliamentary debates on the draft constitution.

Barrow's opening negotiation gambit was nothing less than superb. He took a strong position as the one asking for Independence, not as one who is a beggar, and therefore not a chooser, and made it clear that Barbados would not *"be found loitering on Colonial Office premises after closing time."* Barrow was insistent on a quick resolution of the request for Independence, and punned on the name of the Chairman of the Conference, the Secretary of State for the Colonies, the Rt Honourable Frederick Lee, that nor would there *"be time for the lowing herd to wind slowly o'er the Lee"*.

From early Barrow, who was tertiary level educated in Britain and had fought for Britain in World War II, and whose delegation had many powerful connections also, showed no sense of inferiority. His success in establishing a power superiority led to the removal of Lee as Chairman of the Conference, as a means by Harold Wilson, the then British Prime Minister, of resolving the differences between Barrow and Lee.

The cause of the dispute occurred when Lee called on Barrow to publicly apologise to him for words published in a newspaper, in which Barrow allegedly called Lee "an idiot, who could not chair a meeting". Barrow retaliated that if Lee expected him to apologise before his Ministers on the basis of a newspaper statement, perhaps Lee was truly *"an idiot who could not chair a meeting."*

In terms of the actual negotiation of the contract between Barbados and Britain, Barrow and his team effectively won on the major points of disagreement. Eventually all parties signed their agreement to a new contract between Barbados and Britain, in the form of a Constitution with Ten Chapters which included a Preamble grounded in the 1651 Declaration of Independence and the 1652 Charter.

It is noteworthy that the final report was agreed on 4 July 1966, a date well known in British colonial history. It may be questioned whether Barrow, steeped as he was in history, intended to end the conference on that particular day.

A symbolic crowning achievement of Barrow's negotiation of freedom was in Britain's granting Independence to fall on the 30 November, the day of St Andrew, Barbados' Patron Saint and on the birthdate of his mentor, and uncle, the Rt Excellent Dr Charles Duncan O'Neal.

The second crowning achievement was in the ensuing 1966 General Elections in which the DLP won 14 seats, the BLP 8, and the Barbados National Party, (formerly the Progressive Conservatives and Electors' Association) won the two City seats, a prelude to its demise. No Cabinet Minister lost his seat.

The DLP 1966 Manifesto claimed: *"We now have a country"* which could be translated as, *"Freedom had been won."*

"This is the parting of the ways"

Speech in Parliament, introducing a resolution calling on Britain to convene the Barbados Independence Conference, 4 January, 1966

Mr Speaker, there is in the constituency of His Honour the Deputy Speaker, a monument which commemorates the landing of the settlers in Barbados in 1605. People who are more accurate in their historical facts believe that the settlers came to the island from the United Kingdom in the year 1625. This Parliament was first instituted in 1639.

There are many people, even the Editors of Halsbury's Laws of England, who are not fully cognisant of the nature of the relationship which exists between the dependent countries in the Commonwealth and the metropolitan country.

We have in this island, a flexible constitution in the full and truest sense of the term. Unlike the inflexible constitution of the neighbouring country of Trinidad and Tobago and the constitution of the United States of America, our constitution bears similarity only to the constitution of the United Kingdom, in that it is partly founded on convention and usage, and partly contained in written statutes and constitutional documents known to us in this parliament as the Letters Patent and the Royal Instructions.

When the settlers landed in 1625, they brought the laws of the United Kingdom with them; so that all the laws, customs and usages of Parliament were imported into this Chamber on its foundation in 1639. You may wonder, Mr Speaker, why it is necessary for me to make this excursion into the dim recesses of the constitutional history of this island. It is precisely because there are so many people in this island who are unaware of the long, slow process of constitutional evolution of which the Resolution which we are discussing today is the apotheosis that it is necessary for me to have this debate conducted on a level where the people whom we are addressing will understand the premises from which we speak and the premises on which we stand.

When the Parliament convened in 1639 it was convened under the

Lords of the Council of this island – the Lord Lieutenant General of the island, the Lords of the Council and the General Assembly of this island – to make laws for the better government of the territory under a franchise granted by the Sovereign of the United Kingdom. These territories were run as plantations. We have not fully got rid of the plantation mentality. A franchise was granted to Sir William Courteen, the Earl of Carlisle, who appointed as Governor the Eighth Lord Willoughby and, in exchange for this franchise, a certain tribute was exacted by the Imperial Government in the form of taxation which was levied on the people of this country by a process of sub infeudation from the Lord Lieutenant-General himself, on to the lesser, may I call them, barons and on to the lower order of plantation chivalry that existed in those days, if there is chivalry in the plantation system. In the year 1651 – this was a considerable time before the American Declaration of Independence, precisely perhaps 125 years before the famous Declaration in what is now known as the United States of America, by the 13 British Colonies which we have helped to populate and to develop from these shores in Barbados – the Lord in Council and the General Assembly of this island in protest against the Navigation Laws, the same type of Navigation Laws that the 13 Colonies rebelled against 125 years later, they were a bit slower than the people of Barbados, issued their famous Declaration of Independence, not from this Chamber, because as far as I can discover, this Chamber had not been built, but certainly the Lords of the Council and the General Assembly of this island declared themselves an independent nation. The significant thing about this is that I have not been able to discover anywhere in the records of this House that the Unilateral Declaration of Independence which was made in 1651 has ever been repealed by this House or by any other person.

Shortly after this Declaration – General, Sir George Ayscue bombarbed the township of Oistins, and after two days' fighting a long boat was launched with a white flag and a treaty was signed between the people of Barbados and the United Kingdom government at a place called the Mermaid Tavern in the township of Oistins on the southern coast of this island. In that treaty the people of Barbados agreed to pay four-and-a-half per cent in exchange for the repeal of the Navigation Laws vis-a-vis the merchants and colonists of this country. Our relationship, therefore, with Great Britain has never been a 'status' relation from the very early days which existed in places more properly described as Crown Colonies and which achieved internal self-Government only in the 1950s – territories like

Trinidad and Tobago, the Lesser Antilles, Mauritius, and all the other island territories over which Britain held sway.

Right from the beginning and long before some of these territories were discovered or settled, the relationship between the people of this country and the government of the United Kingdom, had been a relationship of contract and not a relationship of status. That is what has probably distinguished Barbados from any other Westindian island. Its approach has always been a contractual approach and not an approach of status. We continued to make laws. You will find the very earliest Act we have on the Statute Books is, as far as I can remember, in 1667, a law against forcible entry into any lands or tenements.

When the restoration of the monarchy took place, recognition was given to the loyalty of Barbados which is now proverbial – and to me sometimes is questionable in the sense that Barbadians hold loyalty to things which they know nothing about. They do not understand their duty of loyalty to their own country under the Constitution, but this loyalty to the British government was acknowledged. This means that this island was treated with a certain amount of deference to the extent that the island has been left to manage its own affairs. Far from the British government either contributing one penny to the support of the general revenue of this island in a direct manner – from that time until today, all the pro-consular officials have been paid by the people of Barbados although they had no say in their nomination. The Chief Secretaries not only have been paid, and continue to be paid, but the people of Barbados also provided them with living accommodation and with luxuries which are not even vouchsafed to Ministers of Government today, although we are responsible for running the government today. All of these things, Barbadians have accepted, as I have said from that day right on to this, the British government has not contributed one penny towards the general revenue of this island.

Other territories, on the other hand, received and are still receiving substantial annual grants-in-aid, not of development, but in aid of administration and to pay the same Pro-consular officers, the same civil servants, and to pay for the keeping of law and order. They are not for the purpose of paying for the carrying out of development programmes and, unless one appreciates that there are territories who have lived on the 'hand-outs' of the Colonial Office from time immemorial and that Barbados has never been in this invidious position, you cannot understand how difficult it is for us in the Westindies to come together under constitutional arrangements.

We in Barbados have never found ourselves in this position where we had to ask for financial aid from what is fondly – and I say 'fondly' advisedly – described as the Mother Country. We have never been in this unhappy situation. As a matter of fact, I can recount where we have contributed towards the revenues of the United Kingdom.

We have a long history of constitutional government which antedates the constitutional history of the United States, which antedates the constitutional history of any of the Westindian territories, which antedates the constitutional history of the South American countries. It should be that when the Leader of the House rises to his feet and says 'Mr Speaker, I beg to move that this Resolution do now pass,' if the Leader of Her Majesty's loyal opposition fully understood the nature of his functions, he should say 'I take great pleasure in seconding this motion on behalf of the people whom we represent,' and this should be the end of the debate.

But since this Resolution is momentous in the history of the island, and since we have our ignoramuses, our criminals and our cut-throats – we do have our politically ambitious people of flexible views – it is necessary for me to make abundantly clear, and have recorded for all time, the reasons behind the government of this country bringing forward this resolution at this momentous stage.

Mr Speaker, you will be surprised to know that as recently as 1939, the leader of one of the parties on the other side, supported by a former Minister of Government, suggested to the Royal Commission after the disturbances in 1937 that Barbados should revert to a Crown Colony status when Jamaica had regained her original status. It is there in the records where Sir Grantley Adams suggested that, as a solution to the constitutional and economic problems of this country.

Today those of us on this side of the House have every cause, reason and justification to be angry at those people who would pull this island down for their own personal ambitions; we would have every reason to be angry at those people who do not even take time off to think who they are, where they have come from and where they are going.

When the Royal Commission came down here in 1939, exactly 300 years from the date when we began to run our own affairs, it was suggested seriously and supported by people who are in this House today and who are sitting on the opposite side of the Table, that Barbados should revert to Crown Colony status. The economic solution of the island's ills was that the island of Barbados should be developed into half-acre lots and a half-acre lot should be given to each family. That is again the Prime Minister of the late Federation. He did not elucidate on a point raised by Mr Morgan Jones as to whether his half an acre would be in Broad Street and my half an acre would be in Grave Yard, St Lucy,* but the artithmatic was interesting because, at the end of his proposal, Mr Morgan Jones asked Sir Grantley Adams what he was going to do with the other 60,000 people who would be left over. The reply was to 'Get rid of them,'. I am not trying to stir up any animosity against anyone. I am trying to illustrate that 300 years after the establishment of this ancient legislature, you still have people in Barbados who are incapable of thinking rightly, either for themselves or for the people whom they unfortunately represent.

Mr Speaker, despite my former association with that party, the people of Barbados forgave me as they forgave you and re-elected us in 1961 as the constitutional government of this country. We are now witnessing another unsuccessful attempt to take over the running of the country. We are still the constitutional government of this country, and, as such, the people have put us here to implement a certain programme, a programme which was put before the electorate in 1961.

You can compare the constitutional practice here in Barbados today with the practice in a neighbouring teritory, where without any recourse to the legislature, without any public debate whatsoever, without any warnings or discussion even with the closest confidants of the leader of the government himself, or people who considered themselves close to the government, it was announced that Trinidad and Tobago sought their independence. Up to today there has been no debate in Trinidad or Tobago about independence. There was a debate subsequent to the announcement of independence. Criticism of the draft constitution was sought from the Boys' Scouts and Girls' Guides, the Dorcas League, the Odd Fellows and such groups. That was the exercise in democracy that they went through. The exercise in democracy that we have gone through is that we stated our intention before an election. We faltered by the wayside to see if we could collect some of our lesser brethren – in the sense of more unfortunate brethren – together along the road to independence with us; that is where we wasted three and one half years in this exercise. Having been diverted from our main objective, we have merely returned to the mandate of the people and the expression of our

---

* Broad Street is the main street and commercial centre in the Barbados capital, Bridgetown; while the Parish of St Lucy is at the northern extreme of the island, and one of the most distant from Bridgetown.

intentions as demonstrated in the Manifesto of the Democratic Labour Party.

These are the facts. In 1961 on the 4th December when this government was returned, there was a Federation of the Westindies. That Federation was not dissolved until May 1962 by the Westindies Federation Dissolution Act of April of that year, and the Westindies Dissolution Act made provision by order in Council to take away, to confer and otherwise to deal with the constitutions of all territories in this area; and it is rather ironic, Mr Speaker, that the Federation should have broken up on the very day on which, by the recommendation of the 1961 Conference in London, it was supposed to have become independent. The two richest territories seceded with the consent and approval, and I will go so far as to say, with the connivance of Her Majesty's Government. Shortly thereafter we journeyed to London, and the result of our labours was a Command Paper laid before Parliament, and also laid in this legislature, No. 1746, which sets out certain proposals for a Federation.

Mr Speaker, I just want to say that when you hear the talk mooted about in the atmosphere about independence in a Federation, I want to know what Federation they are talking about. It could not be an existing Federation, because there is no Westindies Federation existing today, and there has not been a Federation of the Westindies since 1962...a Federation does not exist in fact or in law between us and the other seven territories in the Eastern Caribbean.

It was clear from 1963 to all of us who were engaged almost in mortal combat with Her Majesty's Secretary of State and his legal advisers that the British government had no confidence in any Federation of the Eastern Caribbean, and no intention to make any capital or other contribution to a Federation. The British government is now prepared to make contributions to individual territories, provided they can keep their eyes on their money; and when you consider the context in which the Constitution of Grenada was taken away, and what was happening in other Windward and Leeward Island territories in financial mismanagement, you cannot blame the British government for keeping a careful eye on the taxpayers' money.

I remember I woke up one morning earlier this year in a cold sweat; I do not know what was agitating my mind, and at the first light of dawn, I telephoned the Honourable Minister of Education (J. Cameron Tudor, now the Foreign Minister, Sir James Tudor) and told him my experience a couple of hours before and I said these four words: 'They nearly had us'. It was because I had been working over the draft Federal Scheme in preparation for a document which was subsequently published and laid in this House. We were going into this exercise in all good faith with our eyes shut, because like in so many other departments of life, we assumed that what we are accustomed to, prevails in other places and will continue to be so for ever more hereafter.

We assumed that we were going into a federation and that there would be the same degree of financial integrity, the same respect for constitutional propriety as exists in this island. Mr Speaker, I just want to say that I am a Westindian, and there is no one who is more Westindian either by birth or by inclination or otherwise than I am. I always refrain from disclosing any legislative matters which I know about, which would be detrimental to the successful carrying out of the federal exercise. I did nothing that an atmosphere of recrimination should be introduced at any stage, and so I suppressed matters which should have better seen the light of day. I do not think by doing so I betrayed the trust of honourable members of the House, because my motives were altruistic.

If I make a statement of fact about our statistics on crime, this is not anything to be anoyed about. If I say that Dr. Williams** said that the proposal to have freedom of movement would create serious problems which Trinidad could not support and did not intend to support even after the end of ten years, is this supposed to be abuse of your neighbours? These are unfortunate factors of colonialism. There are some people in Barbados who would want to tell you that there is no such thing as colonialism and that we are British subjects and that we are happy to be called British subjects. But the worst thing about colonialism is this:- These islands in the Eastern Caribbean only began to get off the ground since they were taken over by democratic goverments in their islands which were responsible to the people. No one is going to be content to be treated as second class citizens in perpetuity. No one is going to be content to sit down indefinitely and watch places like Gambia, Togoland, Malta with only 95 square miles and even the Cook Islands that no school child has heard about, islands with a total population of 11,000 and 12,000 and with populations smaller than many constituencies of ours, being represented and sitting around the United Nations table.

Nobody in this party wants a seat in the United Nations for prestige purposes. Our stand is for the people of Barbados in perpetuity; it is the only state which the Almighty God has ordained.

** Dr. Eric Williams, the late Prime Minister of Trinidad and Tobago.

I should like to make the position of my government abundantly clear. When we decided unilaterally – and I say unilaterally because without any reference to the people of Barbados, I took independent members of the House, the Leader of the Opposition and others to conferences to see if we could patch together the wreckage of the former Federation; I think that we were overly ambitious, but no one can blame us for trying. What I find strange is that having confessed that we are not the creators of mankind and that we could not succeed in doing what the Almighty did not do when he brought certain people into this world, that is to put sense in their heads, I do not think that this government should be vilified for taking the people of Barbados on the road to independence that we had digressed from in 1962 and thereafter. To me this is the strangest situation that could exist in any country with ancient traditions like this one.

You would not expect, Sir, after discussing this matter for three and a half years, how surprised we were to hear all of a sudden that members on the other side were championing the pursuit of the Federal dream. For three and a half years, Chief Ministers of the other colonies were coming up here discussing, not only problems relating to the Federation, but we were giving them advice and encouraging their people to come to Barbados to work to the detriment of the people of this country. In the meantime, not one of them on the opposite side had the decency to ask a Chief Minister to come to his home and have a cup of tea. There are some members over there who would not even ask some members of the House to come to their homes and have a cup of tea. We are living in a country in which you can be sitting next to a boy in Harrison College*** and in the evening after school, he passes you by as if you never existed. That is the kind of people which you find in these islands. We in Barbados, more than any other people in any part of the world, have exhibited how not to live together in unity, and there are no greater practitioners of this than the honourable members on the other side who now claim to be the champions of the people from the other islands.

We would never get together in the Westindies until we fashion something of our own. We have a peculiar situation in the Westindies. There is no political formula that you can translate from Europe or America, that can have application to a situation such as what we have inherited here in the Westindies.

Mr Speaker, I shall continue to read from the Resolution which we have before us: 'any movement towards integration of the people of

*** A prestigious secondary school in Bridgetown.

the area must spring not only from a natural desire for independence, but primarily from a reasonable expectation, if not a certainty of economic advantage. The movement must be sustained by a full appreciation and understanding of its implications and by mutual respect and sincereity of purpose.'

That is what we are being criticised for today. We have said that none of these experiments has been a success. People like the late Professor Ivor Jennings, when they wrote on the Federal Constitution, although realising the difficulties and stating certain prerequisites of Federation, they were not able sufficiently to break down their analysis to be an accurate guide to people who were embarking on this exercise for the first time. Only a Westindian who is working with Westindians, or a Malaysian who is working with Malaysians today will understand the full implications of the Federal exercise. It is one of the most difficult of exercises.

The Federation broke up when two colonies seceded and three others pulled out. I told Sir Stephen Luke that we were not here to work as scavengers; we do not want to have a Federation at all costs with the loss of our self-respect. We were very careful during our campaign not to create any atmosphere of embarrassment for the government that was in power then by campaigning against their breaking up of the Federation.

I do not want anybody to get up and ask any stupid questions in this House. Nobody is going to advise us. There is no provision in this island for a referendum, and as long as this government is in power, there is not going to be one. As long as this government is in power, there is not going to be any proportional representation. We have had a direct franchise all this time. The only electoral reform we promised to do is to abolish the anachronism of dual-member constituencies. As far as electoral reform is concerned, there is no electoral reform to be performed in this island; we have fought and won those battles.

I am merely stating the constitutional position of the government vis-à-vis the electorate of this island. I am not making any proclamation of dictatorship.

I am a penniless politician, but I want to remain an honest one; and if you want to be honest to the people, you have to tell them the plain facts of life. If they do not like the decisions taken by the Government in office, they have recourse to the ballot box. This is what we call a democratic system of government, and as long as this government is in office, we will stick to that.

People must understand that a good government is put there to make decisions. I have to make decisions on the part of the people of this island. You can sleep better in your bed because we make these decisions. As a matter of fact, a democratic government functions best with organised opinion. It virtually amounts to this, that at election time the people place the decision and policy power into your hands. To make you keep on a straight and narrow path, the political party should normally declare its intention in what is called a manifesto.

Therefore, you have two checks. You have the ballot box and you have to publish a programme in what is called a manifesto; otherwise any man can get up on a public platform and say whatever he likes.

If you have a declaration of your intention towards the people of this island, then the people of this island can check your declaration against your performances, and that is the test, and the only test, which will be applied to a government in a democracy. The test is not to buy votes by bribes; and you can never in a democracy hope to get rid of the government in that way. You can only remove the government when the people are dissatisfied with that government. The government has been put there to make decisions and this government has made a decision. I want it to go down on the record of this House because I am an angry man.

Mr Speaker, when you are in a country you owe loyalty first to that country. You can have difficulties and differences, whether the country is an independent country or whether the country is a non self-governing territory or whether it is a grant-aided territory, the society – meaning the government, because that is the policy-making sector of the society – has to draw the line between allowable conduct on the one hand, and insanity or crime on the other.

Some people are talking as if today is the beginning of creation. We have a country and we have a constitution. We have laws, we have police forces, and we are not going to invent police forces any more than we are going to invent crimes or criminals or sadists. We have them in society. If anybody goes to gaol, it is because he has been going to gaol for a long time and because we have been vigilant enough to send him to gaol; but we have a country and this is the meaning of having a country.

People of this country try to set white people against black people. Some members over there would rally members of European descent in this population and tell them that Barrow intends to do so-and-so. They do not have enough sense to ask what is his intention. Never has anybody in this political party expressed or implied any intention that this government or this country should proceed along anything different from an orderly path to independence. The constitution which we are operating now is the type of constitution which we will be operating after independence.

They talk about independence within a Federation; this is the kind of independence which did not dawn on me until I woke up in a nightmare at 3 o'clock in the morning and found myself covered in perspiration, because several activities which were going on in the periphery were beginning to bother me in the back of my mind, and I was watching the behaviour of certain people, and I tried to analyse why it was that certain people were so dead set on certain things. I looked at the Federal Constitution until about 1 o'clock that morning in my office, went home, made a cup of tea and went to bed and woke up in cold sweats. Mr (Vere) Bird (then Chief Minister now Prime Minister of Antigua) has all the seats because the people gave him all. 'The Lord giveth and the Lord taketh away: Blessed be the name of the Lord.' Some of them over there will get their seats taken away; so be it. No one has a claim to political immortality; there are no political immortals under our constitution. You cannot give yourself immortality. As a matter of fact, I would like to say that anybody who made himself President of a country for his life time was automatically signing his death warrant, because that is the only way you could remove him. Only an inept person would make himself President for life. If a man makes himself President for life, you cannot get rid of him the constitutional way, but you can get rid of him by assassination.

We talk of psychological injuries that have been done to our young people by instilling in them a sense of inferiority. There are people in this House who have said they would never employ a black man before they employ a white man. People who are editors in this country would not invite a black man to their house unless they want to sell some idea to him. Therefore, let us understand the various heads of survival. You have survival of being able to fight against the invading hordes of Nazi Germany or any aggressor. You have survival of the human personality. You have economic survival. These are very important factors in human existence. These are very important survivals.

They are not in need of emancipation: they are prisoners in chains. They are the people who respond only to the stimulus of money and they do not care what the stimulus of money will do. There is no political party outside of our party in Barbados which has a clearly defined ideology and perspective for the people of this island, and that is why they are against it.

If you can get independence and economic advantage without having a constitutional superstructure imposed upon you, there is absolutely no inducement and no valid reason why a country like Barbados should surrender to the Lesser Antilles, that is, the less politically astute and experienced politicians of the Lesser Antilles, and I make no apology for saying it. If I say that I do not consider that this government should engage in these federal discussions until after independence, I am merely guaranteeing the independence of the people of Barbados if we go into a federation first. It is as simple as that.

I want to say this: it is one thing to be critical of politicians in the small areas and about the way they function; but these are systems which were set up by Her Majesty's Government when they used to run their affairs and nobody know what they did. These ministers have inherited problems and worries, and the islands were in a condition where all the services and institutions were dilapidated and run-down. These are countries which have been exploited until the last drop of blood has been squeezed out of them, and, under these circumstances, you cannot be surprised if the British government wants to palm off these islands and wants others to take them on.

I have the profoundest respect for the country where I had part of my education, and for the good things in it; but the point is that this is the parting of the ways, and when you come to the parting of the ways, you should be able to continue in correspondence without any acrimony.

I am not going to go into a long recital of all that has not been done in these territories, which is the reason for the present impasse. Colonialism is the reason for the present impasse in Westindian affairs, and we cannot afford to wait. I am not going into a recital of what the British have done and what they have not done. Their relation with our people has not been a happy association. It has been a very unhappy association, and it is regrettable that we will have some of the downtrodden, who feel that they are now slightly privileged, fighting on the side of the people who perpetrated all these acts of inhumanity against our people. When I go to a conference and I want to tell the Secretary of State to go to hell or to know his place, I tell him so because I know the premises, and the position of strength from which I am speaking is not a position of feeling inferior in any way. They are the people who should feel inferior, because they are the people who have broken every single law of morality as far as a relationship with us is concerned. This is all the more reason why we should stand on our own feet, because people are not going to respect you, Sir, if despite the fact that you are financially independent, you still want to be deemed to be a second class citizen of another country.

This is a moment in our history of which we should all be proud instead of being ashamed. If I have any sense of shame, it is shame to know that in my country there still exists an element, that, despite all we have gone through we still have people who are so degrading, and people who are so tantalised by the trappings of colonialism. I do not want my children to grow up as second class citizens, and I do not want the children of any of the ladies who work for me in my house assisting us in the discharge of our daily duties, or the man who works in the garden, or the man who drives the proverbial omnibus to grow up with any sense of inferiority to any persons.

Independence does not mean that you become disrespectful to anyone provided he respects you; and I know that Barbadians have enough good sense; they have a reputation for being polite and courteous to people, and the fact that we have independence would not mean that we are animals cut loose and starting to run around in circles, because we have been operating an independent constitution all these years.

I do not want to embarrass the Secretary of State or any other government. I make the decision about elections and this is a constitutional right. This is not a right which I have arrogated unto myself in my search for dictatorial power or any nonsense like that. How dishonest can people get in this country? When you examine it, you will find that the people who go in for this kind of vilification have not got a single achievement to their credit, a single achievement which has been the subject of impartial examination by anybody inside a school or university or outside; not a single political achievement for the years they are supposed, like the last government, to have spent in here. The only achievement they have is the achievement of slander and degradation; but they underestimate the intelligence of the masses of this country, because the masses of this country want independence. The masses of this country have too much sense to aspire to get into company which is intellectually inferior to the African heritage; but we have a bunch of humbugs in this country whose only ambition is to identify themselves with the hegemony, the presiding power, of Great Britain, people who look like British people and, therefore, are associated with the presiding power, and, if they get into their company, they feel that some of this prestige will rub off on them. That is why they do not want independence, because when you remove the tutelage of subservience and the bonds which keep you down, then every man is the same man. This is a psychological problem.

Mr Deputy Speaker, it depresses me particularly and the members of my Party, because we recognise analytically that this is one of the sad effects of colonialism. I really would be disappointed in a certain way because I thought that with the long tradition we have in Barbados, when we have had to stare facts in the face, and knowing that the people think about us, we would see that they are economically and culturally opposed to the masses of this country. The masses of a country are the true people in every country and they know it, and to try to fool the masses is to underestimate the intelligence of the masses.

What I find rather depressing in the whole exercise, is that they know we have a Constitution, because they have been living under a Constitution and working under the Constitution insofar as it suited them. When it did not suit them, they committed breaches of the constitutional proprieties. If I say, therefore, that I cannot view their activities with any sense of respect as a Barbadian, it is because I am a Barbadian and I am a loyal Barbadian. Anybody who knows me would know well enough that I have no ambition. This is one of my stumbling blocks all my life. I probably would have been a lot further if I had ambition. I have certain principles; they may be Victorian and you may consider them ingenuous. Because of the modern-day thought of 'dog eat dog', some people think that anybody who thinks in Victorian terms is out of date and not 'with it'. Therefore, among some people it is an expedient thing to accept money for political favours dispensed as part and parcel of what they call the game of politics. But it is not a game with us; it is a serious business. I see issues directly in terms of black and white, and there are no gradations between them as far as I am concerned; but there are people in this country and other countries, too, who consider politics a game. They make the pretext that they would do this and that for the people and that kind of thing. They do not want the people to get too much, because if you do all the things for the people that should be done for them, the State would then wither away and you would no longer continue to be an important personage.

If you give a man the right to work for his own living at a wage he considers compatible with his aspirations for himself and his children, then you do not have any more hold over him; but if you can keep him in a state of degradation and make him feel inferior, then they will always use you as the buffer between his oppressors and himself, and this is the role assumed by too many politicians in

Barbados for too long. This is the role which has been assumed by too many of our politicians in Barbados, content to be the buffer element between the masses and the people who do not participate in the society. They only bleed certain people; they do not communicate with them except during business hours. This is the kind of society we are against and they know we are against it. It is not a question of black or white, because we have more black political humbugs than we have white humbugs, and we have them right here in the House (of Assembly), unfortunately. There are certain things, for instance, that some members on the other side would stoop to which the honourable junior member for Christ Church (a white businessman, Fred Goddard) would never stoop to; he does not have to, and he knows he would incur, probably, the animosity of his party if he did them; but other people do these things which are detrimental to the society and they get applauded for it, because to be smart in this society you have to scramble over somebody. It does not matter how you get there; all will be forgiven. It does not matter how many people you assassinate or how many people you put to death or how many people are deprived of their livelihood; it does not matter as long as you get there; when you get there like Morgan the pirate, and all the other rogues and villains of history like Lord Nelson, you will be crowned with imperial honours at the end.

If we go back then in making this analysis of Westindian society, we have been made this way by our history. It has been a history of oppression, and some of us are in a hurry to dissociate ourselves from this long history of oppression, and they are so stupid, they have become so imbued with the spirit of cynicism that they are unaware that the quickest way to get away from this long history of oppression is for all the people to get away, and not a few of them climbing to the top of the ladder and kicking it down behind them.

All of us have to escape; there are not a few of us escaping. What does it profit a man to be Prime Minister of Barbados or of the Westindies? What does it mean? It means nothing if you lose your soul and achieve these objectives. What can you do for a man who is living at subsistence level after you have profited and have acquired all of these material comforts? How many meals a day can you eat? I want to tell some of the young professional people in this country that nobody has ever been revered in history for having become the richest man.

People do not respect you for getting into a certain position. Nobody respects me or would respect the ministers of government or any Premier of Barbados if they go in for corruption. With all the slander and lies which members of the opposition have told on me, if any of them can stand up and say that anybody paid me five dollars, I will hold my peace. I will hold my peace if anybody would get up and say that I have accepted money for doing anything corrupt. A lot of them over there cannot say that. I have never been fortunate enough to win a sweepstake, but I do not intend to get my hands soiled for them or anybody else. I have to discharge my duty to the programme which has been laid down by us and to the people of Barbados and those are the premises from which I am speaking. Some of them are so corrupt that they cannot understand how none of us on this side of the House are not. Corruption is something to them which is crowned with precious stones in these days, when you look around and see 'bauball' going around – to use a good Trinidadian expression. Some people feel that you must try and get as rich as possible in the shortest possible time.

This political conduct appears to be notable today. However, when you have finished, look at Batista of Cuba[****] and all other people like him! Mussolini of Italy was hanged upside down. He was the leader of one of the largest countries in Europe. Look at how Hitler ended up. Where are all of them today? But the names of the liberators, however poor they were, would remain. Simon Bolivar died a poor man on a little island called Margarita off the north coast of Venezuela. Look at liberators like Alexander Hamilton, George Washington, Touissant L'Ouverture. They were in a position where they could have been corrupted, but they did not allow themselves to be corrupted. When the history of Barbados in 1966 is written all the people who have participated in this exercise of trying to pull down what we have built up for Barbados, posterity would have their names desecrated in every sense of the term, and if posterity could dig up their bones or hang them in effigy, posterity would do that – do not let any of them have any illusions. This is a very serious matter. After the country had been exposed during the last three months – three months which we allowed for democratic discussion – to the sort of sordid conduct that has been witnessed and to our having mercenaries like the white bastards in the Belgian Congo – and it is a historical fact that even in the African countries, they employed white mercenaries to shoot down their own people – that even in this country of Barbados you find the white people hiring black people to keep back their own people. I want to tell you this. I rejoice because the Almighty moves in a mysterious way, his

---

[****]Fulencia Batista, Cuban dictator ousted in a populist rebellion led by Fidel Castro in 1959.

wonders to perform, because what this exercise has done more than anything else, is to separate the sheep from the goats, the honest from the dishonest and the liars from the leaders.

What it has done is to separate the sheep from the goats. It has purged the conscience of the community of the disharmonious elements. This has acted as a catalyst to bring up to the surface everything that is wrong in a community like this. We have learnt one lesson, and one lesson alone, that is how not to live together in unity.

We have evolved a formula for living together, but not having any strength. This is one of the paradoxes of our colonial situation in Barbados. Things are improving, but they are not what they should be and there are many things which we have experienced since this Resolution was laid in this House. The White Paper was laid before the legislature in August, and the Resolution was tabled afterwards. We have allowed three months for free unbridled discussion in this country. I know of no other country, including the United States and the United Kingdom, where the people who exhibit these disruptive propensities would be allowed to walk about the capital with impunity. I say that without any reservation. That in itself shows that we have had to purge ourselves of the things which have existed in the community for all of these years. The masses have begun to speak for themselves, and long may they continue to do so.

The soul of this community has to be laid bare, and there is no better time to do that than when we are preparing for independence, so that we know what we are, who we are, and where we are going.

The people who have money in this country are uncultured and they have no use for nine-tenths of the people of this country. Look at their houses. All they want to know is how much profit they are going to make and how much money they are going to lose. They do not understand the first thing of the complexities of the system. '

Who are all these people and what have they contributed to the society? Nothing. They do not like the legislation we pass, and I am not asking them to like it. They are not going to like the Tenantries Bill and they are not going to like the Social Securities Bill. They do not like these things because they feel people are becoming too independent. They have no cultural standing; they have no political ideology; they are only in an entrenched position of privilege and prestige, of prestige inherited by the association with the metropolitan country which is always willing to run to their rescue.

I want to say something about the metropolitan country. Right here in my White Paper I have referred to the Central African Federation which lasted from 1953 to 1963. The Central African Federation was dissolved in 1963 because of Dr. Kenneth Kaunda and Dr. Hastings Banda, the respective leaders of their people. Both of them have been in gaol for agitating for freedom for their people; so what did the British government do? They threw them into a Federation with Southern Rhodesia in 1953, and put Dr. Kaunda and Dr. Banda in gaol, and the effect of this Federation was to give 200,000 white Rhodesians perpetual dominance over four million Africans in South Rhodesia, and God knows how many in what used to be Nyasaland and Northern Rhodesia and which are now Malawi and Zambia respectively.

Sir Grantley Adams' Federation was a dependent Federation, a Crown Colony Federation, and in desperation Mr (Norman) Manley (then Premier of Jamaica) and Dr. (Eric) Williams (then Premier of Trinidad and Tobago) called a conference in England which was to make the Federation independent on the 31st of May, 1962. That was the date set for the independence of the Westindies Federation, but it was broken up on the same date. The British government broke it up on that date.

I have come across in the United Kingdom some of the crudest people I have ever come across in my life and some of us try to ape all the worst features of the English educational system.

When you talk about political immorality, you have to understand that there is a country which has ruthlessly taken hold of the economy of the other countries, people who are more benighted than ourselves and less advanced in what they choose to call a civilisation; they have murdered, detribalised and suppressed their religious activities and that sort of thing, forbidding them to use their own language. You cannot be surprised that the residual effects of that kind of harsh treatment must still be manifested in the behaviour of some politicians of the colonial territories today.   ·

What I want to impress upon honourable members is that there is nothing politically moral in the exercise of this Federation at all. In other words, it was the device to get rid of the incorrigible politicians of the Leeward and Windward Islands who were causing them (the British government) quite a lot of headaches. At the same time, there will be people of a certain mealy-mouthed, holier-than-thou attitude who would say that they have created another territory free to a state of independence, as if the whole experience was some sort of Sunday School exercise, and not one of the worst things which could be perpetrated in the history of mankind.

AT THE CONSTITUTIONAL CONFERENCE
AT LANCASTER HOUSE

With Burrowes, Vaughan, Tudor, Greaves, Brathwaite and Walcott alondside Stow

With Burrowes, Vaughan and Tudor

The Road to Destiny

Sir Philip M. Greaves

No discussion on Independence would be complete without an acknowledgement of the devotion of Errol Walton Barrow, whose life was intimately interwoven with the general concern for the plight of Barbadians, particularly the underprivileged. That was his life's work and he came finally to the conclusion in 1966 that it could best be achieved within the political framework of an independent Barbados.

I first met Errol on my return to Barbados after a 10 year hiatus. He was by then Premier and known to me by reputation. As an attorney, his skill in the court was legendary; an accomplished practitioner who yielded no quarter to judge or jury. His political skills were equally outstanding as he displayed an empathy with the various sectorial interests in the society and had indeed implemented measures that were curative and uplifting. It was therefore not difficult for me to accept his invitation to join his Cabinet towards the end of his first term, following the unexpectedly resignation of one of his Ministers.

In 1966, Independence became his consuming interest. It was the direct result of his frustrations over the tardiness and lack of progress in establishing a federal structure involving the remaining territories of the ill-starred West Indies Federation, following the secession of Jamaica and thereafter Trinidad and Tobago. As Premier of Barbados, he was disappointed that the United Kingdom, the administering power for the Windward and Leeward Islands, was not prepared to commit to a financial package on behalf of those grant-aided territories. Barbados was neither prepared, nor able, unaided, to carry the cost of administering what came to be known as the "Little Eight".

Errol's frustration with the federal exercise deepened due to the lack of any progress after three years of toil both on substantial financial aid from the UK and his further expectation for independence at the outset of the "Little Eight" Federation. There was no longer any choice. In his conviction it had now resolved itself into Independence for Barbados alone and he took recourse in the Democratic Labour Party's 1961 Manifesto which carried this statement on the last page: "*The road to destiny is the road to Independence. Towards this goal the country must press on. As the island has never been a grant-aided territory there is no reason why within or without a Federation, Barbados should not attain the full stature of Independence now, within the British Commonwealth.*"

His decision to proceed to an independent Barbados led opposing factions to attempt to bring about a political divide between Errol's position of an independent and progressive Barbados and those who used the occasion to try to the fan flames of opposition to Errol's ostensible unfitness as Premier and potentially Prime Minister. So the options were:

- Independence for Barbados, or
- Independence but within the larger group of federated states

The battle lines were drawn within the Democratic Labour Party (DLP), of which Errol was President, and beyond the bounds of Party allegiance.

Errol brought the options to a convocation of the Party and before a vote thereon could be taken, three ministers and two other parliamentarians known to be opposed to Errol's position ferociously engaged the debate but later capitulated and Errol's position was adopted as Party policy. One of his ministers promptly resigned from the Cabinet and from the DLP.

As a result of political rift, I was invited into the Cabinet. Several weeks later the Motion for Independence was passed and approved in the House of Assembly; I had the honour as Leader of the Senate of successfully piloting the Resolution for Independence in the Upper Chamber.

With the pathway cleared, Errol assembled a small committee to commence work on drafting a constitution which included:

- Fred Cozier, Permanent Secretary and Secretary to the Committee
- William Douglas, Chief Justice (later Sir William)
- Wilfred Fergusson, former Chief Justice
- Philip Greaves, Minister (now Sir Philip)
- Cameron Tudor, Minister of Education (later Sir James)
- Hylton Vaughan, Attorney General
- Frank Walcott, Member of Parliament (later the RE Sir Frank)

The first draft constitution was prepared by William Douglas based on the Jamaica model as he was working in Jamaica at the time of its accession to Independence. The Trinidad model was also reviewed. Eventually the Committee decided to adopt the Jamaica model with the exception of the Chapter dealing with the Protection of Human Rights for which it preferred the Trinidad provisions. Having satisfied ourselves with the draft, it was sent to Professor O.R. Marshall (later Sir Roy) for his comments and review. Professor Marshall had no difficulty with the draft except to recommend that Barbados should follow the Jamaica Constitutional provisions on Human Rights Protection which were more flexible than the provisions from Trinidad. His recommendation was accepted and the Committee presented the final document for Parliamentary approval.

The White Paper was debated in the Barbados Legislature in January 1966, following which the Resolution passed by both Houses was transmitted to the Secretary of State for the Colonies requesting him to convene an early conference to discuss Independence for Barbados within the Commonwealth in 1966. The Secretary of State replied in February that the British Government agreed to convene a Conference and proposed that it should be held in London in June.

The proposal was accepted and the conference on the issue of the Barbados application for Independence was held at Lancaster House. The Conference was attended by representatives of the three political parties, as follows:

The Rt. Hon. Frederick Lee, MP   *Secretary of State for the Colonies*
Mr J.T. Stonehouse, MP   *Parliamentary Under-Secretary of State*

Sir John Stow, KCMG, KCVO   *Governor of Barbados*

Democratic Labour Party Delegates
The Hon. Errol. W. Barrow, MP   *Premier*
Sen. the Hon. H.A. Vaughan, OBE, QC   *Attorney-General*
The Hon. J.C. Tudor, MP   *Minister of Education*
Sen. the Hon. P.M. Greaves*   *Minister without Portfolio*
Sen. C.L. Brathwaite
Mr F.L. Walcott, OBE, MP

Advisers
Prof. O.R. Marshall
Mr K.W. Patchett
Mr J.A.J. Murray

Barbados National Party Delegates
Mr Ernest D. Mottley, CBE, MP   *Leader of the Opposition*
Mr F.C. Goddard, MP
Sen. J.S.B. Dear, QC

Advisers
Mr E.R.L. Ward
Mr L.A. Lynch, MP
Sen. D.G. Leacock

Barbados Labour Party Delegates
Mr Freddie E. Miller, MP
Sen. H.B. St John

Advisers
Mr H.de B. Forde*
Mr J.M.G.M. Adams

Officials

Mr E.S.S. Burrowes, CMG	*Financial Secretary*
Mr F.L. Cozier, OBE	*Permanent Secretary to the Premier*
Mr D.A. Williams	*Senior Parliamentary Counsel*

(*Sir Henry Forde and I share a unique link to the Conference as he is the sole surviving Adviser and I am the sole surviving Delegate.)

The Conference was opened on 20 June by the Secretary of State for the Colonies, but was fraught with drama from the inception.

At the Opening Session each delegation wanted to be the last to address the session. Ernest Mottley, the Leader of the Opposition then made the opening speech but neither of the other two delegations would yield to the other. Errol's position was that being the Party in Government and Premier he had a right to be the final speaker or to choose the order where he would want to speak. In the end neither Errol nor Freddy Miller spoke.

The conference then got underway the following day and his initial statement was vintage Barrow as he assured the Colonial Secretary that his *"Government will not be found loitering on colonial premises after closing time",* having emphasised that: *"Neither the smallness of their territory nor the slenderness of their physical resources deters [the people of Barbados] in the path to nationhood. They have a modest part to play in the affairs of their region, the Commonwealth and the world, and all they require from you, is that you should speed them to their rendezvous with destiny some time in 1966."*

It became clear from early on that the partisan information fed to the Colonial Office had reached the Colonial Secretary who was the Conference Chair. It became even clearer to everyone that a direct clash between the Secretary and Premier was inevitable. Errol egged it on and the Secretary not being the most astute of politicians inadvertently aided and abetted.

After one of the sessions, Errol in frustration invited a representative of one of the Barbados newspapers to a meeting where he launched into an indictment against the Secretary accusing him of being ill-advised and lacking the capacity to preside over the conference with the full knowledge that what he said would be reported by Government House in Barbados back to the Colonial Office in London.

The Secretary was livid, and as the delegations assembled for the next plenary session that Errol attended, opened the document he had received from Barbados and divulged what Errol was reported to have said about him and demanded that Errol apologise to him in plenary. As I was seated next to Errol I was left with no doubt from his utterances that the Secretary had stepped on a hornet's nest.

When the Secretary concluded his statement, Errol rose and totally annihilated him, letting it be known that instead of embarrassing him (Errol), the Secretary had exposed his own incompetence and the person from whom an apology should be forthcoming was him for his inept attempt to publicly embarrass the Premier of Barbados. The session was adjourned and all other sessions were chaired by the Under-Secretary of State.

At the Conference, all three parties were in agreement that Barbados should proceed to separate Independence. There were, however, a number of differences between the Party in Government and one or both of the Opposition parties over particular provisions of the draft Constitution. Some of these were resolved in discussion but the following areas were the major points of disagreement:

- Composition of the Senate
- Provisions for qualifications and disqualifications for membership of the House of Assembly
- Provisions for an independent and impartial commission charged with the duty of supervising the registration of electors and the conduct of elections
- Constituency arrangements
- Provision for a permanent boundaries commission to keep constituency boundaries under review Emergency Provisions
- Compensation for Deprivation of Property

However, progress was made and at the plenary session on the afternoon of the 1 July 1966, the Colonial Secretary re-emerged, unseen for several days, and made the following statement:

"This Constitutional Conference has now completed the major part of its business. We have examined the draft Constitution produced by the Government of Barbados and I am happy to say that, on much of it, all parties represented round this table have reached agreement. This will be recorded in the report of the Conference where the main features of the Constitution will be described. There are certain matters on which, unfortunately, it was not possible for the Government and the two Opposition Parties to agree, and I appreciate the importance of some of them to the parties in Barbados. They are all matters on which it is understandable that there might be differences of view between the various groups in a democratic society framing a constitution for independence. These disagreements will also have to be set out and recorded in the Conference report.

The Legislature of Barbados in requesting me to call this conference proposed that as a result of it Barbados should proceed to separate independence in 1966.

On this question of separate independence for Barbados I have as you all know had separate discussions with all the parties represented round this table. I understand that, although some of the Barbadian representatives would have preferred their country to seek independence in an association with their neighbours in the Caribbean, all parties are agreed that for the time being this aim is not attainable and therefore they concur in the proposal that Barbados should proceed to separate independence.

In the meetings which I had with the parties separately to discuss this question I made it plain that, having heard their views, I would consult my colleagues and let them have the United Kingdom Government's decision. I am now in a position to inform the Conference that these consultations have taken place and that, subject to the passage of the necessary legislation by the United Kingdom Parliament, Her Majesty's Government agree that Barbados should become independent on the 30th November 1966.

The question of the date of the next elections in Barbados is one for the Government of Barbados to determine, bearing in mind that a Dissolution is in any case due not later than the 19th December 1966. They will doubtless be announcing their decision in due course."

Jubilation followed and the unbelievable happened, Errol and Freddy Miller who had not said a single word to each other for over ten years embraced each other as if long lost brothers.

The Barbados delegates unanimously expressed the wish that on achieving Independence, that Barbados should be accepted as a full member of the Commonwealth of Nations. It was confirmed that the British Government would be happy to consult the other members of the Commonwealth at the appropriate time asking that Barbados should be admitted to membership.

We were now on the road to destiny – the road to Independence!

POSTSCRIPT

On Temperament: Some of Errol's utterances were often labelled as intemperate. There are usually several reasons why someone's pronouncements may be considered as such. But there are a number of reasons why anyone may fail to maintain an even temper. Clearly the more one is before the public eye and more is required of that person – sometimes more than is reasonable – the more one is prone to lose one's cool. A prime minister is no different. Errol did not take a vow of temperance in terms of speech and even then, such vows are broken under particular circumstances. Some persons' intemperance is manifested in different ways. With Errol, he never raised his voice when making mincemeat of another. His use of language was sufficiently wide that he did not need a hammer to kill an ant. When provoked he may say things like *"ushering people out of the state"* or for comic relief refer to someone as being *"all things to all men and very little to any woman"*. But his home was open to all persons regardless of race or creed or hour; often long before the sun announced its presence. He treated everyone equally and that is the kind of Barbados he was sought to create.

"No loitering on
colonial premises"

Address to the Barbados Constitutional Conference
in London, July 1966

Mr Secretary of State,

We thank you for the courtesies which you have so far shown us
and particularly for the kind words of welcome you have just spoken.

The small territory whose fortune and future we are met here to
decide, is unique in many respects. It came into association with the
Crown of England neither by conquest nor by purchase but by
settlement. It is interesting to note that Barbados began its association
with England at the time when English political institutions experienced their severest strain.

When in 1639 your own country had been governed without a
Parliament for 11 years, the English inhabitants of Barbados settled a
Parliament for themselves and thereby created the Legislative
institutions which we have since, without any disturbance enjoyed.
In this respect, Barbados shared only with Virginia, Massachusetts
and Bermuda, the solid comforts of representative government.

In 1651, when Englishmen were cowering in their homes under the
whip of Cromwell's major-generals, and when they who had lopped
off the head of a king sought to enmesh the people of Barbados in
their 'saintly' tyranny, Barbadians stubbornly defended their respective institutions from Cromwell and in the famous Charter of
Barbados which they signed, they have managed to preserve for
three centuries the supremacy of parliaments and the liberty of the
subject.

A century and a half later, the genius of Thomas Jefferson distilled
from this Charter that heady wine of sovereignty which we now
know as the Declaration of American Independence.

Again when in 1668 the crown and the liberties of England were
once more in jeopardy, and the democratic freedoms had to be
enshrined in a Bill of Rights, the Parliament of Barbados celebrated its

golden jubilee and judges administered the same common and statute law which was under a temporary cloud in England.

The strength and durability of our institutions are best demonstrated by the fact that representative government and the rule of law are now administered by people who are different in racial origins from those who established them.

Ninety per cent of our people are of African origin, whose ancestors have experienced the harshness of unfree and unrequited labour. Their descendants have lived through the period since emancipation hemmed in by all the frustrations which a plantation economy imposes upon its labour force.

As opportunities came, they fought and finally broke the political power of the local oligarchy, and now enjoy full internal self-government, based on adult suffrage at the age of 18, a Cabinet system, an independent judiciary, a competent public service, a population which is 98 per cent literate – most significant of all a Treasury which has never needed a grant in aid of administration.

The people who now enjoy these blessings feel a natural affinity with, and are grateful to, those Englishmen who in 1639 built better than they knew. They laid the foundations for that free society, a small part of which we already experience and the greater portion of which we shall establish after independence.

Our relations with the Crown have always been warm and it is the unanimous desire of our citizens that Her Majesty shall be Queen and Head of State of an independent Barbados.

Occasionally in our history, we had to resist the encroachments of British governments in our internal affairs, encroachments designed to lower the status from that of a settled territory to that of a colony.

In 1876, the Legislature of Barbados successfully defeated an attempt by the Colonial Office to force our country into a federation which, if it had come about, would have given the Colonial Office greater control over Barbadian affairs.

In defeating that manoeuvre, we embarked on the path along which our Constitution has been carried to the threshold of Independence.

When, therefore, the Legislature of Barbados in January, in affirmative and convincing manner, requested your predecessor to arrange this conference, the Legislature itself was playing its traditional role of speaking for the people in their great moments.

In our country, as in England, the supremacy of Parliament is zealously upheld and a Government of Barbados, like its counterpart in Britain, would never resort to any subterfuge designed to frustrate the clearly expressed desires of a duly elected Parliament.

In order that you, Mr Secretary of State, should not be incommoded by our problems,we have assumed and discharged the responsibility for producing the constitution under which the people of Barbados will continue to govern themselves after independence.

As you expect in a country with our parliamentary traditions, this constitution was presented in draft, first to our Legislature and then to our citizens. Only as recently as Friday last, it was given final approval in its amended form, and the draft is now submitted for your consideration.

In our view, there can be no question whether Barbados is ripe and ready for independence. Three centuries of history answer that question in the affirmative. You have never had to shore up our finances; you have never had to maintain or preserve public order among us. Even now, without the help of thousands of our best citizens, your own hospital and transport system would be in jeopardy.

In two world wars, hundreds of our people have readily responded to your summons and some have never returned. The People of Barbados have never given you any cause for worry, and no British government has ever been forced, on our account to vindicate its policy at the bar of international opinion.

In assuming the burdens of independence, the people of Barbados have no illusions about their task. They are well aware that in this country, it is commonly believed, although it is not a fact, that people of African origin cannot for long maintain democratic forms of government after independence.

These people conveniently forget that the colonial system was designed not to promote free institutions, but to safeguard imperial interests. They also forget that if in the act of surrendering power, the imperial authority promotes and leaves behind it, a divided community, then some time must necessarily elapse before democratic institutions can take root in countries emerging from colonialism.

Political democracy is a precious concept, but it is not an Anglo-Saxon discovery and it is capable of growth among all sorts and conditions of people. Even in Anglo-Saxon countries, the principles of democracy are not always adhered to when justice is required for persons of different racial origins.

In the face of this, it is not surprising that new countries must take time to develop free institutions. To expect an emergent country to provide a fully democratic system on the morning after a colonial nightmare, is rather like asking a man to explore England with a map of Old Sarum and an 18th Century map at that.

By some fortunate turn of history, the people of Barbados have managed to establish before their independence the solid framework of a free society. Their training and apprenticeship are now complete. They have three centuries of steady maturity to draw on and self-confidence sprung from the management of their own affairs.

Neither the smallness of their territory nor the slenderness of their physical resources deters them in the path to nationhood. They have a modest part to play in the affairs of their region, the Common-wealth and the world, and all they require from you, is that you should speed them to their rendezvous with destiny sometime in 1966.

Mr Secretary, we have a self-imposed curfew on the duration of these discussions in that the government has arranged to leave the United Kingdom on the 5th of July for an equally important meeting with our partners in Canada.

There can be no time in the circumstances for the lowing herd to wind slowly o'er the Lee.

This, Sir, is in accord with your wishes and our intention to safeguard your person even if your office is soon to be dissolved. My Government, I assure you, Sir, will not be found loitering on colonial premises after closing time.

INDEPENDENCE

The 1966 Election Campaign for Independence

Receiving the Constitutional Instruments of Independence from the Duke of Kent

With Governor Stow who became the first Governor-General

Taking the Oath of Office at Government House

No Turning Back

Professor Mary Chamberlain

"To be young and to be alive in Barbados tonight, I feel as if I were in paradise already."

Rapturous words spoken by Errol Walton Barrow on taking delivery of the Constitutional Instruments of Independence, the night of Wednesday, 30 November 1966

The 1961 DLP election manifesto had committed the Party to reforms in almost every sector of Barbadian society. It proposed to implement free and compulsory schooling and to expand education facilities at every level, it proposed to introduce school meals, it promised to overhaul the health care system, to introduce maternity leave and improve pre- and post-natal care, to launch a crash programme to relieve unemployment, and to introduce a Social Security system, including health insurance.

The reforms were an indicative list of the desperate needs of the people of Barbados and a resounding statement not only of the failure of the directed investment initiated over the last twenty years of the Colonial Development and Welfare Fund but also of general British neglect. While the BLP administration had initiated some reforms, notably in the area of social and health administration, progress had been slow and Adams' directorship had been diverted by the issues of Federation and by constitutional matters. The DLPs electoral promises would, however, cost money.

The DLP manifesto also made one thing absolutely apparent. *"The road to destiny",* it declared, *"is the road to Independence. Towards this goal the country must press on."* And Barrow made it clear that Federation could not be allowed to divert attention and resources away from implementing reforms: *"we are not prepared to postpone or abandon our programme of free secondary education or any of other immediate projects."*

It was a view point underwritten by the Barbados Advocate editorial at the time: *"While we believe Federation should be saved and that it would be of advantage to Barbados to associate with, and provide the dynamic leadership the territories of Eastern Caribbean need, it is obvious that, far from being able to support federation, Barbados is hard put to support herself. Only if Britain, America or Canada or all three [together] are willing to subsidise the cost of Federation until it can pay its own way and by a crash programme of economic and technical aid make that a possibility, should Barbados join with grant-aided territories in Federation."*

With the final collapse of the Federation negotiations in late 1964, Barrow set his sights on Independence as the only viable way forward. Despite the poverty and the significant levels of unemployment, Barbados' economy was strong, compared with other parts of the Eastern Caribbean.

Barbados had never received budgetary aid or grants-in-aid from the British government, its debt (from development loans) was relatively small, it had been self-governing for three hundred years, and in the last ten years it had become a fully-fledged semi-autonomous democracy. Moreover, it had turned increasingly and successfully to Canada as a source of aid, reducing Barbados' dependence on Britain. In Barrow's eyes, Barbados met all the economic and constitutional criteria which were necessary and sufficient for Independence.

His vision now, did not include a Federation as a necessary condition of that independence. In August 1965, Barrow issued a White Paper laying out the Government's proposals for Independence and as he was to argue against the opposition to fulfil the DLPs manifesto on which they had been voted into Government. Until then as the British had reported there had been little public discussion on the matter. 'Nothing,' recalled one informant, "had been leaked or released to the press – people didn't take the press seriously then anyhow, about the progress, or lack of progress, of these talks."

In Barrow's view, the drawn-out negotiations on the Eastern Caribbean Federation had effectively diverted interest away from its substantive point: Independence.

Necessarily, the proposals in the White Paper were anathema to long-standing Federalists such as Wynter Crawford (who resigned from the DLP) and to the BLP and Adams who was wounded but by no means ineffectual. Barrow's decision to issue the White Paper without discussion also attracted attention from a group subsequently tagged the 'Under Forties', a coalition of young professionals who had been meeting for some time to throw around political and social ideas and who, with the publication of the White Paper, felt that some formal discussion on the implications of Independence was required.

Neither radio nor newspapers were then used effectively as media for debate. Accordingly, they sponsored a series of public meetings, opening in Queen's Park. The meetings were well attended as less than fifteen years after universal suffrage, public meetings could still excite and attract a mass audience. Public meetings not only engaged a fully committed electorate, they were, and had been, part of popular, dramatic entertainment, a form of 'public spectacle' which had attracted large audiences, long before universal suffrage.

Despite the discussion, and the calls for an election prior to Independence, Barrow put a proposal to the House of Assembly, based on the White Paper, to initiate Independence talks. The decision not to hold an election, or even a referendum, on Independence was quite clear in Barrow's eyes. Against charges of abusing his authority, he argued that he and the Government had been democratically elected on a manifesto pledge of Independence. There was, therefore, no need to hold an election to decide the issue. And, as a sop to the Opposition, he argued in the House of Assembly that Independence did not necessarily rule out a Federation at a later date; but on terms acceptable to Barbados and not imposed by the British, whose enthusiasm for a Federation, any federation, was based on the need to *"palm off these islands [of the Eastern Caribbean]"* by getting others to take over responsibility.

Throughout 1966, the debate and the manoeuvrings continued with Barrow resisting calls for elections and Adams, in particular, attempting to trick him into doing so, not least by demanding an audience with the

Secretary of State for the Colonies in an attempt to persuade the British to delay the date of Independence to 1967, by which time Barbados would have had to go to the country.

The constitutional talks in London in June 1966, confirmed the date of Independence as 30 November 1966 and although Barrow returned bullish and triumphant, as he famously argued at the conference that Barbados *"will not be found loitering on colonial premises after closing time"*, he nevertheless had to concede that elections should be held prior to that date.

On 2 November 1966, General Elections were held and the DLP was returned with a significantly increased share of the vote, at 49.3 per cent, which represented an increase of 13 per cent in support from their 1961 performance (at 36.3 per cent).

It was an outstanding endorsement of Barrow and the DLP and of the progressive ideology of the Party, and of his leadership through the Independence negotiations with the British, and of the popularity of Independence. Sir John Stow, the then Governor (and at Independence, its first Governor-General) had to revise his views, having confided in secret a few months earlier to the Secretary of State, that it would be *"a frightening thought that Barbados may be going into Independence with a near madman at the helm"*.

From a context in which, two years earlier, there had been indifference to the issue of Independence, immersed in the miasma of federal negotiations, when it came, Independence was greeted on the whole with enthusiasm. There were some who were apprehensive, others who bemoaned the loss of a direct link with Britain, and some who left (with their money), but all considered that Independence was inevitable. The levels of public debate, and controversy, had succeeded in raising a general awareness about Independence, about being a West Indian, and also about being a Barbadian in ways that the Federation had not.

Foreign Policy Architect
Dr Peter Laurie

FORGING A FOREIGN POLICY

The main tasks of Prime Minister Barrow and the Democratic Labour Party (DLP) Administration on gaining Independence in 1966 were essentially domestic: to continue the economic and social development of the country so as to create the greatest prosperity for its people and to spread that prosperity as equitably as possible. Nevertheless, it was in the area of foreign policy that Mr Barrow, as the first Foreign Minister of Barbados, placed a stamp of authority that would last for the next fifty years.

When Barbados became Independent there was no burning external issue around which to immediately orient its foreign policy. It faced no threat to its territorial integrity, as, for example, did Guyana, which was confronted with a claim by neighbouring Venezuela for a third of its territory. Mr Barrow however, was acutely aware of the small size of the country, the lack of natural resources, and the urgent need for continued transformation from dependence on a single export crop – sugar – to a more balanced economy.

Small size also meant vulnerability to external shocks whether they came in the form of hurricanes, sudden unfavourable changes in the terms of trade, or military threats. Sensitivity to issues of sovereignty would be an abiding feature of Barbadian foreign policy from the beginning. In addition, he, in view of the country's history, was especially sensitive to issues of colonialism, neo-colonialism and racial discrimination.

Against this background, Mr Barrow, regarded Barbados' foreign policy as having three main goals:

1. seeking to harness external resources for the economic development of the country;
2. trying to avoid entanglements in external relations that might distract from the main task of development; and
3. lending Barbados' voice in support of international equitable economic development, political freedom and democracy.

Barbados became independent at the height of the Cold War, the fierce global ideological rivalry between the United States of America (USA) and the Union of Soviet Socialist Republics (USSR) that characterised international relations from the late 1940s until the breakup of the USSR in the early 1990s. Both superpowers tried to rally as many 'client' states as possible to their side, the USSR finding captive allies in Eastern Europe and the US finding willing clients in Latin America.

It was against this Cold War background that Mr Barrow was to enunciate in December 1966 in his first address to the United Nations General Assembly what was to be a cardinal principle of the foreign policy of Barbados: *"friends of all, satellites of none"*.

Over the years this axiom was much misunderstood. Neither Mr Barrow, nor the people of Barbados for that matter, understood it as strict neutrality between the two superpowers; Barbados after all, had a substantial and friendly relationship with the United States; it had no diplomatic or other relations with the Soviet Union. Moreover Barbados did not join the Non-Aligned Movement (NAM) until the 1980s and never attempted to play any great role in it.

What Mr Barrow wished to signal was that Barbados, as a small state, was determined not to be used as a client, pawn or a proxy by either major power in the Cold War – especially the US within whose sphere of influence Barbados was strategically located. Barbados, and Barbados alone, would decide where its interests lay. And, if necessary, Mr Barrow was ready to speak his mind bluntly when it came to defending the national interest.

However, at the same time he appreciated that a small state located next door to a superpower must always devise and conduct its foreign policy with an eye to how it might impinge on the superpower's interests and how the superpower might react. That was common sense. It did not mean that Barbados could not take independent action nor pursue goals of which the US did not approve. It simply meant that one had to be prudent.

It was from these three broad principles of harnessing external resources for national development, steering clear of entangling alliances that might endanger or constrain its own freedom of action, and supporting international struggles for freedom, democracy and equitable economic development that largely derived the element of pragmatism that characterised Barbadian diplomacy from the start.

Mr Barrow was a man of strong principle and ideals but also a down-to-earth pragmatist. He infused Barbados' foreign policy with this pragmatism which no doubt also rooted in the character of the Barbadian people. Whether shaped by geography, history or culture, the Barbadian is essentially a person of conservative temperament, cautious and pragmatic in outlook.

Barbadians are resistant to radical change and have recourse to rebellion only when the forces of reaction have blocked all peaceful and legal paths to progress. Then they act with determination. The Right Excellent Bussa's 1816 revolt against dehumanising slavery and the 1937 popular uprising against intolerable conditions of life are testimony to the Barbadian's outrage and determination in the face of gross injustice.

But most of the time Barbadians are suspicious of grand designs for the radical remaking of either their society or of the international community of nations. They prefer modest, achievable goals that neither outreach their imagination nor their pocketbooks.

Nevertheless Mr Barrow injected into our foreign policy a strong streak of idealism. This was most evident in his vigorous advocacy of human rights. This too had its roots in Barbados' history of resistance to colonial racial discrimination and oppression. It was therefore not surprising that Barbados was outspoken from the beginning in opposition to racism, especially in the Southern Africa. This opposition was not confined to words, but found expression in tangible efforts to help the victims of apartheid and racial discrimination.

This policy quickly became universally applied to any situation in which people were victims of oppression or had their fundamental rights violated. Accordingly Barbados has defended over the decades the rights of women, children, the disabled, and victims of torture and genocide, among others.

Linked to the defence of human rights was the promotion of democracy, freedom and peaceful change. This again was rooted in Barbados' history. Following the 1937 uprising, the Barbados labour movement, at both the economic and political levels, used peaceful but forceful means to effect change. Much of the struggle for social justice and ultimate independence was focussed on Parliament, an institution that has an ancient history in Barbados. Consequently Mr Barrow, along with most Barbadians, had a fierce attachment to parliamentary democracy and remained convinced that it was essential not only for safeguarding political freedom and social equity, but also for achieving economic prosperity. Hence Barrow saw both at home and abroad a connection between democracy, peace and prosperity.

Barbados' foreign policy was rightly conceived of as the obverse of its domestic policy. Beyond these three broad principles there were a number of other defining themes reflecting national interests that went into Barrow's early mapping of a foreign policy for a newly independent Barbados.

At the political level, Barbados considered that the best guarantee of its security lay with strong multilateral institutions like the United Nations and the Commonwealth of Nations. Barbados also sought to create common cause with other developing countries to advance their collective interests globally: namely continued decolonisation, an end to all forms of racism and colonial oppression, and the alleviation of world poverty. Barbados also tried to harmonise its foreign policy with that of the other independent Caribbean countries: Guyana, Jamaica and Trinidad and Tobago.

At the economic level, Barbados' goals were to secure and maintain preferential access to the markets of the developed countries for its primary exports (sugar, rum and molasses); obtain concessionary financing from international financial institutions and donor countries for its infrastructural and institutional development; encourage foreign direct investment in light manufacturing and tourism; and promote tourism in the markets of the developed countries. In these early years the principal countries for achieving these economic goals were the United Kingdom, the United States and Canada.

Finally, at the consular level Barbados had many nationals residing overseas, mainly in the United Kingdom, Canada and the United States, for whom it wished to provide consular services. A large Barbadian diaspora had developed though massive migration to Panama in the early part of the 20th century (to help build the Canal), to the United Kingdom in the 1950s, and to North America in the 1960s. Over the years Barbados would come to see these overseas Barbadians as a significant resource for the country.

FOREIGN POLICY DELIVERY

Mr Barrow, as the first Foreign Minister, gave a lot of thought as well to the organisational basis of Barbadian diplomacy. Before it could attempt to achieve any of its foreign policy goals, the Government first had to set up a foreign service within the constraints of its limited human and financial resources. The Ministry's early recruitment of available talent, its broadening of the recruitment base to reflect a greater diversity of skills, and its continuous investment in training at all levels over the years, combined to produce Barbadian diplomats of the highest quality, many of whom have and continue to serve with distinction in regional and international bodies.

Mr Barrow decided to assume direct responsibility initially for foreign policy. This responsibility was discharged through a division of the Prime Minister's Office, headed by permanent secretary F.L. 'Fred' Cozier, at Government Headquarters. This arrangement continued until 1 April 1967 when a Ministry of External Affairs was established, although it continued to be housed within the Prime Minister's Office. In August of that year, the Hon. J. Cameron Tudor was appointed Minister of State for Caribbean and Latin American Affairs to assist the Prime Minister in carrying out his duties. It was not until 1971 that a full-fledged Minister of External Affairs, Senator The Hon. George Moe, was appointed.

In its embryonic stages, the senior ranks of the Foreign Service were staffed by talented public servants like Fred Cozier, Jean Holder, Oliver Jackman, Val McComie and Monty Williams who brought a great deal of experience and skills in other areas to the Ministry. These pioneers, operating on a shoestring budget, and inspired by a passionate commitment to the cause of an Independent Barbados taking its place on the world stage, organised the headquarters division and the embassies abroad, and articulated the country's positions on a myriad of international issues often through sheer instinct guided only by the basic tenets of a still-evolving foreign policy.

In deciding where it should establish diplomatic and consular representation abroad, Barbados was severely constrained by limited financial and human resources. Mr Barrow therefore had to exercise both prudence and selectivity, focussing exclusively on those countries and organisations in which Barbados' national interests were paramount. Accordingly, the Government initially decided to set up diplomatic and consular missions in London, Washington D.C. and Ottawa, reflecting the main economic ties of Barbados. A Permanent Mission to the United Nations and a consulate-general were also set up in New York.

Moreover, in all three cases, a novel arrangement for sharing was entered into with Guyana. In Britain, Barbados converted a welfare office for students and nationals it had set up as far back as 1955 into the chancery of its first High Commission on November 30th 1966. Barbados and Guyana shared not only office space but also the High Commissioner, Sir Lionel Luckhoo. A Barbadian, J.C. King, formerly permanent secretary in the Ministry of Trade, Tourism, Cooperatives and Fisheries, was appointed as deputy high commissioner. Similar sharing arrangements were made in Ottawa and Washington D.C. where Barbados and Guyana shared office space and diplomatic personnel.

These shared arrangements lasted until 1970, when Sir Lionel Luckhoo retired and Barbados appointed Waldo Waldron-Ramsey as his replacement. At the same time new premises for the chancery were acquired. Subsequently, Barbados opened an embassy in Caracas in 1974 and by the end of the 1970s Barbados had diplomatic relations with 56 countries and had seven overseas missions. Five countries also maintained resident embassies in Bridgetown.

An important aspect of Barbados foreign relations was the welfare and protection of nationals living abroad. In the case particularly of the UK, where it was estimated that over 54,000 Barbadians lived in the period immediately following Independence, the provision of consular services was central to the work of overseas missions.

Mr Barrow also initiated regular consultations on foreign policy by bringing home all heads of diplomatic and consular missions every two years. These sessions proved invaluable in helping to develop and fine tune external policies as well as prepare positions on the numerous international issues confronting Barbados.

CARIBBEAN UNITY

Mr Barrow was a strong advocate of regional integration. Even before Barbados became independent, he had held discussions with the leaders of Guyana and Antigua on the possible establishment of a free trade area in the Caribbean. In December 1965, the Heads of Government, Barrow, Bird and Burnham, signed the Caribbean Free Trade Association (CARIFTA) Agreement at Dickenson Bay, Antigua.

The CARIFTA Agreement did not immediately come into effect but proved to be the impetus for wider regional integration; the 4th Commonwealth Caribbean Heads of Government Conference in Barbados in 1967, formally agreed to institute CARIFTA which came into effect in 1968.

CARIFTA provided not only for free trade between the parties, but also aimed to tackle underdevelopment from a regional perspective as well as laying the groundwork for expanded functional cooperation in such areas as sea and air transport, health, education, mass communications, and the law of the sea.

Another critical regional economic institution that Barrow spearheaded was the creation of the Caribbean Development Bank. He had raised the idea at a Commonwealth Caribbean/Canada Conference held in Ottawa in July 1966, and then subsequently at a meeting of the Tripartite Conference (sponsored by the UK, the US, and Canada) held in Antigua in November of that same year. Canada, the UK and the US all indicated their support in principle for such an initiative and agreed to give favourable consideration to the provision of technical and financial support.

At the 1967 Heads of Government Conference, Heads accepted the idea of a regional development bank. In 1968, the Commonwealth

Caribbean Finance Ministers, meeting in Antigua, were persuaded by Barrow to choose Barbados as the headquarters for a regional development bank. The agreement establishing the CDB was signed in 1969 and entered into force in 1970. The CDB proved to be a catalyst for the development of Caribbean states and for the promotion of economic integration and functional cooperation in the Caribbean.

In 1972, Commonwealth Caribbean leaders at the Seventh Heads of Government Conference decided to transform CARIFTA into a Common Market and establish the Caribbean Community (CARICOM), of which the Common Market would be an integral part. At the Eighth Heads of Government Conference of CARIFTA held in 1973 in Georgetown, Guyana, the decision to establish the Caribbean Community was brought to fruition with the approval by Heads of Government of the draft legal instruments.

The Georgetown Accord provided for the signature of the Caribbean Community Treaty on 4 July 1973 and its coming into effect in August 1973, among the then four independent countries: Barbados, Guyana, Jamaica and Trinidad and Tobago. The Accord also provided that the other eight territories – Antigua, British Honduras (Belize), Dominica, Grenada, Saint Lucia, Montserrat, St Kitts/Nevis/Anguilla and St Vincent which signed the Accord would become full members of the Community by 1 May 1974. The signing of the Treaty establishing the Caribbean Community, at Chaguaramas in Trinidad on 4 July 1973 was a defining moment in the history of the Commonwealth Caribbean, one that Mr Barrow had worked tirelessly to achieve.

The three main planks of CARICOM were the deepening of economic integration, the strengthening of functional cooperation and the coordination of foreign policies of the independent member states. Mr Barrow, for the rest of his life, continued to be a fervent advocate of regional unity and self-reliance. Shortly after his election in 1986, he addressed the Seventh Annual CARICOM Heads of Government Conference held in Guyana, and in a widely appreciated speech, committed his Government to do all in its power to advance the cause of regional unity.

Barrow also made the accurate observation that the people of the region were far in advance of the politicians. Indeed, he noted, *"The regional integration movement is a fact of daily experience. It is a reality which is lived, but which we have not yet been able to institutionalise. "*

Barrow observed that the reasons for the failure to keep up with the people was that the governments had focussed too much simply on trade liberalisation and had neglected the deeper reasons for coming together: namely the shared culture of the Caribbean, the common heritage and indeed a psyche moulded by the same historical forces.

Barrow also expressed his concern about the militarisation of the Caribbean and called for it to be recognised as a zone of peace. Barrow saw regional cooperation and self-reliance as a means of lessening the dependence of the Caribbean on external powers, a theme in keeping with his 'friends of all, satellites of none' foundational principle of foreign policy.

Although Barrow died shortly thereafter, his vision lived on and helped impel the region towards closer unity.

CUBA

One of the geo-political issues in the Caribbean that Mr Barrow had to immediately deal with was Cuba. Ever since the Cuban Revolution in 1959 and the nationalisation programme instituted by the Government of Fidel Castro, the US had been hostile to it. The US instituted an economic embargo in 1960 which effectively forced Cuba to turn to the Soviet Union for economic assistance.

In 1961 the US launched the disastrous Bay of Pigs invasion and by October 1962 the Caribbean had become the major theatre of the Cold War struggle as the Cuban Missile Crisis took the world to the brink of a nuclear war. Also in 1962, at the behest of the US Government, the Eighth Meeting of Consultation of Ministers of Foreign Affairs under the Inter-American Treaty of Reciprocal Assistance (the Rio Treaty) took a decision to exclude Cuba from participation in the Organisation of American States.

It was this tense situation that Mr Barrow confronted upon Independence in 1966. After joining the OAS in 1967 he was faced with the choice of possibly offending a major economic partner and friend, not to mention superpower, by not toeing the American line on Cuba, and standing up for what he believed to be right. In keeping with its avowed policy of being 'friends of all, satellites of none', he sought to keep maximum room for manoeuvre in the hemisphere and the Caribbean in particular.

Mr Barrow's approach to Cuba was pragmatic. He made it known publicly that he would not support any move to have Cuba re-integrated into the OAS until such time as it publicly committed itself to 'honour and uphold the principle of non-interference in the affairs of other states'. His Government also did not seek initially to establish diplomatic relations with Cuba. At the same time, Mr Barrow considered that it might be useful to explore cautiously the possibilities of trade and functional cooperation with Cuba, especially since Barbados, acting through the British Embassy, had for some time been helping older Barbadian immigrants to Cuba to resettle in Barbados.

From the late 1960s, the Government of Barbados acting mainly through the High Commissioner in Ottawa along with the Permanent Representative to the UN, quietly initiated an ongoing dialogue with representatives of the Cuban Government. In 1971, the two governments agreed to begin low level trade and agricultural exchanges. In October of that year, a special mission from Barbados visited Cuba which opened up discussions on future cooperation in agriculture and trade. The Cubans, in return, sent a technical mission to Barbados in 1972, primarily to look at Barbados' achievements in sugar cane technology.

Despite these encouraging signs, Mr Barrow still moved cautiously. In early 1972, the Cabinet decided that Barbados would make no immediate unilateral move to establish diplomatic or consular relations with Cuba, but that Barbadian diplomats should continue to hold informal consultations with their Cuban counterparts on the facilitation of Barbadian nationals in Cuba, on trade and technical cooperation and other areas of common interest.

Then later in 1972 came what many observers of hemispheric affairs saw as a diplomatic bombshell: the announcement of the intention of the prime ministers of the four independent Caribbean countries – Barbados, Guyana, Jamaica, and Trinidad and Tobago – to establish diplomatic or economic relations with Cuba. At this time the only countries in the hemisphere that had diplomatic relations with Cuba were Canada, Chile and Mexico.

The announcement came at what turned out to be one of the truly historic Heads of Government Conferences, the seventh one, held in Chaguaramas, Trinidad in October 1972. The same Conference that agreed to the establishment of CARICOM. It is worth reproducing the statement in full, since it is one of the seminal documents of Caribbean diplomacy:

"The Prime Ministers of Barbados, Guyana, Jamaica, and Trinidad and Tobago, meeting together during the Heads of Government Conference at Chaguaramas, have considered the state of their relations with the Government of Cuba and the obligations which the OAS has sought to impose upon its members in regard to relations with that Government; and to make the following statement:

(1)   The independent English-speaking Caribbean states, exercising their sovereign right to enter into relations with any other sovereign state and pursuing their determination to seek regional solidarity and to achieve meaningful and comprehensive economic cooperation amongst all Caribbean countries will seek the early establishment of relations with Cuba, whether economic, diplomatic or both.

(2)   To this end, the independent English-speaking Caribbean states will act together on the basis of agreed approaches."

Note, however, the two notes of caution, both of which were introduced by Mr Barrow. He insisted that the proposed relations with Cuba might be *diplomatic or economic*, thereby leaving himself some wriggle room in view of his Cabinet's decision earlier that year not to proceed with diplomatic relations for the time being. He was also careful to ensure that the four countries would act together on the basis of agreed approaches.

In any event, although the reaction of the US was one of disapproval, it was not hostile. The four countries proceeded to establish diplomatic relations with Cuba simultaneously on 8 December 1972.

This was an early triumph for CARICOM coordination of foreign policy, one that would prove hard to replicate later on in similar international circumstances. Barbados would continue to develop cooperative relations with Cuba as well as let its position of principle be known in international forums.

CONCLUSION

Mr Barrow not only crafted a successful foreign policy appropriate to a small island state like Barbados; he also set a tone of caution and pragmatism that would endure through the several changes of government that would follow. At the same time, he spoke out frankly whenever he determined that the interests of Barbados were threatened. This, too, he would pass on to his successors in office.

Mr Barrow truly believed that Barbados should be *'friends of all, satellites of none'*.

Friends of all; satellites of none

Address to the United Nations, on the occasion of the admission of Barbados to membership of the UN, December 1966.

Mr President,
Mr Secretary General,
Distinguished Delegates,

Humility must be the most appropriate feeling for the leader of a state admitted to membership of this illustrious assembly on the basis of sovereign equality.

The people of Barbados, even before their emergence into nationhood, have always tried, not without some success, to arrange their affairs in accordance with the principles of this Charter to which I have, in their name, subscribed their unstinted allegiance. Despite the limitation of their territory, the paucity of their numbers, the slenderness of their resources, the inhibiting atmosphere of three centuries of colonialism, they have provided for themselves stable political institutions and economic activities which will better stimulate their future development.

In their name, we wish to thank the governments of the Argentine, Britain, New Zealand, Nigeria and Uganda for their prompt and generous sponsorship of our country. We also thank the distinguished delegates here assembled for the warm and courteous greeting accorded to our delegation. We should like to record our profound appreciation to all the distinguished members of the Security Council for the alacrity with which they processed our application to make it possible for us to secure membership in the same year that we achieved nationhood.

The people of Barbados do not draw a dividing line between their internal affairs and their foreign policy. They strive in their domestic arrangements to create a just society for themselves. In their Constitution, they affirm respect for the Rule of Law; they also declare their intention to establish and maintain the kind of society which enables each citizen, to the full extent of his capacity, to play his part in the national life; they further resolve that their economic system, as it develops, must be equitably administered and enjoyed and that undeviating recognition should be paid to ability, integrity and merit.

In thus charting our domestic course, we can have no interest in a foreign policy which contradicts our national goals. On the contrary, we will support genuine efforts at world peace because our society is stable. We will strenuously assist the uprooting of vestigial imperialisms because our institutions are free. We will press for the rapid economic growth of all underdeveloped countries because we are busily engaged in building up our own. *In fine*, our foreign and domestic policies are the obverse and reverse sides of a single coin.

We have devised the kind of foreign policy which is consistent with our national situation and which is also based on the current realities of international politics.

We have no quarrels to pursue and we particularly insist that we do not regard any member states as our natural opponent. We shall not involve ourselves in sterile ideological wranglings because we are exponents not of the diplomacy of power, but of the diplomacy of peace and prosperity. We will not regard any great power as necessarily right in a given dispute unless we are convinced of this, yet at the same time we will not view the great powers with perennial suspicion merely on account of their size, their wealth, or their nuclear potential. We will be friends of all, satellites of none.

A disquieting feature of the world situation is the frequent allusion made to the alleged proliferation of small states in this Assembly. Attempts are made from time to time to devise schemes to give the larger countries more voting power in the Assembly. The principle of 'one state one vote' whereby all member states are equal under the Charter, is becoming unfashionable and the proponents of the new theory wish to render some states more equal than others.

The General Assembly should know that the Barbados Delegation will not support any formula based on such a preposterous bit of special pleading. To accept it even for the narrow purposes of discussion at any time, would be to connive at the negation of democratic principle. The whole basis on which this organisation rests, is that of equal sovereignty. If size, wealth or capacity to destroy mankind were the basis for membership, the organisation would not exist in its present form and its Security Council would consist of a mere handful of mutually suspicious countries.

It seems strange to small countries to find their equality challenged by these mutterings of discontent with the form of the Charter. Perhaps the mightier nations genuinely fear that their influence will be swamped in the majority of votes now recorded in this Assembly. This fear can only be real if the mighty are pursuing aims inimical to the interests of the smaller ones. So long as their own national interests and their international commitments can be identified with those of the small countries, they have no reason to fear the admission of small states to this Assembly. Democratic countries owe the stability of their institutions to the participation of the masses in the political life of their countries. In like manner, the emergence of small states into full sovereignty increases the chances of peace.

Even in this distinguished Assembly, it is not always, or not fully, appreciated that the tensions of the cold war have been lessened by the mere existence of nearly forty newly independent states in Africa, Asia and the Caribbean. United Nations opinion is now more often to be found in Delhi, Addis Ababa and Port-of-Spain than it is in London, Moscow and Washington. No longer is there that unique and frightening confrontation of rival power blocs staring and scuffling with each other in the ruins of their respective policies. The independent countries of Africa, Asia, the Caribbean and the other uncommitted countries are making, by their existence alone, an outstanding contribution to international stability.

If the larger countries wish to earn or to retain the confidence and respect of small countries, there will have to be a rapid change of values. They must no longer enjoy squatters' rights in the volume and arrangement of world trade. New concepts of distribution and exchange will have to be worked out, because emergent countries will no longer be content to be hewers of wood and drawers of water while the wealth of the world flows past them into the coffers of some twenty countries.

In a world population of some 2,400,000,000, only 375,000,000 (or slightly less than one-sixth) enjoy the best standards of living. In another segment of the world population, some 425,000,000 (or slightly more than one-sixth) enjoy fairly tolerable standards of living. The remainder of mankind, some 1,600,000,000 souls in Asia, Africa, South Eastern Europe, Latin America and the Caribbean, sweat out their lives in unremitting poverty, without the tools of modern production, with meagre educational facilities, with little expertise in the arts of public administration, with driblets of financial and technical assistance, with a population explosion and with a cataract of gratuitous advice on how to govern themselves.

The stark reality of the international situation is not the possibility of nuclear destruction, but the certainty of dissolution if this mass misery continues beyond this current decade. When 65 per cent of the world's population can enjoy only 19 per cent of the world's wealth, a diplomacy based on power cannot withstand the explosive anger of upheaval based on poverty. Two-thirds of the world's people do not fear a nuclear holocaust because they literally have nothing to live for. The irony of their situation is that they hold the key to the world's prosperity, but that the doors are bolted against them by the participants of prosperity.

This is the background, distinguished delegates, against which my small country enters upon its international obligations. It belongs to the submerged two-thirds of the world. It sees no hope for itself or for its companions in misery except in the efforts made in this Assembly to work out with speed, the new conditions of human progress. The Barbados delegation pays its tribute to the specialised agencies of this body for the solid contribution made both in the past and now, to human well-being in many parts of the globe. But this delegation nevertheless feels that the eradication of world poverty is a function which cannot be discharged by delegation, but must engage the United Nations at their highest levels.

The obligation laid on the Security Council to preserve world peace ought to be amplified by an equally solemn commitment to prevent world poverty. It is not a coincidence that the explosive areas of the world are precisely those areas in which ignorance and poverty most abound.

Mr President,

Mr Secretary-General

Distinguished Delegates,

The people of Barbados will support and uphold the efforts of this organisation to the limit of their moral and physical resources and would wish to record their profound gratitude to the Assembly for this first great privilege of expressing their hopes and aspirations for the unity and progress of mankind. They could best sum up their attitude to this moment of their history in the words of Mr 'Valiant for Truth', an interesting character in John Bunyan's famous book:

'Though with much difficulty I have got hither,
'Yet I do not repent me of the trouble I have taken.'

AT THE UNITED NATIONS

(L to R) With Oliver Jackman, Frank Walcott, Val McComie, Waldo Waldron-Ramsay

Addressing the UN General Assembly

His Ideology

Oliver Jackman

The Harrisonian Tribute, 1987

Everybody who knew Errol felt that they knew him well. Nearly all felt that only they knew "the true Errol Barrow". The sincerest tributes to him began long before his shocking death. They are to be found in the "inside stories" thousands of people have been telling about him for years.

Everybody has his or her own very personal, totally authentic, Errol Barrow story, and future historians are going to go out of their minds as they try to grapple with the volume of contrast and paradox that awaits them. That is the way it is with heroes: they really are several times larger than what you and I call life, large enough that all who come into contact with them can get a piece of them quiet ample enough to make a full-size personal legend.

Proteus of Greek mythology had nearly all the marking of a master politician. Like all politicians, he, "knew all things past, present, and future", like all master politicians he had the capacity to transform himself into anything he chose, a tiger, a tree, fire, a serpent, what you will. He had, however, one failing, which was to get him to tell anything from his wide store of knowledge you had to catch him during his midday nap in his cave and hold on to him very tight. That is not an advantage in politics.

Errol was a protean man. He was a successful and brilliant lawyer who publicly and privately maintained that anybody in their right senses ought to stay as far as possible from lawyers. He was a politician who never hid his contempt for politicians. (Of course, he is now being described as a "statesman", that is, a successful politician who dies in office.)

He was an aristocrat and democrat, third-worlder and monarchist, dilettante and scholar, grass-roots man and internationalist. Introvert and extrovert, street fighter and suave diplomat. And he shifted from role to role, from pole to pole, with the silky smoothness of the finely tuned German driving machines he loved to drive. He wore Bally shoes and Pierre Cardin shirts, drank mature rums and scotches, filled his home with the best writers and artists and scholars and sportsmen and politicians, and bitterly despised the second-rate and pretentious.

However, unlike the classic aristocrat, he was convinced that everyone else, if given the chance could be an aristocrat. It is possible that, despite his erudition and his enormous worldly sophistication, this was his only ideology.

My late mother, who had no truck with politics and little time for politicians when they were plying their wares, considered that there were really only four major events in her long life (from 1902 to 1985): two world wars, the riots of 1937, and the introduction of free secondary education in Barbados in 1961, "Barrow freed the people", she would say; and that was the beginning and end of her politics.

Thenceforward, in her view, Errol could do no wrong, having done such a great right. She would not have been accepted as a professor in any political science faculty on that basis, but the faculty may have been the losers. For Errol Barrow, despite his fulminations (and he was a world-class fulminator) happily got a number of fundamental things right in his political career.

The man who unforgettably termed the Civil Service *"an army of occupation"*, left the Service largely alone, and certainly made no systematic effort to corrupt it. The man who appeared determined to arrogate to himself near-dictatorial powers over both the judicial service and the public service, and lost an election largely because of it, used those powers to help create a judicial bench that must be one of the most respected and independent in the entire Third World.

Most of all Errol gave Barbadian democracy flesh by a series of apparently inconsequential acts and gestures. I recall hearing when in Canada that a former chauffeur of the High Commission had been the chauffeur of a minister in the Barrow Administration. I asked the minister, when he was on a visit to Ottawa whether this was true and he was apoplectic: *"Chauffeur? Chauffeur? Are you crazy? How could I have a chauffeur when the Prime Minister doesn't have one?"*

Of course, the Prime Minister ought to have a chauffeur, as anyone who has ever been his passenger will attest; and he did eventually get one. But his famous reluctance to take on the trappings of high office was crucial to what he was address in his renowned "mirror image" speech. If a Prime Minister can drive his own car, live in a modest residence, shop at the supermarket like everybody else, stop and talk in the street to anybody and everybody who wants to talk to him, and not only during election campaigns, and all without losing 'dignity' or diminishing his 'prestige', then perhaps we ought to re-examine some of our ideas about the nature of dignity and prestige.

More important, if one Prime Minister can do it, all who come after had better learn to do it too.

But he understood the uses of power perfectly well. A physically robust friend of mine who was chairman of a quasi-governmental corporation was seen in the courtyard of Government Headquarters some years ago, white and shaking like a leaf. Since he had previously been black, an acquaintance asked him what the matter was. It seems that he had had a disagreement with Mr Barrow, in whose portfolio the corporation fell, and had been on the receiving end of a particularly forceful explication of the difference between the Prime Minister and a corporation chairman.

I was luckier in my disagreements with him which fortunately were few and because of my diplomatic postings were mostly by telex and telephone. After one such, where for a number of reasons my view was allowed to prevail over his, he visited New York where I was posted, and invited my wife and me to dinner followed by a jazz concert. He was at his convivial best, but the subject of our disagreement, which was inescapably topical and hung obsessively in the forefront of my mind, was never once mentioned during the several hours we spent together. It took me many years to realise that the dinner and the jazz and the silence were all the acknowledgement I would ever get that I had been 'right' and he had been 'wrong'. On reflection, Dipper, I would say that it was really quite enough.

Heroes give the impression that they have invented themselves. It isn't true. Errol didn't invent himself, and didn't spring fully-grown out of the things of Zeus. He was Barbadian to the very marrow. If he took upon himself the task of inventing a Barbados capable of surviving the twentieth century and soldiering on into the twenty-first, he took his inspiration from deep down within his Barbadian psyche. His Caribbean vision, limitations and all, was the vision of a Barbadian, and legitimately so.

Errol was loved, because of the way he used the power we gave him. Unlike so many of his contemporaries, he demonstrated to his compatriots over the years that power could be used to strengthen rather than threaten. He was one of the best, and he was our boy.

AT THE WHITE HOUSE

With US President Lynden B Johnson at the White House

With the US President and their spouses

Visit to the White House

Remarks at the White House, 11 September 1968

President Lyndon B. Johnson spoke on the South Lawn at the White House where Prime Minister Barrow was given a formal welcome with full military honours. The Prime Minister responded as follows:

Mr President, I should like to say how deeply honoured we are that you, without doubt the busiest man in the world, should have time to invite the head of a government of one of the smallest independent countries in the Western Hemisphere to your great Capital, which has been so appropriately named after the first great President of the United States.

I should like to say that in accepting your kind invitation, I thought it was only fitting and proper that the head of the government of the only country which the first President of the United States visited outside of the North American mainland, when over 200 years ago young George Washington spent 4 or 5 months in our salubrious climate, should return the compliment. But I hope, sir, that when you have laid down the honours of office, that we will not be saying that George Washington was the only president of the United States to visit Barbados.

It is time that we had another person who had occupied this high office visiting our country. After your long and strenuous term I shall formalise what I am doing informally in public today and invite you to come and emulate the example set by your great predecessor.

Again, Mr President, we are not unmindful of that great honour and I look forward to very cordial discussions with

you on a variety of topics, as I look forward to the continued
cordial relations between our two countries. I thank you.

Dinner Toasts of the President and Prime Minister Barrow of
Barbados held in the Rose Garden.

Toast by President Lyndon B. Johnson: The Prime Minister reminded
us this morning that George Washington travelled to Barbados in 1751
and he was returning his visit. George Washington was so delighted by
what he found in Barbados in 1751 that he wrote a journal about his
visit. I am not making any suggestions, Mr Prime Minister, and I hope
you don't have your pen and pencil with you, but that little book did
great things for our two nations.

In fact, Mr Prime Minister, we may say that the Father of our Country
was really the father of your tourist trade. Barbados has become the
favourite island under the sun for many Americans. They are called by
beauty and tranquillity. They go there to seek a rest with you, to refresh
their spirits with the joys of nature, and perhaps to recover what they
may have lost in the scramble of modern life in the United States.

Mr Prime Minister, we are very grateful to you and your people for
never failing us in our human needs, for always sending us home happier
and wiser from even the briefest visit with you. As I have told your lady
this evening, I look forward with pleasurable anticipation to accepting
the kind invitation you tendered us earlier today. But this, my friends, is
still only the Barbados of the travel folder. I should like to remind you
all that there is still another Barbados.

There are other reasons for gratitude and friendship between our
two countries. There is the Barbados that our fathers turned to when
they were framing our Declaration of Independence and the Constitution
of our country. Barbados had its own Declaration of Rights as early as
the year 1651 and we, Americans were very grateful and very proud
then to have drawn upon it in our own documents.

There is the Barbados that sent a message across the seas in the first
dark hours of World War II "Go ahead Britain" that message said,
"Barbados is behind you." It was a mighty big statement from a mighty
little country. But in those days no one laughed. Great Britain was a

very little island, too, then. The British people were cheered to know that Barbados stood with them in that trying period against the ugly head of aggression that had reared itself.

They cheered again when the message was followed by a man from Barbados who came to fight with them in the Royal Air Force. That man has been a great champion of freedom ever since. He is our very special guest this evening, the distinguished Prime Minister of Barbados. There is the Barbados, too, that President John F. Kennedy must have had in mind when once he spoke of the role and the duties of small nations in the world in which we live.

President Kennedy said, "No nation, large or small, can be indifferent to the fate of others, near or far." He recalled the testimony of history and went on to say, "All the world owes much to the little 'five feet high' nations. The greatest art of the world was the work of little nations. The most enduring literature of the world came from little nations. The heroic deeds that thrill humanity through generations were the deeds of little nations fighting for their freedom. And, oh, yes, the salvation of mankind came through a little nation."

I thought of those words last night, Mr Prime Minister, when I went across the street to speak to some of my dear friends of the B'nai B'rith, who are the people and the friends of another little nation, Israel. I also thought of you and your people, sir, because I am proud to know that you share my hopes in this Nation's purpose. You share our urgent and genuine desire to work with every nation every nation large or small for just one thing: the peace and the security of human beings.

It is just as I said last night, we seek a world, we in America seek a world where neighbours are at each other's side and not at each other's throat. We act in the belief that no nation, large or small, can or should turn its back on another nation that may be the victim or may be unfortunate enough to be assaulted by aggression. We do not believe from all that we have learned through the years, at such painful cost, that there is ever any such thing, Mr Prime Minister, as harmless aggression, anywhere or any time.

At all times, we Americans believe that the smallest and the most distant of nations, without ever thinking for a moment that we are the world's policeman we still believe that all nations have a claim on

American concern and American conscience. Our concern as Americans throughout the years is a long and honoured one. It is just as your visitor, George Washington, said, more than 2 centuries ago, "It is mankind's cause."

We are concerned only that mankind lives free and mankind lives without fear, governed only by the independent human spirit. And we want to help all mankind in that quest, although in helping them we are frequently misunderstood at home and abroad.

Barbados is helping us find the way. Your people, sir, have preserved the traditions of a parliamentary democracy and justice now for 3 centuries. Within a few days of winning independence, you, sir, declared your intention to work unsparingly for peace by joining the United Nations and doing your bit in that great forum.

You have become, in a very short time, a very valued member of the Organisation of American States. Next year the ties between our two nations will be strengthened again when we join as partners in one of the most ambitious studies ever undertaken of our air and our ocean environment. The United States will assign at least eight research ships and a fleet of scientific aircraft numbering more than 20 that will have its survey headquarters where George Washington went to enjoy the sun.

Other nations are being invited to join in that daring and important project. We expect it to contribute greatly to the World Weather Watch program and to the world's knowledge of the waters and the atmosphere, especially of the Caribbean area.

Prime Minister Barrow responded as follows:

I can imagine the feeling of some official of the United States Government more than a century ago when he was called upon to move the vote of thanks for the Gettysburg Address. I fear as great a sense of inadequacy on this occasion as the unknown, unsung citizen of the United States may have felt when he was called upon to speak after that other great President of the United States had spoken.

This sense of inadequacy could only be matched by one of the disciples, who was asked to deliver a homily after the

Sermon on the Mount. Without in any way entering into or descending into the political arena on the local scene, I am a disciple of President Lincoln. I am a disciple of Jefferson. I am a disciple of President Kennedy and I am an unrelenting disciple of Lyndon B. Johnson.

I have come to appreciate the President of the United States more since I have been, unfortunately, thrust into the position of being Chairman of the Cabinet of Barbados and leader of the government of my country, than when I was deputy leader of the opposition. I have never had the good fortune to be a Senate majority leader, but since I have been leader of the Government of Barbados, I have collected a massive file marked "Suggestions on How to Run a Government." I am sure that President Johnson has a library full of suggestions on how to run a government.

I wish the President of the United States to know that although the country over whose destiny I have the good fortune – and the misfortune at the same time from my personal point of view – to preside, that I understand the problems of someone who is President of the greatest nation on earth and the greatest democratic force that exists in the universe today.

I entirely sympathise with him, especially now that he has decided to lay down the burdens of office. As a matter of fact, 6 months after I became Premier of Barbados, I nearly made a similar decision. I am not surprised that after 6 years he feels that he has had enough, because he has been engaged on the field of political battle for almost the whole of my life span and I am a novice yet in this field myself.

I should like to say that I appreciate, Mr President, all of the kind things you have said about my country. I sat at a gathering just on Saturday evening which detained and postponed my visit to the United States by 24 hours. One of our largest business firms was celebrating its centennial. I said there were too many people who behaved as if every morning was the beginning of creation. What we need in the modern world is a sense of history.

Sir Winston Churchill, when he was delivering a lecture some years ago on the national heritage, said that "If you want to go forward, you have to be able to look back."

I wish to say here this evening that it should be the aim of every democratic society and every democratic government in this Western Hemisphere of ours to have as its motto that if you want the people to look back – and if you do not want them to look back in anger – you have to give them something to look forward to.

This paraphrase, however you may call it, of Sir Winston Churchill's remarks, you will excuse, I am sure. But the United States is a country which is in the throes of social and economic revolution. I think that if the Government of the United States is going to achieve the great ideals which President Lincoln so much desired to be consummated and did not succeed in seeing consummated in his lifetime, that this society will have to give all the people of all races, of all colours, and all religions something to look forward to and then they will be able to look back with pride.

This is what we are trying to do in our small community. This is what I am satisfied, from my examination, my continued interest in the developments of this country that the President of the United States has been striving throughout his tenure of office to do. I hope that President Johnson will not be the last great President of the United States, and whoever is elected to this high office will carry on the great traditions which have been fostered and developed by his predecessors in office and so ably carried out and continued by him.

Mr President, I should like to say again that we in Barbados appreciate the honour which you have bestowed not on me, but on our country, on our citizens, those who have stayed at home and those who have immigrated abroad.

I think I mentioned to you this morning, Mr President, that we have more Barbadians living outside of Barbados than we have living inside of Barbados. So, although geographically we are a country with 106,000 acres and I understand you have 475,000 acres of land which can be used for urban renewal we cannot bring some of your land to Barbados, but we can send some of our Barbadians to your land.

I should like to express my appreciation for the liberalisation of the policies for the Western Hemisphere countries, which liberalisation has taken place within your regime.

No one can quantify or assess accurately what this has done to give hope to the teeming hundreds of thousands of people who are living in the developing countries.

We look forward to the continued cooperation, and the continued good will of the people of this country.

Early Signs of Leadership

Carl E. Jackman

The Harrisonian Tribute, 1987

Errol and I were the same age, had been exact contemporaries at school, Harrison College, and had always been good friends. From his early youth he was prepared to fight for his principles, never afraid to question authority. He slid naturally into a leadership position.

Early challenges to the bigger boys on the Fifth Eleven pitch at school, and as a fourth-former for membership of the Acton Club (a prestigious history club then attended by sixth-formers only) and to Prefects on matters affecting the rights of the Middle School Community, whilst possibly embarrassing to his friends who preferred to remain faceless and unknown to those in authority, impressed us that he would one day be a politician.

Those close to him had no doubt about it. He spoke often and with admiration of his uncle Dr O'Neal, one of the early speakers in Barbados for the rights of the masses, and indicated clearly that he wished to follow in his footsteps. He lived near the uncle of one of his contemporaries in the Sixth Form, Mr C.L. (Crissy) Braithwaite, a politician who frequently lectured him on the needs of the masses.

The closest spell of friendship between Errol and me took place during our days in the Classical section of the Sixth Form. Carlyle Burton, Errol and I both joined this august body at the same time; august because we found scholarly giants in the Upper Sixth, O.R. Marshall, T.P.B. Payne, St Elmo Thompson, Kenneth Stuart, H.A. Cuffley, Johnnie Braithwaite, Cameron Tudor, Val McComie, and Fred Cozier. The subsequent success of these men gives us an idea of the type of brains with which we were competing, just within the Classics Section. All the individuals in this group have done well and their combined influence has sometimes been surprisingly overwhelming.

The first of that group, which got on so well together, spending holidays and week-ends in each other's company, is now dead and must be a solemn reminder to the rest of us that we are in the waiting-room and that our flights can be called at any time. Errol was a common friend to the whole group, largely, I think, because of his geographical location. His mother's house was just outside the gates of Harrison College and we all had to pass it in coming to or going from school and hence it became a place where we 'limed' from time to time.

I once attended a meeting of a University "*Appraisal*" Committee, a select group of West Indian Ministers of Government and Administrators who were forging out a new structure for the University of the West Indies. It was a matter of great pride to find that out of some 50 persons gathered together from all over the West Indies to chart the future of our regional university, seven had received a vital portion of their education in the same place and at the same time.

Participating in that meeting were Errol (the Premier), Fred Crozier, the Permanent Secretary in his Ministry, Cameron Tudor, the Minister of Education, Carlyle Burton, the Permanent Secretary in his Ministry, and representing the University of the West Indies, O. Roy Marshall, Kenneth Stuart and myself.

The end of our school careers coincided with the beginning of the Second World War. Errol was accepted for the Royal Air Force and went off to train. He had a brilliant war service as a navigator and we kept up a fairly regular correspondence during that period. After the end of the war he stayed on in England to study, first to do a degree in Economics and then to read for the Bar.

In England, we met again when I went up to do postgraduate work, and we renewed our friendship; he was by then married with a family and his passion to see an end to injustice had increased in intensity.

His subsequent return to Barbados and his career in Law and in politics are a matter of public record. I merely want to bring out his willingness to defend or fight for the principles of those unable to fight for themselves, his interest in the betterment of the condition of the people of Barbados and his outspokenness all started when he was a small boy at school and that if there is any such thing as destiny, this was his destiny.

I wish on behalf of his schoolmates and friends, to whom he was still known by his schoolboy soubriquet of 'Dipper', a name derived from a famous English wicket-keeper of whom Errol patterned his own wicket-keeping, to express our satisfaction and pride at his illustrious career and to indicate the deep honour which he had bought to our group of whom he was truly *primus interpares*, the best known and most famed of a not undistinguished group.

The Aviator

Ian Dev. Archer

I joined the Barbados Civil Service in 1964 as a junior administrative officer and was assigned to the Office of the Premier, Mr Errol Walton Barrow. In addition to his other Ministerial responsibilities, Mr Barrow was, at the time, the Minister responsible for Civil Aviation.

It is of interest to note that in every Administration headed by him, both before and after Barbados' Independence, Mr Barrow was always the Minister responsible for Civil Aviation. He clearly was not prepared to entrust this subject, in which he was deeply interested, to anyone. This abiding interest in aviation matters was probably due, in part, to his experience as a RAF aviator during World War II.

Since Barbados was not responsible for external affairs matters prior to its Independence, Barbadian civil servants, at that time, had little or no experience in dealing with the international aspects of civil aviation. For example, up to 1966, the air services agreements which permitted foreign airlines to operate to and from Barbados were negotiated and concluded with the governments of these airlines by UK civil servants resident in London.

This fact prompted Mr Barrow, in the period leading up to Independence, to have arrangements put in place which were designed to ensure that a cadre of civil servants, including myself, would be trained in the international aspects of civil aviation.

On the occasion of the admission of Barbados to membership of the United Nations, Prime Minister Barrow addressed the General Assembly in December, 1966 and declared, famously, that an Independent Barbados *"will be friends of all and satellites of none"*. I have no doubt there were sceptics, both inside and outside Barbados, who may have dismissed that declaration as mere political rhetoric.

They were soon to discover that Mr Barrow practiced what he preached.

Having joined the UN, Barbados became a member of many of its Specialised Agencies, including the International Civil Aviation Organisation (ICAO). And as a member of ICAO, Barbados participated in a conference to draft a multinational treaty designed to bring to an end the menacing problem of aircraft high-jacking. At the conference, the USA and its European allies as well as South Africa were insisting that the treaty should include a clause which would provide that any state which became a party to the treaty would automatically be considered as having entered into extradition treaties with all the other states which ratified the treaty.

This discussion was taking place at a time when the laws of apartheid still applied in South Africa. The African states at the conference, opposed to the apartheid regime, made it clear that they could not agree to such a clause. They pointed out that the provision would force an African state to return to South Africa any freedom fighter who, in an effort to flee from the dreaded apartheid system, had high-jacked an aircraft which had landed in that African state. Barbados was one of the delegations which supported this African position, much to the chagrin of the US delegation. The conference was in deadlock and, therefore, the proposed treaty was in jeopardy.

Although I was the Barbados delegate I was not aware that the US delegation had requested the US State Department to attempt to persuade the Government of Barbados to instruct me to support the US sponsored clause. Several months later I discovered that when the US request was referred to Mr Barrow his response was simple, *"If the Barbados delegate needed instructions with regard to this matter he would have asked for them."* Mr Barrow was sending the clear message that his *"satellites of none"* position was not mere rhetoric. The controversial US sponsored clause was subsequently withdrawn and the treaty concluded.

The next occasion, of which I am aware, when Mr Barrow flexed Barbados' "sovereignty muscles" in civil aviation matters occurred when American Airlines applied for a licence to operate to Barbados. Understandably, the tourism officials were eager to have this well-known airline commence air services from the USA. However, while the Barbados authorities were processing the application, Mr Barrow, as Minister responsible for Aviation, was informed that Caribbean Airways, the airline designated by the Barbados Government, under the Barbados/ USA Air Services Agreement, was refused permission by the US Aviation Authorities to operate to the USA. The reason given for this decision was that Caribbean Airways was "not effectively controlled" by the Government of Barbados.

The US authorities incorrectly contended that Laker Airways, a UK airline and the minority shareholder in Caribbean Airways, was in "effective control" of Caribbean Airways because all the aircraft that the Airline was operating were on lease from Laker Airways and the general manager of Caribbean Airlines was a former employee of Laker Airways. This argument was without merit since the Barbados Government owned 51 per cent of the shareholding of the airline company and appointed the Chairman and the majority of the Directors of the Airline's Board, which was responsible for directing the affairs of the Airline.

In these troubling circumstances, a 'quiet word' was passed to the Barbados Air Transport Licensing Authority that, as far as the Minister responsible for Aviation was concerned, the Authority could "take its time" in processing the application of American Airlines. As a consequence, there was a delay in granting the required licence to American Airlines. This delay was of great concern to our tourism officials. So much so, the then Minister of Tourism sought a meeting with the Prime Minister and at the meeting the Minister expressed his strong concern that the delay in granting permission for American Airlines to operate to Barbados could severely damage the efforts of Barbados to attract more tourists from the US. Mr Barrow's calm response was that *"Barbados would not sell itself for the American dollar"*.

As was intended, the message that Barbados was prepared to play 'hard ball', got through to the US Aviation Authorities and, shortly thereafter, Caribbean Airways was granted its licence to operate to the USA. This would not have occurred except for the steely resolve of Mr Barrow. The application by American Airlines was then speedily dealt with and the Airline was authorised to begin its services to Barbados.

Mr Barrow could also be the consummate, persuasive diplomat. He played this role admirably during the discussions leading to the establishment of the original structure of LIAT (1974) Ltd., the regional airline.

In August 1974, Court Line the British airline which owned Leeward Islands Air Transport (LIAT) Ltd, was declared bankrupt and its subsidiary company LIAT was placed into the hands of a liquidator. That month representatives of the Governments of the Leeward and Windward Islands held an emergency meeting in Antigua and Barbuda and decided, among other things, to invite other regional governments to join them in an effort to ensure that the air services within the region, then provided by LIAT, would not come to an abrupt halt. The Governments of Barbados, Guyana, Jamaica and Trinidad and Tobago accepted the invitation and a series of Ministerial Meetings were held at which the formal structure of a new company, LIAT (1974) Ltd., was discussed. Mr Barrow was the Barbados representative at these meetings and as a committed regionalist urged his ministerial colleagues to support his view that the structure of the new airline should be that of a genuine multinational company owned by regional governments.

The then Premier of Antigua and Barbuda chaired the initial meetings of the Ministerial Committee. However, in early 1975 the Ministers invited Mr Barrow to assume the Chairmanship and under his astute guidance Guyana, Jamaica and Trinidad and Tobago not only agreed to become shareholders of LIAT (1974) Ltd., but they, as well as the other participating Governments, embraced Mr Barrow's proposal that no Government should have a controlling or dominant interest in this new regional airline. Accordingly, in 1975, none of the eleven shareholder Governments of LIAT (1974) Ltd. acquired more than 19 per cent of the airline's shares.

It is important to note that in 1975 no air services were being provided by LIAT to either Guyana or to Jamaica, and there was little likelihood that the "new LIAT" would provide such services in the near future. Notwithstanding these facts, the Governments of these two states not only became shareholders of LIAT (1974) Ltd., but they also agreed to join the other shareholder governments in guaranteeing a loan from the Caribbean Development Bank to the new airline.

I am of the firm belief that Mr Barrow's strong advocacy, as Chairman of the LIAT Ministerial Committee, for the establishment by the governments of the region of a regionally owned multinational airline to operate intra-regional air services, played a significant part in persuading the Governments of Guyana and Jamaica to become full shareholder-partners in LIAT (1974) Ltd.

As many would know, there was another side to Mr Barrow's personality. He would sometimes use what I describe as intemperate language in his criticisms of individuals and institutions. An example of this is his infamous accusation that the Civil Service was *"an army of occupation"* made at a Labour Day rally organised by the Barbados Workers Union. That day being a Bank Holiday, I was at home and having listened to Mr Barrow's speech on the radio, I made a promise to myself that at an appropriate time I would take him up on what I thought was his unjustified criticism of civil servants.

The opportunity I was waiting for presented itself a few years later at a CARICOM Heads of Governments Conference in Jamaica. I was a member of the Barbados delegation and at the end of each working day at the Conference the Barbados delegates assembled in the Prime Minister's hotel suite for a debriefing session. One evening, I waited until all the other delegates had departed and, having been fortified by a few drinks, I told the Prime Minister that his speech labelling all civil servants as *"an army of occupation"* was not only manifestly inaccurate but that it caused deep hurt to the many dedicated and committed civil servants of which I was certain he was aware. I was not prepared for the response I got. Mr Barrow just looked at me, smiled and responded with a well-known proverb *"Who the cap fits, let him draw the string"* (meaning that the person who knows he is guilty about something will react accordingly). I could only smile and meekly take my leave, resolving never to raise the matter again.

As Permanent Secretary in the Ministry responsible for Aviation, I met with Mr Barrow in his office on the 31 May 1987, to discuss whether Barbados should put forward a candidate for the post of Secretary

General of the International Civil Aviation Organisation. After a brief discussion Mr Barrow suggested that both of us should think about the matter overnight and we should meet the following day for further discussions. That meeting never took place because Mr Barrow departed the next day.

THE CARIBBEAN MAN

With Dr Eric Williams, Prime Minister of Trinidad and Tobago

With Forbes Burnham, Prime Minister of Guyana

With Michael Manley, Prime Minister of Jamaica

Heads of Governments and officials at the signing of the CARIFTA agreement in 1968. From right to left: (2nd) George Price of Belize, (3rd) Milton Cato of St Vincent, (4th) Eric Williams of Trinidad and Tobago, (5th) John Compton of St Lucia, (6th) William Bramble of Montserrat, (7th) Eric Gairy of Grenada, (8th) Errol Barrow of Barbados, (9th) Paul Southwell of St Kitts, (10th) Forbes Burnham of Guyana, (11th) Hugh Shearer of Jamaica, (12th) V.C. Bird of Antigua and Barbuda.

"The University and The People"

Graduation Address: University of the West Indies, Cave Hill Campus, 6th February 1968

We welcome to our University, the UK Minister of Overseas Development on two grounds. First, he escaped from our common bondage at the same institution of learning (LSE) a brief twelve months before me, and needs your sympathy in the exacting servitude in which we have both ended up as Ministers of Government. But of more importance is that the Right Honourable Reginald Prentice represents on this occasion the Government of the United Kingdom without whose generosity, the construction of these buildings may have been postponed for an indefinite period. The citizens of the United Kingdom deserve our thanks for this their most significant contribution west of Suez.

The Government and people of Canada have made their own very substantial contribution to this University. In addition to funds already provided for expansion at Mona and St Augustine, and apart from the numerous scholarships now enjoyed by students of all the territories, the Government of Canada has already earmarked a substantial sum for further developments at this site, and the sum will meet the cost of constructing a hall of residence for the students of the other territories, who we hope will come here in ever increasing numbers. Both the University and the Government of Barbados have already dispatched their thanks to the Government of Canada, but would still wish to greet our Canadian friends to the public recognition of their assistance.

Since I am addressing the distinguished company as a Member of the University Council, I may perhaps not without some diffidence express the University's appreciation to the people of Barbados for the gift of the land on which the college stands and for the provision of the ancillary services. In a deeper sense, however, the citizens of

Barbados have merely established in a positive way their commitment to and faith in this region. By surrendering so large a portion of their scarcest commodity to a regional enterprise, they have demonstrated that they yield to more in their desire to promote the unity of this region.

When in July 1962, the Common Services Conference made the historic decision to retain and expand the University as a regional institution, it was felt by many that this was a pious hope in view of the political uncertainties then prevailing in the area. At that time none of the subscribing territories was a sovereign state and the peculiar political contrivance [Federation] which had held them together in chafing submission was in ruins.

The breakup of a civilisation is often accompanied by a deceptive amount of social activity. As in a bodily fever, the pulse becomes more rapid, the rate of oxidation faster, even the flash on the patient's cheek may give the deceptive appearance of health: only the glassy eye will indicate that the patient is unconscious of what is going on about him: his mind instead is grappling with phantoms.

Lewis Mumford writing on the condition of man retracing the decline of the classic societies continued:

"In this Hellenistic world, so rational in its surface activities, phantoms and visions appeared in growing numbers precisely at the moment when the Museum of Alexandria was supporting a vast corps of savants and professors who were carrying exact science beyond the realms Aristotle had explored. Theophrastus developed a systematic botany. Hero of Alexandria invented the reaction steam turbine, the first groping toward the modern steam engine. Archimedes founded the science of hydrostatics and made decisive contributions to mechanics. But these inventions and discoveries did little to lighten labour: steam or clockwork was used merely to open temple doors without human hands and thus superstitiously heighten the religious awe of the worshipper. Slave labour, which undermined the ancient polity also reduced the province of the machine. And though the scholars of Alexandria collected, collated, classified, made accessible to other scholars, a growing body of knowledge, the results did not flow out into life: after Aristotle's synthesis, learning tended to fill books and deflate men. Frustrated, cheated, the ordinary man descended to new depths of irrational impulse and superstitious habit."

Have we not seen a similar reaction in our own time? For the context of our rapidly changing times I wish to demonstrate that these reactions are as much in evidence today as they were two thousand years ago. I wish to discuss *The University and The People*.

It is of the utmost importance that our statesmen and scholars, students and scientists should all realise a university institution cannot survive unless it has as its constant goal, service to the communities which support and sustain its activities. At this college of Liberal Arts and Science we have embarked with some assistance on a task of bringing people to the University. It is vital that we should endeavour within the shortest possible time to bring the University to the people. The contributions made by the smaller territories represent in most cases a large proportion of their resources and will be justified only to the extent that commensurate returns in trained manpower are increasingly available.

Occasionally there have been signs that the concept of a regional university is not held with the firmness it deserves. One hears of peculiar interpretations given to the concept which seems to suggest that words have lost their meaning. While I should not wish to see duplication of effort and the resulting financial chaos which this would bring, I think wholly proper that each new development should buttress and extend the regional character of this University. It would be too much to expect the territories to connive at specious definitions of regionalism which cover the hand of selfishness with the glove of extravagance.

While it is conceded that each territory must establish its own priorities for national development, it must never be forgotten that all territories are now firmly committed to important common enterprises, whether for the establishment of Free Trade or a Development Bank or the improvement of communications, it is on the University that they lean most heavily for the studies upon which they reach their conclusions.

Then the University by its accessibility to all becomes the instrument of general progress. It would be a senseless reversal of this trend if new development were to be regarded by anyone as opportunity for territorial aggrandisement.

University costs are rising steadily. More money has to be found for maintaining existing services and for financing properly planned expansion. It now requires nearly $3,500 a year to keep a student at Mona, nearly $3,300 at St Augustine and over $2,500 at Cave Hill. Even with generous assistance from overseas for capital construction and for scholarships and research fellowships, the territories must still provide several million dollars each year for the current operations of the University. The larger territories, apart from their mandatory payments to the central university budget, maintain hundreds of students from public funds in furtherance of their policies for the spread of higher education. This investment on their part cannot be curtailed until there is evidence that it is no longer necessary.

Meanwhile the University itself has to teach more students, do more research, and provide even more special services to governments. All of this activity will necessarily be reflected in higher costs though equally in speedier development. The calculated sacrifice of present comforts to future benefits can only be justified if the fullest use is made of available resources.

When therefore we speak of bringing the University to the People, we should not only mean that more and more people should directly as students enjoy its facilities, we should also intend that the citizens of the region should be encouraged to regard the University as their most important asset. We cannot rightly urge them to sacrifice for it merely by pointing with pride to its facilities or to its achievements or even to its international standing. They must feel for the University the same concern which the fortunes of sugar, tourism, industrial development and national security engender. They must be helped to know, as a settled conviction, that the efficient growth of this University is almost their only path to prosperity.

The University for its part must eschew conspicuous consumption. It is the People's University. In this most exacting role it must lead the territories in the difficult art of making one dollar do the work of two.

Governments have to run the fierce gauntlet of parliamentary approval for public expenditure and they sometimes have to impose taxation which is never acceptable. If the University raises its level of expenditure to a height not easily justifiable by the benefits conferred on the taxpayer as citizen, the Governments will not have a pleasant time with their fellow citizens when they ask for increased provision. The greater awareness of the University's moderation the more generous will be the region's response. Dr Samuel Johnson once said of Scotsmen that they, "sustain their culture on a little oatmeal." I should not live to prescribe this somewhat unpalatable diet for our University, but I think that we can still sustain our culture by the prudent use of a slender purse.

Ahead of all our striving and self-denial lies our goal of a prosperous and civilised community of people in this region. These territories have now awoken after three centuries of neglect to find that the world has nearly passed them by. They must now cover in less than a decade the distances negotiated at leisure by a more favoured people. To make two blades of grass grow where one grew before, to train ten persons in the same time as it would have taken to train one, to remove ignorance and squalor, to offer gainful employment to every citizen and to preserve our cultural heritage in all its richness – is a task which might well discourage even the most stout-hearted.

In addition to these urgent domestic preoccupations, we are all of us subject to the presence of the world outside the region. Other countries more powerful than our own territories in population, economic strength and military capacity, daily make decisions to which we are not a part but from the consequences of which we cannot renege. Already the cost of financing numerous vital public services in each territory has gone up in the wake of sterling devaluation, to mention only one example of our interdependence. Events like this impress upon us by direct experience how very urgent it is to hasten our region's growth by all available means in the shortest time.

It seems to me that we need to press into service all the instruments of our progress. Every resource of mind and spirit must now be fully deployed in all these territories. Not the least valuable to us of these resources is our University now nearing the end of its second decade. In its short life it has shared with our national game the matchless honour of unifying these territories. But it does not engender that feeling of common identity which we all experience when in a Test Match the battle sways from side to side. On such occasions the whole region holds its breath and offers expert but conflicting advice to our captain from which he, I must assume, prudently distils the formula for victory.

If we could feel a similar sense of identity with the fortunes of the University we should not only love it more, but we should also experience our greater need of it. Our support of this institution ought to be based not only on its capacity to serve but also on its success in keeping all together. For the work which the University does is valuable not merely because we get our money's worth, but because through it we know each other better, and, best of all, because it should give the people whom we serve a cause for rejoicing. The physical plant and the amenities which the university has acquired supply a planned degree of comfort if not luxury.

If the graduates whom we turn out on our societies are not conscious of those who in the words of the historian Polybius supplied the luxuries and comforts, those whose harvests or cargoes the money for taxes came then the University will have failed the society – it will have failed the people.

Behind all the rightful glamour and pageantry of this occasion pf Graduation lie the hopes of nearly four million people. These hopes must never be frustrated. These human souls must reap with every passing day the full reward of their patience and sacrifice. They must never have an opportunity to be impatient or embittered. We must keep asking ourselves:

"Who has given me this sweet?
And given my brother dust to eat?
And when will his wage come in?"

I as a proud West Indian steeped in the heady wine of classical culture need not apologise for bridging the span of two thousand years by an appeal to the wisdom of our own West Indian poet Derek Walcott, a distinguished graduate of our West Indian University:

"But let us hope, or bless.
I bless with a maker's hands, with ten clasped prayers
All believers in battle, all strollers through fire,
Who feel a heavy future in their eyes,
Limbs, tongue, tired, but not willing to sit still.
I praise those who see a world among these islands
Where we shall try to live in peace and fail,
The failure nothing. I also fold a prayer
For who climbed ladders to see the wide world stretched
Ringed with eternity and its own terrible power,
Nor shouted down false bulletins of hope, not return giddy
From clouds and the rung of their star circled genius
But returned to live near in humility.
And from the chapels of my cupped hands I ring
The little men, reciters at parties, quadroon bohemians,
The fisherman, trailing the sun in his darkening net,
And the working man in overalls putting up the ladder of the
sun,
All those who dream against reason, who will make us
More powerful than stones in the Atlantic tributary,
But powerless, permanent, lovely and human,
Proud not of overcoming complexion,
But climbing poet and labourer nearer the tireless sun."

FOR QUEEN AND COMMONWEALTH

With Pierre Trudeau, Prime Minister of Canada

With Julius Nyrere, President of Tanzania

With Her Majesty The Queen

Arriving in Canada for the 1973 Commonwealth Heads Meeting

1973 Commonwealth Heads of Government Conference, Ottawa, Canada

At Marlborough House, Commonwealth Secretariat Headquarters, London

"Commonwealth – the Strategy of the New Deployment"

Address to the Empire Club of Canada, Toronto, 19 April 1973

I have chosen a rather obscure title for my remarks here today. It is *"Commonwealth – the Strategy of the New Deployment"*. We could, unprofitably, spend a lot of time debating whether the Empire every really became a Commonwealth of Nations or whether that expression is in truth and in fact a euphemistic term designed to gloss over the difficulty inherent in attempting to define a system of political and economic relationships that has undergone considerable change through the passage of time. And they are still undergoing subtle and sometimes imperceptible alterations from day to day, conditioned by the realities of changing situations in an outside world of which the Commonwealth nevertheless is an integral and important part.

If no man is an island entire in itself then the Commonwealth is even less an island and cannot afford to be a closed circuit system in which communication is limited to its subscribers. We have never shared our wealth in the loose association of independent and dependent countries which replace the conceptual empire after the imperial conferences of the 1930s gave way to the Commonwealth conferences of the 1950s.

We have never shared our wealth at all at any time. We had ease of military deployment but we had no ease of movement of peoples. We had relative ease of movement of goods. We did manage to build up trade and relationships, starting perhaps with the Canada-West Indies Agreement in the mid-1920s, which gave preferential treatment to one another's goods. These preferential arrangements are about to break down and that is why I have chosen the title – the Strategy of the New Deployment.

Is there a strategy and is there a new deployment? I should like to submit, with all due respect, that the strategy may not be one which is drafted as a communique at the end of the Prime Ministers' Conferences which we hold with varying measures of success from time to time, usually at intervals of two years, but a strategy is nevertheless emerging and as a result there is a new deployment; a deployment which has been brought about by the realities of 20th century living.

The realities of 20th century living are, firstly, the development of the nuclear potential, making the sheer might of military power irrelevant to the ability of a country to defend itself against external aggression. The kind of alliances which we now have to develop are not alliances based on the sizes of the armies which you happen to maintain. As a matter of fact, as you are all aware, most of the military establishments have dwindled in size and importance and they are playing a smaller and smaller role in the global strategy which we are witnessing in the last quarter of the 20th century.

We have, furthermore, the development-whether this development is to take its place or not-of new economic and trading blocs. We have witnessed since the end of World War II the establishment of new organisations such as the General Agreement on Tariffs and Trade (GATT), an agreement which perhaps, with the exception of Canada, has been honoured more in its breach than in its observance by the subscribing countries.

We have the new alignments developing in Europe, the community to which the United Kingdom had recently acceded and some of the other European countries such as Sweden and Ireland. We have in the Caribbean itself a new alignment with the Organisation of American States and we have in South East Asia a new development in that with Britain's entry into the community in Europe, the Commonwealth members of that part of the world are having a second look at their relationships with their neighbours in the Pacific and in South East Asia, a look which they were not disposed to entertain before. There is, therefore, some kind of new strategy developing.

And then we have new discoveries, discoveries of new wealth in countries that were considered to be backward countries in Africa such as Libya, and in the Sudan in Nigeria. We have had the independence of most of the African countries either from Great Britain or France since 1.948 and a similar movement has taken place in the Caribbean.

And then we have had, two or three years ago, the last vestige of the imperial connection with the insistence of Great Britain that there was some amorphous, anomalous, unmentionable treaty that the Government of South Africa, which was known as the Simonstown Agreement, under which they felt constrained to sell arms to the South African Government. At the same time, this treaty had never secured the approval of the British Parliament and the discussion of the Simonstown Agreement caused the Governments of Mauritius, Ceylon [Sri Lanka] and India to take another look at their relationships in the Indian Ocean and the part which the British Navy could be expected to play in the event of some external aggression. So all of these things have been taking place.

The Commonwealth, scattered as it is over the whole face of the globe, has been trying to survive under very difficult circumstances under the old concepts and that is why a new strategy has had to develop almost spontaneously rather than by design and, in some respects, has had to be encouraged by the positive actions of the governments themselves. But frequently the governments have only taken action after they had been forced by the situations which have been created around them to take positive action. Australia has been very late but nevertheless with a change of government both in Australia and New Zealand, we are feeling a new kind of sun coming from the Pacific Ocean and we are witnessing new stances being adopted by the Governments of Australia and New Zealand.

To those countries which were considered an almost indissoluble part of the old British Empire, the old Dominion partnerships, the attitude of the Government of Australia, not only on the political level but on the economic level towards the Government of South Africa, let us say, and their new, shall I say, affection for the lesser developed countries in the Pacific and in the Far East demonstrate a kind of grasp of the economic, social and political realities of order which were remarkably absent before.

I should like to come a little closer home, to your home and to my home. Since 1961 when the West Indies Federation was dissolved; it was officially dissolved in 1962 but the September 1961 referendum in Jamaica sounded the death knell of the now defunct Federation. Four countries, four small dependent territories in the Caribbean have now become independent countries and they have sustained their independence without asking for alms from anyone but are grateful for any assistance either on a bilateral basis or multilateral basis which may have been vouchsafed to them by friendly partners either in the western hemisphere or in Europe.

But, nevertheless, we have managed in our four countries, Jamaica, first, Trinidad, secondly, Guyana, thirdly, and finally Barbados to sustain our independence to the extent that we were considered to have committed an act of defiance in October last year when we took a lead in the western hemisphere in deciding to open diplomatic relations with the Republic of Cuba, much to the chagrin of our neighbours to the north.

But it demonstrates that the developing countries can take a lead in conditioning the minds of people who should know better to the realities of the new situations which we have to face in this quarter of the 20th century. And I have no doubt that the other countries which are mightier and more powerful than the four small independent countries in the Caribbean will soon shamefacedly or not, have to follow suit because it appears to me to be a rather ridiculous situation where a country can have diplomatic relations with the Vatican, let us say as an analogy, and cannot correspond with the parish priest within your own frontiers, who happens to be a Roman Catholic. I do not think that the parable will be lost in this audience.

And we cannot sit down in the Caribbean and wait for our strategy to be dictated or governed by the political or other economic or social prejudices of people in other countries because to entertain such a belief would be an abandonment of the sovereignty that we believe in and we have never subscribed to the doctrine of limited sovereignty. And I have been, myself, very firm right from the beginning of Barbados' independence that we would be friends of all and satellites of none.

The Government in Moscow, the Union of Soviet Socialist Republics (USSR), appears to believe that it is alright for a state to be independent and sovereign, so long as the exercise of its sovereignty does not infringe upon the social, the political and economic interests of the Soviets. In the same way, unfortunately, there appears to be a superstition in the western hemisphere, not restricted to the Government of the USA, but also some of the military dictatorships in Latin America, that small independent countries could do what they like provided that what they do is not only not against the interests of the government of the larger country which subscribes to the doctrine of limited sovereignty but actually has to conform to the foreign policy and the objectives of such larger country.

Now when the governments of independent Caribbean countries make decisions on foreign policy, it is not merely an act of defiance, it is an act of realism. We, too, have to look at what our major trading interests and political interests may happen to be from time to time. And in making such decisions, it does not mean that we are underrating the ideologies of the countries with which we wish to have diplomatic relations. Sometimes we do it merely to protect the interests of our nationals who reside in those countries. Sometimes we do it to protect the interests of our major exports because we consider that it is better to be able to sit around a table and discuss the terms on which we exchange our goods with countries in the outside world, with people who are in a position to do us damage, than to keep them outside of the confines of the conference table. And so, it is in this light that one has to view our decisions. To emphasise it again, in the light that we do not agree with the doctrine of limited sovereignty, we will never subscribe to this doctrine.

And secondly, and following from that, that we have to follow a policy which we consider best in our own interests. And that is what Great Britain did way back in 1962, under the leadership of Mr Macmillan, the British Prime Minister, and with the able assistance of Mr Heath then, Commonwealth leaders were summoned to London for the first time, five years after the Treaty of Rome was signed, to discuss the possibility of Britain's entry into Europe.

I regret to say, without in any way reflecting on the leadership of Great Britain at the time, that the reason at the time why we were not willing to buy the European Economic Community was not so much due to the fact that the Community was something bad in itself; one Australian described it as a rich, white man's club but I did not necessarily feel the same way but perhaps the Australians had more to lose than any other country by the immediate accession of Great Britain at that time and the Australian farmers were very bitter about the very prospect of

Great Britain's membership in the Community; but there was unfortunately, the old imperial stance of "listen chaps, we will tell you what is good for you".

Despite Mr Heath's valiant efforts to put matters on a more business-like plane, we were left unfortunately with this impression that Britain had made up its mind and the Commonwealth could take the hindmost. And at one stage Mr Macmillan, appeared to be rather hurt over the attitude of most of the African as sociables, as they are described. He said to the leaders of the African delegations "We are rather surprised that you attack Britain like this because we thought that you wanted to get a united Africa and surely the best way to do it is to become associated with Europe because things that are equal to the same thing are equal to one another."

One of the leaders of the African delegations, who unfortunately has since been deposed, said that African unity was not to be established as a by-product of the European Economic Association. That put Mr Macmillan in his place and I repeated much the same thing last week in Guyana when there was evidence that the associated states, who are as sociables under part four of the Treaty of Rome of 1957, were being confused by their nebulous situation and by the lack of a clear statement on behalf of Her Majesty's Government as to their future that West Indian unity could not be achieved as a by-product of European Economic Association but as a direct result of our own deliberate efforts. And that is part of our strategy. That is part of our deployment.

So we have, on the one hand, developed our strategy towards the Caribbean Community and at the same time we have to pursue a strategy of cooperation with our neighbours in the western hemisphere and I hope that Canada will play its rightful role in helping us to develop this strategy. But Canada has a special position and therefore we cannot dictate to the Government of Canada what Canada should do.

But I am hoping that, as we develop our manufacturers and since Canada does believe in the liberalisation of trade, that I can serve notice that as far as imperial preferences are concerned that I consider them anachronistic in the modern world and I know that until I make a statement like that or someone has the courage to do it, that the Canadian authorities may feel that there is some obligation to perpetuate a system of imperial preferences which can only create a lot of damage and misunderstanding. The have already created a lot of misunderstanding insofar as The European Economic Community is concerned and insofar as United States of America is concerned because since the Kennedy round of talks on trade liberalisation, the United States, whether they are being sincere about it or not, has stated its willingness to grant to the developing countries a generalised system of preferences provided that the other industrialised countries, such as the European Community countries and countries like Canada, do not insist that the developing countries should extend to them reverse preferences.

I've done a little arithmetic on this whole business of preferences and I personally do not think that with modern inflation that the reverse preferences make any difference to the availability of the consumer demand or the country demand for goods from industrialised countries into the developing countries. And since they are ineffectual they might as well be abandoned but it is far better to abandon them when it appears to be an act of generosity on your part than to wait until they are proven to be useless when you get no credit for it.

I am a realist and therefore I am suggesting that the whole system of imperial preferences be abandoned as part of the strategy of the new deployment because that is the one thing that is causing some kind of hang-up against the introduction of the Generalised System of Preferences (GSPs) as they are called, which have been mooted during the past three or four years.

Naturally, until Great Britain has been told the facts of life by her trading partners inside Europe, Great Britain will wish to hang on to imperial preferences for as long as possible because British industry is becoming increasingly uncompetitive. These are the manufactured goods coming from other industrial countries such as Japan and West Germany and even Canada. And they will want to hang on to imperial preferences but the way that I see it, it is fairly obvious that by 1974 most of these will have to go.

What we are concerned about in this strategy is the system of restricting imports by our former trading partners, our friendly developing countries, and the restriction by the USA using quotas and sometimes complete embargoes against the goods of the developing countries. So we will have in future, quite apart from the friendly exchange of ideas, and some of them are really good ideas, which takes place at a Commonwealth Prime Ministers' Conference, to have new exchanges with new groups of people in different parts of the world.

We will have to have more conferences between the Australians and the New Zealanders, the inhabitants and Government of Singapore, Malaysia, what used to be French Indochina, Japan and Hong Kong is one grouping; then all the Indian Ocean countries with the East African countries; and all the countries in the Mediterranean and in West Africa; and then all the countries in the OAS, instead of those lengthy compliments which appear at the Pan American Union, to the illustrious ancestors of the generals who constitute most of the military governments in those countries, before they attack their policies.

We should have realistic exchanges about what is happening to the people over whose destinies we have the honour to preside. What are we doing about improving the standards of living of those unfortunate people in Latin America who do not strut about in military uniforms? What are you buying from us who are members of the OAS? How can we increase our trade? The alliance of progress is dead and it ought to be given a respectful burial. These are the things we ought to be saying to one another and I should like to see the Canadian Government taking a more active interest, other than its contributions made to the Inter-American Development Bank, in hemispheric problems.

There is a considerable amount of bilateral aid passing from this country to the Commonwealth countries in the hemisphere. There is a considerable amount of trade even with Cuba and I applaud the wisdom of the Canadian Government and the Canadian people, in continuing to trade with the country rather than creating animosity with people who have no quarrel with the people of Canada. But there is room for a great deal more dialogue between the countries who are deployed in this part of the world. And I think that if we had the Government of Canada more intimately involved, in our discussions on real terms, that it would do a lot to introduce an atmosphere of realism into the discussions which the Latin American countries and the Commonwealth countries, who constitute most of the OAS, have across the table with their mighty neighbour to the north, the USA.

We have now moved and will be moving on the first of August this year to establish a Caribbean Community. By doing so, we do not remove the four independent countries outside of the Commonwealth. The concepts of change, new strategies are being developed. The thing about the Commonwealth that it is difficult to define, like the British Constitution. But somehow or other it works and it works sometimes more successfully than those things which have been institutionalised and have their constitutions embodied on the four corners of a document. It works because it is flexible and it works, not because it is monolithic, it works because it is everywhere. What we should be doing now, apart from the geographical realities of the Commonwealth being everywhere, is to make sure that the Commonwealth is in everything.

So the Commonwealth is in Europe in the Economic Community. The Commonwealth is now, for the first time, in the OAS and we small countries put it in the OAS. Great Britain has just been refused Observer Status. How have the mighty fallen. Of course, we voted for Great Britain; they couldn't get in anyhow but we voted for them. But even if our vote was going to make the difference, we would still vote for Great Britain and we are prepared to vote for Canada. But the point is that we put the Commonwealth in the OAS. The Commonwealth is everywhere and we want to get the Commonwealth in everything.

This is the message which I have. Because unless you are in everything, people can do things to you. So the Commonwealth is in the Organisation of African Unity. The Commonwealth should now try to get into Rhodesia and South Africa. This is my belief. We are in the Indian Subcontinent. We have never really left Peking, we've been selling them goods all along. We are in the Middle East and we should never leave it, not with soldiers or military presence, but we have to make sure that wherever there is intercourse with human beings, whether it be trade, or social, or cultural, that the Commonwealth is involved. And small countries sometimes can lead the way.

I am hoping that in the Commonwealth conference we have in Ottawa this year, I have been attending them since 1962, we will not see a new heaven and a new earth or that we will build Jerusalem, but that we will witness an appreciation of the new strategy of involvement which is necessary if we are going to be able to understand one another, if we are going to be able to understand not only in a lingua franca, understand what I say, I'm sharing a common language, but understand our problems and be able to advise and do something about them. And by the deployment of getting involved now with people in a peripheral kind of way, not so much involved towards the centre or looking toward the centre, but looking in an eccentric kind of way to the periphery in the areas in which I have mentioned but particularly in our own area.

We have started our drive to get involved in the Caribbean and Canada can start its drive by getting involved in the north. Australia has spearheaded the movement with the Prime Minister of Singapore in South East Asia. The lead has not come from London. The lead has come from us and unless Canada wishes to abandon its role as an equal partner, then Canada must do some spearheading as well, and this is what I am looking forward to at this Commonwealth conference. That new concepts will arise, that we will have new ideas and that we can go forward being able to communicate and understand the problems and to build up a much more lasting peace and prosperity than we have enjoyed up to the present.

THE TREATY OF CHAGUARAMAS

With Forbes Burnham, Dr Eric Williams and Michael Manley signing the Treaty of Chaguaramas

The signed Treaty of Chaguaramas

With William Demas signing the CDB Headquarters Agreement

A West Indian for All Seasons
Sir Shridath "Sonny" Ramphal

'Errol' to many, 'The Skipper' to some, 'Dipper' to others; it is for me a special and substantial honour to have been asked to contribute to this publication that honours the memory of The Right Excellent Errol Walton Barrow. That the book marks the 50th Anniversary of the Independence of Barbados enhances that honour, as does the fact that this year is also the 50th Anniversary of Independence of Guyana; for it was in the Barbados-Guyana context that I knew him best.

1966 was a moment of achievement that Barbados and Guyana shared and through which I came to know and respect Errol, the Father of Independence, as a cherished West Indian colleague and friend. For ten years from 1965 until 1975, the year in which I was selected as the Commonwealth Secretary-General, we bonded in ways that only men who shared common passions could.

Errol had an almost unique way of bestowing his friendship on individuals regardless of their station or origin; and I was favoured thus for the many years that I knew him. These days when I pass the vicinity of Paradise Beach where his cottage, *Kampala*, was nestled, I cannot but reflect on the happy days there drinking Scotch and coconut water while Dipper settled for tonic, and cooking.

Prudence dictates that I not reminisce about Errol in his domestic political scene; but, in any event, I did not know him in that context. I knew him as a West Indian; and in that common belonging we were in a shared regional home. When he came to British Guiana, as Guyana was then, we went duck shooting, strictly in the interest of saving Guyana's rice farmers from the pestilence of ravaging *Wisi-Wisi* ducks, he was in his West Indian home as well.

It was the same when he went sailing in the Grenadines with the former St Vincent and the Grenadines Prime Minister 'Son' Mitchell (now Sir James) or Saint Lucia's John Compton (later Sir John), or 'limed' in Jamaica with Michael Manley (later the Most Honourable). For those occasions, Errol displayed a capacity, rare among politicians, for switching off politics.

Yet, there is no question that the fraternity of those moments enhanced the levels of comraderie and civility that characterised his serious regional political encounters, whatever the 'Barrowisms' that may have coloured his debates. We could do with some of that easy sociability within the region's current political directorate; fraternity beyond the conference rooms.

Those encounters are a significant part of the Barrow Legacy. It is my contention that Errol has not been sufficiently credited for the regional accomplishments that were his handiwork. One in particular stands out for me. The 1973 Treaty of Chaguaramas establishing the Caribbean Community and Common Market (CARICOM) is often regarded as the resumption of West Indian regionalism after the debacle of 'Federation'. The truth is otherwise.

It was in fact the Dickenson Bay Agreement signed in 1965 between Antigua, Barbados and Guyana to establish the Caribbean Free Trade Association (CARIFTA) that marked this resumption, and the credit for that must go primarily to Errol. It was he who initiated the post-federal *détente*.

In his 4 July 1973 speech at the signing of the Treaty of Chaguaramas, after recalling his association with Forbes Burnham and Michael Manley in the early years of the West Indian Students Union in London (both of them now on the platform with him as fellow Heads of Government) and their activist years of the 1940s in London, he testified to his regional role with becoming modesty:

"Occasions for making disclosures of this kind are not frequent. I can now disclose that it was on 4th July 1965, that the Prime Minister of Guyana met with me in Barbados, at my invitation to discuss the possibility of establishing a free trade area between our two countries in the first instance, and the rest of the Caribbean at such time as they would be ready to follow our example…and today, I am very happy to be here, some eight years later to be a signatory to the documents for whose signing we have been summoned by the distinguished Prime Minister of Trinidad and Tobago."

That was indeed modest. Barrow, Burnham and, with Errol's encouragement, Antigua's Vere C. Bird Sr, signed the initial CARIFTA Agreement in December 1965 but suspended its coming into force with a view to making it region-wide from the beginning. When it became operational in 1968, eleven Caribbean countries were signatories. It was by CARIFTA that the regional journey was resumed and was to evolve into the Common Market and Community and, thereafter into the Caribbean Single Market and Economy (CSME).

Errol did not carry federal baggage. He had some scars from the 'agony of the eight' but was so passionately West Indian that as early as mid-1965, just three years after the rancorous dissolution of the Federation, and the eve before Barbados' Independence, he initiated that resumption. I write of these works of Barrow with nostalgia, for I was privileged to be there through them all.

It was then a time of a special relationship between Barbados and Guyana. Jamaica and Trinidad and Tobago were already independent, and so a bit apart. The Leewards and Windwards could not yet entertain that ambition but Barbados and Guyana could, and did, and that put them in a shared constitutional category. But, beyond their aspiration for independence, there were other ties that bound the two countries. For decades, Barbadians had been settling in Guyana. They were notoriously amongst our finest teachers and our most solid policemen and started families there. Burnham, as Errol testified, was the grandchild of Barbadians as was another future President, Desmond Hoyte.

Guyanese too were to have Barbadian grandchildren none more eminent than one of Errol's successors as leader of the Democratic Labour Party and Prime Minister of Barbados, David Thompson. And, of course, many Guyanese businessmen invested in Barbados in a range of enterprises, from the Banks Beer to hotels.

So, when Burnham's People's National Congress (PNC) won the 1964 General Election, the old fraternity of *Knutsford House*, the West Indian Students Hostel in London that Barrow and Burnham shared was transformed into close political, social and economic relations between Barbados and the soon-to-be Guyana. By 1966, when the two countries were to stride out into the international community as independent states they had already co-authored CARIFTA.

Guyana became independent on 26 May and Barbados on 30 November of 1966. I was in Barbados for the flag-raising at the Garrison Savannah as part of the Guyana Delegation along with our then High Commissioner to the UK, Sir Lionel Luckhoo. Out of his congenital practicality, but bolstered by the reality of the special relationship that existed between Barbados and Guyana, the new Prime Minister of Barbados proposed that these two new Members of the Commonwealth of Nations should share a High Commissioner in London. Guyana readily concurred. It was a diplomatic first. It was also much admired as two new Caribbean flags flew together over the joint-High Commission on London's Cockspur Street. It could only have happened on the basis of the close fraternity of our two countries, and of their leaders, a kind that went deeper than regionalism.

There was another element of Errol's character that he exuded with naturalness, an element we claim to be true of all West Indians, though in our broader community it is often more an aspiration than a truth. At the personal level, Errol was wholly devoid of considerations of class, colour, or race. He did not need to assert it as a credo, he simply lived it. The aphorism 'he walked with kings, but kept the common touch' often referenced had, in relation to Errol the man, a larger dimension than is usual in our multi-coloured, multi-ethnic Caribbean community. They are virtues we need to recall and reinstall in our societies as we face the threat of losing them, everywhere.

In our severely challenging and rapidly changing world, the peoples of our region can ill afford to drift, much less be driven, apart, especially now. From the earliest CARIFTA days, and of this I speak with personal assurance, Errol knew well the importance of the West Indian market to Barbados, an importance that has only increased over time. So, while Errol was committed to deeper Caribbean integration because he firmly believed in the validity and importance of a West Indian identity, he also recognised and keenly promoted the value of its economic dimension. Today, we devalue the goals of the CSME at our peril.

What Margaret Attwood once wrote of nations generally at an earlier time is particularly true of us in our Caribbean Community today:

> *It is cold and getting colder,*
> *we need each other's breathing, warmth*
> *surviving is the only war*
> *we can afford*

In the context of this 50th Anniversary of Errol's greatest public achievement, the Independence of Barbados, I honour his memory on behalf of all who dwell in his regional home. The West Indies needs more and more deeply, and urgently, the qualities that Errol Walton Barrow brought to our civilisation. The 50th Anniversary of the Independence of Barbados is a good time to reaffirm our commitment to them, across our region.

"Towards a United Caribbean"

Statement made in the House of Assembly on June 19,
1973, on the establishment of the
Caribbean Community

At the conclusion of the Eighth Conference of Heads of Government of Commonwealth Caribbean Countries, held in Georgetown, Guyana, in April this year, the Minister of External Affairs signed on behalf of the Government of Barbados, the Georgetown Accord which was adopted at that conference.

Under that instrument, the governments of Barbados, Guyana, Jamaica and Trinidad and Tobago undertook to sign and ratify a Community Treaty in order to establish a Caribbean Community and Common Market as between their respective countries with effect from August 1, 1973.

The governments of Belize, Dominica, Grenada, St Kitts-Nevis-Anguilla, St Lucia, St Vincent, undertook to sign and ratify the Treaty so as to become parties thereto on 1st May, 1974, whereas the governments of Antigua and Barbuda and Montserrat, declared their intention to give urgent consideration to joining in the Accord.

The establishment of the Caribbean Community will see the achievement of an aspiration that began in December, 1965, at Dickenson Bay, Antigua, when the governments of Antigua and Barbuda, Barbados and Guyana signed an agreement to establish a Caribbean Free Trade Area. During the two years following this agreement, studies were carried out to see how far the liberalisation of trade could be linked with other regional efforts to promote the development of the area. This culminated in crucial decisions being taken at the 1967 Heads of Government Conference in Barbados. The Conference not only endorsed the framework of the Dickenson Bay Agreement, but also accepted a number of positive proposals designed to carry the regional movement beyond the limited strategy of a free trade area.

The Heads of Government enumerated areas where a regional effort would be likely to allow greater benefits to accrue to the area. Indeed, these were set out specifically in Annex A to the CARIFTA

(Caribbean Free Trade Association) Agreement, indicating that the regional association was intended to be a dynamic institution. Thus the Annex anticipated a Common External Tariff, a programme for the location of industries in the Less Developed Countries, a regional policy on the granting of incentives to industry, marketing arrangements for an agreed list of agricultural commodities and the establishment of regional sea and air carriers, among other things.

The CARIFTA Agreement came into effect on May 1, 1968, and by August 1968 covered the following territories: Antigua, Barbados, Dominica, Grenada, Guyana, Jamaica, Montserrat, St Kitts-Nevis-Anguilla, St Lucia, St Vincent and Trinidad and Tobago. In May 1971, Belize (British Honduras) became a member.

Successive meetings of the CARIFTA Council of Ministers and of the Heads of Government grappled with the problem of further economic integration and functional co-operation. After five years of in-depth studies, of deliberations and of bargaining, the Seventh Heads of Government Conference of October 1972 took the decisions to establish a Caribbean Community embracing efforts at economic integration, but also including the co-ordination of foreign policy and the institutionalisation of existing areas of functional co-operation.

The Caribbean Community will have as its principal organs the Conference of Heads of Government and the Common Market Council. As institutions of the Community, there will be a number of Standing Committees of Ministers. Associated institutions will also be recognised.

An integral feature of the Caribbean Common Market will be the establishment of a Common External Tariff and Common Protective Policy which Barbados, Guyana, Jamaica and Trinidad and Tobago agreed to adopt with effect from 1st August, 1973, as between themselves. Members of this House are aware that by virtue of some aspects of my recent Budgetary proposals, Barbados will already have begun to meet its obligations under the Community Treaty.

The governments, parties to the Accord, also agreed to establish a Caribbean Investment Corporation, to apply an agreement for the Harmonisation of Fiscal Incentives, and to conclude a Double Taxation Treaty by the 1st June, 1973. The three relevant instruments have already been signed by the Minister of External Affairs.

Another measure provided for is the elaboration of a scheme for the Rationalisation of Agriculture in the region, to be introduced by 1st July, 1973.

The Community and Common Market are intended to promote the co-ordinated development of the region and to increase intra-regional trade thereby reducing dependence on extra-regional sources. The community will institutionalise the machinery for the many shared services, which already exist and which even the most prosperous of the More Developed Countries, could not operate on its own. Moreover, the region as a whole will carry more bargaining weight when confronting third countries, trading groups and international organisations.

In order to reap the benefits that the new Community and Common Market offer, Barbadian businessmen – indeed regional businessmen –must undertake a re-examination of the needs of the area and structure their production lines to meet these needs.

The Common Market should provide an opportunity for our industrial and agricultural sectors to leap forward. With the necessary determination, the region's economy can become vibrant within a relatively short period of time.

This government has constantly recognised the desirability of developing closer relationships with the other English-speaking Caribbean territories – not only because of our similar historical, cultural and economic background, but also because of the need to protect our small communities from exploitation by undesirable influences. I need hardly remind honourable members that only two years ago, the Governor-General stated in his Throne Speech:

'My Government will continue to play an active role in the attainment of economic integration in the Commonwealth Caribbean. In particular, no effort will be spared to ensure that satisfactory decisions are reached on such important matters as the harmonisation of fiscal incentives, the rationalisation of agriculture and the location of industries.'

And so the package contained in the Community Treaty places high priority on the strengthening of the economies of the Westindian territories. Within the framework of this Community and the Common Market lies the opportunity for greater and more rapid economic development for the area.

I propose to join with the Heads of Government of Guyana, Jamaica, and Trinidad and Tobago and sign the Community Treaty at Chaguaramas, Trinidad and Tobago on 4th July, 1973, the anniversary of the birth of the late Norman Washington Manley. When the Community Treaty has been ratified in accordance with our constitutional procedure, that Treaty and all other relevant instruments will be laid on the table in both Houses of Parliament.

THE TITANS

With, from left, Prime Ministers James Mitchell, John Compton and Pierre Trudeau

The Era of the Titans
The Rt Honourable Sir James Mitchell

With my five-year sojourn in London concluded, on the last day of 1965 I left England on a banana boat with a young wife for the voyage home to St Vincent and the Grenadines. On route we docked in Barbados.

Philip Greaves (now Sir Philip), the then newly appointed Senator and Minister, collected my wife and I that Saturday morning and took us to meet his Premier, Errol Barrow. The then Minister of Education, Cameron Tudor (later Sir James) was also present. I had previously known Philip as a Latin teacher in St Vincent when I was an agronomist and our friendship resumed in London which included our hitchhiking together across Europe.

Errol's Legend had preceded my introduction. I had previously heard of him and admired the heroic tales of when he was an aviator in the Royal Air Force during the Second World War; a noble distinction held by only a few West Indians.

We met just as he was getting ready to lead Barbados into Independence and unknown to me then, a few months before I would become the Member of Parliament for the Grenadines, on the Opposition bench. I would return to Barbados to attend the Independence celebrations, as a guest of Philip.

St Vincent then became embroiled in a statehood constitutional battle. On the way to London to try to resolve it, my then leader Milton Cato visited his brother Sir Arnott, and I went separately to meet and explain our problem to Errol, who assured me that he would get the Guyana/Barbados High Commissioner Sir Lionel Luckhoo to provide any assistance that he could.

The spiritual link of the Barrow family with the Grenadines, his father serving as Rector in Bequia, seemed to survive in Errol. I remember sailing on the Goddard schooner with Errol and Captain George Fergusson when we ran into a school of Dorado. George's zeal would not abate until dusk by which time we had landed twenty-two fine specimens, more than enough for all those dining at the Frangipani Hotel that evening. When I proposed a toast to Barbados and St Vincent, Errol corrected me saying, *"To Barbados and the Grenadines."*

My subsequent appointments as Minister of Trade, Agriculture, Labour and Tourism, took me often to the Barbados and the summit establishing CARIFTA, and subsequent collaboration with my fishing buddy, George Fergusson in the frequent Guyana meetings.

Errol called one day to say that the then Canadian Prime Minister Pierre Trudeau was honeymooning in Barbados and that he intended to fly the couple to St Vincent and that I should arrange to pick them up on a fast boat to join the Canadian yacht "Passe Temps" in Bequia for a day sail with its owner, Ken Patrick, and the then Saint Lucian Premier John Compton (later Sir John), already in Bequia. A beautiful sail it was to my family island, Isle a Quatre; we moored in Lagoon Bay and the honeymooning couple swam off in the distance.

These friendly and informal occasions rejuvenated our ancestral bondage with Canada, which had survived the historic trade of Canadian cod in exchange for rum and sugar. Personal chemistry between leaders becomes foreign policy among nations. The presence of the international airports in Barbados and Saint Lucia are the fruits of this rich legacy. It was a personal privilege when the then retired now late Sir John Compton was able to represent the Caribbean at the state funeral of Pierre Trudeau in September 2000.

On the last weekend before the second referendum on Quebec Independence, I urged a Caribbean audience to mobilise their influence to secure for themselves a Canadian passport rather than a Quebec passport which helped to ensure a victory for the Canadian identity and blame laid for the Quebec defeat on minorities. Now, with the turn of the tide, I too need a visa to visit Canada.

Jean Chretein, then a Minister under Trudeau, who would become Prime Minister, requested my help to secure the safe return of Canadian armaments from the Balkan wars on a Vincentian registered ship, which I did and for which he thanked me graciously when we attended the

UN Millennium Summit. In retirement, he would invite me to join him on the InterAction Council of former heads of state and government.

In the early 70s, slow responses among my colleagues and the Government to the demands for infrastructure expenditure in my constituency of the Grenadines led to my resignation from Government. The consequence was that the next 1984 General Election ended with a result of a tie between the two major parties election 6:6:1, the one remaining seat being mine as an Independent MP. A government could not be formed without me, and previously both parties now with six seats each, had rejected me.

Fortuitously I had introduced telephones into Bequia; as I needed sound and urgent advice as I was inundated with contrary signals as to what I should do. I called Errol. He was quite clear what I should do. *"Demand the top spot, I will speak to Joshua"*, [the then Leader of the People's Political Party] *"Get them all to sign that they have confidence in you, with a document witnessed by a Justice of the Peace, and you all go and see the Governor."* And so Caribbean history was made on Errol's good consul; that an Independent MP with no political party became Head of Government.

The CARIFTA Council met every three months in Guyana. While ministerial colleagues in the East Caribbean fought over the allocation of industries (which I knew had to satisfy a private sector criteria) I drew on my European experience to forge the Agricultural Marketing Protocol, and other institutions in agriculture. Then the OPEC oil crisis descended on us in October 1973. Oil moved from US$3 to US$33 per barrel overnight. I met with Dr Eric Williams during the crisis and drew to his attention to the looming impact on agriculture with the price of nitrogen fertiliser going through the roof. I explained to Prime Minister Williams how Trinidad could benefit in this exercise and it was in this discussion that the idea of the Caribbean Food Corporation, the Caribbean Agricultural Regional Development Institute (CARDI) and other agricultural institutions were formed.

I remain permanently indebted to Robert Lightbourne, the then Jamaican Trade Minister, from whom I gleaned many negotiating skills and who conceptualised the idea of an OPEC-type organisation for sugar.

One Sunday, Errol summoned me to Barbados. The Big Four: Burnham of Guyana, Errol Mahabir for Trinidad, Hugh Shearer of Jamaica, and himself were discussing a sugar organisation using the OPEC concept and he advised that he was sending a plane to bring me to the discussion so that I could launch the idea to my Eastern Caribbean colleagues. I told Errol that my political partner E.T. Joshua was in Barbados and it was not necessary for me to come. He replied frankly, *"We want your input. We'll take Joshua to lunch."*

I flew to Barbados. I listened patiently for a long time and then chimed in. *"Gentlemen,"* I said, *"with all due respect, I differ. Sugar prices can rise. I agree. But what you propose will work only for two summers. The European beet producers will get back into the game and our protected sugar quotas will collapse forever."* We went on to discuss the changes needed to move beyond CARIFTA to CARICOM. As the East Caribbean territories with colonial status had no foreign policy authority, I suggested that we should seek British approval to join CARICOM only after it was established, and not before. And it was agreed there and then that the Eastern Caribbean States would join CARICOM after the four independent countries. We then went to lunch with Joshua.

It was way back in 1962 on a wide beach in Alassio on the Italian Riviera, one Sunday morning searching for German earnings lost in the sand the previous night, when I found the sheet of a newspaper clipping informing me of the collapse of the West Indies Federation. Now here I was, a decade later translating my experience hitchhiking through farming countryside in Europe into Caribbean policy.

The DLP were out of office, "Bree" St John (later Sir Harold) was the Prime Minister of Barbados and supportive of my quest for the European Union to build an airport in Bequia as a regional project. I had the support of many prime ministerial colleagues but the CARICOM Secretariat seemed to be jeopardising the project with lengthy letters. So to Brussels, Eugenia Charles, the Prime Minister of Dominica, and I went with our officials. Eugenia went off to chair the ACP Council and left me with the CARICOM Secretary General to face the European Commissioner for Development.

Having got the Europeans to define their position, we drafted a memorandum which I proposed to initial the next day. However the

Secretary General advised we couldn't proceed without consensus. I spent that night on the telephone with the Caribbean Heads and secured support from A.N.R. Robinson in Trinidad, Herbert Blaize in Grenada, John Compton in Saint Lucia, Kennedy Simmonds in St Kitts, and Desmond Hoyte in Guyana. I found Errol in Miami but he advised that he was preoccupied with a family illness but when I raised the Bequia airport issue, he simply responded saying, *"'Son', I trust your judgment. I will be the first to fly a plane to Bequia."* Today, the Bequia airport has daily links to Barbados but Errol regrettably is not around to enjoy it.

One night a plane crashed offshore in foul weather off St Vincent on its third attempt to land. Our investigative authority produced their report and I showed it to Errol. *"Rubbish"*, he said. *"The Control Tower should never have allowed him to try a third time. Check and see if the pilot didn't have a date that night...When we were flying through enemy fire to land in France, nobody was going to stop us if we had a date."* I shall not share the outcome of my findings here.

Many an early morning as I passed through Grantley Adams International Airport, Errol would drive himself to the airport just to have a simple chat with me. I regret that Errol is not around today with me to inveigh against the "army of occupation" in the aviation industry who ensure we are confined to a slow boat to China.

Why does a half hour flight from Bequia to Barbados cost the same as a flight from Barbados to Miami or Toronto? Is this the right path for our tourism sector? When will our luminaries allow private sector competition and free choice to be normal policy in a framework of Open Skies? Instead, stale rules and new senseless regulations become the hallmark of a proud but hollow national identity, constructing barriers to opportunity.

Errol addressed my NDP Convention in Bequia. And the following Sunday, I addressed his DLP. He spent the weekend in Bequia, quite tired on one of our antique four posters only to rise and swear at the news that a Barbados Coast Guard vessel en route to Grenada had grounded in the Tobago Cays. That was the last time we were together.

In his demise, it was Cameron Tudor, whom I had met in his office that first Saturday coming ashore from the banana boat, who summoned me to do the eulogy for Errol. It was the crispest I could muster, tinged with Tennyson, not like the sonorous themes later propounded for Sir John Compton and Sir Eric Gairy.

> *"A pillar of our Caribbean had fallen.*
> *Sunset and evening star*
> *And one clear call for me.*
> *And may there be no moaning of the Bar*
> *When I put out to sea."*

One day passing through Barbados airport a luggage porter who was helping me pronounced, *"You are the only politician that made me cry"*; he was referring to my eulogy at Dipper's funeral.

My last sounding in Errol's memory came at a formal banquet, seated beside his sister Dame Nita, then Governor General. Out of ear shot of then Prime Minister Sandiford, I asked her, *"What do you think Errol would have to say about the collapse around Sandiford, with all those ministers resigning?"* *"Thank God"* she replied. *"He's buried at sea so he's not turning in the grave."*

I am proud that I served in the era of the Titans.

"A giant step for all of us"

Address at the signing ceremony of the Treaty of Chaguaramas establishing the Caribbean Community and Common Market (CARICOM). Chaguaramas, Trinidad. July 4, 1973

Your Excellencies,
Distinguished guests,
Comrades and friends,

To those who have not been engaged upon the slow process of Caribbean integration, it would appear that this journey commenced at Chaguaramas a few short months ago, and like a race which takes place in a stadium, the end is where the start was.

But the process, as far as three of us, I would say all of us here, certainly the four Prime Ministers, are concerned, goes a long way further back than that.

To the Chairman of this meeting, and the distinguished Prime Minister of Trinidad and Tobago, it started with his struggles at the University of Oxford, when I can truly say, he wrestled with the beast at Ephesus. That chapter in his life has not really been written, but some of us are aware that those who would distort the whole course of Westindian history set out to thwart the attempts of our distinguished Prime Minister of Trinidad and Tobago, to put the Westindian history in its proper perspective, and to give new hope to the people who had been subjected to colonial tutelage for such a long time.

I think that the writings of Dr Williams, the economic researches of Professor Arthur Lewis, were the first faint glimmerings of the indication that the Caribbean people, were capable of managing their own affairs.

We have been a people who have been imbued with a sense of our own inadequacy. Half a generation later, the Prime Minister of Jamaica, who is on this platform, the Prime Minister of Guyana who is on my left, and I, under the leadership of the Prime Minister of

Guyana, who was the President of the first Westindian association founded in the United Kingdom, that was the Westindian Student's Union; we staged the first public meeting on Caribbean integration in the United Kingdom, and we followed the biblical injunction by staging that meeting in the lion's den itself; in that bastion of imperialism which is described as Trafalgar Square.

A lot of our fellow Westindians were rather amazed at our temerity, and we solicited the assistance of our colleagues from other parts of the world in making a bold stand on the need for Westindian integration. I should like to pay tribute to the President of the Westindian Students Union – the first President, the former President, my colleague, Mr Linden Forbes Sampson Burnham, on having the courage and the foresight to lead us on these bold excursions which we followed from time to time, in protesting against conditions in the Westindies, and indeed, supporting our comrades from Africa and other parts of the colonial empires in their protests against the conditions under which our people suffered.

Occasions for making disclosures of this kind are not frequent. I can now disclose that it was on the 4th July, 1965, that the Prime Minister of Guyana met with me in Barbados, at my invitation to discuss the possibility of establishing a free trade area between our two countries in the first instance, and the rest of the Caribbean at such time as they would be ready to follow our example.

The letter which I wrote was in my own fine Barbadian hand which is sometimes illegible. But apparently, the Prime Minister of Guyana was able to read that letter, because of his, he informs me, Barbadian ancestry. Therefore, the hieroglyphics were not entirely strange to him.

That letter must for some time remain in the archives of the Prime Minister of Guyana because I had a few rather caustic observations to make about the failure of our people to get together in some meaningful kind of association. I regret to say that in typical style, a style which has not been unassociated with my posture either in the courts of law or legislative councils, I had some rather personal statements to make about the failure of our leaders to get together in a meaningful association.

So we have for the moment to draw a veil of secrecy and silence over the contents, or the full contents, of that letter. One day, about 25 years after we have both of us relinquished voluntarily the positions which we now hold, the archivist may be given permission for the sake of future generations to publish the full contents of that letter.

In that letter, I invited the Prime Minister of Guyana to come to Barbados so that we could hold these discussions and today, I am very happy to be here, some eight years later to be a signatory to the documents for whose signing we have been summoned by the distinguished Prime Minister of Trinidad and Tobago.

To me it is the end of a long journey. Neither one of us, either the Prime Minister of Jamaica, the Prime Minister of Guyana, or I, had any ambitions to be Prime Ministers. We had ambitions at that time, to see the Caribbean integrated. Today I hear the young aspiring political contenders stating that they want to be Prime Ministers as if being a Prime Minister is like taking an examination and once you achieve the pass mark you are automatically a Prime Minister.

I remember well that in 1955, if I may reminisce very, very shortly, that the General Secretary of the Barbados Workers' Union and the late Norman Washington Manley, whose birthday we commemorate today, and I hope the Prime Minister of Trinidad and Tobago will forgive me for making reference to this, spent two days trying to persuade the Prime Minister of Trinidad and Tobago that he must take his rightful place on the Caribbean political scene.

This is another illustration of the statement which I made a few moments ago that none of the three of us set out to be Prime Ministers. I can now say that remembering what took place in Kingston, Jamaica, none of the four of us set out to be Prime Ministers. The distinguished Prime Minister of Trinidad and Tobago did not even want to be a politician.

So that today when I hear criticism of leadership in the Caribbean, those criticisms would probably have been justified, and justifiably levelled at some of our predecessors in office; but they certainly cannot be levelled against any of the four heads of governments here who have been dragged reluctantly to the high offices which we now occupy.

I hope that when the time comes that we will not be dragged reluctantly from those high offices which we now occupy. The problem which confronts the Westindian people today, is one of persuasion, to persuade people of the calibre of the Prime Minister of Trinidad and Tobago and other distinguished people who have contributed towards the success of this experiment to remain with us and to make a further contribution so that our countries will be able to progress not because of any predilections on our part to preside over the destinies of our peoples, but it will be dependent upon the willingness of the people of the Westindies to recognise the quality and the nature of the leadership which some of our countries enjoy, and that does not necessarily include Barbados, but it does not necessarily exclude Barbados either.

So, Mr Chairman, it was on the 4th July, 1965 one small step for two countries. Today as a signatory to this agreement, I should like to paraphrase the words of Mr Neil Armstrong * and say it is a giant step for all of us.

*

*The first American astronaut to walk on the moon.

In the Image and Interest of the People
Harold Hoyte

The street is in darkness,
Children are sleeping,
Mankind is dreaming.
It is midnight.

Who will awaken
One little flower,
Sleeping and growing
Hour and hour?

Light will awaken
All the young flowers,
Sleeping and growing
Hour and hour.

Dew is awake.
Morning is soon.
Mankind is risen.
Flowers will bloom.

MARTIN CARTER, *For My Son*

The script for Errol Barrow's political strategy was alluring since it was uncomplicated. And his campaign approach was irresistible because it was fervently evangelical. I think he may have seen it as some sort of missionary duty to awaken his countrymen to Martin Carter's new light and new morning of blooming flowers.

Therein reposes the phenomenal success we now opportunely remember as we enthusiastically embrace 50 years of nationhood following his creation of new standards and ideals for our island. One cannot help but wonder what would be his advice to Barbados at this juncture, were he still alive. To hazard a guess would be to do a great injustice to his singular view of our country's destiny.

The passage of time allows us the freedom to better analyse and appreciate the shrewdness of his speeches and the soundness of his strategies as one of our most fierce combatants.

His is the story of a compelling persona that was this zealot, easily winning and influencing his people. No wonder he could nonchalantly corral the people and then set the society free.

Outstanding civilisations of old, and indeed current power centres like the USA, have all benefited from instilling a sense of worth in their people. That was what Errol Barrow saw as his duty for Barbados. So he infused us with great expectations and then equipped us through free universal education, empowering a whole new generation with a great sense of who we were and who we could become.

His main medium was the public meeting. He was not our most eloquent speaker, but he possessed a refined elegance of delivery and an imposing platform presence, extolling people in their thousands. He was also well esteemed for an uncanny skill of campaigning for causes that resonated with ordinary folk, which lasted right through to his famous "Mirror Image" speech of 1986, his most memorable.

Key to this success was the fact that Errol Barrow intimately knew his folk and spoke the language that they understood. Even though he was regarded as middle-class having been born on a plantation, this did not seem to impact negatively on his appeal to the broad masses. His large working-class base was populated by people fascinated with and absorbed by a leader whose values and foibles were similar to their own. It did not matter if the shared values were positive or negative. Either way, the attraction was strong and the loyalty was secure.

The masses would line up behind him as someone who was seen to be sincere in purpose. Barbadians fed off the energy of his earnest example and genuine endeavour. In the end, the test which proved his durability as a devoted servant of the population was that he remained relevant to the pursuits of Barbadians until the day of his death.

Even as a politician, he took his cue from an acute knowledge and experience of military combat, relying more on discipline than a word of command. For him, what was required was just a gentle urging of his people to advance. Advance, he advised. And the sons and daughters of Barbados marched forward to the beat of their own loyal hearts. Thus Barbados grew and prospered under his tuition and training.

In its simplest form, the mantra of the man and the matters that directed his strategic successes were his commitment to doing, not just speaking. He identified what was relevant to the working class and got on with the job. This is best expressed by Dr Don Blackman, a former Cabinet Minister who said at Barrow's passing: *"Mr Barrow was no mere rhetorician. He acted like a man of thought and thought like a man of action. He subscribed to the doctrine of praxis, uniting theory and practice."*

The evidential result is a developed Barbados and a large number of citizens, educated and equipped for self-realisation.

His was a critical role at a precarious juncture of our history and Errol Barrow knew it. When he was initially elected to the House of Assembly, he observed first-hand the slow pace of change in society and became restless and unfaltering in striving towards an improved living standard for the people.

High on his list of abiding concerns was improving the material and psychological welfare of Barbadian citizens by taking the country beyond internal self-rule into the dignified realm of full political independence. We must therefore never, ever, lose sight of the value of his significant foundational role in the social transformation of our little island into a sovereign entity embodying pride in ourselves as *"friends of all, satellites of none"*.

He was the consummate nation-builder, with none other than the then Prime Minister Owen Arthur defining him, at the unveiling of the Errol Barrow statue in 2007, as "the most complete leader of Barbados". In 1982, Barrow explained his own approach this way: *"I place special emphasis on defending the dignity and self-respect of our people since it must never be thought that poverty is a good enough excuse for abandoning virtues."*

It is this foresight that fed into the strategic goals he set for himself and his party, the Democratic Labour Party (DLP), from its outset.

At the time of the emergence of Errol Barrow in the public affairs of the island, Barbados had reached a certain constitutional threshold. In stepped a man prepared to pervade upon us a new sense that we were masters of our own fate (as against subjects of some faraway colonial controller) and that through self-confidence (and ultimately Independence), we could firmly release ourselves from the clutches of our colonisers and embrace a new actuality above and beyond that pedestrian recourse to the Palace of Westminster and Whitehall to which we had become habituated.

He believed that the concepts of political advancement that he held dear were based on a vision of creating an ideal society, and that this is only possible through well-timed and well-conceived strategies. He also knew that any effective stratagem must almost inevitably involve a struggle and that such a struggle demanded commitment and discipline by its adherents.

He strongly argued that the assumption of political office is consequential on a party doing most of the "right things" in a pivotal time. Observing him at work, I believe he saw some of these to be a strong organisation, relevant vision and a positive spirit.

It is the execution of this mode of thinking which refashioned our island into a dignified nation state. Even then this was no idle boast because we pondered how other newly emerging countries of that era had stumbled along the path after Independence, or the leadership had become so idealistic and self-absorbed as to turn back the fortunes of the people.

Not so Errol Barrow. What manner of man was this?

I do not think Barrow would mind being referred to as a democratic socialist, though it is an overused political generalisation that takes advantage of the clamour for liberal and progressive politics. He was certainly not a doctrinaire socialist, but rather a pragmatic one.

In 1985 he described himself as a "socialist" but qualified it by saying in the DLPs 30th anniversary booklet: *"I have always thought of myself as a socialist in the general terms of the British Labour Party of which I was a member. But I have become suspicious of such labels. On the one hand there is the Union of Soviet Socialist Republics. On the other hand, Hitler's political organisation was called the National Socialist Party. No doubt Fidel Castro would describe himself as a socialist. So did the man who was referred to as Ronald Reagan's closest ally in the Caribbean."*

Barrow enjoyed a nationalist outlook but appreciated the international realities within which he would have to work.

In this context we can now come to understand fully his influence on the development of the new Barbados that we unthinkingly take for granted. On profounder consideration, we discover that here was a political visionary, a man of sagacity and apposite perception. Clearly Barrow followed in the footsteps of his uncle The RE Dr Charles Duncan O'Neal, founder of the Democratic League and a man well ahead of his time in the thirties.

They both shared a desire to inspire an optimistic view of the future based on critical decision-making that was people-centred.

No Barbadian of my youthful spirit in the sixties could ever forget Barrow's impact on our lives. He made us feel that we were somebody, and that we could realise our dreams if we were prepared to work honestly and diligently. He established in us a sense of our true identity as Barbadians and placed us in a position of duty to be fully responsible for our destiny. His remarkably consistent set of ideals about Barbados and the Caribbean enthralled us. They never wavered, and because his appeal and personality copiously typified the very essence and spirit of the Barbadian version of independence, we appreciatively followed.

Errol Barrow's influence was also all-encompassing, and this must be acknowledged in any assessment of his life and times. For me, his unswerving Barbadianness also stood out in the mind of the "man in the street" searching for leaders who mirrored their tenets and expressed their fondest targets. His candour mixed with caring, and his unbridled love for a people he truly cherished, were never disrupted by the heights he climbed, the kings with whom he became acquainted or the glory of his undoubted attainments.

Barbadians of my age group, 20 or so years behind Barrow, were inspired by his model of nation-service and his drive for us to claim genuine self-determination. We revered him for his outstanding leadership and sacrifice. Today, therefore, we should honour his tireless and thankless effort to redirect the destiny of a people then strangled by Britain's imperial encirclement.

His path of progress was distinct and permanent, his instance clear and firm. His influence has rightly become a sounding board for praise, and a springboard for national enrichment and beneficial social or economic transformation. These personal attributes dove-tailed into the unique guiding ideology he adopted for his country and countrymen, an ideology he often referred to as the "right remedies," a simple term that ill Bajans familiar with seeking counsel from the "doctor shop" could relate to. In all of our suffering and sickness we always crave for "right remedies".

Barrow perceived a sick and sickening society and provided the prescription, without any of the snobbish "doctor politics" associated with Dr Eric Williams and that generation of Trinidadians and Tobagonians. I well recall that later in his career, on the eve of the 1986 General Election, Barrow challenged his colleagues to recognise and endorse *"the political will and ability of the DLP to pursue the 'right remedies'."* He qualified this by including his own views on social justice in modern Barbados, different from what prevailed when he was ushered into power in 1961.

He declared that the 'right remedies' were defined as the original hallmarks of the Party, and that as such its re-empowerment started from its own conviction to be true to itself. It was Barrow returning to the foundational values he held in high regard, and that earned him high reward in 1961 and again in 1986. I think Barrow was also saying that the Party's emphasis – its will and its ability – must, as it did in 1961, tilt against unequal shares of power.

For him 'ideology' translated into simple action-oriented theory, approaching politics in the light of a system of relevant ideas. It was Barrow who proffered the belief that Caribbean leaders must not allow themselves to be placed in *"ideological strait jackets, designed and made in Washington or anywhere else."* Or better still, his insistence at the Independence Conference in London when he asserted that he was not prepared to linger any longer on the steps of the Colonial Office.

We should all remember with fond appreciation his 1966 speech to the United Nations, where he declared: *"We will be friends of all, satellites of none. We shall not involve ourselves in sterile ideological wrangling because we are exponents not of diplomacy of power, but of the diplomacy of peace and prosperity. We will not regard any great power necessarily right in a given dispute unless we are convinced of this, yet at the same time we will not view the great powers with perennial suspicion merely on account of their size, their wealth, or their nuclear potential."*

An essential aspect of the Barrow political strategy was securing the region through a common association, be it a federation or community. He was a champion of regional integration and saw it as part of how Barbados could further grow. He joined with Forbes Burnham of Guyana and Vere Bird of Antigua to initiate CARIFTA and later with them and others to launch CARICOM. He once said that Caribbean people must accept that they have a cultural history and a *"common feeling that goes deeper and is much older than CARICOM and negotiations about trade."*

He argued that the islands are *"viable, functioning societies with the intellectual and institutional resources to understand and grapple with their problems,"* adding: *"Collectively, we have the resource potential necessary for our continued development and, of course, we have a heritage of exquisite natural beauty entrusted to us. The Caribbean is, after all, a civilisation."*

William Demas, who as President of the Caribbean Development Bank saw at first hand the movement towards integration, credited Barrow as a leading West Indian nationalist. He said of Barrow: *"He was always in favour of Caribbean political unity. He believed in Caribbean unity as an objective. He was a forthright, fearless and untiring champion of Caribbean sovereignty...not only just national flags and national anthems and so on, but genuine Caribbean sovereignty."*

Among these goals were his ideas on the rationalisation of shipping in the region, both intra- and extra-regional; the strengthening of the University of the West Indies as a regional institution free of political interference; and a novel notion about the creation of common services for all of the islands.

Thus Errol Barrow was wary of the role of the United States in Caribbean affairs and said: *"The utmost priority has to be attached both by the Caribbean and the United States to the movement for regional co-operation...,"* for him self-reliance in the situation of the Caribbean must necessarily mean collective self-reliance. *"With all the money, all the technology and all the will in the world, the US cannot solve the problems of the Caribbean."*

Strange as it may suggest, I do not think Barrow entertained the current popular belief that a political party is a machine geared primarily to win elections. He regarded this obsession as a temporal approach that devalued the benefit of creating an institution that was capable of surviving bad times to leave a positive and indelible mark on the country and its people.

On the matter of leadership, Barrow recognised the presidential nature of our elections and so paid due attention to how leadership positions were dispensed, sometimes offending those close to him. He knew that settled leadership was a pre-condition for electoral approval and to that extent he found himself wrestling, at least on two occasions, to take control of the DLP when at least one other person, Branford (later Sir Branford) Taitt, had his own ambitions.

In 1980, in the lead-up to the 1981 General Election, Taitt was Party president and it was assumed, as is the tradition in the two great parties of Barbados, that he would have given way to Barrow, the genuine Party leader. Taitt did not relent and Barrow humbly withdrew. In Barrow's place, his lieutenant, Cameron (later Sir James) Tudor, contested and lost to Taitt.

Barrow then led the DLP to its second successive defeat. Again in 1984, as we moved inexorably to the 1986 poll, Taitt was in the chair, but Barrow signalled his wish to take over at the annual conference. Taitt got support from some ridings and took on Barrow in a toe-to-toe contest. Barrow won a rather close contest, 199 votes to 154.

Barrow moved on to take the DLP to its most resounding victory ever and later Taitt would confess *"It was brave of me. And in retrospect, a little foolish too."*

Leadership style was not a matter about which Barrow seemed consciously to pay much attention. Unlike some modern-day politicians who seek advice on attire and platform dramatics and so on, he was himself and not a creation of consultants or public relations advisers. Barrow's style was appropriate to the days when we were emerging from colonialism and a strong adversarial style was appealing to people searching for a messiah.

Barrow's approach, like that of his contemporaries Forbes Burnham, Michael Manley and Dr. Eric Williams, was to adopt a combative flair consistent with what was effectively used by the labour union movement then as many political parties had emerged from trade unions.

Some of his colleagues regarded Barrow as uncaring and ruthless because he was capable of harshly expressing his views to and about colleagues. On one such occasion he disposed of two men who strayed from the Party's articulation on the fundamental issue of the payment of salary increases to parliamentarians. This cost the two senators their places in the Upper House without even a prior hint about his disgust. Barrow announced their dismissals at a public meeting, following it up with a letter to the Governor-General the following morning. On another occasion he chided his associate Speaker Neville Maxwell: *"The Lord giveth and the Lord taketh away."*

Indeed, Barrow is on record as saying: *"I will not pretend that we all agree on every detail. Neither will I pretend that we are all-perfect and abide by our high ideals in every circumstance. Every church has its share of backsliders and we have had ours. Some of them are now in important positions in the other party."*

Beyond his polished aggression, Barrow carried natural charm and a certain humane spirit that helped define his popularity at all levels of society. Spirit may not be a typically descriptive 'political' word of choice, but as deliberately applied here, it is that intangible sense of accomplishing which excites people into wanting to be part of a successful movement. Barrow had the knack for doing just that in the most unpretentious fashion.

The way in which he was able to coalesce people of all economic and social classes and colours into the unit that the DLP became shortly after its founding, spoke to the spirit of this man, even though he was not yet the nominated leader of the emerging organisation.

It should be noted that the DLP went into the 1961 election with no designated leader and its manifesto failed to carry the traditional tone-setting statement of a party head. However, in the course of the election campaign Barrow emerged as the obvious choice when they won, but J.E.T. Brancker (later Sir Theodore), who was Opposition Leader and seen as the most senior of the stalwarts, said he would not serve in Barrow's Cabinet and took the post of Speaker instead.

This winning spirit of Barrow was no accident. Central to the Party's success was his vibrant personality which attracted to the Party's fold, by contrast, the likes of the eminent businessman Douglas Lynch (later Sir Douglas) and English hotelier Peter Morgan, on the one hand, and taximan Livvy Burrowes and entrepreneur C. Leroy Brathwaite on the other.

All sorts of persons, regardless of ideological perspective, scrambled to be part of the new DLP experience in the early sixties. This spoke to the Party's spirit. People put aside their individual "isms" and differences to get on board the train, unconcerned about the route and undaunted about the cost, caring only about the destination. Many dismiss spirit as unimportant, but it is what ignites emotions when logic and argument fail. Barrow knew it binds people in a common aim when dogmas or adversity set in and failure is at the doorstep.

A Party's spirit is the sense which it develops in people of wanting to belong, created by sharing big ideals and appreciating quality leadership. The body language of its principals, the contagious camaraderie that lends to a feeling of family and oneness are key contributors. Barrow abounded in these attributes.

Spirit leads to a feeling of passion about the party and infuses the electorate with a desire to realise its dreams because they see themselves in or contributing to those dreams. The essential element of spirit is based on a party being identifiable with something. The Party must define what that something is, and it must be believable.

Was anyone ever in any doubt about where Barrow stood on anything? Even when he changed his mind, as he did (with cause) on the Federation of the "Little Eight", he could make the switch because he recognised that conditions had changed, and he was confident that his judgment would be trusted by the people.

But merging disparate persons into a single political unit where ideology plays an intrinsic part, creates a risk of introducing friction between extreme causes and priorities. It was Barrow's challenge to resolve this as bloodlessly as possible. It was something only he could achieve.

In creating a balanced path for all, he lost some founders like Owen T. Allder and Lloyd Brathwaite, who had little tolerance for the other race, whites, in the early scheme of things DLP. Barrow and others in the leadership of the DLP never deviated from the course of racial forbearance. They also wisely sought a central point between extremes of ideology and race.

The effort was to have a harmonious arrangement of all the forces and factors that impinge on a party's operations, and thus its enduring success. Clearly Barrow understood the dangers of one group having an undeserved advantage in the affairs of a party seeking the endorsement of all.

His building blocks of success came not only from seeking a perfect balance, but also from having an open mind. Barrow was quick to work with people who believed in this goal. He must therefore have been emboldened by the insatiable drive of A.E.S. (T.T.) Lewis, the passion of Owen T. Allder, the eloquence of Cameron Tudor (later Sir James) and the dedicated democratic socialist moorings of Wynter Crawford and Edwy Talma (later Sir Edwy).

He recognised that a party seeking to emerge from the unknown, and fighting against an entrenched entity like the Barbados Labour Party and the apparently indomitable Sir Grantley Adams (later The RE Sir Grantley), required a desire, nay passion, to assimilate and integrate new thinking, theories and comportment.

To this extent, Barrow gave a keen listening ear to Crawford whose experience in the establishment and running of the National Congress Party would prove invaluable, and who was a fount of new, bright ideas and astute on political manoeuvring. No assessment of Barrow's early success should ignore the Crawford factor which also added a dimension of anti-Adams bombast crucial to dismantling this political pillar.

How was success achieved?

On the way to creating the conditions for acceptance, empowerment and, ultimately holding office, Barrow developed a political party that provided people with a sense of their own liberation from real or perceived shackles, and offered a way out from their induced feeling of indolence. In many respects he must have seen this as a personal undertaking, but knew it had to be achieved outside of the BLP whose leadership had a far too gradualist approach to the full emancipation of the people.

As one who closely followed Grantley Adams, Barrow knew that the people of Barbados, by their consistent record, had demonstrated a loyalty to a proven leader, but were clinical in the way they executed selection. He knew Barbadians set very high standards for those who would run their affairs. There were no shortcuts to obtaining endorsement. They would not be fooled into accepting imitations of the real thing, and insisted on commitment to hard work.

On the road to seeking the approval of the masses, a political leader had to understand that a perceptive people would see past the smoke and mirrors, through the gloss, and around the façade. Thus he was prepared to ignore the trappings and offer substance. That substance was people empowerment. It went further, though. He adopted a self-effacing projection of self.

This Errol Barrow political strategy is well grasped by comparing the manifestos of his DLP in his heyday with those of the BLP during Owen Arthur's prime.

While for the DLP it was never about Errol Barrow the man, for the BLP it was only about Owen Arthur. No DLP manifesto carried a picture of Errol Barrow on its cover for any of the elections between 1961-1986 when he was leader. (In 2008 David Thompson's picture featured as did Freundel Stuart's in 2013). On the other hand, for every election in which Arthur led the BLP in 1994, 1999, 2003, 2008 and 2013, Arthur's picture dominated the cover of each manifesto.

And when one looks at the slogans used, again the thrust of the DLP was about what it could do for the country. Like "Operation Takeover", "Advance with the Dems", Design for Living", "Putting it Back Together", "Into the 90s and Beyond", "Barbados Into the 21st Century", "Fighting for Your Security" and "A Fair Share for all".

For BLP sloganising, the direction differed: "The Great Combination", "A Team for the Times", "Going with Owen" and "Arthur

Now more than ever" all spoke to individuals. In fairness though, during Arthur's time the BLP also carried slogans such as "Your Choice for Change", "Only the Best for Barbados", but by juxtaposing Arthur's picture next to these titles, they still sent a certain message about the man.

Thus look and character of the manifestos of the DLP during Barrow's tenure spoke volumes about his modesty. They did not seek to make him out to be the people's saviour, even if this was what people clamoured after. There was nothing of the tawdry boast that the BLP used in the Owen Arthur era. For Barrow, his picture as their leader needed no reinforcement because his likeness was engraved in their hearts. It was not the messenger, but the message.

Another fine attribute of Barrow's campaigning was the fact that he was an intense listener. Although, as I know only too well, his retorts could be devastating.

Barrow did not like canvassing in his own riding, St John, and discouraged it by imploring colleagues not to "contaminate the night air" with blaring loudspeakers because the people of that parish needed no political meetings to make informed decisions. However, at a national level he liked to be innovative.

Two examples stand out in my memory because they were so visual. The first was his use in 1971 of a horse to do house-to-house canvassing. People liked the idea of "The Skipper" riding a horse in their neighbourhood. On another occasion, he flew a light aircraft over the island, dropping off bundles of the DLP's newspaper, The Democrat, from the air.

As he came to his last years, Barrow left with Barbadians his concerns for our future when he delivered his well-known "Mirror Image" speech 1986 at a memorable public meeting. It was a message that expressed his concern for the misplaced values of citizens he helped fashion in a very precise manner.

At this juncture, we may well want to reflect on his words and not just gloat over his phenomenal strategies that took us "over the bridge," as calypsonian John King so eloquently shared with us.

Barrow was not just a man of personal charm who inspired loyalty from colleagues and admiration from supporters. He was committed to the transformation of the society. As he spoke in anguish on that night in 1986 in Independence Square, Bridgetown, his overarching concern was the evaporation of the self-confident, self-reliant Barbadian he envisaged and indeed, inspired. He regretted the disappearance of the strong, assertive and independent Barbadian spirit and mourned the new value system that made mendicants of us all.

He said what he wanted for Barbados was a people able to run their own affairs, pay for the cost of running their own country and have an educational system which was as good as what could be obtained in any industrialised country anywhere in the world. As we reflect on his strategies and style, Barbadians have an onus to regain the lustre which Errol Barrow bequeathed to us, urging that we abandon our opportunistic cravings and become firm craftsmen of our fate.

"A true man does not seek the path where advantage lies,
but rather the path where duty lies.
And that is the only practical man,
whose dreams of today will be the law of tomorrow
because he knows that without a single exception,
the future lies on the side of duty."

JOSE MARTI, journalist, poet and National Hero of Cuba

Speaking for the confraternity of pain and deprivation

Address to the 29th Annual Governors' Meeting of the World Bank and International Monetary Fund (IMF) in Washington, D.C., 3 October, 1974.

I have the distinctive honour to address this meeting on behalf of the Governors of the Bank for the Bahamas, Guyana, Jamaica and Trinidad and Toabago, as well as for my own country, Barbados, and if they should so wish the rest of the Caribbean Community not represented here at this Twenty-Ninth Annual Meeting of the International Monetary Fund and of the World Bank.

I should like to congratulate Mr McNamara (Robert)[*] for his very constructive and thought-provoking speech to us and for the efforts which he and the Executive Board extended on behalf of us all in the developing world during this past year. The institutional developments relating to the World Bank Group and specifically the Development Committee, which we support, should provide material assistance to the Group in the years ahead and enable it to achieve the realistic goals which it has set for itself.

Since the meeting in Nairobi last year developments in the international economy have introduced new financial crises and have placed additional obstacles in the way of developing countries as they strive to provide more jobs and improve the standard of living of their peoples. We in the Commonwealth Caribbean have not escaped these convulsions; and we are striving, through regional co-operation as well as through our own individual efforts, not only to meet the present difficulties, but also to provide for the necessary long-term restructuring of our economies. But in these efforts, we require the full support of the international institutions and particularly the World Bank Group.

We believe that if the international institutions are to play their expected role in the modern world they must work with the support and the efforts of the peoples in the developing world; they must

[*] Then President of the World Bank.

encourage them through financial and technical support to redouble their efforts and so provide more jobs, more school places, better health facilities, more houses, and a more diversified production structure than would otherwise have been possible. But the relationship between the World Bank group and the developing countries can be productive only if it is conceived in terms of a partnership at the highest; but more properly as principals working through an agency for the fulfilment of the collective and individual objectives of the members of the organisation.

We in the Commonwealth Caribbean welcome constructive comments and advice on the policies we pursue and on the methods of introducing feasible modifications. We recognise that the World Bank Group can bring to bear on our development problem advice and experience drawn from a wide cross section of the developing world. At the same time, since development is about people and for people, development processes work only through the institutions and systems that have become part of the country's way of life; and they will work only if the people are satisfied that they respond to their real needs and circumstances. In this sensitive area, therefore, the views and practices of the recipient countries cannot be lightly ignored or, worse still, discarded. It is the antithesis of co-operation and counter-productive in the extreme for the World Bank Group to impose as preconditions for its support, policies which we in these countries are convinced are inappropriate or impossible to implement at any particular point in time. What clearly is necessary is for a continuing dialogue, without preconditions, between the World Bank Group and the client country through which an acceptable package of policies and financial support can be worked out. The World Bank Group must accept as a fact that the government and people of· a country are most concerned about their own future and fully realise that the primary responsibility for achieving the highest rate of economic development rests on themselves. But in this they need the support of the institutions based on effective consultation.

This need for continuing dialogue has always been necessary. But it is even more necessary now as we in the Caribbean strive to cope with the development problem complicated by the energy crisis. These circumstances call for the closest possible co-operation and genuine sympathy from the World Bank Group. It is, therefore, disturbing to us to find that, in the current aggravated circumstances that we face, the World Bank Group seeks to impose preconditions for its support which are unattainable even in normal times. To give an example, the high imported inflation from which we all suffer calls for special measures to assist the lowest income groups. This must affect the level of public savings. Quite clearly, we must find intolerable, a precondition which imposes on us a level of public sector savings unattainable even in the absence of such pressures. A similar situation arises in respect of our public utilities, severely affected by the higher prices for oil, machinery and equipment. If they are required to achieve the same rate of return as before, even when they are adding to their fixed assets, then they too will add to internal inflation. But how can the underemployed rural dweller absorb higher utility charges when he is already burdened with higher prices for rice, flour and meat? Yet measures such as these, including completely new concepts relating to credit worthiness, are being imposed on some developing countries as preconditions for Bank assistance. If these measures are insisted upon there can be only one result – the destruction of the social fabric and cohesiveness in the societies which will make any form of development impossible.

This is why we emphasise the need for constructive dialogue. We believe that the World Bank Group must always be guided by the spirit of its Charter which emphasises the role of the Group as agents in the development process. Such a role is inconsistent with the adoption of preconceived policies and concepts which are insensitive to the real problems that we in the developing countries face.

If, as we hope and should believe, the Bank really wants to assist us, the small developing countries with special problems, then a special approach is clearly necessary. I have referred to the need for dialogue. There is also the need for special measures to speed up the disbursement of the Bank's assistance. We are mindful of the strictures in the Bank's Articles of Agreement, which limit the extent to which non-project lending can be undertaken. We are also aware, and we appreciate, the excellence of the Bank's project preparation work and the contribution which this can make to financial discipline and institution building in small developing countries such as our own. Nevertheless, we believe that the pressures which the present situation creates for an early transfer of real resources on the scale required and within the time period necessary cannot be effected solely through project lending. If the Bank is to be effective a much greater proportion of its resources must be disbursed in the form of programme loans to accelerate economic and social development and make an early contribution to the creation of jobs.

There is a further reason why programme lending must be adopted in dealing with small developing countries such as our own. Many of the projects which we have are small and discreet, but they all add up to a development programme which has meaning to our population. The Bank can assist us in meaningful ways only if it adapts its policies to suit the special circumstances that we face. Regrettably, this is not now the case.

One of the ways in which the World Bank Group can adapt its policies to meet our special circumstances is to provide additional assistance through our Caribbean Development Bank. However, in using the regional institution to channel World Bank funds, two important guidelines must be observed. First, such assistance as is provided through the regional financial institutions, should be supplementary to, and not at the expense of the other financial and technical support, coming directly from the Bank to its members; in other words, the Caribbean Development Bank should be used as a vehicle for increasing the financial assistance which the Bank will provide for countries in the Commonwealth Caribbean. I wish to emphasise, as Chairman of the Board of Governors, that the Caribbean Development Bank should not be regarded as an alternative vehicle for providing the same amount of support. Second, in providing through the Caribbean Development Bank the World Bank should not impose criteria and restrictions which would inhibit the regional institution and make it ineffective as a vehicle for transmitting such support. Assistance should always be provided on the most concessionary terms in order to meet the needs of the poorest countries of the region.

The financial crisis in which the small developing countries of the Caribbean are now being tempestuously tossed around adds new urgency to questions which we have raised in the past – one of these is the introduction of third window[**] in the Bank. We are not unmindful of the problem of finding additional resources which could be made available on special concessionary terms. We do, however, feel that when all of us are recoiling from the special problems of imported inflation and the general problems of underdevelopment, then the needs of all of us, and not only a few of us, in the developing world must be taken into account. It may well be that an essential prerequisite for mobilising the resources required will be a restructuring of the shareholding in the Bank to reflect the realities of the circumstances that face us today and of the special position of the oil producing countries in particular. There is in our view no justification for the international community not facing up to this issue.

[**] 'Third Window' refers to the lending section of the bank. A first window might represent, for example, loans at ordinary, i.e. non-concessionary rates, while a second window offered easier terms.

We propose that special devices be adopted now to alleviate the heavy debt burden that the developing country clients of the Bank now bear. This burden is now critical; it will become increasingly so in the light of the current excessively high borrowing rates. We, therefore, propose for consideration, the establishment of a compen-satory tranche*** of soft funds to alleviate this burden on developing countries whose development efforts are being threatened by burdensome debt service payments. We are prepared to submit a detailed formulation of this proposal to the Bank.

We acknowledge that under the dynamic leadership of Mr McNamara, the Bank has discarded many of the shibboleths that formerly impaired the quality of the assistance it provided in the overall development effort. This evolution must continue and the Bank, recognising the principles of national sovereignty over natural resources, must play a constructive and positive role in ensuring that countries with such resources obtain the best possible returns, measured in national terms, from those assets which they are fortunate to have.

The Bank can assist in a number of ways. Firstly, by financing the infrastructure required for the exploitation of these resources. Secondly, by participating directly in the financing of natural resource projects and in assisting developing countries in negotiating the best possible terms in their exploitation; and third, by invoking the powers provided in the Articles of Agreement of the World Bank to guarantee market loans raised by the developing countries for participation in the projects themselves. We are convinced that through these devices the Bank can make a signal contribution to international economic stability and development and enable small countries to obtain a fair and just return from their national assets.

I should now like to make a few observations on behalf of the government of Barbados and based largely upon my personal experience.

As with most institutions, whether international or governmental, that may owe allegiance to several masters the International Bank for Reconstruction and Development has developed a personality of its own which does not necessarily bear resemblance to the demeanours, physiognomies, or outlooks of all or any of its members; and what is probably more alarming, the Bank has developed a will of its own which more frequently than not, fails to reflect the individual will and

---

*** 'Tranche' refers to the reserve of money contributed to the institution and then available for on-lending to members.

aspirations of any of its members, or the collective will of all as concluded in the annual statements of the Governors or in the resolutions which we may pass from time to time.

Like most bureaucracies, the Bank has developed its own theology with accompanying ritual of canons and liturgy and its own hierarchy of saints and priests and novices. We the Governors are expected to attend the celebration of the mass on the saint days which usually extend over the last week in September and first week in October, dependent, for all intents and purposes, on the phases of the moon.

I am aware that the Bank was designed to engineer the reconstruction and development of the European countries which had been devastated by World War II. In that regard the Bank succeeded in restoring the mighty to their seat, without having to worry itself morally or otherwise with exalting the humble and meek.

In its preoccupation with what it considered to be its prime objective of restoration, it not only restored the gap between the rich and the poor, but by accident rather than by design continued to exacerbate the growing economic disharmonies between the absolute rich and, what has been described at this very meeting, as the absolute poor.

We in the Caribbean are not classified by this or by any other international institution among the congregation of the absolute poor.

Our countries do not figure among those selected for redemption because we have managed by our own efforts to raise the per capita incomes of our peoples and because we have succeeded in developing our health and educational services to levels which frequently equate, and sometimes surpass, those of more prosperous countries.

We have done so despite the low prices hitherto paid for our primary products and despite the lack of encouragement and assistance from the countries which constituted our traditional trading partners. We have been imbued not with righteousness but with hopelessness, but we have managed to muster our courage to take our destinies into our own hands.

I speak for the median minority; for those hitherto silent members who have come out of great tribulations but who recognise the soul-destroying tribulations of those who are still members of the confraternity of pain and deprivation. These are the one billion persons to whom Mr McNamara referred who suffocate and suffer with per capita incomes of less than $200 per annum.

We come from the Caribbean not as supplicants at the gate – the gates of the IDA[****] have long been shut in our faces – but as members of the co-operative anxious to do business and with bankable assurances.

It is at this stage that the inquisition begins. And after the inquisition, a period of instruction on how we should amend our wicked, wicked ways of trying to overcome unemployment and raise our living standards. We must do penance on our knees, create more unemployment, devalue our currencies, freeze wages at levels which are demonstrably below subsistence in order to preserve our comparitive costs advantages, and read the economic sermons of the Reverend Dr Malthus[*****] in all our churches twice a day at matins and vespers and four times on a Sunday.

If I appear to be critical of the current policies pursued by the World Bank Group, it is not because I am unaware of the important strides which the Bank has made over the past several years and of the dynamic plans that it proposes for the five years ahead. We in the Caribbean are pleased to support the adoption of the proposal for a lending programme of US $36 billion over the period 1974-78, a programme which, in our view, calls not only for increased borrowing by the Bank but also for an increase in capital subscription. Our comments derive entirely from the fact that we are inordinately dependent on the international institutions for our economic viability, and for the preservation of our independence; we, therefore, feel compelled to urge this important institution to adapt its policies and programmes to meet the specific circumstances which we face, so that the assistance which it can provide to us will produce the results which both we and the Bank expect, sufficiently and in time.

.

[****]IDA is the International Development Association, an institution of the World Bank which specialises in providing soft loans to developing countries.

[*****] "Rev. Dr Malthus" is a reference to Robert Thomas Malthus (1766-1834), a British economist best known for his warning that unless world population growth was controlled it would outstrip world food supply.

Co-operation to survive and advance

Address to the Annual Governors' Meeting of the Caribbean Development Bank (CDB), held in Barbados on 26 May, 1975.

Your Excellencies,
Fellow Governors and Advisers,
Mr President,
and Directors of the Caribbean Development Bank,
Distinguished Guests and Observers,
Ladies and Gentlemen,

The normal procedure at these Annual Meetings of the Bank is for the Chairman of the Board of Governors to invite the Head of Government of the host country to welcome the visitors and to declare the meeting open. There is then a vote of thanks and the Prime Minister leaves, after which the Chairman of the Board of Governors delivers his report and the more practical aspect of the Board's business is embarked upon with the President's address.

This year, Providence has ordained that you should be spared at least three of these addresses, but nevertheless, it is still my duty and pleasure as Chairman of the Cabinet of Barbados to say welcome to you all. As Chairman of the Board of Governors of the Bank, I should like to say a special word of welcome to the representatives of the Republic of Colombia, which is being represented at the Board of Governors Meeting for the first time since being admitted to full membership and, happily for us, by a long established friend of the Caribbean, the distinguished Dr Carlos Sanz de Santamaria.

I should also like to record with pleasure the presence, as observers from our neighbours in the Caribbean, of Sr. Julio Imperatori, Vice President of the Banco Nacional de Cuba, Sr. Andres Julio Espinal of the Central Bank of the Dominican Republic, Sr. Luis E. Agrait and others from the Commonwealth of Puerto Rico; Sr. Wenceslas Salas of the Bank of Mexico; Mr Braam of the Ministry of Finance of

Surinam and also His Excellency E.O. Kolade, the High Commissioner of Nigeria to many CARICOM countries.

In every respect, with all respect, and in my multiple capacities – welcome.

I have no intention of leaving the meeting at this stage, neither will I permit a vote of thanks.

It is my sincere wish that you are by now quite certain of your welcome to our friendly island. I say this, not only because I know the people of Barbados wish it to be so, but because it is important that we should be sufficiently composed to reflect, for the next day or two, on the course travelled by this important regional institution during the past year, and to set its course, together, for the year ahead or more. Occasions like these are important and necessary if we are not to feel, with justification, that we are but the victims of events and institutions alike, rather than the framers in large measure of our destiny and our fate. This is our Bank, and if we would have it serve us, we must first serve it.

In my view, it is timely to remind ourselves that this institution was created, not so much to fulfil some hallowed and time-bound concept of development, nor the dream of one visionary or another, but to foster and contribute to the improvement in the welfare and living conditions of the peoples of the region. The precise methods by which this goal of human upliftment is accomplished may, and indeed must, vary with time and circumstances. But the goal itself cannot change.

The Annual Report of the Directors reminds us that recent developments in the wider world around us have made attainment of our goal more difficult rather than easier. For many years, instability and uncertainty have been the main features of the international financial and monetary system. This has been followed by inflation and shortages – especially in food and energy. Recession and growing unemployment now threaten to overshadow the severity and seriousness of the former crises. Because of this it is perhaps understandable, though not necessarily excusable, that more attention would appear to be given to individual survival, rather than to international co-operation and development. Our responsibility in the developing world is to continue to remind the international community that the transfer of resources from areas of relative abundance to areas of relative scarcity and need, is not only a social and economic, but the moral and practical imperative of our times.

This Bank, like others of its kind, was created to assist the transfer of resources to this region as well as the re-distribution of resources within the region. I am particularly encouraged by two recent developments which, among others, give clear evidence of the continued success of the Bank in attracting resources to the Region. I refer to the interest expressed by General (Yakabu) Gowon, President of the Republic of Nigeria, in channelling funds to the region through the Bank, and the re-affirmation of a decision by the Governors of the Inter-American Development Bank to make funds available fo the Caribbean Development Bank for on-lending to all member countries, whether or not members of the Inter-American Development Bank.

The loan by the government of Trinidad and Tobago on soft terms to assist the LDCs (Lesser Developed Countries) in providing counterpart funds for projects financed by the Bank, and the creation by the government of Venezuela of a Trust Fund in the Bank are without a doubt our most outstanding examples to date of use of the Bank to redistribute resources within the region.

I need hardly remind you that this effort to attract resources is crucial to the success of the Bank, and that we must individually and collectively pursue policies that will make the attraction and distribution of resources a continuingly successful exercise.

A review of the activities of the Bank during the past year reminds us, however, that development, even when aided by indigenous institutions and inspired by native genius, is a complex process requiring sustained effort and the tackling of many different problems simultaneously. Resources, scarce and necessary though they are, are by our own experience more difficult to disburse than to mobilise. The Annual Report reminds us yet again that disbursement of resources is our least distinguished accomplishment. Some member countries, like my own, are even less distinguished in this regard than most. Because of this I might perhaps venture a few observations on this recurring and vexing problem.

It is a widely held view, though perhaps not as widely expressed, that loan disbursement procedures appear to be designed not just to safeguard the interest of the lender, but to tax the ingenuity of the borrower. (For my part I remain convinced that they are designed to tax the ingenuity of the lender as well!) Much can and is being done by the Bank to improve and simplify its disbursement procedures. But as has been observed before by the Bank and its borrowers alike, what is done in this direction must always be consistent with maintaining the integrity and viability of the institution itself. It is, after all – however regrettable member countries find it – a loan institution. The maxim 'Neither a borrower nor a lender be' is not emblazoned on the escutcheon of the Bank.

It is recognised too that disbursement is as much a function of lending procedures as of the absorptive capacity of borrowers. Generally, though not invariably, lower absorptive capacity is associated with low levels of development. Unsuitable and inadequate institutional arrangements, fiscal constraints and scarcity of skilled manpower all contribute to the inablility of our countries to absorb financing at the rates that we would wish. It is clear that these bottlenecks must be tackled vigorously and conscientiously if we are to succeed, and the Bank with us and through us. In my view there are a number of things that can be done now to reduce these obstacles to disbursement.

Firstly, there is training in appropriate project skills of persons whose jobs it will be to formulate and implement projects. I would urge your support then for the proposed Project Training Courses at the Centre for Development Studies with the assistance of the Bank and under the supervision of our former President, Sir Arthur Lewis who has consented to be the Centre's Director. Shortage of skilled and experienced project specialists is a universal, not just a regional, phenomenon. This alone would suggest that we should attempt to develop these skills here in the Region with the assistance of this our own financing institution, the Caribbean Development Bank.

Secondly, the process of identification and formulation of viable regional projects must continue. We have made an encouraging start in this direction, but it is only a start. Those who are impatient with results in this area to date, should reflect on the complexity of the exercise and the cost to the region, should adequate research and preparation not precede implementation.

Thirdly, I turn to the thorny problem of institutional reform. Here the problem of skilled manpower shortages confronts us again. More important than this, however, is the question of political will. The dismantling and reform of institutions invariably involves tampering with vested interests of one kind or another. All institutions, however efficient, serve some purpose and some interests – though not always the right ones. Experience would suggest that the tackling of this problem is necessary to our success in raising the living standards of the broad mass of our people. We neglect it at great costs and to our own peril.

I observed earlier that the temptation is perhaps for some, especially the relatively better off, to avoid co-operative effort and pursue individual survival. In this way some or a few might indeed survive. It is unlikely that any of us would advance. Ever-widening co-operative efforts are called for now more than ever. Our problems no longer come singly, as we know only too well from recent experience with inflation and recession.

We must strengthen the inner circles in order to survive.

We must strengthen the inner circles in order to survive and move to wider circles of regional co-operation, if we are to hold our own in this era of crisis and strain.

We must strengthen the inner circles in order to survive; move to wider circles of regional co-operation if we are to hold our own; and press on to ever-widening circles of international co-operation if we are to concern ourselves not merely with survival and keeping up with the rest, but with the advancement and relentless onward march of the people whom we claim to represent and who expect us, through this institution, to show them clearly the way ahead.

Come Unto Me

Dame Maizie Barker-Welch

1987 Parliamentary Tribute (abridged)

I met Errol Walton Barrow first in 1952, when I was introduced to him as, believe it or not, the teacher of my husband. I did not know at that time that I was in the presence of the greatest Caribbean man of this century.

I, then, became very interested in the Democratic Labour Party and realised that Errol Barrow had tremendous dreams and vision for Barbados. I realised that he would stop at nothing to carry out the ideals and objectives as stated in our Constitution, the Constitution of the Democratic Labour Party, which he founded in 1955.

I was able, thereafter, to watch the progress of the man, politician and statesman, and it was with great rejoicing that I witnessed his plans unfolding. I know that I am speaking for all the women in Barbados who care about their families when I say that the he did not go about flaunting banners, he did not have any gimmicky speeches about women but he cared so deeply that he instituted the sort of legislation that would make the women of this country very happy.

When you feed a woman's children, you are feeding her. When you make school books available to them, you are helping her. When you give free education, you are making all the women of Barbados know that their sons and daughters can achieve and aspire to the great heights of the politicians and the statesmen of this country. I remember very well how some people did not believe it could have been done, but he knew, and today we are reaping the benefits when we watch the engineers, agriculturalists and all the various professions of the young Barbadians.

I do hope that a lot of them, most of them, who do not yet know about this man, will be able to read about him. I feel we should commission people to write books, books so that the smallest child can understand, so that instead of reading "Dan is the man in the van" from some outside source, they will read about Errol Walton Barrow, a hero of Barbados.

I remember, too, his great concern for women, in that he was a little impatient with women's organisations because he did not see them as drawing in all of the women, he saw them as a sort of middle-class institution, and in my eagerness to, what shall I say, talk for the cause of women's organisations, we had several arguments. But I had to admit that he was right. A lot of time that is spent in just socialising could far better be spent in making sure that the women of all walks of life are drafted in, that their suggestions are sought, that they are brought up with all of those others who already have had an advantage.

I also respect him as a great Caribbean man, and it was the measure of his influence that even though he was in Opposition, the leaders of the Caribbean and the politicians of the Caribbean still listened to him.

I scarcely am able to finish the National Anthem these days, I usually sing it on occasions when it is played, but every time I sing that National Anthem, I remember who caused us to have that Anthem, I remember the Father of our Independence. And so, it is with humility, but still a very great pride, that I, too, pay tribute to this great man.

"Development and Democracy"

Anniversary lecture to the Democratic Labour Party's
Academy of Politics on 25 April, 1980

What is democracy? The word is a combination of two Greek words
DEMOS (People) and KRATEIN (to rule). In other words, rule by the
people either directly or through elected representatives, as distinct
from rule by a person, a monarch, a king, an emperor, a dictator, an
oligarchy, or a few people – rule then by the majority.

I should like to make my language unambiguous from the outset by
saying that democracy as most political scientists understand the
term, is not a philosophy in itself nor a body of beliefs on which one
can simply pin abiding faith by declaring I believe in democracy and
done with that. All you have established is a commitment to a system
in arriving at decisions but not the nature of the decisions themselves
nor the criteria by which they may have to be evaluated.

The democratic process is supposed to ensure that the decisions
which are made, enure to the benefit of the greatest number and that
there is some substantial support for actions and programmes
embarked upon in the name of the people. Development is described
in the 'New World' Dictionary as economic, social and political
progress after emergence into statehood.

The terms have been most frequently used internationally with
reference to Third World countries and specifically we have had the
Development Decade and the United Nations Conferences on Trade
and Development, the Inter-American Development Bank, the
Caribbean Development Bank and so on ad infinitum. The government of Puerto Rico named their most successful development
institution Fomento. In whatever language, in whatever country, in
whatever forum we speak, when we say development, we immediately stimulate the interest of all classes and races and ideologies, the
interest of the banker, and baker and candlestick maker, the gluttons,
the scholars and even the dunces. There is always the promise in
development of something for everyone, a little more for some, a little

less for others, rich man, poor man, beggar and thief.

In order to understand the objective of developmental process which, I take it, is to become developed, it is necessary to know what is the antithesis – 'underdeveloped' or 'undeveloped'. Economists and sociologists tend to employ definitions which are mainly concerned with per capita incomes, extent of industrialisation, consumption of electricity, number of telephones, television sets and motor vehicles and other particularly North American criteria which are demonstrably irrelevant to the kind of societies that such humanists as Dr Kenneth Kaunda and Dr Julius Nyerere are trying to reconstruct in their respective countries. Von der Mehd, himself a distinguished American political scientist, had this to say, 'The average American has built a stereotype of an underdeveloped country. According to this stereotype, a state is considered underdeveloped if it cannot be related to a model based upon a Western European or North American polity which is democratic and which has several political parties, widespread literacy, a high standard of living, wide circulation of newspapers and books, consensus on the fundamentals of government, a long history of peace, and (in some models) a white population'.

K. H. Pfeffer of the University of Punjab wrote in 1960, 'The term underdeveloped country is based on the assumption that there exists a commonly accepted standard of development. A person or a group or a nation can only be called underdeveloped when there is general agreement what a developed or a fully developed person, nation or group ought to be like. Thus, the very category underdeveloped should be tested before use, since it is loaded with values and prejudices'.

When I accepted the invitation to deliver this first of the annual Anniversary Lectures, which happily coincides with the celebrations of the 25th Anniversary of the founding of the Democratic Labour Party, I had no idea that the title chosen for this lecture would be one over which I would have had to agonise for such long periods of time or that it would be fraught with so many semantic, philological, and philosophical difficulties. In order to escape from the entanglement of time consuming academic quarrels, I wish to crave your indulgence to allow me to adopt for our own limited purposes some definitions more relevant to the human situation in our own country.

Firstly, I wish you to accept that since 1980 is neither the beginning of creation nor, as far as I can discern, the end of history, that all countries are developing countries and all peoples all over the world are evolving in different ways under different systems towards conditions of perfection or imperfection which human ingenuity at this early dawn in the history of mankind cannot foretell.

Secondly, that for the time being, for lack of better, we as a people, prefer a democratic system of arriving at decisions. The problem of political development, in theory at least, is not one which inhibits us, since we are actors ourselves and not acted upon as we were before independence.

Thirdly, that the development which concerns us all immediately is social and economic in quantity, and personal and human in quality.

And that brings us straight to the examination of the way in which this development is to be achieved and sustained under the democratic process.

On the 15th January, 1941, President Franklin D. Roosevelt delivered these words in his message to the United States Congress: 'The basic things expected by our people of their political and economic system, are simple. They are: Equality of opportunity for youth and others. Jobs for those who can work. Security for those who need it. The ending of special privilege for the few. The preservation of civil liberties for all. The enjoyment of the fruits of scientific progress for a wider and constantly rising standard of living'.

These things cannot come automatically, they must result from an economic relationship in which all (the citizens) have a shared interest and concern.

Article Three of the Constitution of the Democratic Labour Party sets out the objects of the party. Three (b) is to raise the standard of living of the people of Barbados and create the greatest measure of social betterment by sound management of the financial and economic resources of the country. Three (e) is to create and maintain a social and economic atmosphere conducive to the enjoyment of equal opportunities and of the democratic way of life by all.

The founders of the Democratic Labour Party twenty five years ago and the President of the United States of America forty years ago, both spoke clearly about equality of opportunity for people. Real equality and real opportunity must open the door to real personal and real human development. Not the kind of opportunity calling at 8.15 a.m.* for requirements and qualifications with which our educational system has not provided the average citizen. I respectfully submit that these government programmes have been systematically de-signed to give the impression that opportunities for employment are

*This is a reference to a government-sponsored short radio programme advertising training and job opportunities.

being created by a government which is in fact, doing nothing more than disseminating advertisements clipped for the most part, from bulletins and information sheets of overseas organisations.

President Franklin D Rooselvelt, the product of a wealthy American capitalist family, speaking to a Congress dominated by the concept of unbridled capitalism and the inestimable benefits of the free enterprise system, did not apologise for stating unequivocally that the first basic that the people expected of their political and economic system was –'Equality of opportunity for youth and others'. How else can people develop? The Gross Domestic Product of a country at factor costs, or market value can grow from year to year. Yet people can stagnate, suffer and succumb. 'Ill fares the land to hastening ills a prey, where wealth accumulates and men decay'.

We in Barbados tend to take cover and run for shelter as soon as the C.Gs, D.Ds, E.L.C.** and the other cohorts of unbridled capitalism deliver their periodic attacks on the principle of socialism which they little understand but feel it their duty to assail.

When he was Chief Minister of Jamaica in the fifties, the late Norman Washington Manley said, 'What is the essence of socialism? It was never put better than by Professor Arthur Lewis when he said with stark simplicity, Socialism is about equality. A socialist believes that the purpose of human history is to achieve a society dominated, dominated, dominated by the concept of equality'.

After all that is what FDR says the people expect of their political system. And he was not speaking about Czechoslovakia or the Union of Soviet Socialist Republics. He was speaking about the broad masses of registered Republicans and registered Democrats living in the free enterprise capitalistic United States of America. This concept of equality – Mr Manley went on – involves a society where the exploitation implicit in the class system has ceased. A society where there is equal opportunity, not (merely) opportunity, but truly equal opportunity for all to share in a rich and varied life and to develop the many and varied solid talents of the human individual. That is development.

Secondly, a society where each person will have equal access to the essential human freedoms, and this involves a society rooted in economic and social security consciously maintained and reinforced by creative human effort, foresight and skill and, lastly, a society where there will be equality of status without which the belief in the supreme significance of the individual is meaningless and largely

**C.Gs, D.Ds are regualr pro-American letter writers to local newspapers. ELC is the pseudonym of former newspaper proprietor Jimmy Cozier, who has a column in the local press.

hypocrisy.

As we enter the decade of the eighties, there is no need for us to contrive new formulae or spin out new high-sounding phrases in an attempt to attract support to our basic philosophy. We leave it to others of baser metal to indulge in calculated political chicanery and to attempt to suborn and subvert the public purpose. True personal development cannot take place if the political leaders of a country believe that the masses are there for manipulation. The Brazilian educator, Paulo Freire wrote, 'A real humanist can be identified more by his trust in the people which engage him in their struggle, than by a thousand actions in their favour without that trust'.

The distribution of largesse which the 'Larousse' English dictionary describes as the distribution of gifts by a superior to inferiors cannot be development. Conspicuous consumption by politicians, particularly undertaken at the expense of the taxpayers, is not development. The construction of office buildings may boost the profits of importers of builders' hardware and provide some jobs at a low technological level in a short time span, but it is not development. The purchase of warships and armoured cars is not development, particularly when no local skills have been mobilised in their acquisition, also at public expense. Gambling is not development. The perpetuation of the persistent poverty of military agriculture, in idealising the plantation system, is not development. The denial of the right to work, the right to eat and even the right to life cannot be development.

It stands to reason that any political party seeking to fulfil the expectations of the populace for equality, jobs, security, the ending of privilege, the preservation of civil liberties and so on, must set about to accomplish these objectives in a planned and organised manner, working along with the people and not in a whimsical opportunistic and patronising manner of which, unfortunately, we see growing manifestations these days. The record of the Democratic Labour Party in fulfilling these objectives has made it possible for real human development to take place.

The elimination of the inequalities of the school fees system and text books, the provision of hot meals, the introduction of National Insurance and social security, severance pay, the systematic expansion of job opportunities through the development of tourism and industry, training in the hotel industry and in the Samuel Jackson Prescod Polytechnic, the Community College, the provision of free university education, the enactment of trade union legislation and tenantry development and control – all of these, and many more too numerous to mention, illustrate that our living has not been in vain.

Let us conclude by summing up Democracy and Development in my terms. Since democracy is rule by the people and in our system, not directly but through elected representatives then the people must tell the representatives and those seeking to represent them what they expect of our political and economic system. Particularly, the young people must be made to feel, however inarticulate they may be, 'right' that someone is prepared to listen to them 'right'. They are tired of being told what they are expected to do. It is time we asked the young people of Barbados how best do you think you can develop as a person, how best can we help you to be creative and to realise to the maximum your human potential.

If I may be allowed to conclude with another quotation from the 'Pedagogy of the Oppressed' by Paulo Freire, 'A revolutionary leadership must practice co-intentional education. Teachers and students (leadership and people) co-intent on reality are both subjects not only in the task of unveiling that reality, and thereby coming to know it critically, but in the task of creating that knowledge. As they attain this knowledge of reality through common reflection and action, they discover themselves, as its permanent recreators. In this way, the presence of the oppressed in the struggle for their liberation will be what it should be, not pseudo participation but committed involvement'.

"Begging will not solve our economic problem"

On the Caribbean Basin Initiative (CBI) at a news conference on 22 April, 1982 (abridged version)

I wish to turn, out of a sense of duty, to at least one, probably two or three, of our great Caribbean leaders to disabuse the minds of the public on what Mr (Ronald) Reagan has called, the great Caribbean Basin Initiative (CBI).

My understanding of the English word 'initiative' is something which has been inspired, undertaken, instigated, if you like, put into motion, for the first time by some person or persons.

Therefore, the impression has been spread abroad that the whole concept for an economic plan, if you can dignify it by that name, for the Caribbean area, was initiated either by the President of the United States (Ronald Reagan), by the Prime Minister of Jamaica (Edward Seaga), or by the Prime Minister of Barbados (Tom Adams); and that this initiative with one or two or all three of those persons, is a means of doing something for the benefit of the people of the Caribbean as a whole.

The whole concept of a Caribbean basin was formulated first by the late Dr Eric Williams, Prime Minister of Trinidad and Tobago, in the presence of Dr Willam Demas (the Secretary-General of the Caribbean Community, but now President of the Caribbean Development Bank) and myself, at a private meeting which Dr Williams held at his home, between the three of us in the early '70s.

At that stage we were satisfied that the Caribbean Community was well on its way to becoming an established fact, and Dr Wiliams was looking around to see what further concepts could be initiated for the benefit of the Caribbean region. I remember well sitting around with the two of them, that is the Secretary General of the Caricom Secretariat and the Prime Minister of Trinidad and Tobago and discussing how the region, as a region, can become more integrated.

We had already integrated the Commonwealth Caribbean in the Caribbean Community, that is, all the former British colonies in the

Caribbean and some of the territories which were still British colonies, nearly twice the number that had been members of the ill-fated Federation; had brought them together in an economic grouping.

Dr Williams was a Caribbean integrationist. He had already made overtures to the other Greater Antilles, such as Haiti, the Dominica Republic, Cuba, (about) the idea of eventually embracing them into a wider community. Dr Williams sat down and drew three concentric circles.

The first circle he described as the Caribbean Community, former liberated colonies, now constituting the Caribbean Community. The second concentric circle was the territories in the Caribbean Sea which would include places like Haiti, Santo Domingo, the Antilles – French and Netherlands Antilles. The third circle was the largest, and included all the territories which had coastlines on the Caribbean Sea and the Gulf of Mexico.

If you look at the map behind me, you will see that Guyana is just on the edge. These are the islands including Jamaica; then you have Venezuela and Colombia, which are already members of the Caribbean Development Bank (CDB); then you have Panama, which was formerly part of Colombia; then next to Panama is Costa Rica, Nicaragua, Honduras, Guatemala, Belize and Mexico. Then to the north you have Cuba, Haiti, Santo Domingo, Puerto Rico, and you come all the way down to the American Virgin Islands.

The expression Caribbean Basin countries was one which was formulated. It was formulated in a very restrictive way by Venezuelan publicists earlier in the 50s, as the Venezuelan basin. But, certainly the concept of a Caribbean basin was one which was formulated by Dr Williams and Dr Demas and not by anyone in the United States.

I wish to tell you about a true Caribbean initiative now, because I think we owe it out of respect to the memory of Dr Williams that other people should not try to steal the wonderful ideas which we had for the upliftment of the peoples of the Caribbean, and make us the subject people of other imperialistic powers.

You will notice, gentlemen, that there is a country down here which is called El Salvador. El Salvador is not a Caribbean Basin country. El Salvador is a Pacific country. El Salvador rightly belongs with Japan, and the Philippines, and Hawaii and that group. So if the President of the United States really wanted to do something for the Caribbean, he would not spend half of the money on El Salvador, because $128 million out of $350 million which he is asking the Congress of the United States to appropriate under his Caribbean

Basin Initiative, is for a Pacific country.

But let me go back to the original Caribbean Basin plan. Dr Demas said, we cannot call this wider community, the Caribbean Community; we'll have to look at it from the point of view of the litoral countries.

I want to tell you now of the Caribbean Basin plan. The Caribbean Basin plan asked for no assistance from Great Britain, from the United States of America, from France, from West Germany, from Japan, or any country outside of the Caribbean Basin. It was literally an 'Operation Bootstrap' by which the people of the Caribbean would definitely take over the commanding heights of the economy which President Reagan now wants to hand back to American businessmen.

Dr Williams said that he will spend two thousand million dollars on one project alone. The first project ...

(Journalist, interrupting: "U.S. dollars?")

My recollection is T and T (Trinidad and Tobago) Dollars. When we are in the Caribbean, we do not think of the United States treasury. We were in Port of Spain. So I would have to take it he meant T and T dollars. When I say dollars in Barbados, I do not mean American dollars. I have not become so slave-minded yet.

...Two thousand million dollars which he would find out of Trinidad reserves, in order to build an aluminium refinery if you speak English, aluminum smelter if you speak American, smelter in Trinidad, using Trinidad reserves of natural gas, to process the bauxite which was leaving Jamaica, leaving Suriname, leaving Guyana and going up to places like Kittymack in Canada to be made into aluminum products.

This was the Trinidad government's contribution; no money from the United States; two billion Trinidad and Tobago dollars.

The second thing was that the government of Mexico, at the time the President of Mexico was a gentleman by the name of Alvares Echevarria put forward the idea of a shipping service which would complement the service which we have, and would do all the external shipping for the area.

Let me give you some figures. When I last did a calculation of this two-and-a-half, to three years ago, I calculated that Barbadians were paying $80 million per annum in freight charges to foreign shipping companies. I am sure it is much more than that now, because shipping costs have (gone up) considerably. Let us say around $100 million –Barbados alone. Can you imagine the amount of money that countries like Venezuela, Colombia, Trinidad and Tobago, with heavy equipment, are spending on freight and insurance of goods brought into their countries?

So President Alvares formulated the idea of NUMACAR and asked us to join; that was part of the Caribbean Basin Plan. Unfortunately, I do not think that the present government of Barbaos ever gave very serious consideration to NUMACAR, the external shipping line, because all the statements made by government ministers have been very derogatory, in the same way that all the statements they have been making about the litttle sop that the American Government is throwing at the Eastern Caribbean, have been very adulatory. Anything that is initiated within the region, meets with derision. I think it is a great pity that we do not recognise the talents that we have in the persons like Dr Demas, and Dr Williams and Sir Arthur Lewis, and people of that kind of ability who, in my opinion, have more ability than all the people that they have at the World Bank, International Monetary Fund, put together.

Here was Trinidad offering to put up this money to help the economies of Jamaica, Suriname, and Guyana and to integrate the processing of basic raw materials, because we are always complaining about primary products receiving only low prices, and then our having to pay high prices for manufactured goods coming from the industrial countries.

Here was a great opportunity to industrialise the Westindies. Here was another great opportunity to get control of our shipping. But the efforts of the government of Mexico met with derision, and, recently within the past 12 months, the government of Trinidad and Tobago, has pulled out of the exercise of the international shipping company, for reasons best known to them– but after Dr Williams died. The government of Barbados never really put their hearts and minds in the exercise at all, and they were very easily persuaded by British shipping and British commercial interests, that it is not in our best interest to venture into these deep waters.

The third project which has not got off the ground yet, much to Dr Williams' dismay, he must have died of a broken heart, is the Caribbean Food Plan. Every now and then we read something in the newspaper about the Caribbean Food Plan. We read about the large sums of money which are being spent by all the territories on the import of foodstuffs.

There is no reason why the Caribbean countries, places like St Vincent, Dominica, which claim to be poor countries, and always stretching out their hands asking for money from other people, should not be feeding the whole of the Caribbean and getting money for it, and developing their economies. Dr Williams formulated the idea of the Caribbean Food Plan.

What happens in the Caribbean is that when you have a good idea, either the British or American commercial interests kill the idea or the Westindian governments appoint committee after committee and the experts who sit on these committees, or the civil servants are the main beneficiaries of these well thought out ideas, and spend 15 or 20 years ...

The civil service and British officials and American officials are the main beneficiaries of all our efforts to stimulate economic growth in these countries; too much talking and writing and minutes and that kind of thing.

So the Caribbean Food Plan was the third thrust towards making the region economically self-sufficient.

What I wish to reiterate, for the last time, is that none of these Plans called for any outside expertise, or any outside financial assistance. As a matter of fact, the main rationale of the plan was to make us independent of refineries of aluminium outside, make us independent of external shipping, and make us independent of the imports of food from countries which were outside of the Caribbean.

Now, where did Venezuela come in on this? The Venezuelans, round about 1974, made an offer that they would sell crude oil to the territories at a price of $6.00 per barrel. The price is now $32 per barrel, a barrel is roughly 43-44 gallons. The price in 1972 was round about $1.80, and all the countries were being affected by the OPEC decisions.

The Venezuelans, being members of OPEC, could not break the agreement; so what the Venezuelans said they would do was to give us credit; in other words, we would pay them $6.00 a barrel and, let us say the price was $12 a barrel just for the sake of argument, they would sell us at $6.00 a barrel and the other $6.00 we could use locally for economic development, and it would be a book entry which we would owe the Venezuelan government – theoretically they would owe the Venezuelans this money, but I doubt that the Venezuelan government would ever want to collect that money. There again an initiative coming from within the Caribbean.

You will ask me now, what happened to the plan. It is a very sad story.

Some Foreign ministers got together in New York. I have to speak the truth on this even though I may offend certain people. These Foreign Ministers, having heard about the plan from some of their leaders, like Mr Burnham (Forbes Burnham of Guyana), myself, Dr Williams, and the President of Venezuela, decided that they would summon their own meeting and they invited *Marish and Parish, Sam Cow and Duppy,* everybody. All the OAS (Organisation of American States) people, I believe the Argentinians – they didn't invite the Falkland Islanders – the Chileans, the Salvadoreans, the Ecuadoreans, everybody, because they wanted to get the international spotlight.

(They) held a meeting at the time of the (United Nations) General Assembly in New York, without any authority whatsoever from Dr Williams, the President of Venezuela, or anybody else. At that meeting, they spoke about the Caribbean Basin Plan without anybody telling them to do so. (They) called in the American press, and decided that they were going to have the first meeting in Caracas, Venezuela.

Our understanding between the President of Venezuela, myself, and Dr Williams and Mr Burnham, I believe Mr Manley (Michael Manley, Prime Minister of Jamaica), was that the first meeting was to be held in Port of Spain, since it was Dr Williams' idea; and that Dr Williams would send out the invitations, and that Dr Williams would be chairman of the meeting.

When Dr Williams heard about this meeting which was to be held in Caracas, all hell broke loose, and he said he would have nothing more to do with it. The President of Venezuela sent and called me and asked me to go and speak to Dr Williams and tell Dr Williams that he knew nothing about the meeting which was held in New York; that he had given no one any authority to convene a meeting in Caracas and it was still his understanding that Dr Williams was to send out the invitations; and that the meeting was to be held in Port of Spain under the chairmanship of Dr Williams.

I went to Port of Spain, and I went to see Dr Williams by myself. I explained in great detail to Dr Williams what had happened; how the meeting had been held in New York; who had convened the meeting; their motives for convening the meeting. They meant well, but they wanted to get a little of the limelight, a little of the credit for the Caribbean Basin Plan.

I explained to Dr Williams what the President of Venezuela had told me. Dr Williams sat down for 45 minutes and listened to me, and when I finished speaking, there was a little silence, and he said: 'Have a drink, Errol'. That is the only thing he said for the whole time. He didn't even ask me what I was going to have to drink; he mixed the same thing he was accustomed to drinking which I don't drink, but for politeness, I drank, and that was the end of the

*A Barbadian dialect phrase meaning all and sundry.

Caribbean Basin Plan. That's all he said. He didn't even say, as he said on another occasion, 'I dun wid dat.'

Our motto is 'Pride and Industry', and I think that in Barbados we have lost our pride. This is what I particularly want to say: we do not have any pride anymore, because we are joining the ranks of the beggars. We have developed a mendicant mentality, and we are even boasting now of our mendicancy, our success in begging. We have never been a nation of beggars.

I told some American reporters once that I was shocked that countries like Egypt and Israel would have a man like Henry Kissinger (former U.S. Secretary of State) running between their capitals, saying he was making peace. I said that if Henry Kissinger was ever so crazy as to come down to the Caribbean if we ever had any dispute, say with Trinidad and Tobago, that he could be so drunk as to say he was shuttling between Port of Spain and Bridgetown, settling a dispute between Dr Williams and Errol Barrow our people should throw us out of office overnight. We here in the Caribbean should settle our own problems, whether they be political problems, or whether they be economic problems. We do not have any right to our independence, unless we are prepared to settle our economic problems without going cap in hand to other people joining in their sterile ideological disputes, even with some of our own brethren, running cap in hand begging them for money.

No one from outside the region should be able to come in here saying they are settling disputes in the Caribbean. The Caribbean peoples have got to settle their own disputes. If that is alright for Egypt and for the Middle East and for the Israelis, it is because these people want to buy a lot of sophisticated armaments to kill one another, and, therefore, they have to be dependent on the United States, and, therefore, they have to suffer the ignominy of having a United States Secretary of State telling them what to do. But Dean Rusk (U.S. Secretary of State when Barbados became independent in 1966) could not tell me what to do. Dean Rusk could not tell me to accept money from President (Lyndon) Johnson. I think President Johnson was the greatest of American Presidents.

But I will not accept any arms from President Johnson for myself or Barbados; and, therefore, we have no right to be joining this queue of mendicants.

We never had a cent from the United States government, and I am proud of it, and I do not think the Barbadians were worse off then, than they are today. Begging from the United States is not going to solve our economic problems.

"The Danger of Rescue Operations"

From Caribbean Review, Volume 12, Number 4 (Fall 1983). Florida International University

On 9 April 1898, the Government of Spain, which had for four years been waging battle against Cuban Independence in the face of growing threats from the United States, agreed to an immediate cease-fire in the campaign against the insurgents, freed all US citizens held in prison, and permitted American relief units and supplies to enter Cuba. The withdrawal of Spain from Cuba and Puerto Rico – the last vestiges of her imperial dominion of the New World – was thus only a formality.

On 11 April, President McKinsey proposed to Congress "the forcible intervention of the United States as a neutral to stop a war…to end the barbarities, bloodshed, starvation, and horrible miseries, and to protect American and property in Cuba."

The Spanish American war spread from the Caribbean to the Pacific and lasted for three months. The Assistant Secretary of the Navy, Theodore Roosevelt, astride his horse, Little Texas, achieved some undeserved historical immorality by leading a band of volunteer adventurers known as the "Rough Riders" at snail's pace up San Juan Hill in the wrong direction after it was all over bar the shouting. In the mythology of United States military exploits this became glorified as the "charge at San Juan Hill". Spain withdrew from Cuba just as she had declared she would before the US invasion or "rescue operation".

The US remained, and still has a base, at Guantanamo, by virtue of the treaty signed by the new Cuban Government granted leases to the liberating government. As so "democracy" came to the Cuban people along with the reservations of the Platt Amendment, stipulating that the Government of Cuba consents that the United States may exercise the right to intervene for the presence of Cuban Independence and the maintenance of a government adequate for the protection of life, property and individual liberty. The first American intervention took place a short five years later in 1906 under the order of Theodore Roosevelt, by then President of the United States. In 1912 and 1917, the US troops were back again to protect American lives and property.

A debt is owed by all students of Caribbean and American political history to the late Senator Everett Dirksen of Illinois who, in June 1969, entered into the Congressional Record a formidable list of more than 150 military adventure and interventions – all in the name of freedom and protection of life and liberty. No wars have been waged on the soil of the continental United States in the past 100 years by any foreign power.

In December 1823, President Munroe, in the message to Congress, declared "The American Continents, by the free and independent condition, which they have assumed and maintain, are henceforth not to considered as subjects for further colonisation by any European powers." Designed originally in London by British Foreign Secretary George Canning as a joint Anglo-American warning to France and Spain, the Munroe Doctrine developed into a battle cry for US intervention in the affairs of Western Hemispheric countries. From Havana to Panama to Guatemala to Chile – the Congressional Record is replete. And now, on to Grenada.

Darkness at dawn. Around four o'clock on the morning of Tuesday, 25 October 1983, those of us who live within sight or sound of the runway of the Barbados airport were roused from our slumbers by the thunder of multiengine aircraft and helicopters warming up and taking off in what turned out, in the next three days, to be an almost endless procession.

If one lives by the sea, the sound of waves crashing against the shore or cliff does not impinge on the conscious mind or even keep one awake. Similarly one grows accustomed to the roar of jet engines during normal traffic hours. Four o'clock in the morning, however, is not normal. The invasion was on. No one taking an intelligent interest in the sad events of the previous six days in Grenada looked forward to military intervention in a situation that was now not dissimilar to Cuba of 1898 after the Spanish Government had already capitulated to the demands of both the Cuban nationalists and the United States. "The war is over, Honey Bun".

On Saturday, 22 October, representatives of the US Government and the deputy British High Commissioner had gone into St George's, the capital of Grenada, had spoken with the leaders of the so-called provisional military government, and had been given the assurance both by General Hudson Austin and by the administration of the medical school that there was no threat to American citizens in the island and that they could be evacuated if it was so desired. The shooting appeared to be at an end; an announcement was made that the curfew which had been imposed was being lifted.

It is alleged that Mr Montgomery, the deputy British High Commissioner, saw the Governor General of Grenada, Sir Paul Scoon, but no suggestions had been made public that the Governor General took advantage of the visit of Her Majesty's representative to solicit the help of the US, Caribbean or even Her Majesty's Government in carrying out a rescue in this territory.

Meetings of some Caribbean Heads of Government were held on that Friday in Barbados and Trinidad on Saturday and Sunday, 22-23 October. The Prime Minister of Trinidad and Tobago did not attend the first and the Prime Minister of Barbados did not attend the second. The delegations from the Lesser Antilles must have remained at the meeting in Port of Spain, since the Government of Trinidad and Tobago was unaware that an Agreement had been entered into Between Barbados, Jamaica, and the members of the Organisation of Eastern Caribbean States invoking an unregistered treaty of mutual assistance to carry out precisely what the treaty was designed to protect against.

While the Japanese forces attacked United States fleet lying at anchor in Pearl Harbour on 7 December 1941, the US Government and media described it as an act of treachery since the Japanese Government has not issued a Declaration of War against the United States of America before the attack. The British Prime Minister on 2 September 1939 demonstrated his respect for these formalities by informing the House of Commons that he had summoned the German Ambassador and had informed him that the British Government, as of then, considered a state of war to exist between Her Majesty's Government of Great Britain and the Third Reich.

Who were the US forces and their camp followers fighting? Who were the rescuing and from whom? No rescue operation was attempted before the assignation of Bishop and his ministers except by the people of Grenada themselves.

Even if one is tempted to believe the belated excuse that Sir Paul Scoon invited the intervention – a story that not even the most uncritical follower of the events is tempted to entertain – it must not be forgotten that Sir Paul, the famous Vicar of Bray, had been appointed by dictator Sir Eric Gairy and maintained his office under a left-wing Marxist regime which seized power only five days after his ascension to the largely ceremonial post. He remained in residence, although not in power, for more than four years unheralded, unsung and unknown to the world. It should not have been difficult for Sir Paul to adjust himself to a third authoritarian regime which had not, up to that stage, either inclined or displayed any intention to remove or replace him.

The Government of Canada which had a representative in St Georges throughout, leased a plane to evacuate its nationals on Monday 24 October. According to Prime Minister Pierre Trudeau, the Grenadian authorities – whoever they were for the time being – had given permission, but the US Government interdicted the landing on that day and the satellite governments obediently ordered the withdrawal of the lease of the Leeward Islands Air Transport (LIAT) *Hawker Siddeley 748*. Ownership of LIAT is also shared with the governments of Guyana and Trinidad and Tobago. Not only was the Government of Canada treated with disdain, but the Prime Minister of Great Britain, America's traditional and staunchest ally, was only told on the Monday, 24 October of "options" and she strongly advised against military intervention.

But Ronald Reagan's mind was made up; like a sheriff whose posse was ready to mount, some of them on donkeys, he rode into town with guns ablaze looking for an enemy.

The US Ambassador to Paris claimed that he knew of the plan two weeks before the event. He subsequently retracted. The Prime Minister of Barbados claimed that he was aware of the plot to kill Prime Minister Bishop two weeks before the events. He also said that he offered political asylum to the Grenadian Foreign Minister Unison Whiteman because he had reason to believe that Mr Whiteman's life was in danger.

Ms Eugenia Charles is an ingenious political neophyte, in no way a pejorative description for an academically well-qualified, highly intelligent member of the legal profession from a sound God-fearing upper middle-class background who *faute de mieux* found herself drafted into the maelstrom of Dominica politics at a late stage in life and struggled to create some kind of order out of that ungovernable situation – very much *le roi malgré lui*.

Ms Charles is a "no-nonsense" person. She is neither power-hungry nor power-drunk. The same cannot be said for some of her fellow politicians in the area; that is why it was so sad to see her being conscripted by the US to give credibility to the decaying political image of the American President. Whether his motivation was to send messages to Nicaragua, Cuba, and El Salvador or to other left-leaning forces in the West, or whether it was to bolster his chances for re-election, he has left a lot of dead bodies in the Caribbean, bereaved families in the United States, Cuba and Grenada, and disunity in the Commonwealth Caribbean whose governments now deeply distrust one another.

He has nearly succeeded in destroying the inner strengths of the Commonwealth as was evident from the bitter exchanges which characterised the daily deliberations in November in New Delhi. The Prime Minister of Singapore, Lee Kuan Yew, expressed his disappointment by saying that the bland press releases did not reflect the true sentiments of the governments.

It would take a master with the statutes of Sophocles to properly dramatise the tragedy of the people of Grenada, or to illustrate the inevitable damage to Caribbean sovereignty and self-respect, not to speak of the systematic dismantling of the Caribbean Community.

> *"By avenging blood for blood so that this storm-tossed city may once again emerge."*
> *"Oedipus Turranos!" Sophocles.*
> *Thebes did not emerge.*

The Caribbean will never be the same again.

Barbadian of the Century
George A. Pilgrim

The publication of the *Speeches by Errol Barrow* represented a treasure in the literature on our much loved late Prime Minister and National Hero. The text in its present form created a repository of political knowledge and insights into the man who took Barbados from colony to Nationhood. Proclaimed the "Father of Independence", it was often said that he "found Barbados a collection of villages and transformed them into a proud nation". In the 50th year of our country's celebration of Independence, the update of this publication is excellent Independence project in itself.

The attainment of Independence and its meanings are wrapped up in what helps to guide and influence the political direction of the late, great leader. He believed and he wrote in the forward of a publication by the Democratic Labour Party titled *30 Years and Onwards*, *"We have tried to ensure, so far as possible that every child born in Barbados has the opportunity to develop the talents with which the Lord has blessed them with regardless of the family circumstances in which they happened to be born."*

The desire to transform was evident in his tenure and posture as he took Barbados on its journey to nationhood. His iconic statement, *"We did not intend to be caught loitering on the premises of the Colonial offices after closing"* is testimony to the mission of man with a clear purpose.

The Democratic Labour Party's leadership was instructive in building up a region through strong bonds and ties. The start-up of the Caribbean Free Trade Association (CARIFTA) and his passion for regionalism was guided in his strong belief of the "collective wisdom" of our people. He acknowledged *"the integration movement is a fact of daily experience.*

It is reality which is lived, but which has to be institutionalised" while this reality was lived, he saw the fragility in our political ecosystem as he opined *"...the slightest discord between two Prime Ministers...can plunge citizens of two countries into verbal and electronic warfare."* His concern then and now was *"...our winning the battle of communication in defence of the unity of the region."*

Professor Gordon K. Lewis, after the death of Barrow commented *"He was, all in all, a politician who turned statesman, who gave to the political career a dignity and prestige which sometimes, in other practitioners of the art, it does not deserve."*

Today, we have at our disposal a platform of options for communication. The prospects of closer ties then have increased reality. This publication must be listed as an attempt to contribute to the communication efforts of binding our region.

I commend the efforts of the team in this regard and extend success on behalf of the Democratic Labour Party in this endeavour, and hope that, as Barbadians, we continue to honour his memory through our service to God, neighbour and country.

By the People

Sir David Simmons,

1987 Parliamentary Tribute (abridged)

Some time ago, during the debate on the O'Neal Resolution, I urged the then Members of the House of Assembly to be circumspect in respect of the assessment of political figures whom we have known, and who have passed on. I urged that we should not seek to tear down each other by baseless or mischievous comment, but rather, to acknowledge the gifts of those who have made fundamental contributions to the development of our people, and at the same time, to be objective, critical and fair.

I pay tribute to Errol Walton Barrow, mindful of those precepts which I expounded during the O'Neal debate. I will have to be objective and critical because I believe that in all things a balanced view ought to be given, free from sentimentality or sycophancy. There is no doubt that Errol Barrow, as a political figure in this island, proved himself to be a very great Barbadian worthy of a ranking as a national hero. Far be it from me to play down his role in Barbados or in the wider Caribbean for he was a courageous and outstanding Barbadian and Caribbean leader.

I got to know Errol Barrow in the middle Fifties when he was a regular visitor to my parents' then home in St Philip. In those days, I was at Lodge School and he took an interest in my development and that of my siblings. After he became parliamentary representative for St John in 1958 by virtue of his parliamentary position he joined the Board of Governors of Lodge School and I saw him quite often there.

In another tribute I mentioned that he introduced me to alcoholic beverages. One Sunday night in August 1960, while preparing to go to England to study I met him at the then Seawell Airport and told him that I had been accepted to the London School of Economics. He warmly congratulated me because that was his alma mater, and took me around the airport and then we went to a bar upstairs, and he bought me a beer. Although 20 years if age, I had never had a beer before.

That half an hour together I treasure because he was by then an established political and parliamentary figure, a man who was destined to lead this country but who took the time to give me valuable insights into life in London; what to expect, what to avoid and how to study for my law exams. I am eternally indebted to him for educating me as to how I should pursue my legal studies and the approach I should bring to bear on them in the succeeding years.

I left in September 1960, and next met next him during the 1966 Constitutional Conference at Lancaster House. I was covering the conference for the Barbados Rediffusion and the Daily News and that brought me into regular daily contact with him and some of the quite substantial skirmishes and clashes. He had a certain intolerance of the Press and a certain unwillingness to accept criticism. But there was an endearing aspect of his character that I have found since we became parliamentary colleagues and that is, that even though at times he may have been quick to anger, he was also conscious of the need to build bridges and reconcile.

I remember one afternoon approaching him in London and said to him, "Mr Premier, on lobby terms, could you give me a statement about today's proceedings?" Cameron Tudor was with him and he said: *"Cammie, you see what David wrote in the Daily News; 'Uproar in Lancaster House'?* He had got a copy of the Daily News whose headline was "Uproar in Lancaster House". Of course, I drew to his attention that the headline really is a matter within the purview of the sub-editor and not the author. Even though he appeared angry at the headline that same evening he invited me and my wife to join him at his hotel for drinks. The whole matter was forgotten; an attitude that carried through in many other subsequent dealings with him.

Errol Barrow led the DLP with great distinction from 1955. Our parties were against each other when I was a candidate in 1971, 1976, 1981 and 1986. Politically I suffered like so many in the BLP from the sharpness of his tongue, from his effusions of fact, and the occasional fiction, on political platforms. But even when we were political opponents I found a certain magnanimity in our relations. In the 1976 by-election in St Philip North, when it became fairly apparent that I was going to win the seat, he drew me aside and he said to me. *"I wish to congratulate you now before the Press. This is a great personal victory."* Then he left me and he repeated those words to the Press and since then members of the DLP teased me suggesting that I was a favourite of his.

He was essentially a charismatic personality with presence akin to Sir Grantley and J.M.G.M. 'Tom' Adams the two Prime Ministers who preceded him. If you walked into a room with Errol, he stood out; you knew he was somebody special. Apart from his physical stature, there was that mien which he had that betrayed the attributes of leadership, outstanding leadership. That he was charismatic and succeeded so well in politics is reflective of a view I hold that Caribbean politicians, certainly up to Errol Barrow's era, have followed a historical pattern of personality dictatorship. I do not use the word 'dictatorship' in a pejorative sense. What I mean is that if we look at Jamaica, Trinidad, Barbados, or elsewhere, there has been an outstanding personality in these various countries who dominated the political scene, and given the strength of personality and nature of their leadership, the political party tended to follow in a secondary role.

He was a patrician, he liked the finer things in life, he could posture well and he understood the psyche of the Barbadian people. Others have spoken of his ability as a yachtsman and as a pilot of his own private aircraft. Some may find an incongruity in the fact that while at the time he was flying an aircraft, the Mini Minor and the donkey cart were more the order of the day. He could posture but he succeeded because he had that character that allowed him to convince the majority of Barbadians, from time to time, of the correctness of his policies, and they were prepared to forgive or ignore the particular personal idiosyncrasies.

He tried to instil in us Barbadians a sense of self-reliance. We are aware of his frequent comments that we must not be a nation of mendicants, and that is a legacy that we should carry on in his memory and pass on to those who follow us. He enhanced the image of Barbados and its people regionally and internationally, and his contribution in this island and in this region will not be diminished by the passage of time.

The time will come when we will have to stop playing cheap politics in the role of parliamentarians and adopt a bi-partisan attitude and policy to a number of the matters which affect us all.

I wonder what lessons can be drawn from the fact of his death in office, at not an excessively old age of 67, and that of Prime Minister Tom Adams at 54. I don't think that the general public realises how burdensome is the Office of Prime Minister. But I do know that it is most regrettable that his death means that whereas one would have preferred for someone of his stature, and indeed that of Tom Adams, to have retired and been available to share his practical experience in politics, to the university perhaps, we are prevented from having this.

In his passing we have lost a leader and colleague who, particularly in his private life, was one of the friendliest, most charming, and even disarming people that you could meet.

Undoubtedly, he will go down in history as the Father of Independence. In 1966, he gave us the ability to hold our heads high and proud as a people worthy of respect in this world and I will always revere him and his name for that.

"What is your Mirror-Image"

*Address to a political rally 13 May, 1986, at which the
Democratic Labour Party's 27 candidates for the
general elections of 28 May, 1986 were introduced*

What I wish to speak to you about very briefly here this evening is about you. About yourself.

I want to know what kind of mirror image do you have of yourself? That is what I am concerned about. What kind of mirror image do you have of yourself? Do you really like yourselves? Because you can never really like anybody unless you first like yourself. There are too many people in Barbados who despise themselves and their dislike of themselves reflects itself in their dislike of other people...people who live next door to them, members of their family, husbands, and wives, and the ox and the ass and the stranger within the gates.

I would like to say that in 1951, 1956, 1961 the Conservatives used to do a few favours for people.

A planter would send a man who had a little influence, let us say in Ellerton Village in St. George, send him down to Plantations Limited or Manning and Company and get some lumber to repair the old house, or if he had a cheap canvasser you would send him to Detco Motors and let him trust a new car. And those people would be motivated into giving their support to the Conservative candidate because of the favours which used to be given out to them.

But it really did not matter because the people who accepted that kind of help thought that they would be beholden to the rich people of this island, because the rich people were in a position to do personal favours for them. But what the rich people in Barbados did not realise is that they did not have money to do favours for everybody who had the right to vote after universal adult suffrage.

That was all right when you had 250 people voting in St. Thomas, and probably 178 voting in St. Andrew, and probably 311 voters in St. Lucy, but when you have 38,000 voting alone in St. Michael – voting for two candidates, not even John D. Rockefeller himself would be able to do enough favours for 38,000 people to persuade them to go and cast their votes and exercise their suffrage against the Labour Party's interest, in favour of that wealthy person.

Which group is wealthiest in Barbados then? Who has the most money to spend? There has never been anybody in the history of Barbados with six million dollars at his disposal. The Tom Adams government had $600 million in each and every year at its disposal to bribe you with your own money, and then spit in your face.

So the Conservatives now can save their money. They are not going to France and Italy anymore because of terrorism, but they are going to Tampa, Florida, Vancouver, British Columbia and California, because they have people now who will spend the workers' money to bribe the workers and they could save their money and thus go off and live like true politicians, while they use your money against you.

Now what has bothered me in this society is that every time after elections, people expect certain things to take place. And although the law says that he that giveth is as much guilty of bribery and corruption under the Corrupt Practices Act as he that receiveth, we know that even on the polling day, people are given envelopes with $100 bills in them.

Philip Greaves* and Asquith Phillips* and I sat down trying to get people to bring affidavits, so that we could lock up some of them. Our own people, registered Democratic Labour Party people, said they were not prepared to go into court and swear.

So what kind of mirror image would you have of yourself? If there are corrupt ministers in Barbados tonight, you have made them corrupt.

I am not trying to make any excuses for you, but I realise what has happened in this society. You have people who are living on the brink of, and at, subsistence level. I look around and see people who have not done an honest day's work in their whole lives driving around in MP**cars, having an ostentatious standard of living, unlike my poor families in St. John, who the Welfare Officer gives $50 to feed a family of ten for a whole week.

What kind of mirror image can you have of yourself?

*(Philip Greaves is an attorney-at-law and is now Deputy Prime Minister. Mr Greaves, Mr Asquith Philips and Mr Barrow worked out of the same chambers in the 1976-86 period during which Mr Barrow's Democratic Labour Party was out of office.)

**(MP is the prefix on the licence plates of Government registered motor vehicles).

Let me tell you what I mean by 'image you have of yourself'. You so much despair of this society that you queue up at Trident House (United States Consulate) day after day. Those of you who have read Julius Caesar would know the passage that says: 'You have sat the live long day with patient expectation to see great Pompey pass the streets of Rome.' And you have stood the live long day with patient expectation for the man to tell you down there that you can't get the visa to get on the 400 to New York next week.

Your greatest ambition is to try to prove to the people of the United States Consulate that you are only going up to visit your family, when you know very well that when you get up there, you los' 'way. And you are surprised when the people at the United States Embassy tell you that you do not have a strong reason to return to Barbados. And you are the only person dishonest enough with yourself to realise that you do not have a strong reason to return to Barbados, because Barbados has nothing to offer you. You are not being honest with yourself, but you tell the man down there, 'Oh yes, I'm returning.'

If I had to answer that question now I would be in trouble, because under this dispensation for the past ten years, I never had a strong reason to come back here.

But I want to tell you this, that I believe that I am as much Barbadian as they are and I do not like my country being run down the way it has been run down since 1976, and that is the reason why I return.

When I went to Mexico, I had to make a decision, and I returned; I went to the Pacific and I had to make a decision and I returned. I had a strong reason. My reason is that I did not want to see my country go down the drain but you who are not in politics, don't have a strong reason. Tell me one good strong reason you have to return to Barbados.

Your mirror image of yourself is that your ambition in life is to try and get away from this country. And we could call ourselves an independent nation? When all we want do is to go and scrub somebody's floors and run somebody's elevator or work in somebody's store or drive somebody's taxi in a country where you catching your royal when the winter sets in?

What kind of mirror image do you have of yourself? Let me tell you what kind of mirror image I have of you, or what the Democratic Labour Party has of you. The Democratic Labour Party has an image that the people of Barbados would be able to run their own affairs, to pay for the cost of running their own country, to have an education system which is as good as what can be obtained in any industrialised country, anywhere in the world.

It is only now that you are reading that in the state of Texas, the government of the state has asked to make the teachers pass an examination – you know what kind of examination? To see if they can read and write!

The gentleman of the Texas teachers' union came on the news and he said that he was very proud of the result because only eight per cent of the teachers couldn't read and write!

If (President Ronald) Reagan had to take the test, I wonder if he would pass. But this is the man that you all say in the newspapers, how great he is for bombing the people in Libya and killing little children. I am no (Libyan leader Mu'ammar) Qathafi supporter. I don't know Qathafi and I have never had any desire to go to Libya. But this is the man that you all go up to at the airport and put down a red carpet for, and he is the President of a country in which in one of the more advanced and biggest states eight per cent of the teachers cannot read and write, and he feels that they are better than we. And you feel that we should run up there and bow.

What kind of mirror image do you have of yourself? Why don't you sit down there and start trying to put people on the moon, too? Instead of using $100 million to develop the potential of the young scientists that we have, and the young doctors that we have, we spend it putting up an expression of a momumental edifice behind the Cathedral and call it a Central Bank Building, because we think that people develop by ostentation, by showing off, and not by developing people.

But when a government steals from people in the way of consumption taxes and takes that money and spends it on their own high lifestyles, and unnecessary buildings, then that government' not only has contempt for you, but what is most unfortunate, you have contempt for yourself, because you allow them to do it.

And you get the Prime Minister of the country saying that his ambition is to have the same kind of lifestyle as the people in the United States enjoy. I wonder what kind of lifestyle he is enjoying now? And then his successor goes outside of Barbados and says we are drifting away in Barbados from the Westminster model of parliamentary democracy, and we are easing into a presidential system; that we want a presidential system, so that, like Reagan, they can go and bomb. They can go and bomb the mental people in the hospital in Grenada and the little children in Benghazi, in Tripoli? Is that what we want a presidential system for?

We don't have a Presidential system yet. But you have people who are employed and paid with your taxes who could buy a boat and give it to an Englishman to smuggle arms into Barbados. I can give you the name and the place and everything you want.

We don't have a presidential system, but you can have people removing money from a Canadian Imperial Bank account and people who are in charge of the institutions in this island, and transferring it to the Barbados National Bank without the authority of the people from whose account the money was being withdrawn. I know it is so, because I told (Prime Minister Bernard) St John who it was and that man has not been locked up yet.

I told him then that you should never appoint a person to a responsible statutory corporation in this island who is accustomed to forging people's signatures. And then he went outside and came back and never said a word. And you allow that to go on in Barbados.

And there are poeple in high places in this island who conspired to allow that to happen, because the gentlemen was fined $1,000 for so doing, and not by the law courts, but by a private group of people who got together and said, 'You committed forgery; we are going to fine you $1,000.' So you circumvent the Director of Public Prosecutions, and you hold your own dumb-head court martial and then you present him with a big bowl and congratulate him on his achievements.

What kind of an image do you have of yourself if you allow this kind of thing to happen?

What kind of an image do you have of yourself when you allow the mothers of this nation to be beasts of burden in the sugarcane fields? In Mexico where people suffer under a lower standard of living than in Barbados, they use donkeys to freight canes out of the fields.

In Antigua, they use a small railway; but here the mothers of the nation with sons at Harrison College, the Alleyne School and daughters at Queen's College, St Michael and Alexandra – they are used as beasts of burden and there is no shelter in any of those sugar cane fields. I have talked time and time again to the Barbados Workers' Union about this and you allow that to continue. What kind of image do you have of yourself?

I suggested, and I was inspired by the work done by the late Mr Ernest Bevin, who was (British) Foreign Minister, who went to work at eight – I don't mean 8 o' clock in the morning, I mean eight years of age – and those dock workers in London used to turn up during the winter and summer from 5 o'clock in the morning waiting for a ship, and if a ship didn't come in for three weeks or three months, they wouldn't get any pay. And Ernest Bevin introduced the guaranteed week for dock workers. I set up a commission of enquiry into the sugar industry and made the examination of the guaranteed week for agricultural workers one of the terms of reference of that commission, and the commission reported that nobody gave any evidence before them in support of this recommendation.

What kind of mirror image do the people of the Workers' Union, of whom we have members, have, even of you or themselves? And I had to wait until there was a dispute in the sugar industry and we had television and get on a blackboard and say, well these will be the wages from next week and on Tuesday I went into the House (of Assembly) and introduced the guaranteed wages for agricultural workers.

Why should only one man have a mirror image of you that you do not want to have of yourself? What kind of society are we striving for? There is no point in striving for Utopia, but you do not realise your potential.

You have heard the opportunities which our members have taken to improve themselves by going to certain institutions and so on – not that we believe that people with good education are the only people who can be in politics. The very fact that a man has made the effort and taken the time to improve himself shows that he has the kind of calibre which would make him a useful representative of the people.

I lived in a little country when I was young, the Virgin Islands. It was just bought from Denmark by the United States of America. My father was a Chancellor. I was too young to go when he was transferred. So when I was three months old, I went.

There is no unemployment in that country. They don't manage their affairs as well as we did in the past. They don't receive any big lot of grants and loans and that kind of thing, even from the United States.

They have to bring in workers. They have the largest oil refinery in the western hemisphere run by a man called Hess. But that is a small country. But there is another small country which is run by a friend of mine. The country has 210 square miles; it is 40 square miles bigger than Barbados. If you took the Parish of St Phillip and put it right in the little curve by Bathsheba that would be the size of the country of Singapore of Lee Kwan Yew.

But you know the difference between Barbados and that country? First, Barabdos has 250,000 people. You know how many people Singapore has on 40 more square miles? Over two-and-a-half million, on an island just a little larger than Barbados.

They don't have any sugar plantations; they don't have enough land to plant more than a few orchids on. It is one of the orchid centres of the world. They grow orchids in Singapore. They don't have enough land to plant a breadfruit tree in the backyard and nearly every Barbadian, even in the metropolitan area of Bridgetown, would have some kind of fruit tree in the backyard.

Sixty per cent of those three million persons have been housed by the government of Singapore.They don't have any oil for ministers to steal. They don't have any beaches like we have here. There are people here in this audience, Barbadians who have served in Singapore, who can tell you about Singapore. There is no unemployment in Singapore.

They have developed an education system but they are teaching people things that are relevant to the 21st century. They are not teaching people how to weed by the road. They are in the advance of the information age.

But you know the difference between you and them? They have got a mirror image of themselves. They are not looking to get on any plane to go to San Francisco. Too far away. The government does not encourage them to emigrate unless they are going to develop business for Singapore.

They have a mirror image of themselves. They have self-respect. They have a desire to move their country forward by their own devices. They are not waiting for anybody to come and give them handouts. And there is no unemployment.

Is that the mirror image that you have of yourself? Anyhow, ladies and gentleman, I done.

For the People

David A. Comissiong

In May 1986, I received a telephone call from the then newly elected Prime Minister of Barbados – Errol Walton Barrow. He proceeded to ask me a series of questions that were designed to elicit personal information about me, and then ended the conversation with the following statement: *"Oh, and by the way, I am appointing you to the Senate."*

I had just turned 26 years of age, and therefore at that time became the youngest Senator in the history of Barbados. Needless to say, it was a great honour for me to be asked by Errol Barrow to serve his Administration in the Upper Chamber of Parliament and I eagerly looked forward to many years of political interaction with this legendary Barbadian statesman.

Alas, it was not to be! Almost exactly one year after that unforgettable telephone conversation, this great man passed away, leaving this earthly scene. And, many years later, our nation is still reeling from the effects of his most untimely passing. In celebration of the legacy of the RE Errol Barrow on the 50th Anniversary of Independence, I offer the tribute that I made to this great Father of our Nation in the Senate on 11 June 1987.

There will never be another Errol Barrow. I believe that a number of very unique and special circumstances coalesced to form the character and personality of that great Barbadian.

From his very birth, his life was a special one. He was the nephew of the RE Dr Charles Duncan O'Neal, the great socialist. From very young he must have imbibed the great socialist principles and the principle of identity with the interest of the working people.

He was the son of Bishop Reginald Barrow, and I, as a son of a minister of religion, know the special and unique influences and pressures that are brought to bear on the child of a minister of religion; and if you are lucky, you have held up before you the great moral values; and I believe Errol Barrow was lucky.

At a very early age he experienced not only the confines of Barbados, but the variety and diversity of the Caribbean region. He lived in the United States Virgin Islands as a youngster, and his family had tangible links with St Vincent and the Grenadines and other Caribbean islands. So at a very early age he would have become exposed to the uniqueness, vitality and the specialness of being a Caribbean person.

He attended Wesley Hall Boys' School, where he was imbued by the spirit and personality of Rawle Parkinson, and he must have imbibed there, also, the principles of self-reliance and industry that were the hallmarks of the late, great headmaster of Wesley Hall. He was exposed in 1937 to Marcus Garvey, and that, too, must have left its mark.

He was exposed to the phenomenal 1937 riots that played so large a role in creating the new Barbados. That, too, must have opened his eyes to the need for change in Barbados and to the possibilities of the new society that he was to play so large a part in building later on.

He was exposed to World War II, to the Nuremburg Trials, great issues of human suffering, to the great problems of the 20th century of racism and nationalism. He was exposed to these things at perhaps the most profound and fundamental level in the days following the end of World War II.

He attended the London School of Economics at a time when it was traditional for Barbadian Scholars to opt instead for Oxford and Cambridge, law and medicine. It means that even at that age he had his mind set on the future, because at that time economics was a relatively new academic discipline, in the direction of the modern world, of a modern Barbados.

He came back to Barbados and practised law, and became involved in politics in the era of the late 1940s and early 1950s, the era when the energies of the masses of people were being released, following the end of World War II, the time of the great achievement of universal adult suffrage, when the ordinary Barbadian man and woman came forcefully on to the political stage in Barbados.

I think that all these powerful circumstances created a unique individual, and I will not say that we will never see a greater person, but certainly we shall never see a person who so admirably represents the best qualities of the Barbadian people.

It is a pity he did not find the time, to write his own autobiography. I think it is crucial to the development of the youth of this country that we have access to a properly documented, well written official biography of the life, times and work of the man Errol Barrow.

If we want to find a concise and cogent statement of where he wanted this country to go especially during the last year of his life, we need look no further than the text of the two outstanding speeches that he made during the past year: the speech he delivered to the CARICOM Heads of Government at their meeting in Georgetown, Guyana, and the speech that he delivered in Miami. I think he was making three fundamental points.

He was telling us that our future lies in the Caribbean integration movement. He made this point very forcefully in Georgetown, Guyana. He said that we should not even confine that integration process and movement to mere matters of trade and economics, but we have to begin understanding ourselves, appreciating ourselves, appreciating the wonderful achievements, unique institutions and the unique personality and character that we, as a Caribbean people, have developed over the centuries. We need to begin understanding that and developing it.

He also made another fundamental point, that we have, as a people, as a nation, and as a region, to protect the sovereignty and integrity of our nation and of our region. He was very strong in his pride as a Barbadian and as a citizen of the Caribbean. He made the point that we had to defend our Independence and stand tall as a people; that we were not here to accept largesse or freeness from anybody; that our principles must be those of self-reliance and doing things for ourselves.

In fact, at the Miami conference he told his friends in the United States Congress that if they wanted to assist Barbados, the way to assist us was not to give us Aid or largesse, but to free up their markets to Caribbean exports. He said that they should do that not as any favour to the Caribbean people, but as a practical measure to redress the phenomenal imbalance in trade between our countries and the US, and that that was not asking for a favour.

That is how Errol Barrow thought and spoke. In fact, the Americans themselves are now asking Japan to correct the imbalance in trade between their two countries, and this is no favour. He was not looking for favours.

The first fundamental point that he made during the past year, and the third fundamental lesson he was trying to teach us, is that we need to embark upon the urgent task of resuscitating our economy and making our economy more competitive internationally, with all classes, all people, and all sectors of the economy working towards that common goal.

Errol Barrow was trying to say to us that we exist in a very precarious environment, we are a small island developing state, and that if we are to survive, every sector, every class, all people must be involved in that process and we must pull together.

I believe that these are the three fundamental lessons that he tried to leave with us over the past year. The third one is perhaps the most fundamental, because in making that challenge to the Barbadian society, he was saying that our salvation lies in our own hands, in the skills, the determination and the will of the people of Barbados to succeed, and I believe he was throwing out a special challenge to the young people of Barbados, the ones he had done so much to educate.

As we celebrate the 50th Anniversary of Independence, I would just like to echo that the greatest tribute we can pay to Errol Barrow is to make sure that we continue his life's work, and by our so doing bring it one step closer to fruition.

Caribbean Integration:
The reality and the goal

Address to the Caribbean Community Heads of
Governments Conference, 3 July 1986,
Georgetown, Guyana

Mr Secretary General,
Mr President,
Your Excellencies,
Distinguished Colleagues,
Fellow Prime Ministers,
Ladies and Gentlemen,

> "The Street is in darkness,
> Children are sleeping,
> Mankind is dreaming,
> It is midnight.
>
> "Who will awaken
> One little flower
> Sleeping and growing
> Hour and hour?
>
> "Light will awaken
> All the young flowers
> Sleeping and growing
> Hour and hour.
>
> "Dew is awake
> Morning is soon
> Mankind is risen
> Flowers will bloom."

The celebrated national poet of Guyana, Martin Carter, in his poem 'For My Son' reminds us in these moving stanzas that we represent the expectations of five million human beings, and what is more that what we achieve or betray concerns not only the living, but those who are not yet born.

There are many critical questions on our agenda. There will be many different, even conflicting views. We have a long experience in surviving such differences. And we will survive them again. But there is a fundamental theme on which I should like to think there can be no difference. And that is the absolute necessity to promote and defend the solidarity and the sovereignty of this regional Caribbean family, and also the absolute obligation to discover those strategies and mechanisms which will ultimately lead to unity of action in all major areas of our economic, social and political life. If we have sometimes failed to comprehend the essence of the regional integration movement, the truth is that thousands of ordinary Caribbean people do, in fact, live that reality every day. In Barbados, our families are no longer exclusively Barbadian by island origin. We have Barbadian children of Jamaican mothers; Barbadian children of Antiguan and St Lucian fathers. And there is no need to mention Trinidad and Tobago which has always been tied to us not only by the inestimable bonds of consanguinity, but by the burgeoning cross fertilisation of cultural art forms. We are a family of islands nestling closely under the shelter of the great Co-operative Republic of Guyana. And this fact of regional togetherness is lived every day by ordinary Westindian men and women in their comings and goings.

The small traders, and some not so small, who move from Jamaica to Haiti on what I believe, is their legitimate business. The same with Grenada and Trinidad, Barbados and St Lucia and Dominica. What some people call the underground economy. It is true that the laws of each territory may sometimes get in their way, but for the majority of these decent and industrious sons and daughters of the Caribbean, I believe their business is spontaneous though unassisted, and legitimate though unregulated. I should like to believe that we are all committed to the principle of mobility and people interaction. To the principle, I repeat. And that we have an obligation to think and go on thinking out ways how such a principle might be applied without imposing on any territory a greater strain than its resources are able to support.

The point I want to emphasise is this: the regional integration movement is a fact of daily experience. It is a reality which is lived, but which we have not yet been able to institutionalise. What is the source of our failure? I should like to share some of my own misgivings. The first has to do with communication and the ways in which we communicate. For many of our people, the regional integration movement has come to mean matters which relate exclusively to trade. Who will buy my shirts and on what conditions? Whose markets will open up for my pepper sauce, my guava jelly, who will buy my white sand, who will buy my grey sand? These are realistic questions; but we have made them the exclusive justification for our being together. And this has been a grave shortcoming. Whether we recognise it or not, we have a cultural history, a common experience of feeling which goes deeper and is much older than CARICOM and the negotiations about trade.

My attention was drawn recently to an essay by the Jamaican artist and scholar, Rex Nettleford, who articulates what I am trying to say about the essence of the regional movement which transcends mere discussions on trade. Jamaica is the occasion, but it is the Caribbean he is addressing. I quote:

> *"The public opinion polls can tell you what are the feelings of a day or moment; they cannot tell you what are the deeper social and psychological needs of our people who have had to devise strategies and stratagems of survival against the ravages of severance and suffering, and the continuing deprivation in economical, social and political terms ... Such strategies are the result and clear sign of a collective intellect, a collective wisdom that resides among our ordinary folk. But that collective wisdom continues to be ignored on account of the arrogance of planners trained in the North Atlantic or even at the University of the Westindies, especially when the UWI forgets that it is not an extension of Oxbridge. The collective wisdom and intellect of our people are yet to be tapped and given central place in the development strategy of our nation. But we are so busy Westminsterising ourselves into becoming a clone of the Anglo-Saxon world and its American extension that we forget that we have a life and history of our own to be examined, dealt with and used as a source of energy for the development of this nation/region and the shaping of a civilised society."*

In every territory of our Caribbean region – and it has been my own experience in Barbados – I believe we have been failing to find a way of using the 'collective wisdom' of our people. We have not been able to communicate the essence and the cultural infrastructure of the regional integration movement. We have not been able to get people's minds to move beyond the constraints of trade. As a result, the slightest discord between two Prime Ministers over some restrictions affecting a type or quantity of wearing apparel can plunge citizens of the two countries into verbal and electronic warfare. The promise of the regional integration movement, even in the area of trade, cannot be realised unless we find new ways of communicating to the mass of our people the meaning and purpose of all our regional institutions. And that's one reason (if no other could be found) why the University must move from the confines of the campus more and more into the heart of the communities which constitute our region. This battle of communication in defence of the unity of the region, must be won if our efforts during this week and hitherto are to survive beyond the confines of conferences. Every institution and organisation should feel the obligation to accept this challenge: the national and regional media; the schools at all levels of instruction;the Church, every gathering that goes by the name of Caribbean should feel this obligation to accept this challenge of communication; to propogate the message that the region is a larger concept than trade, and that the future of trade arrangements may be favourably influenced by that conviction among the mass of ordinary people whose 'collective wisdom' I believe, with Nettleford, is a fact and very much alive.

The University of the Westindies has provided us over more than one generation with some very remarkable social scientists. I recall with a certain pride the excellent work which was done by the New World Group over the 1960s. Every major sector of our economic life has come under their scrutiny: Sugar, Bauxite, Oil, Tourism. Girvan and Thomas and Carrington, Brewster and Beckford, and, of course, Lloyd Best; Investigation which has always concerned the Institute of Social and Economic Research whose former Director, Allister McIntyre, is with us today. They proved beyond any doubt that this region is not lacking in intellectual human resources. But in spite of all this excellent work, an important link was missing. All this analysis, all this valuable organisation of information never got very far beyond the small circle of specialists for and by whom it was written. There was no link between that great storehouse of knowledge and the toiling mass of workers who are the motor force of any society. The analysis may be brilliant, the recommendations very ingenious; but these will serve a very limited purpose if their content does not become an essential part of the consciousness of the working population. This has been the curse of our societies: that division between those who work exclusively with their brains and those who, we think, work only with their hands. The truth is all men and women, irrespective of occupation, have to work with their brains. But this division of labour has made us most vulnerable where we needed to be most resilient. I am speaking of food and food production. We are worse than vulnerable. It is as though we had chosen to betray the blessings which God and nature has bestowed upon us. Surrounded by the richest of seas, we condemned ourselves to importing fish. Our lands can provide almost every known food crop, yet we persist in the luxury of imported vegetables.

I should like to recall a voice and a great mentor who was never without ideas about this danger and who tried to reverse this suicidal tendency which pervaded all our history. Dr Eric Williams will have to be heard again and again, whenever we say agriculture. He had a conception of food production which was regional. I quote him on the Caribbean Food Crisis:

> 'Food production must be approached as a basic industry to be run on commercial lines by a corporation collectively owned by the governments of the area and making approved investments in the different territories. This in practical terms, means a Caribbean Community Market ... I remind you that, last year, 1973, the Caribbean Community countries imported 24 million dollars worth of fertiliser of which only two million (or 10 per cent) came from Trinidad and Tobago ... Production must aim to satisfy not only the food needs of the local population of the Caribbean. It must also take into account the needs of the extensive tourist trade in such countries as Barbados and Jamaica, as well as the export market beginning with the Caribbean region: Suriname, the Netherlands Antilles, Haiti, the Dominican Republic ... and the commercial co-operation I envisage for the production of food on a large scale must keep the needs of those Caribbean areas in mind...'

Dr Eric Williams wanted to correct the preference for imported foods which has been a major cause of our psychological dependency before and after independence. And he wanted to help make agriculture a respected occupation because we needed it to make food production a respected industry because we cannot survive without it and because it also required gifts of intellect and high technical competence. He wanted to help put an end to the insult he heard school children exchanging about their past. I quote:

> 'I myself encountered .. a group of young people to whom I was speaking and who assured me they wish to have no part of any agricultural programme related to the small farmer and local foodstuff because commodities like eddoes and dasheen were slave food.'

338

The Colonel from the Confederate South has won the battle for the minds of our children. I'm happy to say I don't think this would happen in Dominica where school children are making agricultural work a normal part of their curriculum. And it is here we need to begin (in the schools) if we are going to correct this hostility directed towards the production of the food which is the very fuel of our existence; and if we are going to help another generation to understand why self-sufficiency may be one of the greatest forces of resistance to any form of external penetration.

But no amount of analysis, however brilliant, can save us from this danger without an informed and highly technical work-force in agricuture and the industries it generates.

My position also remains clear that the Caribbean must be recognised and respected as a zone of peace. In this connection, I should like to make further references to Eric Williams by saying that his speech, From Slavery to Chaguaramas, made in 1960 over the issue of the United States base, should be required reading in every school of the Caribbean and in every language of the Caribbean. Europe, and by extension the United States, have always thought it a perfectly natural duty to invade and occupy these territories. Columbus did not dicover the new world. He invaded it. Goerge Beckford asks the question, 'How can you discover somewhere, where people are already living?' We started our history as naval and military bases; that is, in our association with the modern world, each territory was there for capturing and recapturing. Eric Williams had this factor uppermost in mind in his argument over Chaguaramas; and he always argued from history. I quote him to emphasise why this document is so important today. He said:

> *'And as Europe went out, the U.S.A. came in. After getting their independence, which had been based on large scale trade connections with the Westindies, most of them illegal, most of them involving smuggling, the new U.S.A. began from the very start to look upon the Westindies and the Caribbean Sea as their sphere of influence.'*

They began shortly after independence by publishing the Monroe Doctrine, stating that they would not want to see any extension of European colonialism in the Westindies. The ambition clearly stated in those days was to dominate the entire hemisphere.

But if the whole Westindian movement is towards control of its own affairs, I, too, should like to know the clause in Adam's will which denies the Westindian people a share of this world, especially a share of the world that rightly belongs to them.

Puerto Rico has become a launching pad for neo-colonisation of the region. We have also seen it used as a base for a number of military exercises whose purpose is clear. There have been joint manoeuvres of very great magnitude, Ocean Venture '81 and '82. A high ranking officer, in fact, the highest ranking U.S. officer of the U.S. Navy in Puerto Rico, based at Roosevelt Roads, explained their purpose when he said: 'the orchestra practised before playing in public'.

I have said, and I repeat that while I am Prime Minister of Barbados, our territory will not be used to intimidate any of our neighbours: be that neighbour Cuba or the U.S.A.

And I do not believe that size is necessarily the only criterion for determining these matters. But it is important to let people know where you stand if they will support you in what is a moral commitment to peace in our region.

So I return to Eric Williams and the great speech From Slavery to Chaguaramas:

> 'The enemy is not the submarine, or not the weapons which would be changed in 10 years and then changed in a 100 years after that ... the enemy is poverty, the enemy is the suppression of the talents of our population...'

Recently, I have been reading William Demas' very stimulating address to the Institute of International Affairs at the UWI, St Augustine; and I recommend it for serious study. But my attention particularly caught a quotation from the British economist, John Maynard Keynes, on the importance and power of ideas:

> 'Indeed, the world is ruled by little else. Practical men who believe themselves to be quite exempt from intellectual influence, are usually the slaves of some defunct economist ... Soon or late, it is ideas, not vested interests, which are for good or evil.'

And that's why I believe in encouraging young people to acquaint themselves with the great variety of prevailing ideas; for it is only through knowledge and critical acquaintance that they will be able to discriminate which ideas are relevant or subversive to their interests.

And the university must never be restricted, impeded, or harassed for fulfilling its intellectual function of introducing its students, critically and honestly to the great body of ideas which constitute the storehouse of human knowledge. The government of Barbados, of whose Cabinet I have the honour to be Chairman, will never circumscribe the University by demanding that the members of its staff should subscribe to some form of conventional wisdom or be uncritical of the government itself.

The Englishman, Keynes, recalled the importance of ideas. And in our own sea, the great Caribbean poet of the nineteenth century, Jose Marti, spoke of the relation of truth to dreams.

'A true man does not seek the path where advantage lies, but rather the path where duty lies; and that is the only practical man, whose dream of Today will be the Law of Tomorrow; because he knows that without a single exception, the Future lies on the side of Duty.'

I wish to add my personal welcome to you, Mr President, on your assumption of the mantle of leadership of your country, following the untimely passing of our colleague Forbes Burnham. I know that you share the vision which inspired the founding fathers of our integration movement, and which has served to sustain our Community in its moments of gravest difficulty. I wish you every success in your tenure both as Chairman of this Conference, and, as President of the Co-operative Republic of Guyana.

I take this opportunity also to commend our out-going Secretary-General for the sterling contribution he has made to CARICOM throughout his mandate. I wish him well in his future endeavours.

On behalf of the government of Barbados, I take this opportunity to acknowledge publicly all the warm messages of congratulations and good wishes I have received from my Caribbean colleagues both in Bridgetown and here in Georgetown.

Such expressions of goodwill have strengthened the commitment of my government to the principal foreign policy objective which it has set itself, namely: to strengthen the structure of the Caribbean Community by promoting mutual understanding among its members for the benefit of all peoples.

Mr President, Your Excellencies, Ministers, Distinguished Guests, Ladies and Gentlemen, permit me to conclude on a personal note by thanking you for your patience and to borrow from John Bunyan the words spoken by Mr Valiant for Truth in Pilgrim's Progress:

'Though with much difficulty I have come hither, yet I do not repent me of the trouble I have taken.'

He Kept the Faith

C. Asquith Philips

The Harrisonian Tribute, 1987

Errol kept the faith. For my part, I am proud of my close association with him. I am proud that that association is clear testimony of my early independent recognition of his sterling qualities as a man. I am no latter-day convert to an appreciation of his worth.

My tribute to him began long ago in his life time – from the time I joined his Chambers as an aspiring lawyer in 1960/61 in James Street – Lower James Street or James Street West as he jocularly called it in contradistinction to the East End of James Street where the other better off lawyers were.

In those days, seemingly so far away, to praise Mr Barrow was not quite in fashion. Then he was more readily described as a radical (a communist even) or a wild man or mad man. What is now applauded as his forcefulness of advocacy was then decried as bullying. What is now cited as "instances of his tenacity of purpose" was then frowned upon as dictatorial.

I was warned against joining his Chambers. I was told that he would never get work from the solicitors because of his politics – that was true. I was told that we stood of good chance of getting sent to prison, perhaps for sedition – that was not true.

But I was attracted to him by his forthrightness, his outspokenness, his penchant for the outrageous remark. Often, he was saying no more than we all thought but didn't have the guts to say, nor his special way of saying it. I was attracted by his unswerving dedication to serving people.

To be represented by him in the Law Courts as in Parliament was to have his total commitment. And who can forget his clashes with his colleagues at the Bar, on the Bench and in the House of Assembly? He would push your tolerance and your patience to the limit; but you always came around to forgive him because you respected his sincerity of purpose and his unselfish dedication to the service of others.

From my time as General Secretary of the Democratic Labour Party in the early 1960s, I was associated with his political career. I have never seen him waiver in his service to people. Lesser mortals like myself got exhausted along the way. But nothing deterred him, not insult nor vilification; not the occasional defeat at the polls; not the constraints of family life; not even the infamous Duffus Commission (though I knew as his senior counsel in that enquiry how much it wounded his soul); not even ill-health could hold him back, only the Grim Reaper.

Now we come to the heart of the matter. His whole life, career at the Bar, in politics and everything else was nurtured and sustained by love of humanity. Love, not in the maudlin and sentimental sense, but love in the true Christian and deep spiritual sense; what Dr Martin Luther King Jr defined as: *"that force which all the great religions have seen as the supreme unifying principle of life."*

That is why Errol was not just a Barbados man nor a Caribbean man but a universal man. That is why he could at one and the same time be the genial host, the generous friend and the grim uncompromising defender of the oppressed and underprivileged. That is why with his many, splendored personality he could by turn charm and exasperate friend and foe alike.

At the end of it all, Errol, like St Paul could truly have been able to say: *"I have fought a good fight, I have finished my course, I have kept the faith."*

All Were Welcome

Sir Henry Forde

1987 Parliamentary Tribute (abridged)

Errol Barrow deserves to be numbered among the builders of Barbados. I believe that he has contributed significantly to the improvement of our country and to the respect which Barbados holds in the international community.

He came from a tradition which obviously inspired him to reach for the heights. Many people do not recognise the tremendous influence which his uncle, the RE Dr Charles Duncan O'Neal, had on his life. On examining some of the historical records of 1930s, it came to my notice that, when Dr O'Neal died in 1936, the member of the family who went forward to make his funeral arrangements was no other than Errol Walton Barrow, aged 16.

He took the responsibility for that occasion, and it underscored for me the fact that the work of his uncle had impressed itself on his mind from an early age, and, no doubt, in those days he made the decision that he would wish to follow in that tradition.

He was educated at one of our best primary schools in those days, the Wesley Hall School. Later, of course, he went to Harrison College, and then on to the London School of Economics and Political Science. There he came under the influence of one of the great men who believed in democratic socialism and who wrote extensively about it, Professor Harold Laski.

He returned to Barbados in the early fifties, and very soon threw himself into the struggle with another great man who had been influenced by the democratic socialism and Fabianism of the 1930s – the RE Sir Grantley Adams. Alongside Sir Grantley he first won a seat to the House of Assembly as the Member for St George. Between the years 1951 and 1955, he took an active part in the promotion of the working class, principally through his association with the Barbados Labour Party.

It is a matter of record that the breach between himself and the Labour Party came about in 1955. In fact, it is sobering to read the debates for that period to see the exchanges which took place between those dubbed as the "Young Turks" and the hierarchy of the Labour Party. It is also useful reflect that Freddie Miller was among the Young Turks but remained with the BLP. I think the main difference, certainly as highlighted by A.E.S. Lewis, came over the organisation of the Party, the lack of consultation between the hierarchy and elders in the Party and the younger members, and, of course, over their different views about the development of Barbados.

But what I want to underscore is that after that break, it was part of Errol Barrow's determination to contribute to the future of Barbados and he was instrumental, along with others, in forming the Democratic Labour Party. His contribution to the two-party system ought to be recognised. It is part of the democratic tradition of our nation that we should maintain those principles as firmly as we possibly can.

Today, therefore, Barbados is singular among the nations of the world in having the two political parties sprung from the same tradition and both of whom influenced by almost the same political philosophy. And we have two parties in which the two main leaders of these parties have now passed to the Great Beyond, and, for the first time, those of us who have been their sons, their relatives, their friends, have taken over a tradition which I hope we, both Parties, will uphold.

Errol remained in the wilderness for about five years, and they were five stormy years in the history of our country. It is significant, I think, that in 1956, for instance, he did not win a seat back to Parliament and he again failed in the Federal elections 1958. But he was not a person to take defeat lightly. It seemed to inspire him to try again, as he had his goal ahead of him. He came back with flying colours and won a seat for the parish of St John in 1958, a seat which he has held continuously up to his death. Twenty-nine years of parliamentary service is a long time for any one man to give to the nation. In his case it was more than 29 as he had also served from 1951-55.

I first got to know Errol on a friendly basis when I returned to Barbados as a young man in 1959. Our families were connected and I spent several Saturday afternoons at his home. He was a fine cook with a tremendous knowledge of the culinary arts. He was a very good host, and he always welcomed everybody of all social classes to his table.

I visited him on many occasions in the company of diverse political foes. It is one of the things that one does not always recognise in Barbados. I have seen at his house members of the Barbados Labour Party, Barbados National Party, the then Congress Party, even when it would appear to the public as though our political daggers were so drawn as to slaughter each other. But the friendship that inspired us on those occasions belied the divisions which some people believe existed in our personal association and lives. I think that Errol in this respect carried on a tradition that is very valuable in the life of a small country such as Barbados.

I had seen him before that period in the law courts and I admired the tremendous legal skill that he possessed. He was one of the most incisive cross-examiners I have encountered. He had a tremendous grasp of facts, and he was extremely devastating with a witness and equally commanding in addressing the jury. I remember the tremendous clashes which occurred at the Bar in that period. There were times, in fact, when cases were adjourned and not heard, when Errol was lined up against Jack Dear, William Hanschell or Hutson Williams. Always, one could learn from the deep legal knowledge and most certainly the court craft and skill which he brought to the Bar.

By then I had formed my own an interest in his politics. In fact, in the election of 1961 many of us followed intimately the clash between the Democratic Labour Party and the Barbados Labour Party. Once again, one recognised that Errol towered above the other members of his party. He won his victory in 1961 and became Premier and set about immediately on a crash programme to relieve unemployment and continued with what has now been characterised perhaps as his greatest contribution, implementing free education. I believe that this with his leading Barbados to Independence will go down as the two most outstanding contributions of his long and distinguished career.

I came up against Errol at the time of the Federal debate and on the issue of the "Little Eight" Federation. In those days, there were many of us who were strong Federalists who believed that Barbados should seek independence, not on its own, but in association with others, because we did not see the Caribbean tarrying at the gate of colonialism forever. I believe his pragmatism told him that if he had waited for each territory of the Caribbean to reach that stage, it would have been a longer process. So he urged and implemented Independence for Barbados.

It was not for him an easy period. There were others, both within his own Party and without, who held opposing views including Erskine Ward and Wynter Crawford, two of his Ministers who left him over this very issue. But I also recall that Philip Greaves (now Sir Philip) and Erskine Sandiford (now Sir Lloyd) joined him, respectively in his Cabinet and as his Personal Assistant and under his tremendous influence and played their own significant roles.

I very much regret his passing. Those who were his Parliamentary colleagues will miss him. Even when you disagreed with him you had to show him the respect which he so easily commanded. We have national heroes that we do not recognise adequately, in my opinion, and certainly he will be numbered among the national heroes as he is numbered among the builders of Barbados.

'Caribbeanising'
our legal system

*Address to the graduating class of the Sir Hugh
Wooding Law School of the University of the
Westindies (UWI), St. Augustine, Trinidad
23 September, 1986.*

Mr Chairman,
Lord Chief Justice,
My Lords, Your Excellencies,
Distinguished guests,
Members of the graduating class of the
Hugh Wooding Law School – 1986,
Ladies and gentlemen,

Lawyers are not supposed to speak without briefs and since I have no brief, I will be brief. It gives great pleasure in having been invited to address the graduates on this occasion. It must indeed be a happy occasion for all of you and for your families and friends assembled here who, during your period of study at Cave Hill and at St. Augustine, have given both moral and tangible support during a period of what you yourselves may have regarded as an odd year of fire, but you can now look back justifiably upon this experience as most worthwhile and a giant leap forward into the future.

Most people who enter the legal profession have done so because they consider being a lawyer as a congenial and socially acceptable means of earning a living. At times like these we have, from our benchers and guest speakers, a recital of high ideas to be aspired to, which even the Archangel Gabriel himself could not perform. I do not consider that lawyers are necessarily more ethical or have higher standards than any other honourable profession or vocation, and for that reason, I think that I can discard all the lofty sentiments about what lawyers should do and what lawyers should be and say to you that the essence of the performance of your duty should be based on humility, that, to be successful in this as in any other profession one has to like what one is doing and what is more important, particularly in law and to some extent medicine, you must know what you are doing. And in order to achieve these two objectives, a lawyer has to remain a student all the days of our lives. Legal training is essential to the development of our societies. It must be relevant. It must create an understanding of our constitutional and social histories. I hope that what I have to say now is not taken as a criticism of the practitioners here in the Caribbean, but I should like to give you an idea of the genesis of the Faculty of Law in the University of the Westindies and the two Law Schools which are so necessary a part of our legal training.

Some time in the late '60s, the authorities in the United Kingdom became somewhat concerned over the graduation of large numbers of persons from the Commonwealth, and they discovered or they claimed to have discovered, again due to their own fault, (their own fault in the sense that when we went as students to the United Kingdon, they claimed that we all looked alike) that some students were getting examinations taken for them by substitutes.

The system of legal education was very, very deficient. There was no contact between the lecturers and their students. The students could turn up periodically at examination time without having attended any lectures at all, and strange enough some of them passed. But in the early days, most of the persons who went to the four Inns of Court to become barristers were either the brilliant recipients of scholarships from their governments or graduates from one of the great universities in the United Kingdom. I do not have to call any names, such persons as Sir Hugh Wooding, Sir Lennox O'Reilly, Mr Norman Manley – you can name them. There was no danger at that time. But when the winds of change began to blow, and people flocked to the United Kingdon to seek job opportunities, many of them quite rightly felt that they should try to improve themselves and many enrolled at the Inns of Court. But many of them tried to work and to study at the same time, and anyone who has had a sojourn in that foggy climate (I'll try not to be pejorative) will understand that, whereas we have had great success stories in the United States of people, who by the sweat of their brow were able to pursue some courses of study and become successful professional persons, it was virtually impossible to do so in England. And due to the ingenuity of some of our compatriots in the Commonwealth from Far Eastern countries, some legally qualified persons who were reluctant to return to their own countries because of the turmoil which was going on at that time, and possibly for other personal reasons, decided that they would indulge in the profession of examination sitters. And under this scheme, any London Transport worker who had to work too hard by day and could not study by night, or some scion of a rich parent who never had the ability at all, could go to one of these examinees and for the payment of a small fee, get someone to take the exams for them. Now I want to make it abundantly clear – I am not aware anywhere in Trinidad and Tobago that there are such persons masquerading as lawyers. I wish I could say the same thing for Barbados because from the performances and the irrelevancies that I have witnessed during the past twenty years, I am not sure, I will not put it higher than that, that some of them were not the beneficiaries of the people whom I call practising examinees. But the Benchers at the Inns of Court became very concerned and urged upon us and upon what was then the Colonial Office that something should be done to rid them of these nuisances (to use the words of King Henry) – these turbulent nuisances, and encourage the establishment of the Law Faculties and these professional schools not only here in the Caribbean, but in Africa and the Far East as well.

We have been the beneficiaries of these malpractices. I say that because, from my experience, it would not be possible for anyone to attend the Hugh Wooding Law School or the Norman Manley Law School – we are such a small, close compact society – without his name, his abilities, and his physiognomy being well known to his tutors and to his fellow students. That is one reason and we can be certain that all the graduates who came on this platform here this evening are persons who rightfully deserve to be given the certificates which they have gained. So that the general public in Trinidad and Tobago and the Eastern Caribbean can be assured that our graduates are people who have faced the starter and completed the course and breasted the tape.

But there is another reason why the establishment of these facilities here in the Caribbean has been beneficial to the societies which they serve and it is this – that I personally found, even after practising in the Middle Temple although I am a Lincoln's Inn man, in London and coming back here, that the situations which I had to face as a young barrister or advocate were entirely different from those which prevailed in the United Kingdom.

I knew a fair amount of constitutional law, I like to think so, but I certainly did not know much about the constitutions of the Caribbean territories because it was no part of our curriculum. The law relating to Real Property here and Conveyancing was based on a system which had been introduced in the United Kingdom in 1925 – the great law reforms, when we were labouring in Barbados under the antiquated system predating 1868. So I had to start learning Real Property and Conveyancing all over again as a practitioner. And in many other respects I found that what we had had to study in the United Kingdom, while being of considerable advantage to practice in that country, these subjects were totally irrelevant. The only concession that I can remember that was made to the benighted colonies by the authorities at the Council of Legal Education was that they taught Roman-Dutch law as an optional subject for those persons who came from Guyana and Ceylon and countries who had had a history of Dutch occupation. And I am assured by my colleagues, such as the late Forbes Burnham, and later on by President Hoyte (of Guyana) that that was the one part of their training which they found to be beneficial to them on their return to their country. But all the other matters that we learnt particularly in our finals, because in Part I we had Contract and Tort and Roman Law – whatever that is –that in our final examination, we discovered that we could better have spent our time learning something about the constitutions of the Caribbean, learning something if we came from St. Lucia, or Dominica about the Napoleonic code and so on.

I will tell you my personal experience. There was considerable doubt, as we Westindians always underscore our own potential, as to whether we could produce people of quality here in the Caribbean by undertaking our own legal education. And there was in the early days, a certain amount of – I won't like to call it snobbishness, but lawyers are traditionally reactionary – and I used to say, priding myself on not being a reactionary lawyer which I probably was anyhow. The only thing was that I was less reactionary than the others that they ought to crown the lawyers with laurels and usher them out of the State. (I think that is what Cicero said he would like to do with the poets). Perhaps, I was a bit rash in my judgement, but later events proved that there was this reluctance on the part of some of our older practitioners to accept that all training here in the Caribbean could be as beneficial as that they had been exposed to in the United Kingdom.

When I returned in 1976 to a civil practice in Barbados, having become disenchanted with the criminal elements in our society, and having taken on at least three graduates from the Hugh Wooding and Norman Manley Law Schools – I discovered that they had a greater appreciation and a better concept of what the practice of law should be here in the Caribbean than I or any of my contemporaries had had.

Their training has been more relevant, it has one or two defects which I should not like to enter into here and now, but certainly, they have produced better attorneys – now I have avoided using the word 'advocates' because I think what we used to produce in the Caribbean with the English legal background was a variety of brilliant advocates, people who could dazzle a crowd of onlookers, or people sitting in a courtroom with their rhetoric.

I saw some of them graduate to becoming politicians. But when it came to a sound knowledge of office management, of what a lawyer's duty to the general society, the business community, and so on should be, I regret to say they were sadly lacking. I know one of my contemporaries who considered office business so irrelevant to the practice of law that his office was at the top of a staircase in a drugstore, and he had one chair. He could be seen with his gown flying, busying himself from court to court and he had a very successful practice, but he kept no books, so he never knew what he worked for, he never even knew if he had been paid for the cases in which he so brilliantly performed. I shall not call any names but I had to rescue that gentleman, organise his office for him so that he could be relieved for other duties. And one of those contemporaries of mine became a judge and he has the all time record of 15 years waiting for a judgement. I had the record I was waiting for the judgement and he was supposed to deliver it. And there was no prerogative writ that I could take out myself in order to enforce him to give a judgement, because in Barbados that would not be considered playing the game. I was very pleased, therefore, when two years ago, one of the graduates of the Hugh Wooding Law School brought a writ of *mandamus* against a statutory body – the Dental Association– in order to inspire them to enrol a qualified dentist on the register in Barbados – and that is the first time that I know in 40 years that anyone had had the courage to take out a writ of *mandamus* against a statutory authority in my country.

I referred just now to what I consider a defect. If you wish to involve practising barristers in the training of your students it will be necessary for you to set up here in Trinidad, in Port-of-Spain, close to the law courts, some kind of lecture facility whereby the practitioners will not have to spend two hours on the Eastern Main Road unless you give them special passes on the bus route, because no one is going to leave his office and spend two hours to come out to St. Augustine to find that the students have already gone home and, therefore, the students are being short-changed in this respect unless you have a lecture facility close to the offices of the lawyers. The

Norman Manley Law School in Jamaica is much better off in that respect and the members of the profession in Jamaica have pulled their full weight because they are not confronted with this ordeal of having to spend half the day on the road. This is something which I feel could be rectified.

The other defect which I should like to draw attention to is the question of attention being given to the abolition of appeals to the Judicial Committee of the Privy Council. I should like to confess that I am one of the back-woodsmen who fought strenuoulsy to retain the right of appeal to the Judicial Committee. And this was not based on any logic. But I had appeared before the Federal Appeal Court and it appeared to me that I bored the judges for two-and-a-half days and at the end of the first half-day, one of the celebrated judges asked me how long I had to talk and I told him that I had five points of appeal and I just finished the first point so by simple deduction I thought that I had two and a half days.

I was informed by His Lordship (whoever he was), we were then in October – that I could talk until Christmas – it was alright with them – that they had already written their decision. And this was a discipline in which neither one of the judges had been exposed to any kind of training at all because it was not a compulsory subject. So I spent my two-and-a-half-days and I had to go to the Judicial Committee, and I had the satisfaction of knowing that the five points that I had raised now constitute a leading case in the law reports in England reversing the Federal Court of Appeal. So I had, let me call it a gut sort of resentment, against having a Federal Court or a Court of Appeal in Caribbean being the final Court in which matters concerning my clients should be decided – and that was personal. But when I discussed the matter with the late Sir Hugh Wooding, he produced some statistics to me and he pointed out that, as of that time there had been thirty-three appeals to the Judicial Committee of the Privy Council and only two decisions had been reversed. One of them was the decision in the case in which I had been involved and I was right from the beginning. So let us say that there was only one out of thirty-two and you have to be impressed by that kind of statistics and Hugh Wooding said, 'Well if you are taking a one in thirty-two chance, there is no justification for making people spend the money to carry an appeal to the Judicial Committe.' And so I became converted by his logic.

The whole procedure of Appeals and getting leave to appeal to the Judicial Committee is a very tedious one and very expensive for the litigants unless you get permission to appeal in *forma pauperis*. So I think that we in the profession ought to give some attention, probably, to establishing our own Court of Appeal and having no limitation on the age of retirement of the judges because, in my humble opinion, when a judge attains the age of sixty-two or sixty-five as the case may be, provided he is physically fit, I think that he is at the stage where he has just begun to mature – he has just begun. We have had the cases of Oliver Wendell Holmes in the United States, the case of Mr Justice Douglas who became more radical as he got older (not to be confused with our own Sir William Douglas in Barbados). So you see there is a case for our having our own Court of Appeal. As a matter of fact, I should like to make it a qualification that no one under the age of sixty-five should be a member of that court, and therefore, in that way we would get the most experienced persons who will be available.

I made a promise when I started here this evening and I intend to keep it. The law schools themselves have to come to grips with these problems and change their programmes or amend their programmes effectively to meet the challenges of the profession in this day and age. Office management is going to involve more and more the use of computers, word processors, satellite and laser communications, micro-fiche in the search for not only records of property transfers, but also in the search of precendents of cases. When you go into a law library in the Caribbean and you look for a work which you wish to use in the arguments for your cases, you'll find that there has been one copy. Either the judge has taken it or the people on the other side have possession of it, and since we cannot all of us afford expensive law libraries, as a matter of fact, I do not know of any lawyer – no matter what pejorative statements are made about this – I do not know any lawyer who can afford the luxury of having a complete law library and at the same time own race horses – you have to have one or the other.

I should like to conclude in the words of Mr Wesley Williams who wrote in The Law – a Dynamic Profession – the American Bar Association Journal of 1955. Mr Williams is a member of the American Bar, the Pennsylvania Bar, and the Philadelphia Bar Association. He specialised in Corporation, Insurance, Commercial and Estate Succession Law. He said that the profession of the law must be a dynamic one. We cannot worship the status quo. It is the lawyer who has a competence to direct the progress of our remedial law. And if through apathy, indifference or fear of change he fails, we may be sure that others without the knowledge and experience and with little thought for the consequences will undertake this task.

Mr Chairman, My Lord Chief Justice, My Lords, Ladies and Gentlemen. I said right at the beginning that it was not my intention to do what I was being exposed to when I was admitted to the Bar by the Senior Bencher, Lord Henry of Moreton. There were only three of us from the Caribbean. My colleague from Trinidad, I understand, has two children who are also engaged in the practice of law. He is now, I understand two years deceased – but Lord Henry of Moreton admonished us that if we were going to be good lawyers that we should not get mixed up in radical politics and none of us took his advice. I should only like to advise you as graduates here today, that somehow or the other, there is a popular superstition that lawyers have a natural addiction, not necessarily qualification, for politics and if you are so inclined , if you think that in the pursuit of your careers that you can make some kind of contribution to your societies by taking up the challenge of the causes that lack assistance, against the wrongs that need resistance then I should respectfully like to submit that you will be fulfilling those high traditions which your predecessors in the Caribbean so successfully observed.

Thank you.

Statesman and Caribbean Visionary
Alicia Nicholls

On 21 January of each year, the day of his birth, Barbadians celebrate Errol Barrow Day. Our first Prime Minister, the Rt. Excellent Errol Walton Barrow is one of our ten national heroes and our beloved 'Father of Independence'. His likeness graces our fifty dollar bill, while a majestic bronze statue commands the attention of those walking through Independence Square in Bridgetown.

It could be said that one testament of a politician's greatness is when he or she is able to draw praise from both sides of the political aisle. Politicians and ordinary Barbadians, whether BLP or DLP, frequently speak of Mr Barrow and his contribution to our country with the deep reverence one usually reserves for religious figures. Respect for Mr Barrow goes far beyond these shores.

But Mr Barrow was more than a politician. He was a statesman and a visionary who saw it as the region's birth right that the Caribbean should have a share in the world.

I was born the year after Mr Barrow died but I feel no less passionate about our 'Father of Independence' than those Barbadians who had had the privilege of watching him in the House of Assembly getting on with the people's business.

While I may not have had the privilege of hearing his dry wit or seeing him mingle unassumingly with regular folk over a 'bread and two' and some mauby, I like many subsequent generations of Barbadians have benefited from the myriad of far-sighted economic and social welfare policies he instituted which have provided a pathway for economic and social mobility for the underprivileged and have set the foundation for the high standard of living and prosperity that Barbados today enjoys despite its small size and few natural resources.

Thanks to Mr Barrow, Barbadians benefitted from free education from the primary to tertiary levels, free school meals, the National Insurance Scheme and countless other social safety nets. His foreign policy emphasised principles of regional and international comity but also a strong sense of sovereignty and independence encapsulated in his oft-quoted phrase *"friends of all and satellites of none"*.

Mr Barrow enjoyed excellent relations and close friendships with his regional contemporaries. This is not surprising as Mr Barrow, along with regional greats like Norman and Michael Manley of Jamaica, Dr. Eric Williams of Trinidad and Tobago and Forbes Burnham of Guyana, just to name a few, belonged to a cadre of immediate post-colonial leaders who were imbued with a sense of national pride, but also recognised that their countries' economic survival required development within a regional framework.

However, for Mr Barrow, the necessity of Caribbean integration went beyond the possible economic gains. In extolling the desirability of developing closer relationships among the countries of the Anglophone Caribbean, he recognised the *"need to protect our small communities from exploitation by undesirable influences"*. Indeed, self-reliance was a strong theme underlying his vision for the region.

His anti-colonial fervour is encapsulated in another oft-quoted saying of his *"no loitering on colonial premises after closing time"*. He took a strong non-aligned stance during the Cold War, arguing that the Caribbean should be a 'zone of peace' and strongly opposed the US invasion of Grenada while he was in opposition. Mr Barrow recognised that political sovereignty was of little consequence if economic control was surrendered to foreign interests. Pushing for less dependence on developed countries, he criticised what he saw as a "mendicant mentality" in the region, arguing forcefully that begging from developed nations would not solve our problems.

While psychology was not one of Mr Barrow's professions, his speeches reveal his great thinking on the Caribbean psyche and its impact on the state of the region. Despairing over the slow process of regional integration, he spoke of the need to overcome our imbued sense of inadequacy if we are to progress as a region. He lamented that while Caribbean integration was a 'fact of daily experience', it was something that yet was not institutionalised. Indeed some of the reasons for the failings for Caribbean integration which he outlined in his 1986 speech to the CARICOM Heads of Governments Conference in Guyana ring true today.

To Mr Barrow, one of the biggest shortcomings of the integration movement was the failure to communicate that the regional integration movement was more than trade. There was the need to better communicate the regional project to the peoples of the region, by emphasising the strong cultural ties which bind us, and educating them on *"the meaning and purpose of all regional institutions"*.

As a law student, I have sat in lectures and nodded emphatically when I listened to my lecturers speak passionately of the need for 'Caribbeanising' our legal systems and the role of the Caribbean Court of Justice in developing our Caribbean jurisprudence. It should be noted that in 1986 Mr Barrow spoke on this issue in an address to the graduating class of the Sir Hugh Wooding Law School of the University of the West Indies St Augustine in 1986.

Although confessing that he had initially supported the retention of the right of appeal to the Judicial Committee of the Privy Council, Mr Barrow acknowledged the tediousness of this appeal process and suggested that the region instead establish its own Court of Appeal. I believe if he was alive Mr Barrow would celebrate that we now have the Caribbean Court of Justice (CCJ). Unfortunately, while all CARICOM members have accepted the CCJ in its original jurisdiction, only four members including Barbados have made it their final court of appeal.

It is impossible in one piece to do justice to Mr Barrow's legacy. While a proud Barbadian, Mr Barrow also held a deep attachment to the region, an attachment which regrettably seems lacking among many of our leaders of today. His speeches on Caribbean integration should, in my humble submission, be required reading for all Barbadian and Caribbean secondary school students doing social studies or history. Though delivered more than twenty years ago, his statements on self-reliance, self-confidence, regional unity and independence could be transposed to the current dispensation and still be relevant. Indeed, I believe they are needed now even more than ever.

"Speaking to the Future"

11 November 1986 interview with Ayana Gibbs, then a first form student of Harrison College

AYANA GIBBS: Good morning, Honourable Prime Minister, I am very grateful that you have kindly consented to let me speak with you about the independence of our nation, not only because you are now Prime Minister but also because you were the major figure in the achievement of our Independence. Mr Prime Minister, how do you feel when you are referred to as the "Father of Independence?"

ERROL BARROW: Well. It makes me feel as if I'm some sort of patriarch with a long beard. When we achieved Independence I was 46 years old and I suppose a person of that age is old enough to be the father, if not the grandfather of anything, to produce something. But it is just one of these journalistic expressions, which I suppose in a way it is a compliment because George Washington, who was the first president of The United States of America is referred to as "The Father of the Nation" because he was largely instrumental in winning the War of Independence against Britain. We didn't have to fight a war it is true, but we did have to do a lot of talking and arguing because a lot of people were unsure of themselves and were not sort of positive that they were able to run their own affairs.

AYANA GIBBS: Mr Prime Minister, what influenced you to seek Independence for Barbados at the time you did?

ERROL BARROW: You may ask what would influence anyone to be independent at any time. We think that Independence is a natural state of affairs and people should not be ruled over by other people. So it isn't something that you would think of doing at a particular time, it is something which all human beings in any society should strive towards from the time they are born. The people who rule over us usually tend to try to make us feel that we cannot run our own affairs, and that is all independence means – that you wish to run your own affairs without having to wait for other people to tell you what to do.

AYANA GIBBS: Mr Prime Minister, what do you consider to be the main difficulties you encountered in leading our nation to Independence?

ERROL BARROW: The main difficulty I think that my colleagues and I encountered was the lack of self-assurance of the people in Barbados and the people who had political axes to grind, which is the result of a long period of colonial domination, and I think that other societies have suffered from this self-doubt; and whereas the Americans, let us revert to them again, had to fight the British to get Independence we had to fight our own people to persuade them that it was time that we looked after our own affairs.

AYANA GIBBS: Mr Prime Minister, what, in your opinion are the main achievements of Barbados since Independence?

ERROL BARROW: It is difficult for me to pinpoint any one particular matter. I'll tell you why. When my political party took over the Government in 1961 we had a programme and that programme did not hinge on attaining Independence although Independence was part of our programme, in other words, being a self-governing country in 1961 and even before that, we did not depend on anyone for any money to carry out any of the programmes that we wished to carry out in this country; the people of Barbados paid their own way. So when we drew up a programme in 1961 for the improvement of the country, like free secondary education and a National Insurance Scheme and matters of that kind – although some of them came after Independence, they did not come as a result of Independence. It is only a question of timing that we were able to get through some of the matters on our agenda before Independence and others came in shortly after Independence. After Independence, of course, the only difference was that we were responsible in the international community for running our own foreign affairs as well. So that was about the only thing that Barbados accomplished by Independence along with the expense of running these foreign legations and so on that we did not do before Independence.

AYANA GIBBS: Mr Prime Minister, we will shortly be celebrating our 20th year of Independence, is there a special message on Independence which you would like to give to children of my age?

ERROL BARROW: Yes, I should like the children of your age and all the children in Barbados to realise that when you reach the age of 18 you have the right to vote and when you reach the age of 21 you have achieved full maturity. A lot of children today, nearly all the children today, were not even born when we achieved Independence but the future of this country is in the hands of those children who were not born when we achieved Independence. Next year we are going to be 21 and therefore the future is going to be firmly in your hands and you should make the most of your educational opportunities and all the other facilities which you have available for self-development in order to carry this country upward and onward.

AYANA GIBBS: Mr Prime Minister, I would like to thank you again for making this interview possible and I wish you success as you continue the leadership of our nation. Thank you.

ERROL BARROW: Thank you.

"The Caribbean is not an American problem"

Address to the 10th Annual Caribbean/Central American Action-Sponsored (C/CAA) Miami Conference on the Caribbean. Miami, November 20, 1986

I wish to thank Mr David Rockefeller and the Caribbean Central American Action for the invitation to attend the 10th Annual Miami Conference and exposition on the Caribbean and to address the luncheon today.

This is the first of these annual conferences that I have had the opportunity to attend, because the past decade in which they have been held, coincided with the ten years that the political party that I am privileged to lead spent in opposition in Barbados. I emphasise the word 'coincided' because I am sure that there was no connection between my departure from office in 1976 and the institution of these annual meetings.

One of the advantages of being in political opposition – and, believe me, there are more than you may imagine – is that, free from the daily demands of government, one has more time to look critically at the working of our economic and political system. In the past few years, I have given some thought to the evolving relationship between the Caribbean and the United States of America and I must confess that there are elements that have crept into that relationship that frankly disturb me. I say this, without apology, as one who is convinced that close co-operation between the Caribbean and our neighbours in the Western hemisphere is both necessary and desirable. The United States of America is not the least among these. Indeed, our government has proclaimed the expansion of friendly relations with the United States as one of the main goals of its foreign policy. Yet, as I say, there are elements in the recent evolution of U.S.-Caribbean relations that I find disturbing.

First and foremost, it seems to me that U.S.-Caribbean co-operation is being based – or at least being justified – increasingly on negative rather than positive considertions. Let me explain precisely what I am referring to.

If one examines many of the arguments used over the past few years, both by American and Caribbean persons, to persuade the American people of the desirability of assisting with the economic development of the Caribbean, one finds that essentially negative themes have tended to predominate.

If I may be allowed to summarise rather crudely, the case for cooperating with the Caribbean is put something like this: if the US does not help the Caribbean

(1) the communists, who are conveniently hiding behind every palm tree, will take over and surround the US with a ring of hostile islands;

(2) if the communists don't succeed, then the drug traffickers will take over and use the islands as bases to flood the US with 'dope';

(3) in either case, the entire population of the islands will flee to the US legally or illegally and take away jobs from American workers.

This may be a caricature but it is not, I suggest, a misrepresentation of the kind of negative reasoning that is frequently used to justify US-Caribbean co-operation.

The first thing that strikes one, or ought to strike one, about this line of reasoning is that it paints a terrifying, degrading and totally false picture of the Caribbean. For it suggests that what America has lurking offshore is nothing but a sea of troubles, with waves of disasters threatening your domestic tranquility. And unless one throws a whole lot of money and possibly guns at the situation, it might blow up in the face of the US. The cynical view, of course, is that in the context of American domestic politics such rhetoric is needed to 'sell' the idea of helping the Caribbean, to the American electorate. The problem is that you might end up believing such nonsense.

It is dehumanising and false to view the Caribbean as potential American problems. We are peoples with an identity and a culture and a history – the Parliament of Barbados will be 350 years old in 1989. We don't need lessons in democracy from anyone. However severe the economic difficulties facing the Caribbean, we are viable, functioning societies with the intellectual and institutional resources to understand and grapple with our problems. Collectively, we have the resource potential necessary for our continued development and, of course, we have a heritage of exquisite natural beauty entrusted to us. The Caribbean is, after all, a civilization.

The second thing that strikes one about the negative justification for American-Caribbean co-operation is that it paints a less than flattering portrait of the American people. Whatever the demands of political realism, it is, in my view, demeaning to suggest that Americans can be motivated to co-operate with their Caribbean neighbours only by fear for their own security. This is certainly not true of the many American tourists and businessmen I meet in the Caribbean. Indeed, the negative line of argument seriously short-sells the idealism, generosity, and sheer good sense of the American people.

In more practical terms, such negative considerations will tend to engender crisis-oriented and "quick-fix" attitudes to the region – attitudes which will be detrimental to the future of Caribbean-American co-operation.

There are many strong ties between the American and Caribbean peoples – ties of history, culture, and shared values. It is these positive considerations that should be emphasised as the basis of our mutually beneficial co-operation.

The second disturbing element that I have detected in the evolution of Caribbean-American relations is the trend towards an excessive reliance by the Caribbean on the US: the patronage mendicancy syndrome. The Caribbean is not the responsibility of the US, and it is totally unfair and unkind to Americans to ask them to shoulder all our burden. However poor we may be, however severe the economic difficulties we face, it must be clearly understood that the well-being and security of our peoples are our own responsibility. Let us face it, with all the money, all the technology and all the will in the world, the US cannot solve the problems of the Caribbean. In the first fifteen years that my political party managed the affairs of Barbados, we received no aid from the US of A, financial or military, neither did we ask for any. The US can contribute, and can contribute enormously, but only if the people of the Caribbean are themselves determined in a spirit of self-reliance to grapple with those problems.

The utmost priority has to be attached both by the Caribbean and the United States to the movement for regional co-operation in the Caribbean. For self-reliance in the situation of the Caribbean, must necessarily mean collective self-reliance.

Thus the most useful role that the US and other industrialised states can play in co-operation with the Caribbean is by strongly supporting multilateralism in the region and by channelling as much of their assistance as possible through the appropriate regional institutions. This approach offers the best prospects for self-sustaining development in the Caribbean.

It is a pity that the original multilateral approach to the Caribbean Basin Initiative (CBI) was never fully realised in practice, so that the CBI is now almost exclusively associated with the U.S. But I believe there is still hope for greater co-ordination of all the programmes of co-operation undertaken by various industrialised countries, such as Canada and the European Community with the Caribbean. Those same countries might also use their influence in the international financial institutions to get them to change their policies on lending to very small island states. Right now, because of an inflexible application of the per capita income criterion, access of the English-speaking Caribbean countries to soft loans from the International Development Association is being limited and several of them are being told that they will soon not be eligible for any type of loans from the World Bank. In the light of the serious economic difficulties facing the Caribbean today, this is a situation that is nothing short of shameful and demoralising.

I am convinced that the encouragement and support of multilateralism in the Caribbean, and among those friendly countries co-operating with the Caribbean, is the most productive and positive path to follow.

Let me say something about the CBI itself. I doubt that any similar initiative has generated such a torrent of words. Indeed, the CBI is a victim of its own rhetoric in that it has created expectations beyond anything that it could realistically be expected to fulfil. When one examines the actual Caribbean Basin Economic Recovery Act of 1983, one finds a very modest but useful effort at helping the Caribbean by providing restricted preferential access for Caribbean exports to the American market. And we really have to stop judging the CBI on what it ought to have or might have been. Political realism perhaps also dictates that with the Gramm-Rudman-Hollings balanced budget amendment, the current American trade deficit and the tide of protectionism sweeping the U.S., there is little prospect of getting Congress to improve the CBI. Thus, if the CBI is producing only very modest results, it is not because it is a failure, but because it is a very modest instrument. It is regrettable that the media in the Caribbean and the U.S. and our own medicant politicians find it convenient to forget that the whole concept of the Caribbean Basin as an object of economic development originated with the late Dr Eric Williams of

Trinidad and Tobago when he put forward his Caribbean Basin Plan involving one billion dollars to be raised totally from our own resources.

I can only say and say again to my friends in Congress: if you are serious about wanting to help the Caribbean, the best thing you can do is to allow all of our exports free and unrestricted access to the American market. Not as a matter of largesse or aid but as a means of redressing the unfavourable balance of trade which enures exclusively to the benefit of the U.S.A.

One area that offers considerable scope for growth in the Caribbean is the service sector. In a country as small and resource-poor as Barbados, the service sector is and will possibly become even more so a vital component of economic survival. Barbados has, therefore, developed both a tourism sector as well as an offshore sector designed to attract only legitimate business enterprises, whether bankers, foreign sales corporations or captive insurance companies.

Through our own tax treaty and tax information exchange with the U.S., we co-operate in the investigation of tax fraud and related illegal activities. The tax treaty was designed to strengthen economic co-operation between our two countries and any attempt to undermine the treaty will strike a severe blow at this co-operation. I, therefore trust that the U.S. government will honour its commitment to this international instrument and not take any action to alter the lengthily negotiated provisions of the treaty, for any action to alter the provision of the treaty would be a set back to investment tax co-operation and trade not only between Barbados and the U.S., but possibly between the U.S. and other Caribbean countries contemplating the signing of tax and information agreements with the U.S.

Upon assuming office in May of this year, my government commenced upon a programme of economic restructuring aimed at revitalising the economy of Barbados. Our economic policy goals were, and are, the reduction of high levels of unemployment, overcoming persistent economic stagnation; the restoration of private business confidence and performance; the curtailment of substantial losses in public sector commercial ventures and the rebuilding of export competitiveness.

The achievement of these goals has been tackled, initially, under the purview of budgetary measures which have sought to restore incentives to individuals to work, save and invest; reduce the costs of business operation; provide incentives to encourage reinvestment of capital; provide for business to build up healthy reserves, place resources behind small business and reduce the tax burden of private individuals and business.

Most salient of the measures was the reduction in the maximum rate of personal income tax from 60 per cent to 50 per cent; with all persons earning BDS$15,000 a year or less, being exempted from paying income tax. In addition the maximum rate of corporate tax was reduced from 45 per cent to 35 per cent, and will soon move to a graduated tax ranging from 15 per cent to 35 per cent. The tourist sector, in particular, was relieved of an onerous tax burden.

We took all these actions because we were convinced that the personal income and corporate tax regimes were stifling the creativity and entrepreneurial talents of our people, and also because of our firm belief that the private sector has a big role to play in bringing the economy back on track. The rate of return to the community of investment by the private sector is more efficiently realised, and that sector subsumes more importantly the individual working with his own hands.

These measures will, in the short run, generate substantial impact upon disposable income, demand for goods and services and the growth of government revenue from indirect taxation. Over the medium term the growth in purchasing power, correctly chanelled, will lead to the emergence of new businesses and expansion of those already established, thereby creating more job opportunities. Over the long run as businesses expand and new ventures develop, additional rounds of revenues and employment will be generated.

One other complementary area of reform which the government is pledged to undertake as a matter of urgency in order to restore economic health, is the problem of wasteful expenditure and inefficiency in the public sector generally and particularly in government-owned commercial enterprise. Our own enterprises policy recognises that government must play a role in the provision of private goods and services for purchase by individuals, and, therefore, government will continue to invest, appropriately in, and promote the production and distribution of private goods. However, we intend to put an end to the practice whereby publicly-owned enterprises, producing non-strategic goods and services are permitted to operate at a substantial loss with little likelihood of ever making a profit. In the extreme case where complete divestment is the appropriate course, such action will be taken.

Much of the infrastructural and institutional framework for business activity in Barbados was laid down during the years 1961 to 1976, when I had the privilege of heading the government of Barbados for three successive terms. Just as we in Barbados do not need instructions on the virtues of democracy, neither do we need instructions on the virtues of free enterprise. The government is committed to fostering the most healthy and positive climate for private sector investment, both domestic and foreign, in Barbados. We recognise that the ability to produce and export at internationally competitive prices will be critical to our success, and we welcome the foreign, and especially the American, investor, as one who can make an important contribution to that objective.

I look forward to close and friendly co-operation with the people of the United States during my tenure in office. I am convinced that such co-operation is to the mutual benefit of both the Caribbean and American peoples. But I feel equally strongly that such co-operation must be based on positive and not negative considerations and should reinforce the self-reliance and independence of the Caribbean. It has become fashionable in American domestic politics to invoke the name of Franklin D. Roosevelt in order to inspire Americans with a unity of purpose and vision and faith in this great country. I would urge that in the field of foreign relations, you also invoke the spirit of that great American statesman in dealing with your good neighbours in the Caribbean.

Comrade and Brother

E. Evelyn Greaves

The relationship between Barrow and the labour movement is one that spans most of his political career and was such a natural synergy that it might be compared to the relationship between Brazil and soccer. Indeed, the former Prime Minister of Jamaica Michael Manley, had this to say in 1987 on Barrow's passing: *"Errol Barrow yielded pride of place to no person in his support for the workers' causes. The long friendship and close association between himself and Frank Walcott of the Barbados Workers' Union, in the eyes of many the dean of Caribbean trade unionists, is ample evidence of the late Prime Minister's commitment."*

An early contributing factor in the shaping of this National Hero was his familial context. His father, the Rev Reginald Barrow, was a controversial minister of religion who was not averse to using the pulpit to challenge the prevailing dominant white social order and injustices against the underprivileged. In addition, his uncle, the RE Dr Charles Duncan O'Neal, a medical doctor, was a passionate social reformer who waged an ongoing battle against the entrenched establishment for the improvement of the living and working conditions of the poor.

Dame Nita Barrow, his sister noted: *"Uncle Duncan turned his attention from a good private practice to look after the poor…I remember one of our matriarchs who held court every afternoon, even after she had a stroke, saying he is a traitor to his class."* Such was the impact of O'Neal's efforts to assist the underprivileged, even on his own relatives.

Added to his early socialisation, Barrow, while studying at the London School of Economics benefitted from his interaction with the avant-garde thinker Professor Harold Laski, a prominent intellectual whose thinking and moral compass pointed towards radical socialism and a concern for pro-labour reform.

In 1950, the Barbados to which Barrow returned, having completed studies in Law and Economics, was one in which the issues and conditions that led to the social upheavals and riots of 1937 were still very evident. It was one in which, following the recommendations of the Moyne Commission, the Barbados Workers' Union (BWU) had emerged but was struggling for legitimacy.

The fledging Union was being sustained by the sheer grit and determination of Grantley Adams (later The RE Sir Grantley), Hugh Springer (later The RE Sir Hugh) and a then young Frank Walcott (later The RE Sir Frank). It had begun to gain a foothold among some workers, especially at the Foundry and among workers offloading cargo from the ships (the lightermen and longshoremen) and in the sugar industry, the key areas of economic activity.

In addition, the BWU and the Democratic League, with which it was inextricably bound, had attained successes in areas such as: increases in old age pensions; the introduction of a Workmen's Compensation Act; an amendment to the Trade Union Act to limit the liability of the union; an Education Act; a Wages Council and a lowering of the franchise that also allowed women to vote and seek membership of the House of Assembly.

This was a time of great ferment when many changes were taking place throughout the Caribbean. 1951 was the first year in which general elections were being conducted in Barbados under universal adult suffrage which provided an opportunity for some of the young bright coloured intelligentsia to seek membership of the House of Assembly under the banner of the Barbados Labour Party (BLP).

It was in this environment that Barrow entered the political arena and was elected as Senior Member for the constituency of St George under the double member arrangement.

Barrow's relationship with the Barbados Labour Party did not last long as there were a number of instances in which he took issue with the leadership of the Party. He quickly became disenchanted with the slow approach to change advocated by the Party leaders. In addition, he was not satisfied by the way in which Grantley Adams treated Frank

Walcott, his trusted lieutenant, by not offering him in 1954 a place in the newly instituted Cabinet system.

Barrow resigned from the Barbados Labour Party and was among those who were instrumental in forming the Democratic Labour Party (DLP) in 1955.

Between 1956 and 1961 when Barrow and the DLP were largely unsuccessful at the polls, he spent his time building the Party and establishing critical links with workers in the sugar industry. The two opportunities which presented themselves and strengthened Barrow's position were first his re-election to Parliament in 1958 as one of the representatives for the constituency of St John, and the second one was the seemingly intractable fight that the BWU was having with the Sugar Producers' Association in 1958 over the payment of improved wages for sugar workers.

When a strike was called by the BWU, Barrow took the opportunity to intervene by leading a delegation comprising himself, W.A. Crawford, J.C. Tudor, E. Talma and two sugar workers: George Forde of Sunbury Plantation in St Philip and Darnley Jones of Pool Plantation in St John, to meet and bargain with the Governor Sir Robert Arrundell. Following the capitulation by the Sugar Producers, Barrow was regarded as a saviour of the situation.

With the momentum from the sugar workers settlement, Barrow could have formed a separate union for sugar workers, as Grantley Adams and his allies would do subsequently over the issue of the Sugar Workers' Provident Fund, but he did not. Barrow held steadfastly to the view that political parties and the trade unions should be separate institutions governed by their own executive council and rules. Rather, he continued to reach out to and work with Frank Walcott, by then the BWU General Secretary, to strengthen the influence of the Union in the sugar industry. This action cemented his support with the BWU.

Interestingly, during this period, Barrow was also active on the wider Caribbean union scene as legal adviser to Vere Bird who was President of the Antigua Trades and Labour Union and to Robert Bradshaw, President of the St Kitts Trades and Labour Union. As the trade unions in these two countries were based mainly in the sugar industry and were experiencing serious problems with the owners of the industry, Barrow's experience from the Barbados situation was central to the advice that he gave. Incidentally, both these trade union leaders were also political leaders in their respective countries.

The 1961 General Election saw the success of the Democratic Labour Party and the emergence of Barrow as Premier. This period, with subsequent successful elections in 1966, in which he became Prime Minister and then again in 1971, witnessed the pursuance of policies that were aimed at creating employment and also at improving the wages and working conditions of the workforce, with specific emphasis on the sugar workers. Indeed the period 1961 to 1976 can be referred to as the "golden age" of labour legislation.

The December 1961 Throne Speech at the Opening of Parliament outlined the Government's policies and programmes for the 1961-1966 period set the stage by including the following labour proposals:

- *to provide substantially increased Workmen's Compensation benefits and for extension of the range of persons who will benefit under the Act.*
- *to provide for the grant of paid maternity leave to women employed in the public, industrial and commercial undertakings or in any agricultural undertakings.*
- *amend the Trade Union Act 1939 so as to make it clear that agricultural and domestic workers are covered by the Act.*
- *bring the law relating to peaceful picketing up to date with United Kingdom legislation.*
- *to implement a comprehensive scheme of social security benefits for workers in the sugar industry including provision of severance pay for factory workers.*
- *to acquire plantation tenantries for re-sale of the land to the tenant occupiers.*

One of the very first acts of the new DLP Administration in December 1961, was the introduction of a crash programme that provided work for a number of previously unemployed persons and for some sugar workers who were working reduced hours. The single-minded approach with which Barrow introduced this programme created a new dynamism in the country. There were many critics, but the working class felt that Barrow cared for them and was prepared to do something about their plight.

Consistent with the Throne Speech, Barrow began in earnest to implement and modernise some of the labour legislation for which the BWU had been clamouring for a number of years. As a consequence, the relationship between Barrow and Walcott grew stronger. This was further evidenced in May 1962 when there was a looming strike in the transport sector. Hansard records show that Frank Walcott brought a resolution to Parliament to move the House to debate a Matter of Urgent Public Importance relating to the threatened strike.

Walcott was about to leave the country for Europe to attend an international trade union meeting and needed to have the matter settled before he left. Shortly after he began his presentation, Barrow asked that he give way as he had a statement to make. The Premier indicated that only that morning had the matter been brought to his attention. He asked to be given a few days to speak to the transport owners towards having the matter resolved. Walcott agreed and proceeded on his travels and the matter was amicably resolved. This spoke volumes of the trust that had been built up between these two men. It should be mentioned though, that at times, the relationship was strained as subsequent events will show.

The impact of updating and modernising labour legislation during this "golden age" saw many significant benefits accrue to workers both in the public and private sector. Between 1961 to 1971, the DLP under the leadership of Barrow:

- Upgraded the Holidays with Pay Act to improve holiday entitlement from two weeks per year to three weeks per year after working at the business for a continuous period of five years and stipulated that employers were required to allow each worker who qualified to take his vacation.
- Made changes in the working conditions for single women in the public service that put them on the same footing as married women. Previous to this development, single women who became pregnant and had a civil service job had to give it up.

- Introduced the five day work week for public servants.
- Introduced Christmas loans for public servants. These loans had to be repaid by March of the following year – the end of the government's financial year. This was a popular measure especially among the low paid public workers.
- Replaced the 1939 Trade Union legislation in 1964 by a new Trade Union Act. This new legislation allowed peaceful picketing at the workplace and at or near the residence of owners of a business that was the object of the dispute. In addition, the legislation provided for civil servants to form trade unions. Before this, civil servants were limited to forming ineffective and docile Associations. Hence one saw emerging in the 1970s the National Union of Public Workers; the Barbados Secondary Teachers' Union and the Barbados Union of Teachers as significant militant organisations representing their members in salary negotiations and working conditions.
- Introduced legislation to provide for a guaranteed minimum work week for sugar workers during the out of crop season.
- Implemented the Tenantries Act that prevented a plantation owner from giving notice to a tenant on plantation lands who ceased to work for the plantation.
- Introduced the Sugar Workers' Pension legislation that allowed sugar workers who had worked on a plantation for five years and who had attained age 65 to receive a pension from the Sugar Industry.

The latter three measures alone brought a new level of stability to the lives of sugar workers and their families. These also reflected Barrow's deep concern about the situation of workers in the sugar industry. He was relentless in his quest to draw public attention to these difficult conditions and was critical at times of the BWU for not seeking more robustly to effect changes in the working conditions of sugar workers, especially the female workers. Indeed this concern was captured in his 1986 "Mirror Image" speech.

In the 1971 to 1976 period, three fundamental pieces of legislation were introduced by the Barrow Administration that the BWU had been relentlessly lobbying Government for. These three pieces of legislation which probably had the most significant impact on the social and economic life of Barbados were: the National Insurance Act, the Severance Payment Act and the Employment of Women (Maternity Benefits) Act.

For the first time in Barbados, workers were able to benefit from the provisions of National Insurance that covered sick leave and maternity leave and provided for a pension on the attainment of retirement age. Workers and employers would contribute to a Fund that would be administered by a Board that had, among its membership, representatives of workers' and employers' organisations.

Both Barrow and Walcott felt that workers and their representatives should be involved in the national development effort in a meaningful way. It is consistent therefore that they were both advocates for the education of workers.

The Throne Speech in December 1961 included the following: *"... consultations will shortly be held with the Barbados Workers' Union on the establishment of a college for the education of trade unionists."* The BWU began a Residential Summer School programme at Codrington College in September 1961 which lasted until 1974 when the Union built its Labour College facilities at Mangrove in St Philip. The College was officially opened by Prime Minister Barrow and the Government also provided a modest subvention and granted the Labour College duty-free concessions.

When Barbados joined the United Nations on Independence, Barrow appointed his trusted and internationally experienced friend, Frank Walcott, as the country's first Permanent Representative (non-resident) to the UN. By 1967, Barbados became a member of the ILO and on joining ratified over 20 Conventions. This was a landmark occasion for the BWU and Walcott who had previously attended ILO meetings as an Observer from the International Confederation of Free Trade Unions (ICFTU). Now with Barbados being fully a member of the ILO, he could attend as a Workers' Delegate from Barbados. It made a great deal of difference to Walcott and the ILO as he became a member of the

ILO Governing Body in 1969 and was systematically re-elected until his retirement in 1991.

From the above, it was clear that Barrow held Walcott in high esteem which was not only a personal tribute to Walcott but a reflection of the high regard Barrow had for the labour movement. In the Caribbean, there are several examples of politicians using trade unions to gain political office and then ignoring them.

As indicated, the relationship between Barrow and Walcott was sometimes strained. One notable occasion was the issue surrounding the proposed Sugar Workers' Provident Fund in 1964. Walcott was concerned about the lack of a pension scheme for sugar workers and was able to convince most of the sugar workers that, rather than taking all of the BWU negotiated windfall payment, the workers should agree to place a percentage in a Fund for the rainy day that Walcott felt was surely coming given the state of the industry and the unreliable changes that were taking place with sugar prices on the guaranteed market in Britain and the world market.

With the Sugar Producers agreeing, albeit reluctantly, to the proposal it was decided that the Fund should be legally established and a meeting was set up by the BWU and the Sugar Producers with Premier Barrow who endorsed the idea and instructed the Attorney General to draft the necessary legislation.

However, some workers were unhappy about the idea and were easily persuaded to oppose the arrangement. The BLP saw an opportunity to split the BWU and seized it. Grantley Adams having recently returned to Barbados from the failed West Indies Federation joined the fight against the establishment of the Fund. Barrow backed away from the measure since, as Government, he was only facilitating the Union and the Sugar Producers. It was clear that Barrow and members of his Cabinet felt that this issue could spell danger for the Government

The still birth of the Fund meant that all the money was paid out to the sugar workers, which was a huge disappointment to Walcott and gave the BWU an uphill task of trying to regain a foothold in the sugar industry. This was particularly difficult on the plantations as the BWU was now contending with a challenge from the BLP which, unlike Barrow's DLP previously, formed the Sugar and General Workers'

Union. By 1966, the damage done by this episode had its effect on Walcott's bid for re-election for his seat as a member of the House of Assembly representing the rural constituency of St Peter. He would lose to the BLPs Burton Hinds.

As an observation, one can argue that this may have been providential for the labour movement, since it allowed Walcott the time needed to rebuild the BWU and transform it into the modern organisation and strong voice for workers that it became in the years to follow. Incidentally, the relationship between Walcott and Barrow became stronger after this.

With the passage of the 1964 Trade Union Act, public servants could form trade unions which they did with acted with a militancy never previously displayed. The establishment of the Barbados Community College (BCC) in 1969 was the occasion for a strike by the Barbados Secondary Teachers' Union over the fact that BCC Tutors were being paid at a higher rate their members. The Government argued that the two were dissimilar since the BCC was not a secondary school.

When discussions broke down the teachers went on strike which was unprecedented for public servants in Barbados. Barrow was clearly displeased and adopted a strictly legalistic position arguing that by going on strike the teachers had vacated their posts and as a consequence lost their pension rights. This drove fear into some of the teachers and ended the strike with Barrow, appearing to be magnanimous, introducing legislation to restore the pension rights of teachers in the secondary schools.

In 1971, elections in Barbados were contested, for the first time, as single member constituencies. I had the honour to carry the DLP banner for St Lucy and Walcott for the St Michael West constituency. The DLP won this election convincingly but very soon had to confront the serious economic storm that followed the OPEC-led oil crisis brought about by the horrendously high increase in the price of fuel. Barbados was heading for troubled economic waters as oil imports were integral to the economy.

The 1976 General Election fell in the middle of this economic downturn, one of the worst that Barbados had faced up to then. Prices were rising drastically and with this came a fear that salary increases to be negotiated that year would not satisfy the high prices that workers were seeing every day. The National Union of Public Workers (NUPW), the BWU and the other public sector unions submitted proposals for their respective members'. The NUPW's submission included a 100 per cent increase for lower paid workers while the BWU submitted a proposal of 55 per cent for its members.

The first conflict came over salary increases for workers at the Caribbean Broadcasting Corporation (CBC). Barrow, as Minister of Finance and as Minister responsible for Broadcasting, indicated that CBC as a state subsidised agency could not afford what the BWU was asking for. Instead, he offered a 35 per cent increase across the board and further stated that this was the extent to which he was prepared to go in all negotiations for public servants.

When this proposal was rejected by all the unions, the Government went to Parliament and, for the first time, legislated the salaries for public servants. The Government's termination of the negotiations left a bitter taste in the mouths of public servants who were encouraged by the BLP not to accept the proposal and to demand more. However, the legislated position was reluctantly accepted by the workers.

An interesting factor in this scenario was that Walcott, BWU General Secretary and I, a Deputy General Secretary, were DLP backbench Members of Parliament. As a matter of principle both Walcott and I indicated to Barrow that we could not support the move to legislate salaries as it was setting a dangerous precedent. Barrow's approach to this dilemma was sanguine. Indeed, he maintained his strongly held view that the trade union and the political party should be separate but supporting entities and stated his position to DLP colleagues as follows: *"I have a Government to run; Walcott and Greaves have a Union to run and we will not always see eye to eye."* He then proceeded to caution his General Council and Members of Parliament that union leaders should be free to exercise their conscience as they *"were only doing their job"*.

In the above political climate, it was no surprise that the BLP defeated the DLP in the 1976 General Election and would remain in office until 1986 when the Democratic Labour Party won a landslide victory on its return.

The final chapter in this relationship between Barrow, Walcott and the labour movement was written when Barrow invited Walcott to serve as President of the Senate and Knighted him for his excellent work in the labour movement and his contribution to the development of Barbados. This was vintage Barrow. It was done from his heart because it should be clear from the discourse that above all the Right Excellent Barrow Walton Barrow had a deep feeling for the workers of Barbados and contributed immensely to their wellbeing.

"Travelling down the road of social justice"

May Day Address to the Barbados Workers' Union May Day Rally at Queen's Park, Bridgetown, May 1, 1987.

Your Excellencies,
Mr President,
Mr General-Secretary,
Fellow workers, dear loving people,

This year, 1987, is of great significance to all workers' organisations in the Commonwealth Caribbean, since it marks the 50th Anniversary of the events that indisputably led to the legalisation and recognition of workers' organisations in the region.

A lot of young people here, and many more who may not be here today, may not be aware that prior to the year 1939, when the Trade Union Act and Trades Dispute Act were placed on the statute books, any organisation of workers, which set about to change their condition of labour were not only illegal at common law, but actions taken by workers, to bring about alleviation of their conditions, ot to bring attention to their grievances, were liable to be crushed ruthlessly by the full impact of the penalties of the statute law contained in the Conspiracy and Protection of Property Act and other oppressive laws which reflected the social and economic prejudices of the times, and the fears which the political directorates of the day entertained in relation to the natural impulses of the masses to consolidate in order to seek redress to the many disadvantages which encompassed them at home and at work.

The Democratic League in Barbados with the Working Mens' Association, Captain Cipriani in Trinidad with his Working Mens' Association with which the Barbados organisation was affiliated, Hubert Crichlow in Guyana with his organisation, all surreptitiously, gave some leadership and opportunity to the masses to ventilate their grievances during the '20s and early '30s.

But when the voices of their leaders were stilled, and the economic pressures created by the Great Depression made life unbearable here in the Caribbean in the middle '30s, there was a spontaneous outburst of indignation on the part of the unrepresented and underprivileged of the region, which spread like a brush fire in the dry season, from the north in Puerto Rico to the south in Guyana, and from the east in St Kitts, to the west in Jamaica.

No middle class politician or professional person can either claim credit or responsibility for the events of 1937. The leaders who emerged after 1937, were not the supporters of Cipriani, Critchlow or O'Neal,* but rather persons whose consciences were jolted by the events in which so many innocent workers lost their lives at the hands of the militaristic cossacks, who held the thin red line of unenlightened British colonialism and imperialism.

Workers in Barbados were shot down for picking potatoes, by their own families in the police force. Similarly, in other areas in the Caribbean.

A commission under the chairmanship of Sir George Dean was set up by the governor of Barbados and in its report, the commission fully exposed the appalling economic conditions which prevailed in this country and which directly contributed to the uprising of the workers.

In other places, at other times, such assertions of the peoples of their fundamental rights have been glorified – sometimes quite justifiably –and enshrined in their histories as glorious revolutions. In France, in the United States, in Latin America, in the Soviet Union, in Mexico, and even in the Union of South Africa, this has been done.

Here in Barbados, our Barbadian teachers, appallingly ignorant of our own economic and social history, are continuing to teach our Barbadian children that we had riots in 1937. We committed unlawful acts by unlawful means so that the law enforcement agencies had to shoot hungry people digging potatoes, which they had not planted, in order that these law enforcement agencies might be able to maintain something called law and order.

If people in Barbados were not outraged, public opinion in the United Kingdom and elsewehere, was outraged. The British government appointed a Royal Commission under the chairmanship of Lord Moyne, who subsequently lost his life in the Middle East, to investigate the causes of the uprising; and that Royal Commission

*Charles Duncan O'Neal, founder of the Democratic League, and an uncle of Errol W. Barrow.

conducted its public hearings right here in Queens Park. The only days in my whole school career from the age of two-and-a-half in the American Virgin Islands, to age 19-and-a-half on the other side of Queens Park**, that I have failed to attend in sickness or in health, or otherwise, was when I attended hearings of the Royal Commission here in Queens Park.

The commission did not publish its findings until after World War Two, as it would have been embarrassing to the British government if it had published its findings ... its report was submitted to the so-called 'Colonial Office' in which it recommended immediate legislation to establish trade unions in all the Westindian colonies; and that is how the Barbados Workers' Union was born.

The events of 1937, the protest of the leaderless workers, and not the submissions of middle class intellectuals or professionals, were directly responsible for the genesis of trade unions and trade unionism in the Commonwealth Caribbean.

I know because I was there. I was here, and I saw it for myself. I do not rely on the distortions of the workers' history with which this country has been afflicted in recent times, by persons who were not there, and were not interested at that time; and if they had been there, they would have run away, because they would not like to be associated with actions unacceptable to the social directorate of the era.

Mr President, Mr General-Secretary, compañeros, or compañeras, the union has come a long way in its 48 years – in its 48 unbroken years. There has been much social reform during this period. And just as important, the Barbados Workers' Union, has for a long time been internationally recognised.

In returning to the celebrations of May 1st, an order for which the Governor General signed in December 1986***, the labour movement is showing its solidarity with the workers in 70 other countries who have adopted the designation of the first of May as a labour holiday which the Second Socialist International so designated as far back as 1889, 100 years ago.

In ancient times, May Day celebrated the return of Spring, with festivities and dancing. Today we are doing much the same thing. We are celebrating not the return of spring, but the return of hope which

---

**This is a reference to Harrison's College, a prestigious secondary school, located just outside Queens Park in Bridgetown, which Barrow and all Barbados' other political leaders have attended.

***In 1984, the previous Barbados Labour Party Administration shifted May Day celebrations to the first Monday in May, despite protests from the unions.

springs eternal in the human breast.

But I should like to say that the government of Barbados, which is a social democratic government, shares with the workers' organisations, the same objectives; and the main social objective which we share with the workers' organisations and why we find it easy to travel down the same road together, is the objective of social justice.

Social justice cannot be achieved in a society where there is inequality and discrimination either at the work place or outside of it. Social justice cannot co-exist with hunger and unemployment. No matter what achievement may be made by the workers' organisations in securing better conditions of work, better wages, better benefits for their members, as long as you have, outside of the workers' organisations, the industrial reserve army, as Karl Marx described it, or the unemployed, there can never be any social justice in the said society, even for those who are organised within the ranks of the workers' union.

I am submitting, and I think the workers' union has accepted, that it is the common duty of the government and the workers' organisation to see that the whole spectre of unemployment, as far as possible, is removed fom this society, in the first instance, and from the wider Caribbean association in the second analysis.

We are striving towards the elimination of want and distress. People who do not have jobs are a drain on those people who have jobs. Fortunately for us here in Barbados, we have still retained some of the survivals which we brought from our mother country. We have still retained the institution of the extended family. We have still retained those practices of looking after those less fortunate among us, even if they are remotely related to us, or not related at all.

So that I am satisfied that despite the fact that we have unemployment in excess of perhaps 18 per cent of the total labour force, that there are very few people, except your humble servant, who go to sleep hungry at night.

I go to sleep hungry at night by choice, and not be necessity. If I eat a heavy meal late at night, I cannot sleep; so mine is by choice. But I am happy to say that ... despite our indoctrination by the metropolitan cultures, we have managed to retain some of those ancestral practices in the society by which we ensure that members of the family are looked after. By the very token, we are impoverishing ourselves by having to feed those persons for whom the society is not creating the opportunities to feed themselves.

I am sure the Barbados Workers' Union, along with the other workers' organisations, are as much concerned over the alleviation of unemployment as we are as a government. It is very nice for one to get up on a platform and say that we want to relieve unemployment. But it is a far different thing to devise the instruments and create the social engineering by which unemployment is going to be alleviated, if not eradicated.

I do not have any ready formula. But what I want to say is that we are all concerned about it. In the past 12 months, unemployment has dropped by one per cent; but the labour force has increased by 4,000 persons. That really means that in the same period that over 5,000 jobs have been created. I do not think that the government would be so arrogant as to claim credit for having created all of those jobs. But by natural processes of economic growth, 4,000 more jobs have been created during the past 12 months which on the 28th of May would have been the 12 months that this government has been in office.

We are satisfied that we are making some progress in holding the line. But if we are going to reduce the 18 per cent to six or seven per cent, or an acceptable level in other words, then all of us have to work together to ensure that we do something in our own way to help those who are looking for jobs and who cannot secure them.

The government has taken steps by its budgetary measures to encourage the creation of jobs in the society ... The government has also established a task force, including representatives of the workers, in order to investigate ways and means by which we can create more employment opportunities in the society.

I am pleased to see here on the platform with me this afternoon no less a person than the Minister of Labour and Employment himself [Wes Hall]. Somebody criticised the government for setting up a task force to see if we can create jobs. They claimed that we said in our manifesto that we will create more jobs and when we called in all the branches of the society to help us, they say we did not know what we were doing, we had to ask other people.

I will deal with that particular approach to the problem of the society in which we live, because it is our desire to try to bring into consultation in all aspects of the management of this society, everyone who is engaged in the productive activity of the society itself, including the workers and including the employers.

No one group of persons in this society is endowed with all the assets, or the ingenuity whereby they have all the answers to all the problems in this society. We recognise as a government that in order to mobilise all the talents that we have in Barbados, we have to have consultation with all the people in the society all the time. We make no apologies for that.

Mr President, we are now in the last quarter of the 20th century... In the same way that by the social engineering brought about by devices such as National Insurance and Social Security, and by the insistent demands made by the workers' organisations that they should have a just share of the fruits of their labour, that the whole aspect of economic relationships in the society must undergo, and are undergoing a fundamental change.

I think that in the final 12 or 13 years of this century, the unions and the governments and the employers, have a very basic function to perform; that is, instead of regarding the elements in the society from the point of view of we the employers on one side, the government in the middle and the workers on the other side, we now have to look upon ourselves as all participants in the economic process.

The union now has to concentrate on training its members in management skills. That does not mean that I am advocating an immediate takeover of the commanding heights of the economy, as they used to be called in the 19th century, by the workers.

But I am looking forward to the gradual withdrawal of the government involvement in trying to bring about these changes and greater participation by the workers in the managerial functions of the society.

We are not going to achieve our common objectives of social justice if the workers are going to be there on the other side of the fence, having an antagonistic attitude towards the people who control the capital. We are only going to have harmonious relationships in this society if the people who now control the capital realise that the workers themselves are entitled to a share in the control of that capital, both in the managerial and ownership levels.

Therefore, greater shares in the businesses of the society must be available to the workers. Greater participation in management must be available to the workers and we have to abandon this concept that if a worker, through his exceptional talents manages to catch the eye of the selectors, the description that Wes***** will understand, and get a pick as a captain that he no longer can be regarded as a player and cannot take part in the union activities.

The captain must always be a worker himself. You cannot isolate a manager from the workers and say he cannot take part in the work, because my concept is that the manager is as much a worker as the

***** This is a reference to former Westindies cricketer and team manager, Wes Hall, who as Minister of Employment and Labour, shared the platform with Mr Barrow and union leaders during the rally.

man from whose ranks he sprung ... the employers must understand that if we are to have harmonious relationships in this society.

They are asking us now to subsidise the sugar industry. I do not want to go too far down that road, because 20 years ago, at a May Day meeting, I warned the workers in this country of what was going to happen and I was criticised.

I did not say what they said I said. But I warned the workers to watch out, that the thing was going downhill. But I am saying this: we want a share in the management.

They are now asking us the tax payers, you and me, to take up our money and subsidise an industry that is on its way out. But they do not want us to have a share in the management.

When we came into office in 1961 one of the first things that I insisted upon with the British government was that the workers' organisation should take part in the negotiations for the price of sugar under the sugar agreement, because they were getting up there behind closed doors as producers and negotiating with the British government for a price of sugar that would affect the level of wages that workers were to get here in Barbados, in Jamaica, in Guyana and Trinidad and Tobago. I put an end to that.

If year after year they are going to come to the government and people of Barbados and ask them to underwrite the losses of the Barbados sugar industry which we can ill-afford, then they must understand that we must have, for the workers, a share in the decision making at the very highest level, or no can do!

If your leaders are afraid to say it, I am not afraid to say it. I am not ashamed, as one of the former ministers told me, that I come from the plantocracy. I told him, yes, I come from the plantocracy. My grandfather did not take my grandmother behind any field of canes. He took her in church, and, therefore, I am not ashamed and, therefore, I can tell them that if they want the workers of Barbados to take part, to give up their hard earned taxes to support the sugar industry, all I am saying now 20 years later, is that we must have a share in the decision-making and look at the inefficiencies and the efficiencies of that particular industry.

What I say here today about the sugar industry applies to every single branch of economic organisation in Barbados and I say it without any compunction whatsoever. We have to change the whole aspect of economic relationship in this society, if we are going to move forward into the 21st century.

Otherwise, we are going to have this attitude: we are here in the pulpit and you are there in the pew, and you have to do what we tell you and listen to our interpretation of the holy scriptures.

So Mr President, Mr General-Secretary, brother workers, you did not come here to listen to a long speech from me. You came here to allow me to congratulate you on returning to the place where your organisation had its birth, here in Queens Park 50 years ago as a result of representations made by certain people. We should not forget the struggle of those early pioneers. We must not forget the representations made by Israel Lovell, and Roland Edwards; we must not forget the early sacrifices of people like Louis Sebro; we must not forget people like George Reid; we must not forget people like Claude Skeete, McDonald Blunt and others.*****

We have retuned to the cradle, and it is only by returning to our roots, that we will get the inspiration to go forward to greater and better things.

Thank you.

*****Editors note: Lovell, Edwards and Sebro were Workers' Rights Activists in pre-World War Two Barbados. Skeete was the third President of the Barbados Workers' Union and is credited with unionising the country's large corp of postal employees. Blunt was the union's second President, while Reid was one of its more recent activists.

"Financial self-help"

Address to the Caribbean Development Bank Board of Governors' meeting in Grenada on May 13, 1987

Mr Chairman,
Fellow Governors,
President of the Bank,
Distinguished guests,
Ladies and Gentlemen,

This annual meeting is taking place at a time when there is a widespread interest in, and a dire need for the exploration of new initiatives and fresh approaches to the promotion of economic and social development in the Caribbean.

Last year, the Bank completed a comprehensive review of performance and the outlines of a future role until 1990. Also of major significance was the statement of the President of the Bank[*] at the Sixteenth Annual Meeting in Caracas, Venezuela. That statement addressed the important issue of the place of people in, and their potential for contributing to, and benefitting from, the development process. These events coincided, more or less, with the return to office in Barbados of the political party which I have the honour to lead.

New fiscal and general economic management initiatives have been taken in Barbados which are designed to promote economic growth and long-term social and economic development. The government of Barbados has also been taking part in a series of new initiatives at the regional level, which are aimed at strengthening and advancing the integration movement, at a time when there is a renewed interest in the future of that movement.

The Caribbean Development Bank was established in 1970 as an instrument of regional development and regional integration, and to perform the roles of a development agency as well as that of a development bank. I first drew attention in 1963 to the need for such an institution in a speech made at the University of New Brunswick,

[*] Mr William Demas, a Trinidad and Tobago economist, and former Secretary General of the Caribbean community.

Fredericton, which was shortly afterwards read into the record of the Canadian Senate.

We, all of us here, have reason to be proud of the invaluable work done over the years by our institution headed and staffed by experts produced in the region. In recent years, the Bank has been striving to improve its performance in an unfavourable external environment. There is uncertainty over the prospects for higher rates of growth in the major industrial countries in the medium term. There is even greater uncertainty as to whether a return to higher growth rates in these countries will result in the spread of benefits and consequent stimulation of growth in the Third World, including the countries of this region. There is evidence to suggest that these major industrialised countries have been restructuring their economies in ways which will lead to internal growth and development. Resuscitation of these economies will not necessarily generate external spin-offs at a rate which used to be evident in past decades. Furthermore, the prospects for world trade do not suggest that the stimulation of international demand will necessarily bring benefits to small countries like ours, except if new exports are developed quickly which can be marketed on competitve terms.The prices of traditional Third World exports are unremunerative, while the prices of the goods they must buy are rising. The terms of trade continue to move relentlessly against the primary producers.

There is greater demand being exerted on our foreign exchange resources because of the need to service external debts. Foreign investment and capital inflows have been declining.

These problems have, in turn, brought trading difficulties at the regional level, as shortages of foreign exchange have led to increased protectionism.

I need not recount all the other difficulties facing the countries of the region. The staff and management of the Bank have done a commendable job in presenting these in the recent review of the performance of the economies of the borrowing member countries. What I should like to stress is that every indicator points to the need for urgent strategies which will move our countries and the region onto a path of self-reliant and self-sustaining growth if we are to prevent a further decline in the standards of living of the peoples of the Caribbean. We cannot sit passively and wait to reap the elusive beneifits of a return to growth by our major trading partners. Our efforts have to be redirected to internal restructuring and revitalisation of our economies, in ways which will utilise more fully the indigenous human and physical resources of the region.

The Bank's document which outlines its future role through 1990 makes the observation that dependence on the traditional economic sectors will no longer work for the countries of this region. This observation can be extended further. Traditional strategies and measures will no longer work.

There is an emerging philosophy of development which could guide the Bank into a new and more effective development agency role and function. But the new strategy which is needed for our region will be valueless if people are not placed at the centre – both as a means and an end – of the development process. Such a strategy must rest on a confidence in the ability of the region's people to exploit our indigenous resources in a positive and socially profitable manner.

Greater importance needs to be placed on a basic needs and participatory approach to development in the region.I am happy to note that the leadership of the Bank is becoming increasingly aware of the importance of the full mobilisation and development of the human resources which reside in our wider communities, and of channelling these resources into the stimulation of economic growth and national development.

An approach which needs to broaden and enhance participation is in keeping with a policy of decreasing the role of government while stimulating the private sector – using the term 'private sector' in the widest sense.This is the policy which has been adopted by the government of Barbados. The strategy encourages the traditional private sector, but also seeks to elicit greater participation from smaller, community-based entrepreneurs and non-governmental organisations which are seeking to make their contribution in appropriate ways. Mr Demas called for such an approach when, in his statement at last year's annual meeting, he referred to '... the need for the entire society to give more attention to the expansion of self-employment and small-scale enterprises'.

The new strategy which we need must also seek to reform education and training programmes to impart new skills and upgrade old ones. Education and training programes should also be designed to promote a technological development which is appropriate to the industrialisation programmes of the countries of the region. Our educational systems are necessarily thirty years behind our require-ments because our educators are merely passing on what they absorbed thirty years ago. Who is going to educate the educators?

Sir, a strategy which focuses on enhancing the region's human resources and on harnessing those underutilised resources for greater contribution to the national development effort need not be costly. Excessive costs can be avoided, especially if collaboration is developed with those non-governmental organisations that are already involved with groups who are doing things in non-formal, appropriate and cost-effective ways. To this end, the bank should explore the possibility of developing supportive programmes with such non-governmental development organisations.

There is much self-help action which is taking place in our credit unions and co-operative movements, our workers' organisations, in farmers, women and youth groups who are participating in rural development programmes, programmes of literacy and adult education, running small income-generating projects and providing services like day care centres. With a little more help, the developmental contribution of these independent self-help initiatives can be maximised.

In short, Mr Chairman, the development agency function of the Bank needs to be turned in new directions, and a greater emphasis needs to be placed on this aspect of the Bank's activities.

Placing more emphasis on the development agency role and function of the Bank does not mean that the banking functions should be reduced. The Bank as a bank still has an important role to play in supporting such new strategies as can be devised to deal with the problems confronting the countries of this region.

Indeed, the banking role of the CDB assumes greater significance in the face of the pending graduation by the World Bank of some of the borrowing member countries. World Bank graduation will present the affected countries with challenges additional to those already created by the adverse international economic environment and the problems which are evident at the regional level.

On the bright side, however, World Bank graduation may yet point to another avenue which the CDB might explore to assist member countries to move along the path of self-reliance. There might be prospects for exploring with member countries ways in which increasing amounts of domestic and regional financing can be mobilised to lessen the demand for international lending. The way to respond to the decrease in World Bank lending is not necessarily to seek greater amounts of private and/or bilateral resources. Funds secured on such terms may only worsen the debt servicing problems faced by some of the member countries. The Bank needs to meet the challenge of pending World Bank graduation, by finding new and innovative ways in which the Bank's aid co-ordination services can be made available more readily to the member countries.

The challenge to help forge a self-reliant and self-sustaining strategy suggests that the Bank, as a Bank, also needs to look again at the ways in which available assistance is deployed. The need for new initiatives, such as the proposed Caribbean export financing mechanism is clear, as are programmes of lending through private and public sector financial intermediaries, for on lending to the private sector.

I should like to single out for particular mention and support, the call for increasing sectoral concentration of lending. Sectoral lending would allow for comprehensive consultative planning with respective governments and would help to identify project financing gaps which can be filled with effective aid co-ordination.

The role of the Bank as a bank will be threatened, however, unless an urgent solution is found to the problem of arrears. I observe that this problem remains grave and is more likely to affect the Bank's future financial viability. The arrears problem is a symptom of the economic dislocation from which some of the borrowing member countries are suffering. This problem needs to be tackled vigorously in the short term, but there is also the need for a longer-term perspective to be taken. The problem of arrears can only be dealt with effectively when the fundamental causes are addressed.

This is why the theme and focus of my statement have been the need for a strategy which promotes self-reliance and which helps to bring about internal economic restructuring.

In conclusion, Mr Chairman, I should like to record the appreciation of the Barbados government for the continued dedication to the service of the region by the President and staff of the Bank.

Thank you.

The Quintessential Barbadian

The Rt Honourable Owen S. Arthur, MP

It was once said of Barbados, by no less a person than Sir Frank Worrell, that *"Barbados has one exceptional feature. It is the only territory in the world without a local hero. This obtains in all aspects of life. What is the future of a country without heroes?"* Since the 1998 Order of National Heroes Act which my Administration had the privilege of introducing, we do have heroes; and great ones by any standard.

In the entire history of Barbados, it may well be that the most significant single event will forever be the attaining of our Independence. It established us in our true identity as Barbadians. It laid upon us the duty to be fully responsible for our destiny. Just as the attainment of Independence may come to stand as the single most significant event in the history of Barbados, so too the Right Excellent Errol Walton Barrow can lay claim to be the most complete leader, and the most outstanding citizen Barbados has ever known.

Let me remind you of some of these traits which on the 50th Anniversary of our Independence we should revere and honour. Barrow was, first and foremost, driven by a passion to make the Barbadian people great, not only insofar as the region was concerned, but also in the family of nations, both developing and developed. He possessed an unwavering dedication to a vision of world-class status for the Caribbean region's most industrious small nation.

As early as 1950 he visualised the possibility of Barbados becoming a world-class society. Thus, this dedicated nationalist let down his bucket in Barbados of the 1950s, first as a lieutenant to the venerable RE Sir Grantley Adams, the first Premier of Barbados, sole Prime Minister of the West Indies Federation and National Hero, then striking out on his own and creating his own mass-based political force – the Democratic Labour Party.

The question may be asked – what distinguished Errol Barrow from other Barbadian (and Caribbean) leaders of his era? Let me identify five and possibly six areas in which Barrow so acquitted himself as to be regarded by most people as the "Father of modern Barbados."

Firstly, Barrow was a crusader on behalf of the common man. His care and concern for our working class was almost legendary. His was a lifelong campaign to eliminate poverty and wretchedness from Barbados. He was no Bussa or Clement Payne, because he was born on a sugar plantation and knew not the pinch of poverty.

Nonetheless, he had ample vicarious experiences of the material wants and environmental degradation which afflicted the vast majority of our people in the 1930s, 40s, 50s, and 60s. He therefore spent 34 years in Parliament fighting to improve the lot of the people in the villages and tenantries (plantation communities), through legislation and major programmes of education and economic transformation. For this he has earned our eternal gratitude.

Then there is Barrow the great revolutionary and Father of Independence. Many thousands of words have been written and spoken of his bold decision in 1965 to press for constitutional independence for Barbados. Barrow correctly gauged the eagerness and enthusiasm of the Barbadian masses for their freedom from Britain's imperial embrace and led us to that glorious date with destiny on 30th November 1966.

Time has not diminished nor dimmed the lustre of that wonderful occasion, nor have events conspired to make our recollections of November 1966 bitter ones. To the contrary, the new nation which he ushered in that year is now standing near the threshold of First World status and is currently pressing for acceptance as a world-class society.

Thirdly, we must take note of Errol Barrow the visionary educator, the man who completed the Grantley Adams programme of liberating education from the clutches of class and racial prejudices. We laud and magnify his name whenever our children write the Barbados Secondary School Entrance Examination (11+ Common Entrance Examination) each year and whenever they contentedly eat their complimentary school meals each school-day.

We continue to express our admiration for the man who introduced the pioneering concept of the Barbados Community College in 1968, and we stand in awe when we remember that he single-handedly introduced University education to Barbados in 1963 with the opening of what was to become the UWI Cave Hill Campus.

Fourthly, Barrow was a builder. All around us we can see examples of his work. There is the Treasury Building, the first National Insurance Building, the middle-income housing developments of the 1960s and the 1970s; the Industrial Estates, the expansion to the Airport and the Seaport and a number of secondary schools such as Ellerslie, Parkinson and St Lucy Secondary.

Barrow's magnanimity and passion for harmony also inspire us with respect and admiration. This is the fifth area of glorious achievement during his term of office 1961 to 1987 and particularly after 1966, when several voices questioned the wisdom of his decision to take Barbados into Independence alone.

Barrow assumed the mantle of a statesman and held out the "olive branch" to the former plantation and commercial elite who had ruled Barbados up to the 1940s. To them he became the harbinger of democracy, progress, harmony and cooperation. He practiced the politics of inclusiveness long before it became a total force in the 21st century, making whites, Jews, Muslims, Hindus and other racial and ethnic minorities feel comfortable and safe in our society. At the same time he overturned the culture of racial discrimination and secured for all Barbadians their fundamental rights. To all Barbadians he was "the Great Reconciler".

There is a sixth arena in which he shone like a beacon of progressiveness and cooperation – the pertinent sphere of regional integration. It is an important aspect of the traditions of Barbadian leaders, that a significant part of their lifework should be dedicated to the cause of advancing Caribbean unity.

No tribute to this National Hero and Caribbean man would be complete without a generous mention of his valiant efforts to promote cooperation among Britain's former colonies in the Caribbean. Along with Forbes Burnham and Vere Bird, he was one of the Founding Fathers of CARIFTA in 1965; then in 1973 along with Burnham, Manley, and

Williams, he founded CARICOM. In these endeavours he dared to be in defiance and in advance of popular opinion.

Barrow was, if nothing else, confident in himself and about the Barbadian personality. He entertained no fears that in opening our society to stronger cooperation with our regional neighbours Barbados would be overwhelmed or taken over by them. In an action that might be a little difficult for a Barbadian leader of today to contemplate, far less undertake, he made a Guyanese, Barbados' first High Commissioner to the United Kingdom.

He encouraged citizens of our sister Republic to the south to come here to work and invest. Some of the enterprises thus encouraged, notably Banks, are still functioning. In a similar vein, unlike other leaders of his day, he refused to introduce Alien Landholding Legislation, to regulate the ownership of land by foreigners, into Barbados, understanding fully that those who came from abroad to invest to help build this nation would be absorbed by us, rather than we being absorbed by them.

In his every action, his every utterance, he was the confident representation of the Barbadian personality on the regional and global stage, setting in train a practice that has been followed by others, that has enabled this nation to enjoy a respect and to exercise an influence entirely out of all proportion to its small size.

We run the very grave danger in Barbados of savaging the memory of Errol Barrow by reducing his life and his work merely to the fact of free education and to the fact of his having led this country into Independence.

I would like to believe that Barrow saw free education not only as simply absolving my parents and other parents of the payment of school fees, but as an act to enable this country to give the broad mass of children of this society the opportunity and the freedom to develop their intellect, to develop their various talents, so much so that at the end of the day they could exercise their right of free choice, their right to choose the profession they wanted their right to choose the political party of their choice and their right to take a place in this country as worthy citizens.

Independence for some people can become only an event involving the raising of the flag at the Garrison. But it is not only important to have led us into Independence, it is also important to lead this country into unity and also to lead this country into its fullest development. I think that if we are to understand the life and the times of Barrow, we must understand that he has left this country an unfinished agenda. We have achieved Independence but we still have a long way to go to unite our country and to develop this country in accordance with its full potential.

I very deeply regret that he did not leave a wealth of writings behind. It is now, for me, a sad fact that the principal characters in the post-war development of the Barbadian society have died without leaving their memoirs behind for generations. Sir Grantley did not do it, J.M.G.M. 'Tom' Adams did not do it, and now Barrow has gone, taking with him a large part of our political and social history unwritten.

As a testimony to Barrow, let me conclude with a reflection akin to his philosophy. At a time when there is too much conflict in our national affairs, to all Barbadians I must say that we diminish ourselves if we refuse to see the good in others.

Errol Barrow may have functioned on one side of the political bar, but it does not prevent his extraordinary contribution to our nation and its people from being recognised and acknowledged by all as being worthy of emulation.

Although I never got to know him in the personal way in which others may speak, I feel that I know the man well enough that I shall tell my children that he was a fine man and a very great Barbadian in every sense of the word.

Is the Project Completed?

The Honourable David Thompson

The 2000 Errol Barrow Memorial Lecture (edited)

Permit me to start with a quote from a speech delivered by the Right Excellent Errol Walton Barrow: *"We were far on the road to achieving a level of understanding in this country where every man, woman and child felt that he or she counted for something; where he or she felt that here in this country existed possibilities for self-realisation and fulfilment; where mendicancy and dependence were not regarded as the inevitable fate of those persons who were not born to wealth and position."*

How disappointed The Rt. Excellent Errol Walton Barrow must have been when the vagaries of electoral politics often slowed and halted the long march on which he embarked in 1961 to achieve the goals I just read from his speech to the 30th Annual Conference of the Democratic Labour Party on 25 August 1985.

The riveting frankness of his description of the Barbadian condition economically, socially and politically, is matched only by some mission he had to transcend his class origins. Errol Barrow was born to a black, middle-class family and he was extremely comfortable with that fact. But it was not the circumstances of Errol Barrow's birth that were relevant, nor those of his socialisation. What was important was those who his policies empowered and liberated.

In 1961, the Democratic Labour Party won the election with a majority of six and Errol Barrow's DLP embarked on a mission with great tenacity. Dr Pedro Welch says, *"Under his inspired leadership, social initiatives launched by the DLP captured public imagination and linked a growing middle class and an aspiring working class to the fortunes of the Party. The first of these initiatives to bear fruit was the lowering of the voting age from 21 to 18 and the decreeing of "free" education at all government-supported secondary schools the abolition of tuition fees at government schools opened up opportunities for thousands of Barbadians to enter the local "Grammar Schools" and had such a profound effect on the Barbadian voting public that it cemented their allegiance to 'Dipper'."*

At the personal level, I can recount my own mother's views on Errol Barrow and the DLP. We were living in England and, like the thousands of nationals who returned, like the gold rush, my mother lived for the day she could return. We knew the calypso *"Archie brek them up,"* and the National Anthem and we knew about the great Dipper Barrow and the development of Barbados, about which she was extremely proud. She wrote a poem, *"I wonder how the folks all are at home."*

We all got a Geest boat and took the long 10 day trip from the Preston docks to Bridgetown. I left England never wanting to set foot there again. I remember the racial taunts, the rock which was thrown through the window one night, the flat tires, the skinhead who bounced a football in my two-year old sister's head. When you are part of an immigrant minority you can understand it, even endure it.

But to this day, there are things that not even history can explain about the kind of racism I discovered in my country Barbados and to which I have committed myself to obliterating.

Having dealt with the historical and personal, the question must be asked, what were the tangible advances under the Democratic Labour Party? My task is to identify whether the vision of Errol Barrow was fulfilled and if not, how we might complete the process.

The twentieth century has, in my view, been a century of rapid advancement for our country on most fronts. I refer to the establishment of modern democratic government, diversification of our economy through the development of the tourism sector and restructuring of the agricultural sectors, the creation of the manufacturing and off-shore sectors, the strong emphasis on development of human resources, the creation and rapid expansion of the social security scheme and the improvement of the physical infrastructure.

There was a galloping pace of reform and development and the human capital of our country was firmly and solidly built. These were possible because Errol Barrow was able to help Barbadians redefine themselves as "firm craftsmen of their fate". Every achievement set in train "expectations great". The path of development occurred against a background of strong economic management leading, by the end of the 20th century, with Barbados within the top five or so of developing countries according to UNDP's Human Development Index.

What we cannot forget as Barbadians is that this advancement took place against a background of the century starting its first thirty-five years in grinding mass poverty and much institutionalised racial discrimination. We had no natural advantages visible to the naked eye.

The first time that I thought seriously about what it meant to be a twentieth century Barbadian was when I was about fourteen and found a copy of the New World Journal heralding Barbados' Independence in the Combermere School library.

John Hearne writes about the Barbadian as follows:

"the Barbadian is a 'problem'." "Every other West Indian who knows him at all has searched hard for words, at some point, that will pin him down. His elusiveness has aroused as much irritation among his fellow West Indians, as it has clear-headed speculation....any slave society takes its tone and customary behaviour from the masters. And this was particularly true of the West Indians societies in which the slaves were reborn, literally naked, into a world that must have been, also literally, unimaginable, until they saw it, and in which their tribal and past family associations were broken or discouraged, so as to lessen the danger of revolt...it gave to the West Indian, generally, a flexibility of mind, an almost instinctive capacity for creative response to fresh situations and challenges that can be very clearly seen operation in us today. I don't think it is entirely accidental that our greatest cricket captains, Worrell and Sobers, two of the most subtle strategists the game has yet seen, both came out of Barbados. The early black Barbadian had a greater variety of fresh situations and more sophisticated challenges to his mind than was often the case elsewhere.

There is 'wholeness' to the Barbadian that I have not found in any other English-speaking Caribbean territory; an awareness of himself as a person that is remarkable, enviable and, in every sense of the word, good. There are no other children in West Indian fiction like George Lamming's growing boys in the Castle of My Skin. Whatever problems of poverty, race prejudice, lack of social structure they face, they operate out from a powerful individuality. They have a cultural reference point that is truly original. The virtues of industry, thrift, honesty, the care of inheritance, cooperation, a strict regard for orderly debate, a compelling sense of your neighbour's rights and integrity had to be acquired by the Barbadian. These were not simply pious actions inspired by sermons. They were the only possible instincts for survival in such a territory. People, in Barbados, could not remove themselves from another as they could in, say Jamaica, until very recently"

What do other Caribbean people think of us? What about Barbadian values? John Hearne concludes:

"Many of the Barbadian virtues I have tried to analyse above have been, and continue to be harshly criticised by other West Indians as virtues that have become decadent. The wonderful and (for is some of the rest of us) truly inspiring sense of self is often referred to as self-satisfaction. The habit of thrift, good husbandry and industriousness are often called meanness, unimaginative materialism or ruthless self-centred ambition. The quite unique nurture of personal and public discipline is often regarded as mere dullness. The capacity for cooperative action and civil, dialogue is often hypocrisy and compromise, especially when applied to race and colour relationships. The well-known "Englishness" is often seen as smug insularity. The regards for the necessity of good order, protocol and traditional procedure is often dismissed as an infuriating love of conformity for conformity's sake. The careful fashioning of a community in which checks and balances had to be respected, if the Barbadian society were to survive decently, is often felt to be, somehow, a betrayal of the more haphazard, ad hoc approach to social tensions which tends to be the method in other West Indian islands."

He concludes: *"it is better for a country to have an ordered abundance of qualities that can spoil or go sour than to have none at all."*

What Errol Barrow and the DLP did was to declare the Barbadian ethos, to say what Barbadians were thinking and build on the essential character of the Barbadian. The DLP conspired and aspired with the people to make every conceivable sacrifice to ensure that the next generation of Barbadian was better off with thrift, sacrifice, creativity, pride and industry.

Again, I will refer to my personal experience which has conditioned my own view of the family and family responsibility for building our society. When I entered Combermere School in 1972, more than half of the class were being raised by a grandmother or an aunt who was willing to stand back to see others progress. My classmates' parents lived overseas – England, the US and Canada – and were working to improve their lot and those of their children. Errol Barrow's education policies meant that parents and children – two generations at the same time – could make use of opportunities to improve their lot. This in the year 2000, would be called "fast-tracking the process."

This could not have been achieved if a previous generation of Barbadian leaders had not instilled in our grandparents and great grandparents that they would have to be the anchors of our enterprise. To them much credit is also due. There was another element not to be lightly dismissed. Errol Barrow's task was to ensure that his stewardship was so effective that those Barbadians who left, improved their lot and increased their horizons, could return to a Barbados in which they could live comfortably.

In his lecture on Democracy and Development to the Academy of Politics in April 1980, Errol Barrow said, *"It stands to reason that any political party seeking to fulfil the expectations of the populace for equality, jobs, security, the ending of privilege, the about to accomplish these objectives in a planned and people and not in a whimsical opportunistic and patronising manner. The record of the Democratic Labour Party in fulfilling these objectives has made it possible for real human development to take place."*

Before Errol Barrow went to his Maker, he declared his unfinished business for all to hear at the 1987 Annual May Day celebrations when he said, *"I think that in the final 12 or 13 years of this century, the unions and the governments and the employers, have a very basic function to perform; that is, instead of regarding the elements in the society from the point of view of we employers on one side, the government in the middle and the workers on the other side, we now have to look upon ourselves as all participants in the economic process."*

Errol Barrow saw this as the natural direction for natural governance to take saying, *"We are not going to achieve our common objectives of social justice if the workers are going to be there on the side of the fence, having an antagonistic attitude towards the people who control the capital. We are only going to have harmonious relationships in this society if the people who now control the capital realise that the workers themselves are entitled to a share in the control of that capital, both in the managerial and ownership levels,"*

In a simple insightful lecture delivered as the Inaugural George Beckford Lecture in 1995, Dr Kari Levitt made the point that, *"We are told that macroeconomic stability is an essential condition to attract investment and restart economic growth. This is true, although there is no reason to expect foreigners to invest in a country whose local moneyed classes are not prepared to risk their own savings in productive activities. But macroeconomic stability is not a technical matter of programming appropriate monetary and fiscal variables. Stabilisation in a liberalised environment bears down primarily on the poor and the disadvantaged. I suggest that it is a political impossibility without a more egalitarian, participatory and cooperative relationship between the major classes and interest groups in society."*

Two points emerge, one of which is trite: Growth is not enough. We need to capture the balance between sustaining growth and distributing its benefits and to promote social justice. The second is that the national partnership must be genuine, balanced and visionary. It must be under-girded by a vision that speaks not just to its form but to its substance.

On the issue of distributive justice, let me repeat the injunction given by Errol Barrow in 1985: *"our politics are not conspiratorial to be sprung on a surprised electorate only at election time. Our core policies are the same yesterday, tomorrow and for evermore. I do not believe in gimmicks. In human behaviour and economic inter-relationships, there are only so many scenarios. What is often lacking is the political will and ability to pursue the right remedies."*

We have the political will to achieve a level of understanding in this country where every man, woman and child can feel that he or she counts for something; where in our country exists possibilities for self-realisation and fulfilment; where mendicancy and dependency are not regarded as the inevitable fate of those persons not born to wealth and position. The bedrock of this must be to develop even further our human capital.

If we educate our people to weed the road, then that is all they will be able to do. We have to educate them for these challenges and change their thinking to do it. As countries have to adapt to changes, so too organisations like political parties must adapt and individuals must adapt.

There is a formidable agenda for us but the words of my hero, Errol Walton Barrow, *"We have no space on board this shuttle for people who are looking for social status or economic benefit. The money is on the other side. Those who are weary, those who are languid, should go to the Lord and be at rest. There will be no rest for the valiant. No turning back; no time for self-doubt. No time for sell-pity. No time for mistakes."*

The idea of Barbados

The Honourable Ralph E. Gonsalves, MP

Barbados is an idea which has, over time, become manifest in reality. The idea of Barbados encompasses more than a nation-state or a national community. To be sure, it flows from a national community which has been in ownership, not residence, of an especial or particular landscape and seascape.

Still, it is more than this; and it assumes a veritable autonomy as a category beyond the community. The Barbadian diaspora, scattered overseas, has come to draw from this 'specialness' known as the "idea of Barbados". This "idea" acknowledges that Barbados is unique, *sui generis*, of its own kind. It is connected to – nay, derived from – the physical and historical condition of Barbados, yet transcends it.

The unique "idea of Barbados" does not, and cannot, make Barbados immune from the universal 'laws' of history, society or political economy. Indeed, the idea of Barbados has been fashioned through a parallelogram of historical forces and contemporary circumstances, global and regional, which have shaped and conditioned the home-grown evolutions, adaptations, alterations, and changes.

More than any other Caribbean society, with the possible exception of Cuba, Barbados has arrived at a place where its uniqueness represents a model of governance, political economy, way of life, and social order, which invites emulation elsewhere in the Caribbean and further afield, albeit with appropriate amendments. Barbados' high quality governance and level of human development have been a marvel to objective observers, including reputable international agencies.

On a wide range of governance and developmental indices, Barbados is in the top rank globally; indeed, overall, it is a developing country with developed nations' governance and human development attainments. All this is extraordinary for a country of 166 square miles and a quarter million people, which is less than 200 years removed from slavery and less than 50 years as an Independent nation!

This idea of Barbados is not coterminous with a narrow chauvinism, island nationalism or a jaundiced arrogance, though some within and without Barbados may mistake or confuse these with the uplifting "idea" itself. The "idea of Barbados" has saved Barbados in the past and will surely enable Barbados to meet successfully its current economic challenges brought on largely, though not exclusively, by the prolonged global economic slowdown from 2008, and continuing.

Barbados is at once the most conservative and the most progressive society in the Caribbean, bar none! It extols continuity yet engineers, and embraces, change. It is the only Caribbean country that has had, since conquest and settlement, unbroken representative government, albeit on a restrictive franchise until universal adult suffrage in 1946.

It is the first Caribbean country to have attained mass adult literacy, free universal primary and secondary education, and tertiary education. It is the first Caribbean country to have transformed its economy from sugar to tourism, international financial services, and other services. Very early it embraced the Caribbean Court of Justice and cut its judicial umbilical cord with the British Privy Council, yet it values its connection with the British Crown.

Barbados is possessed of "a starched Anglicanism", to use Gordon Lewis' telling phrase, but is more relaxed, informally, about homosexuality than any other Caribbean society. It places a premium on the maintenance of law and order, yet zealously guards individual rights and freedoms. And the list goes on!

In Barbados, there is an invisible "genius of the people" which is the foundation of the idea of Barbados. Modern social scientists refer to this social foundation as "social capital" but it is more than this. I find the category of "social capital" an inadequate proxy for the grounded common sense of Barbadians, their social solidarity, their ability to enhance their capacity to come to terms with their condition and environment, and to address in an efficacious way any set of challenges that arise. Other Caribbean societies, including St Vincent and the

Grenadines, display these qualities, but Barbados seems to have them to an extraordinary degree.

There is an undoubted Barbadian sensibility that informs or shapes the individual and collective responses of the Barbadian people. Many other Caribbean nationals perceive this, quite wrongly, as a sense of "Bajan superiority". It is not that; it is an attribute of quiet assurance, a manifestation of the virtue of self-mastery. That is the wellspring of a civil, and civilised, people steeped in progressive values, but on the bedrock of core values lodged in the social consciousness.

More than any other Caribbean nationals, they appreciate that a progressive society is not built on leisure, pleasure and nice time, but on hard, smart, productive effort. All this is part of the "idea of Barbados".

An acute and dispassionate observer of Barbados notices a distinctiveness that goes beyond, and is partly evident from, an especially unique accent in speech, a restraint in the use of bombast in day-to-day language, an intolerance of slipshod work, an insistence that Government delivers basic services of quality, a settled but not unsettling "mirror image" of themselves, and an elemental patriotism devoid of gaudy exhibitionism.

These observances are evident in the outlook of Barbadians of all walks of life: rank-and-file Barbadians, intellectuals, businesspersons, Rastafarians, writers/performers in the field of the creative professional imagination, civil society leaders, and assorted professionals,

It has always struck me, for instance, that Barbadian entrepreneurs, be they the offspring of the traditional planter-merchant elite or of the newer type, commit themselves to Barbados in a way which appears to be different and better when compared to the commitment of most of the other Caribbean entrepreneurs to their respective countries. Examples abound from Barbados: The "Big Six" owners, Simpsons, Goddards, Williams, Rayside, Nassar, Husbands, and Tudor of blessed memory, and other entrepreneurs of more recent vintage.

Likewise, I have noted that Barbadian writers of the creative imagination, an invariably restless breed who roam regionally and globally, return and stay in the land of their birth and socialisation. The most striking example of these is the iconic George Lamming. They simply conclude that Barbados is their natural place to be in very much the same way that international organisations and embassies with assignments to the nation states of the Eastern Caribbean comfortably set up shop in Barbados.

They, too, acknowledge the convenience and modernity of Barbados, but it is their unarticulated recognition of something special: the idea of Barbados.

I have observed that, generally speaking, the best and brightest of Barbados enter public service whether in the Judiciary, Civil Service or public sector, university, or politics. At the leadership levels Barbados has been blessed by brilliant and grounded personalities such as Grantley Adams, Errol Barrow, Tom Adams, Bernard St John, Henry Forde, Richie Haynes, Erskine Sandiford, Owen Arthur, Mia Mottley, David Thompson, and Freundel Stuart. Surely, this constellation constitutes and abundance of riches over a 60-year period.

Of this galaxy, I am of the considered opinion that Errol Barrow is the greatest leader that our CARICOM region has thrown up since universal adult suffrage. In national and regional impact and influence, Barrow compares with Lee Kuan Yew of Singapore. This high quality leadership over a sustained period is a manifestation, and a buttress, of the idea of Barbados.

In the complex and competitive modern global circumstances, the nurturing of continued quality leadership is an awesome challenge for Barbados. The idea of Barbados is in danger of being undermined if the political system fails to renew and replenish, on an ongoing basis, its leadership stock from the best and brightest of Barbados.

I am satisfied that the "idea of Barbados" in tandem with a mature regionalism in CARICOM is the vehicle through which Barbados will successfully meet its current and prospective economic challenges. The idea of Barbados is a shared experience of Barbadians; it belongs to them. However, this shared experience must become a conscious expression and a fully articulated language for action.

It is the frame of reference for continuity and change, orderly governance and profound alterations in the political economy to accommodate the circumstances at hand. The maturing regional matrices and an alive internationalism provide the context, space, and nexus for the full flowering of the "idea of Barbados".

The query for Barbados is this: can the socioeconomic model initiated by Errol Barrow, perfected by subsequent governments, and which came to maturation under Owen Arthur, be sustained in a period of prolonged global economic slowdown and continued economic uncertainty? An appropriate strategic framework, balancing prudence and enterprise, coupled with specially targeted interventions, is likely to foster economic growth and fiscal consolidation.

The correct answer to the overarching query which I have posed, within the articulated context of "the idea of Barbados" and its regional-international linkages, is likely to yield uplifting results. Thus, rather than propose a particular policy without an articulated context, the policy should be put within the appropriate strategic framework.

Once it is appreciated that the extant socioeconomic model is not sustainable at a time of a prolonged global economic slowdown and that Barbados has always triumphed in challenging circumstances, the people are likely to respond understandingly and favourably. So, for example, a contribution from students to their own educational investment at the tertiary level is less likely to be opposed.

If the answer to the overarching query, articulated context and strategic framework (including targeted interventions) are fully elaborated, references to "Barrow's legacy" or "Bajan's birth right" would be seen as intellectually/practically untenable and demagogic.

The challenges many Caribbean nations now confront include efficient public expenditure; the containment of recurrent expenditure; efficacious debt management; optimal tax administration; economic growth; job and wealth creation; social cohesion and a reduction in social inequality. These are very challenging and not amenable to quick fixes, particularly in small, open, resource-challenged economies in the context of a global economic slowdown. The *chatterati,* with their feet firmly planted in the air, have all the facile answers, but no responsibility for their invariable wrong-headedness.

Fundamentally, "the idea of Barbados" faces enormous challenges from the process of globalisation and its attendant discontents. Globalisation facilitates an increasing homogenisation of culture propagated by a dominant cultural imperialism. Globalisation is impatient of "localisation", but the idea of Barbados strengthens the quest for a particular space within a wider universalism.

This dialectical engagement between "the local" and "the global" does not necessarily presage an undermining of the 'idea of Barbados', but an enrichment of it. Still, it is a challenging endeavour. We must have faith that the 'idea of Barbados' will endure, but faith is made complete or perfect with deeds.

Mirror Image Revisited

Dr Ayana Gibbs

In 1986, when only 11 years of age, I had the opportunity to interview The Right Excellent Errol Walton Barrow for a school project forming part of the celebrations of the 20th Anniversary of the Independence.

About 30 years later, reflecting on the interview, I now recognise three key themes in Mr Barrow's answers to my questions that may not have been so readily perceived by my then young mind, but would be instantly recognisable to all who have heard him speak publicly or privately. The themes are (i) the importance of self-belief, (ii) the meaning of independence and (iii) the value of education.

Today, I recognise all three themes to be of equal importance. Yet at the time, due to a curious trick of memory known as the "recency effect", it was his parting advice to *"make the most of the educational opportunities and all the other facilities available to you for self-development"* that I recalled best and acted upon most vigorously. I studied diligently and won a Barbados Scholarship and went on to study medicine and specialise in psychiatry.

But perhaps due to another equally intriguing feature of memory, obscurely known as "fuzzy-trace theory", I recalled the gist, but not the detail, in that advice. It wasn't until almost three decades later with a PhD and string of other epithets, that it dawned on me that I had forgotten a key part of that advice which was **"***and all the other facilities available to you for self-development"*.

I realised that formal education and qualifications, in fact, represented only a fraction of the self-development facilities available, and needed, for effective leadership – the ability to create a vision of the future and inspire others to engage with it, an instantly recognisable quality in the man aptly dubbed 'The Father of Independence'. Yet Mr Barrow displayed a tremendous degree of modesty in his response to my first question about how he felt about this sobriquet, brushing it off as 'a journalistic expression'.

This brings me to the very first theme that emerged during the interview: the importance of self-belief. Mr Barrow displayed that delicate combination of humility and self-belief that defines true leaders. I am often asked whether I was nervous to be interviewing the Prime Minister of Barbados at such a young age and the answer is 'no'. Along with the now alien sound of my childhood voice, the fact that I gave the impression that this momentous occasion was a most ordinary event is one of the key features that resonates with me as I listen to the recording. This was no doubt due in large part to the successful efforts of Mr Barrow to put me at ease, along with my innocent lack of self-doubt.

It is unfortunate that many of us, myself included, gradually lose that natural self-assurance that comes with childhood, due to a subtle combination of individual personality and life experiences. That is often not fully regained through education may reflect wider cultural factors such as the perception of education as the attainment of qualifications rather than a small segment of the broader path to self-development. This is a fact that has often been lamented by The Hon. George Lamming, CHB, as a prevailing attitude towards education as "something to have rather than something to use".

Nevertheless, moving on to the other key theme of the importance of education, or more accurately, self-development, we all have the capacity to relearn and redevelop that self-belief. In fact, Barack Obama has said that the most important lesson he learned from working with the most powerful person on the planet was "to always act confident", and he was able to use that knowledge to himself become the most powerful person on the planet. This notion of projecting absolute self-belief is actively taught to Harvard Business School students in the mantra "Even if you believe something only fifty-five per cent, say as if you believe it a hundred per cent".

While the longer-term value of the latter approach can be debated, it underpins the fact that feeling and projecting self-belief can be taught, both individually and collectively. This is also the rallying cry implicit in Mr Barrow's famous "Mirror Image" speech of, *"If you don't like your mirror image – change it. "* How does one do this? As an individual, I joined Toastmasters and took classes in improvisation acting, praised by Twitter's former CEO and others as 'the best management training'.

However, collectively, as a nation, we need to better recognise the benefits of the transferrable skills that these activities that have traditionally been view as 'extra-curricular', and therefore less relevant, can bring. Although this is gradually changing with a few pioneers and champions of approaches such as Theatre-in-Education, to remain true to the legacy of Mr Barrow we need to ensure that these opportunities for broader self-development are available for all.

Now I turn to the final theme to emerge, Mr Barrow's thoughts on the meaning of independence – *"the wish to run your own affairs without having to wait for other people to tell you what to do".* Although not the independence to which Mr Barrow was directly referring, this statement embodies the essence of entrepreneurship. Yet, as a nation, we still have some work to do on the relative value that we assign to the pursuit of conventional education and career paths versus higher risk entrepreneurial activities.

Embedded in this is an unhealthy attitude towards 'failure'. Here, I reprise the previous theme of self-belief, of which one of the most crucial aspects is the capacity to learn from failure, that is in turn the cornerstone of success. Recently, I have watched significant others use this capacity to reject traditional career trajectories in favour of social entrepreneurship, defying statistics to join the less than ten per cent of start-ups that survive three years.

During last year's Independence Day honours, I was immensely proud that my father Bentley Gibbs (who was fortunate to have known the Mr Barrow far longer and better than I) was accorded the Gold Crown of Merit. In a subsequent radio interview, he spoke of the seismic shift in his perspective on my brother's career path and some of very themes contained in my interview with Mr Barrow: the need to recognise the changing concept of education, the value of self-learning and enhancement and the need to view the our marketplace not as Barbados, or even the region, but the entire world. What was truly remarkable was that he said that he had also learned these things from his observations of his children (my brother and I), despite the fact that they not yet fully grown and blossomed into conscious awareness in my mind from the seeds sown by our Father of Independence nearly three decades previously.

My 15 years of practice in psychiatry and research in neuroscience has taught me that, as human beings, we have a remarkable capacity to learn, develop and evolve. With this in mind, I will end this reflection with a question to my fellow Barbadians that I have no doubt would be posed by Mr Barrow if he were with us today, which is "What mirror image do you want for yourself and our Nation in 2066 when we celebrate the 100th Anniversary of Independence?"

FAREWELL

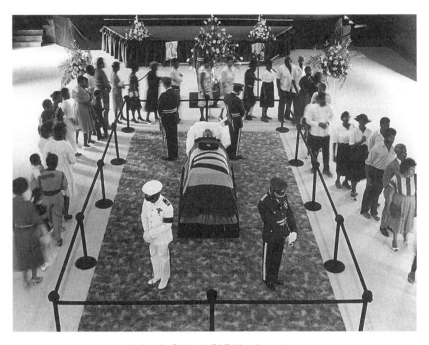

Lying in State at DLP Headquarters

Statue in Independence Square

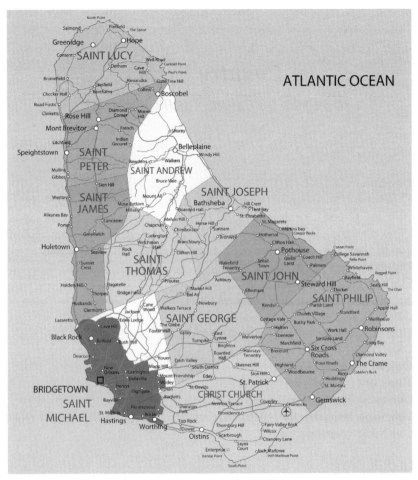

Map of Barbados

Country Facts

Extract from the Commonwealth Yearbook 2013

Population: 285,000 (2013);
32 per cent of people live in urban areas; growth 0.4 per cent p.a. 1990–2013; birth rate 13 per 1,000 people (22 in 1970); life expectancy 75 years (69 in 1970). The population is 93 per cent of African descent, three per cent of European descent, and the rest of Asian or mixed descent (2000 census).
Population per sq km: 661
Life expectancy: 75 years
Net primary enrolment: 97 per cent (2011)
GDP: US $4.2bn
GDP p.c. growth: 0.9 per cent p.a. 1990–2013
UN HDI 2014: World ranking 59
Official language: English
Time: GMT minus 4 hrs
Currency: Barbados dollar (Bds$)
Language: English is the official and first language. An English-based Creole is also widely spoken.

GEOGRAPHY
Area: 431 sq km
Coastline: 97 km
Capital: Bridgetown
Barbados, the most easterly of the Caribbean islands, lies south of Saint Lucia, east of St Vincent and the Grenadines, and north of Trinidad and Tobago.
Topography: Barbados is a comparatively flat island, rising in a series of terraced tablelands to Mount Hillaby at 336 metres. The north-east (Scotland area) is broken, eroded and rocky. The rest of the island is coral limestone crossed with deep river-bed gullies which fill with water during heavy rain. There are no permanent rivers. On the east coast, much of the shoreline is rocky, pounded by a strong surf; elsewhere, natural coral reefs surround turquoise seas and beaches of white sand.

Climate: Mild subtropical. In the December–June dry season cooling northeast trade winds blow steadily; the wet season is humid and hotter, but the climate is generally pleasant even then, thanks to sea breezes. The island is on the southern edge of the West Indian hurricane zone.

Vegetation: Sugar cane and food crops predominate in rural areas. There is a rich diversity of tropical flowers and flowering trees.

Wildlife: Natural wildlife has largely been displaced by sugar cane but the Barbados Wildlife Reserve was established in 1985 in the Scotland district, its 1.6 hectares of mature mahogany trees being the home of the Barbados green monkey and the red-footed Barbados tortoise.

Main towns: Bridgetown (capital and only seaport, pop. 94,200 in 2010), Speightstown (2,400), Bathsheba (1,600), Holetown (1,500) and Oistins (1,500); extensive spread of hotels and apartments along the coast.

Transport: A good road network of 1,600 km (virtually all paved) covers the entire island, with a trans-insular highway from Bridgetown to the east coast. Bridgetown is a deep-water port with a cruiseship terminal and yacht harbour. Grantley Adams International Airport is 13 km south-east of Bridgetown.

SOCIETY

Religion: Mainly Christians (Anglicans 24 per cent, Pentecostals 19 per cent, Adventists six per cent, Methodists four per cent), with small Hindu, Muslim and Jewish communities (2010 census).

Health: Public spending on health was four per cent of GDP in 2012. Barbados has a national health service and the general health profile and life expectancy of a developed country. Infant mortality was 13 per 1,000 live births in 2013 (74 in 1960). In 2013, 0.9 per cent of people aged 15–49 were HIV positive.

Education: Public spending on education was 5.6 per cent of GDP in 2012. There are 11 years of compulsory education starting at the age of five. Primary school comprises six years and secondary five. Computers are widely available to schools. Some 93 per cent of pupils complete primary school (2010). The school year starts in September. The University of the West Indies has a campus at Cave Hill, Barbados, as well as in Jamaica, and Trinidad and Tobago. A UNESCO Chair in Educational Technologies was established in 1999 at the Barbados campus of the University of the West Indies. Other tertiary institutions include the

Barbados Community College, with its Hospitality Institute; Samuel Jackman Prescod Polytechnic; and Erdiston College (offering teacher education). The female-male ratio for gross enrolment in tertiary education is 2.50:1 (2011). There is virtually no illiteracy among people aged 15-24.

Media: Newspapers are privately owned and include *The Barbados Advocate/ Sunday Advocate, The Nation/Sunday Sun, the Barbados Today* and *Business Weekly.* CBC TV (the only terrestrial television channel) and MCTV (a multichannel pay-TV service) are operated by the public Caribbean Broadcasting Corporation. There are several private commercial and faith radio stations. There are 158 personal computers per 1,000 people (2005).

Communications: Country code 1 246; internet domain '.bb'. Mobile phone coverage is good on the island. For every 1,000 people there are 523 landlines, 1,081 mobile phone subscriptions and 750 internet users (2013).

Public holidays: New Year's Day, Errol Barrow Day (21 January), Good Friday, Easter Monday, Whit Monday, National Heroes' Day (28 April), Labour Day (1 May), Emancipation Day (1 August), Kadooment Day (first Monday in August), Independence Day (30 November), Christmas Day and Boxing Day.

ECONOMY

GDP: US $4.2bn

GDP P.C.: US $15,172

GDP growth: 0.80 per cent p.a. 2009-12

Inflation: 5.0 per cent p.a. 2009-13

Barbados has an exceptionally high 'quality of life' rating for a developing country. The economy, formerly a sugar monoculture, was developed over three decades to achieve a balance of growth and social development, and diversified into three main sectors: services, light industry and sugar. An international financial services sector, launched in 1985, has become the country's second biggest source of foreign exchange after tourism. Despite its economic success, Barbados experienced little growth in the 1980s and a recession in the early 1990s, when sugar and tourism earnings slumped. It had to call on the IMF for economic adjustment support and the government introduced economic austerity measures.

By 1993 the economy was recovering and it continued to grow well throughout the 1990s, driven by tourism and construction. Action against drug-trafficking since the 1990s has made security and defence a significant item of expenditure.

With a small and open economy Barbados lacks scope for further diversification and remains vulnerable to economic downturn in its trade partners. After 2000 the economy went into recession due to the downturn in the USA and Europe and resulting falls in tourist numbers. It picked up in 2003 and grew steadily until 2008 when the world economic downturn again caused a sharp fall in tourism and pushed the economy into reverse. After a sharp recession in 2009 when GDP fell by 4.1 per cent, the economy hardly grew at all in 2010-14.

POLITICS
Last elections: 21 February 2013
Next elections: 2018
Head of State: Queen Elizabeth II, represented by Governor-General, Sir Elliot Belgrave (2011-)
Head of Government: Prime Minister, The Rt Honourable Freundel Stuart, QC, MP,
Ruling Party: Democratic Labour Party
Women MPs: 17 per cent

HISTORY AND GOVERNMENT
Prehistoric Barbados is believed to have been inhabited by cave-dwellers of the Siboney culture, from Florida. At an unknown later time, Arawaks arrived from South America. The latter were agriculturists, and excellent weavers and potters. They survived invasions and raids by the warlike Caribs (also from South America), which took place before the 1490s. By the early 1500s, Spanish and Portuguese sailors had sighted the island. It was invaded in 1518 by Spanish colonists from Hispaniola. No Spanish settlement was made, as there appeared to be no mineral resources, but the island acquired a Spanish name – *Barbados* (or 'bearded'), apparently a reference to local fig trees.

By 1536 the island was deserted, either because the slavers had depopulated it or because the remaining inhabitants had fled. In 1625 it was formally claimed for King James I of England. In 1627 English immigrants settled there and King Charles I granted a Barbados patent to Lord Carlisle; after 1660, this patent was surrendered to the Crown and a 4.5 per cent duty on exports levied, which, bitterly resented, was levied until 1838.

Between 1627 and 1640, the island was settled by British colonists, who brought with them indentured labour from Britain and some enslaved Africans, to produce tobacco, cotton and indigo. The introduction of sugar in the 1650s had led to the development of large plantations, and by 1685 the population was around 50,000, consisting mainly of African slaves. By the end of the 18th century, Barbados had 745 plantations worked by more than 80,000 African and African-descended slaves. Harsh working conditions led to slave revolts in 1702 and 1816. Slavery was abolished throughout the British Empire in 1833-34.

Barbados had a house of assembly since 1639 but, due to the property qualifications for the franchise, this was dominated by plantation owners until the franchise began to be widened in 1944. Universal adult suffrage followed in 1951, a full ministerial system in 1954, and cabinet government in 1958.

The Barbados Labour Party (BLP), which developed out of the trade unions, was set up under the leadership of Grantley Adams, and began working for economic improvement and the extension of political rights. The BLP, led first by Adams, and after 1958 by Dr Hugh Cummins, gained a majority in the House of Assembly between 1944 and 1961. In 1955 a split in the BLP led to the formation of the Democratic Labour Party (DLP), led by Errol Barrow, who won the 1961 elections. Thus, by 1957, Barbados had virtual self-government under a democratic system, a status formally recognised in 1961.

Barbados had been a member of the Federation of the West Indies, set up in 1958. When the Federation was dissolved in 1962, the Barbados Government announced its intention to seek independence separately. Arrangements were agreed at a constitutional conference in London, and Barbados became an independent sovereign state within the Commonwealth on 30 November 1966.

The DLP was in power from 1966 to 1976, and the BLP from 1976 to 1986, led by Tom Adams, Sir Grantley Adams's son. In 1986 the DLP, still led by Errol Barrow, won a decisive election victory, maintaining its majority in the 1991 elections. Erskine Sandiford became Prime Minister in June 1987 after the death of Barrow. There was a breakaway movement by DLP dissidents who formed a new National Democratic Party (NDP) but failed to win any seats in the 1991 elections. Sandiford and the DLP were ousted in September 1994 by the BLP led by Owen Arthur.

The BLP won 19 seats (48.3 per cent of the vote), the DLP eight and NDP one. The BLP remained in power until 2008 when they were ousted by the DLP led my David Thompson. The DLP won 20 seats (53.2 per cent of the vote) and the BLP ten ending the BLP's 13 years in government. Thompson was sworn in as Prime Minister but subsequently died in office on 23 October 2010. He was succeeded by Deputy PM and Attorney-General Freundel Stuart.

In the February 2013 election Freundel Stuart and the DLP were returned to power by a narrow margin. The DLP won 16 of the 30 elective House of Assembly seats (51.3 per cent of votes and the BLP – led by former PM Owen Arthur – 14 seats.

CONSTITUTION
Status: Monarchy under Her Majesty Queen Elizabeth II
Legislature: Barbados Parliament
Independence: 30 November 1966
Barbados is a parliamentary democracy and constitutional monarchy, recognising Queen Elizabeth II as head of state. She is represented by a

Governor-General appointed on the recommendation of the Prime Minister. There is a bicameral legislature and party system, based on universal adult suffrage. The Senate has 21 members appointed by the Governor-General, 12 on the advice of the Prime Minister, two on that of the Leader of the Opposition, and the remaining seven at the Governor-General's discretion.

The House of Assembly has 30 directly elected members. Leaders of each Chamber (President and Deputy President of the Senate and Speaker and Deputy Speaker of the House of Assembly) are elected by the members of the respective houses. The Governor-General appoints as Prime Minister the parliamentarian who commands – in the Governor-General's opinion – the largest support within the House of Assembly, and the Prime Minister heads the cabinet. Other ministers are appointed from either house by the Governor-General as advised by the Prime Minister.

The Governor-General appoints the Leader of the Opposition – the MP who, in his/her judgement, leads the party commanding the support of the largest number of MPs in opposition to the Government.

The normal life of Parliament is five years. The constitution may be amended by act of Parliament passed by both houses, except for entrenched clauses which require two-thirds majorities in both houses. These clauses relate to citizenship, rights and freedoms, the governor-generalship, composition of Parliament and its sessions, prorogation and dissolution, general elections, senatorial appointments, executive authority, judicature, civil service and finance.

Sir Henry Forde's Constitutional Commission's much-delayed report was published in December 1998. Its main proposals were to introduce more checks and balances on the government, to create the institutional structures to ensure politicians behave with greater probity, and to replace the British monarch as the head of state by a ceremonial President. In the General Election of January 1999, the Barbados Labour Party (BLP) had a strong endorsement of their management of the economy and a mandate for their proposals for constitutional change.

They gained 26 seats, with 65 per cent of the votes, while the Democratic Labour Party (DLP) took only two. Owen Arthur began his second term of office as Prime Minister. During 1999 and 2000 the new Government pressed on with the proposed changes to the Constitution, adding further issues to the agenda for public debate, for example limiting the number of terms a Prime Minister may serve, equal rights for women, and the independence of the judiciary. However, the debate proceeded slowly.

The BLP after 2003 still had the two-thirds majority needed to enact constitutional amendments, although constitutional issues, such as replacing the British monarch as the head of state with a ceremonial President, had not been prominent in the election campaign. But in 2005 the UK Privy Council was replaced as the final court of appeal by the Trinidad and Tobago-based Caribbean Court of Justice.

INTERNATIONAL RELATIONS

Barbados is a member of the African, Caribbean and Pacific Group of States, Association of Caribbean States, Caribbean Community, Commonwealth of Nations, Non-Aligned Movement, Organisation of American States, United Nations and World Trade Organisation.

GOVERNORS-GENERAL OF BARBADOS

SIR ELLIOTT FITZROY BELGRAVE, G.C.M.G., KA.
Govenor-General 2012 - Present

SIR CLIFFORD S. HUSBANDS, G.C.M.G., KA.
Govenor-General 1996 - 2012

DAME RUTH NITA BARROW, G.C.M.G., DA.
Govenor-General 1990 - 1995

**SIR HUGH W. SPRINGER, G.C.M.G.,
G.C.V.O., KA., C.B.E.**
Govenor-General 1984-1990

SIR DEIGHTON WARD, G.C.M.G., G.C.V.O.
Govenor-General 1976 - 1984

**SIR ARLEIGH W. SCOTT, G.C.M.G.,
G.C.V.O.**
Govenor-General 1967-1976

SIR JOHN STOW, K.C.M.G., K.C.V.O.
Govenor-General 1966-1967

PREMIERS AND PRIME MINISTERS OF BARBADOS

SIR GRANTLEY HERBERT ADAMS,
C.M.G., Q.C.
Born April 1898
Premier of Barbados 1954-1958
Prime Minister of the West Indies Federation
1958-1962
Died November 1971

DR. HUGH GORDON CUMMINS
Born February 1891
Premier of Barbados 1958-1961
Died October 1970

THE RT. EXCELLENT
ERROL WALTON BARROW,
Q.C.
Born January 1920
Premier of Barbados 1961-1966
Prime Minister of Barbados 1966-1976; 1986-1987
Died June 1987

THE HON. FREUNDEL J. STUART, Q.C., M.P.
Born April 1951
Prime Minister of Barbados 2010-

THE RT. HON. J.M.G.M. (TOM) ADAMS,
Q.C.
Born September 1931
Prime Minister of Barbados 1976-1985
Died March 1985

SIR HAROLD BERNARD ST. JOHN, Q.C.
Born August 1931
Prime Minister of Barbados 1985-1986
Died February 2004

THE HON. DAVID J.H. THOMPSON, Q.C.
Born December 1961
Prime Minister of Barbados 2008-2010
Died October 2010

THE RT. HON. OWEN SEYMOUR ARTHUR,
M.P.
Born October 1949
Prime Minister of Barbados 1994-2008

THE RT. HON
SIR LLOYD ERSKINE SANDIFORD
Born March 1937
Prime Minister of Barbados 1987-1994

NATIONAL HEROES OF BARBADOS

Rt. Excellent
Bussa

Rt. Excellent
Sarah Ann Gill

Rt. Excellent
Samuel Jackman Prescod

Rt. Excellent
Dr. Charles Duncan O'Neal

National Heroes of Barbados

Rt. Excellent
Clement Payne

Rt. Excellent
Sir Grantley Adams,
Q.C., C.M.G.

Rt. Excellent
Sir Frank Walcott,
K.A., O.B.E., LL.D.

Rt. Excellent
Sir Hugh Springer,
G.C.M., G.V.C.O., K.A., C.B.E.

Rt. Excellent
Errol Barrow
Q.C.

Rt. Excellent
Sir Garfield Sobers